Nelson

ACCOUNTING AND FINANCE *for* WA

Ken KRACHLER   Chris DURRANT   Alan PHILLIPS   John CANNON

2A
2B

NELSON
CENGAGE Learning™

Australia • Brazil • Japan • Korea • Mexico • Singapore • Spain • United Kingdom • United States

NELSON
CENGAGE Learning™

Nelson Accounting & Finance for WA 2A-2B
1st Edition
Ken Krachler
John Cannon
Chris Durrant
Alan Phillips

Publishing editor: Deborah Barnes
Project editor: Katharine Day
Senior designer: Ami Sharpe
Text designer: Santiago Villamizar
Cover designer: Leigh Ashforth
Cover image: Getty Images
Photo researcher: Georgina Wober
Production controller: Damian Almeida
Typeset by Q2A Media

Any URLs contained in this publication were checked for currency during the production process. Note, however, that the publisher cannot vouch for the ongoing currency of URLs.

For product information and technology assistance,
in Australia call 1300 790 853;
in New Zealand call 0508 635 766

For permission to use material from this text or product, please email **aust.permissions@cengage.com**

National Library of Australia Cataloguing-in-Publication Data
Ken Krachler ... [et al.].
Nelson Accounting and Finance for WA 2A-2B

1st ed.
9780170182041 (pbk.)
Includes index.
Bibliography.
For secondary school age.

Accounting--Textbooks.
Finance--Textbooks.

657

Cengage Learning Australia
Level 7, 80 Dorcas Street
South Melbourne, Victoria Australia 3205

Cengage Learning New Zealand
Unit 4B Rosedale Office Park
331 Rosedale Road, Albany, North Shore 0632, NZ

For learning solutions, visit **cengage.com.au**

Printed in Australia by Ligare Pty Ltd
1 2 3 4 5 6 7 13 12 11 10 09

Contents

Foreword

Welcome to the world of accounting – from budgeting to profit analysis, you will learn important skills you can use every day and as part of your future career.

Chartered Accountants enjoy one of the most highly regarded careers in the business world today. Why? Because money makes the world go round – and accountants are the ones who understand money, numbers and whether an organisation is profitable. Accounting and finance professionals are the first to know how well an organisation is doing and what needs to happen to keep it that way.

Chartered Accountants use financial information to make decisions about an organisation's prosperity and direction. These accountants are professionals who have completed a degree and the Chartered Accountants Program to become a qualified accountant.

The depth of experience and training required to be a Chartered Accountant makes it an ideal step into senior management roles. It's not surprising that many heads of business start off with a professional Accounting qualification to properly understand how businesses operate.

Chartered Accountants work everywhere – from fashion houses to charities, government organisations to local accounting firms – every company or organisation needs an accountant. Accounting can also provide opportunities to work overseas; professional accountants are recognised around the world.

Whether you see yourself investigating fraud as a forensic accountant, dealing with personal finances as a financial planner or managing personal or business tax as a tax accountant, the role of a Chartered Accountant is diverse. Your course will help you to decide which area you want to go into.

I hope you enjoy learning about all the different aspects of accounting and embrace this first step towards the rewarding and varied career of professional accounting.

Michael Spinks FCA
President (2010)
The Institute of Chartered Accountants in Australia

charteredaccountants.com.au/students

Chartered Accountants

NUMBER ONE IN NUMBERS

About this book

This textbook is a stand-alone resource for Units 2A and 2B of the Accounting and Finance Course of Study (COS) developed by the Curriculum Council of Western Australia. The first five chapters cover content of Unit 2A, and the remaining seven chapters deal with 2B, although there is some cross-referencing.

A word on **ledger account layout:** in the real world, the use of T-form ledger accounts has been largely replaced by three-column accounts, and is the format used in computerised accounting systems. However, many textbooks, even at university level, still use the T-form account. Consequently, although we will use three-column form in this textbook, the use of T-form accounts is still acceptable and, where appropriate, is shown in the solutions.

The same can be said about **accounting terminology.** In this book we use terms currently favoured by the profession and the regulatory authorities. However, using these terms is not mandatory, and many organisations continue to use alternatives, such as 'Balance sheet' for 'Statement of financial position'. Using these alternative terms is, therefore, perfectly acceptable.

CHAPTER FEATURES

- Chapter-opening-page objectives: '**What you will learn**'.

- **Key concepts** picking up on new and important terms to make revision easier.

Key Concept 3.3

Closing entries

Closing entries are the journal entries used to transfer balances from revenue and expense accounts to the profit-determining account at the end of the financial period.

- Graphical summaries in chapters, to aid student understanding and revision, and help visual learners.

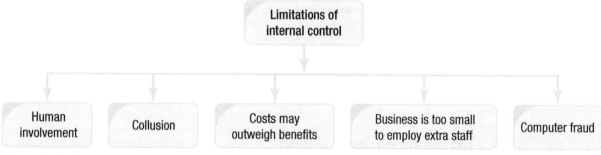

Figure 4.4 Limitations of internal control

- Frequent practical **worked examples** to help students grasp the understandings and skills involved in the chapter topic.

Example 3.1

EXAMPLE:
Tran's Transport was set up on 1 September when Tran deposited $50 000 in a business bank account and contributed his personal vehicle worth $25 000 to the business. At the same time, he purchased another vehicle costing $30 000 from Vin's Vans, paying $10 000 deposit, the remainder being on credit terms. Both the cash ($40 000 left in the account) and the vehicles ($55 000) are resources controlled by the business, having a defined value and future economic benefits for the business. They will therefore be recognised as assets on 1 September. The $20 000 owing to Vin's Vans is a quantifiable present obligation that will, in

due course, result in an outflow of economic benefits of that amount from the business. It will therefore be recognised as a liability on 1 September. Tran's capital (owner's equity) is the difference between the assets ($95 000) and liabilities ($20 000), i.e. $75 000.

This may be summarised as follows.

Assets	
Cash	$40 000
Vehicles	$55 000
	$95 000
Liabilities	
Loan from Vin's Vans	$20 000
Equity	
Capital: Tran	$75 000

- **Reality-check case studies** and newspaper articles, which give real-life scenarios to tie down the theory.

Woolworths defend security after shoplifting job uncovered

Woolworths has defended its security systems after police arrested two men over a major shoplifting operation in Sydney.

Police were patrolling the inner-city suburb of Alexandria just before 6:00pm (AEDT) last Saturday when they noticed two men looking suspicious in Euston Road.

A search and subsequent questioning led police to a warehouse where police say they found cosmetics worth millions of dollars stacked in boxes, some of it stolen from Woolworths.

What other processes have you noticed in place at your local shops to safeguard the store's stock?

www.amazon.com

- Website **URLs** where relevant.
- End-of-chapter comprehension questions '**Test your knowledge**'. These check students' understanding of the objectives.
- End-of-chapter comprehension practical questions, '**Test your understanding**'. These are so extensive they have their own menu to assist classes to quickly find the exact questions relevant to a particular lesson. Most students will probably not need to do them all; time constraints and student ability will determine how many exercises you complete.

Test your understanding

Topic guide

- Ethical dealing with lenders, customers, employees: 5.1–5.3
- Resource conservation and environmental concerns: 5.4–5.8
- Community involvement: 5.9–5.10
- Taxation responsibilities: 5.11–5.12

- At the end of each chapter there are also an **Investigation, Essay topics** and an **Ethics case study**.
- The book's **teacher website** at nelsonnet.com.au includes easily accessible solutions to all the practical questions and suggested responses to the other questions. There are also extra multiple choice questions.

Acknowledgements

The authors and publishers would like gratefully to credit or acknowledge the following sources for permission to use copyright material.

Photographs

Alamy: p. 173; iStockphoto; p. 228 (bottom right)/Tomas Bercic: p. 126 (bottom)/BMPix: p. 16/Diego Cervo: p. 15 (top)/Dainis Derics: p. 231/Christine Glade: p. 228 (top)/Niko Guido: p. 124 (bottom)/Tom Hahn: p. 342/H-Gall: p. 175/David Joyner: p. 301/Volker Kreinacke: p. 352/Derek Latta: p. 297 (top)/MBPHOTO: p. 122/Felix Möckel: p. 349/Tom Nulens: p. 3 (bottom)/Skip ODonnell: p. 300/James C. Pruitt: p. 315/Nadejda Reid: p. 314/Alina Solovyova-Vincent: p. 303/Linda Steward: p. 130/Tony Tremblay: p. 298/Frances Twitty: p. 126 (top)/Konstantin Voznikevich: p. 172/Igor Zhorov; Jupiterimages Corporation: pp. 2, 3 (top), 5, 129, 177, 178, 296, 297 (bottom), 305; Shutterstock: p. 124 (top): p. 132 (bottom)/Marcin Balcerzak: p. 170/Diego Cervo: p. 345/Maria Dryfhout: p. 308/Elena Elisseeva: p. 15 (bottom)/Milos Jokic: p. 127/Adrian Matthiassen: p. 139/Konstantin Shevtsov: p. 132 (top)/Paul Tobeck: p. 4/Liz Van Steenburgh: p. 228 (bottom left)/Vibrant Image Studio.

Text & Illustrations

Extract from ABC News 'Police issue fake credit card warning' first published by ABC Online, 22 January 2009/ABC News 'Woolworths defend security after shoplifting job uncovered' first published by ABC Online, 30 January 2009, both extracts reproduced by permission of the Australian Broadcasting Corporation and ABC Online. © 2009 ABC. All rights reserved; Australian Financial Review, 24 March 2009; Victor Violante, 'Bookkeeper stole $235,000 to feed poker machine addiction' Canberra Times, 18 July 2008; Centrelink WA media release, 'Centrelink crackdown on skimpy cash fraud', 11 January 2007; Glenis Green, 'Pregnant, 25 and in jail for fiddling with the books', Courier Mail, 30 June 2009; The information as seen on p. 348 is provided by CPA Australia Ltd, www.cpaaustralia.com.au; © Financial Planners Association of Australia; Data available from: www.roymorgan.com; © MYOB; Small Business Development Corporation, media release, www.sbdc.com.au/publications/mediareleases.asp?newsid=210, 26 October 2007; Harriet Alexander, Sydney Morning Herald, 11 March 2009, www.smh.com.au.

Every attempt has been made to trace and acknowledge copyright holders. Where the attempt has been unsuccessful, the publisher welcomes information that would redress the situation.

About the authors

Ken Krachler is the Dean of Business at Canning College. Over the past 26 years he has taught Accounting at TEE, TAFE and Diploma level (equivalent to first year university) in Western Australia. He has provided leadership in accounting and finance curriculum in WA for 20 years through his involvement in the Accounting Syllabus Committee and Accounting and Finance Course of Study Committee (including spells as chairperson of these committees). He has written accounting exam papers and prepared other accounting support material for use by teachers and students in WA.

Chris Durrant taught Year 11 and 12 Accounting for 20 years in WA. During that time he was on the Accounting Syllabus Committee and was one of the writers of the Accounting and Finance Course of Study. He co-authored a textbook on the previous accounting courses and has written numerous exam papers and other accounting support materials. Before becoming a teacher, Chris worked in a variety of commercial enterprises as an accountant or manager and set up and ran his own animal husbandry business.

Alan W Phillips MA BA DipEd has worked across the three secondary sectors in Western Australia. He is currently responsible for accounting at Wesley College in Perth. Recent Masters studies at Curtin University Business School renewed his interests in the legal underpinnings of financial reporting and the inevitable mandating of matters related to corporate social responsibilities. He is an advocate of computer-based processing of data and a leading curriculum renewal practitioner.

John Cannon has taught accounting for more than 20 years at upper secondary, TAFE and university levels to local and international students. He has been involved with the development and implementation of new courses of study for accounting and other business education subjects. For many years he has undertaken the writing and marking of accounting exams and accounting support materials. John is a CPA and was part-owner of farming and service businesses before becoming a teacher.

This book is dedicated to the hard-working business educators of Western Australia. The authors wish to thank Robyn Ricket and Teresa Althorpe for their input and advice on computerised accounting, their colleagues for their encouragement, and most importantly their families for their constant support.

Thanks also to our excellent reviewers: Dr Len Therry from Edith Cowan University and Christina Habib from Penrhos College.

Chapter 1

INTRODUCTION TO BUSINESS FINANCIAL MANAGEMENT

What You Will Learn

After studying this chapter you should be able to:
1 Identify and compare the main classifications of business: merchandising, service and manufacturing
2 Explain, compare and evaluate the main types of small business ownership: sole trader, partnership and small proprietary company
3 Describe the impact and importance of legislation relating to the formation of sole traders, partnerships and small proprietary companies
4 Explain the accounting assumptions: accounting entity, monetary, accounting period, historical cost, going concern and accrual basis of accounting
5 Explain the definitions of the elements of financial statements as per the Framework for the Preparation and Presentation of General Purpose Financial Reports ('The Framework')
6 Explain the concept of 'double entry' and show how this is applied in the recording of financial transactions
7 Explain business obligations in relation to the goods and services tax (GST)
8 Discuss the need for finance by business proprietors
9 Identify, compare and evaluate possible sources of external and internal finance available
10 Identify and explain the factors that financial institutions consider in granting finance
11 Explain the meaning of ethics and outline how the concept applies to the financial operations of small businesses

Introduction

Accounting is a long-established and colourful profession. One of the most memorable accountants in literature is Ebenezer Scrooge, the main character in Charles Dickens' story *The Christmas Carol*. Scrooge is a grumpy and mean accounting partner of the late Jacob Marley. His downtrodden worker Bob Cratchitt has the daily tedium of entering the ledgers – no doubt with quill pen! So readers are introduced to a partnership, ledgers, exploited workers and perhaps – as in recent times – large performance bonuses to executives whose businesses are in financial trouble. Whether accounting is really like Scrooge's Counting House we will discover as we work through this textbook.

Accounting involves people and – like Scrooge – some earn disreputable names, but most carry out their duties competently and faithfully, as did Bob Cratchitt. In this book you will explore, learn and apply knowledge about financial structures and procedures that will be useful in your personal, business and professional life.

This first chapter focuses on understandings of common forms of business structures and the language (concepts, terms and their meanings) used by accountants in their daily professional life. Specific themes in the chapter will focus on exploring the types, characteristics and advantages and disadvantages of sole traders, partnerships and proprietary companies. This will include consideration of legislation influencing the formation and operation of these business organisations. We will also investigate the purpose and importance of accounting assumptions, including the accounting entity, accounting period, historical cost, going concern, monetary and accrual accounting and the definitions of the elements of financial statements. Later in the chapter we will introduce ethics in accounting and principles and legislative background to the goods and services tax (GST).

TYPES OF BUSINESS

There are essentially three types of business, the characteristics of which will to some extent modify the financial recording and reporting that is required. These are merchandising (retailing), service and manufacturing.

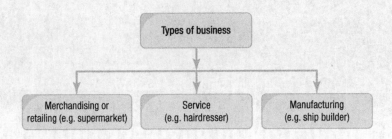

Figure 1.1 The three types of business

Merchandising (retailing)

Merchandising businesses (also called retailing or trading businesses) generate profit by purchasing stock and reselling it at a higher price. Coles, Bunnings, Harvey Norman, a petrol station and the local neighbourhood deli are examples. The main cost for such businesses is stock (inventory) so reports will focus on this item and the efficiency with which it is being managed. The income statement will identify the margin (gross profit) that is being achieved over the cost of purchasing the stock related to the sales price achieved. Retail businesses need to efficiently manage inventory as well as other operating expenses.

Service

Service businesses generate profit by providing a service to their customers. Examples include Telstra, Ace Cinemas, a plumber and an accounting firm. Service firms' main costs are usually the wages of the people providing the service; the valuation and management of stock is usually insignificant. The Income statement for a service business will not include a gross margin or profit as such, although many businesses will separately identify the direct costs of providing the service (such as wages of those

Accounting and Finance: 2A   ISBN 9780170182041   Cengage Learning Australia

directly involved and materials used) compared with the overheads (such as administration salaries and rent).

Manufacturing

Manufacturing businesses earn profit by purchasing raw materials or components and converting them into products, which are then sold on to other businesses or, in some cases, directly to customers. Examples of this sort of business include Houghton's Wines, General Motors Holden and a surfboard maker. The emphasis for the financial system will be on the cost of the inputs and the efficiency with which these are converted to the final product. In many ways, this combines the requirements of retailing and service businesses.

Many firms, of course, combine elements of more than one type of business. A petrol station (retail) may also provide a service in the form of vehicle repairs, a hairdresser (service) may also retail products such as shampoos and hair dyes and a wine producer (manufacture) may also sell its products directly to the public through sales from its cellar door. Businesses that do this will normally try to separately identify the costs and revenue of the different elements of their undertaking so that the profitability of each can be assessed.

Key Concept 1.1

Business classifications

Businesses may be classified as merchandising, service or manufacturing, depending on whether they earn most of their revenue by selling goods, providing services to customers or manufacturing goods for sale. This classification influences the nature and focus of their financial systems and reports.

BUSINESS STRUCTURES

There are many forms of business organisation, from sole traders to partnerships, companies and groups of companies to multinational conglomerates. There are also not-for-profit and public-sector organisations. In addition, there are other, less common, forms, such as co-operatives, friendly societies and provident societies. Some businesses operate under a franchise arrangement and others are branches of single entities.

Three very common small business organisational structures are sole traders, partnerships and proprietary companies. Proprietary companies are the most common business structure in Australia.

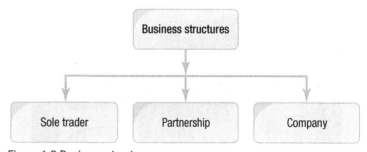

Figure 1.2 Business structures

Sole traders

Characteristics

A one-owner business (a sole trader) is a common form of business organisation. It is simple to set up – all that is required is a business bank account. A sole trader is not a legal entity as it is not a registered (i.e. incorporated) body. This means that it cannot own property, enter into contract or sue or be sued in its own name. Its owner has unlimited liability for all the debts of the business.

```
         Characteristics of
           a sole trader

   One owner   Not a legal entity   Unlimited liability
```

Figure 1.3 Characteristics of a sole trader

```
         Advantages of
       being a sole trader

   Ease of formation       Gain all the profits
```

Figure 1.4 Advantages of being a sole trader

```
         Disadvantages of
        being a sole trader

 Unlimited    Limited         Not a legal    Bears all the
 liability    sources of      entity         risks and losses
              finance
```

Figure 1.5 Disadvantages of being a sole trader

Legal considerations

In Western Australia the *Business Names Act 1962* is relevant if a sole trader operates under a name other than the owner's personal name. A business name is registered and a fee is charged for renewal of a business name. Most businesses also require an ABN (Australian Business Number) for taxation purposes (a requirement under Australian legislation), such as the GST (see later in this chapter). Other legislation that may need to be observed by sole-trader businesses include health laws and occupational health and safety requirements. Many of these are state and local government laws. They are designed to protect the interests of businesses and the community within which they operate from the consequences of fraud, deception and malpractice.

Advantages and disadvantages

The sole-trader business structure is easy to form and simple to operate. When business is going well the owner will gain all the profits.

The fact that the business and the owner are not seen as separate legal entities creates a problem for the owner when the business meets financial difficulties: the owner is liable for all the debts of the business and might have to sell personal possessions, such as the family home, to meet them. This latter concept is called *unlimited liability*.

In addition, the sole trader relies heavily on the owner for finance and this can cause problems if the business expands. Owners tend to have limited funds at their disposal. A sole trader provides all the inspiration and effort; though, of course, employees can assist in sharing the work and providing ideas. The profit of a sole trader is taken as drawings and viewed as income for taxation purposes. The sole trader bears all the risks and losses of business operation.

Accounting and Finance 2A   ISBN 9780170182041   Cengage Learning Australia

Key Concept 1.2

Sole trader

A sole trader is a business that is not a legal entity, owned and operated by one person.

Partnerships

Characteristics

A partnership is a relationship that exists between two or more people to carry on a business in common with a view to profit. A partnership is not regarded as a legal entity separate from the partners who comprise it. All business property and transactions are carried on in the name of the partners. Partners have unlimited liability for all the debts of the business.

Legal considerations

Partnerships are similar to sole traders in that the owners have unlimited liability. The partners have full financial liability, jointly and severally (not necessarily equally), for the obligations (the debts) of the business. In 1909 a category of limited liability partners was created in Western Australian legislation. Such partners can take no part in the business and avoid the unlimited liability shared by the remaining partners. However, such arrangements are very uncommon and we will not consider them in this book.

Partnerships have been recognised in Western Australia since 1895 with the *Partnership Act 1895* providing the legal framework. The law specifies the rules that will apply to a partnership in the absence of a formal agreement to the contrary. For example, profits are shared equally and consequently partners will not be entitled to a salary or interest on capital and cannot be charged interest on drawings. Further, if a partner lends money to the partnership, such a loan (usually termed an *advance*) attracts six per cent simple interest. An advance is essentially similar to any other form of borrowing and is treated as a liability not equity.

The WA Partnership Act makes other provisions about the operation of a partnership, including the admission and retirement of partners, mutual agency and rights of partners. The Act, for example, states that the partnership records must be kept in a location that is accessible to all partners, that partners are entitled to an equal right to partake in the management of the business and that a person cannot be introduced into or expelled from the partnership without the agreement of all the other partners.

Australian Corporations legislation limits partnerships to 20 members, though exemptions exist for large professional partnerships, such as lawyers and accountants. When a partnership operates under a name other than the owners' personal names, a business name needs to be registered and a fee is charged for registration and renewal of the business name.

Other legislative requirements (such as the need for an ABN, GST obligations and health and safety laws) are the same as those outlined for sole traders. These apply to all businesses however they are structured.

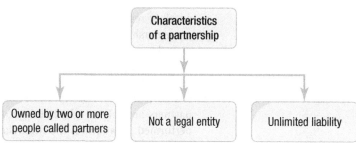

Figure 1.6 Characteristics of a partnership

Partnership agreement

If the partners wish to override or amplify the provisions of the Partnership Act, they may do so by entering into a *partnership agreement*. A partnership agreement is a legally binding contract between all the partners so that their wishes are applied to the running of the business. In order to modify the provisions of the Act, an agreement must be in writing and signed by all partners.

Possible contents of a partnership agreement

- Partners' duties
- Salaries and drawings
- Decision-making
- Admission of new partners
- Exiting of partners
- Interest entitlements on capital and drawings
- Treatment of advance
- Division of profits
- Resolution of conflict
- Life of the partnership
- Review of the agreement

As previously stated, the partners can override part or all of the provisions of the Partnership Act that they do not see as being in their best interests. This is particularly important if the partners do not wish to share the profits or losses equally. This may be necessary to take account of the different capital contributions from partners: their differing qualifications, skills, knowledge and experience and the extent to which each withdraws their share of the firm's profit. This can be done, for example, by providing for interest on capital, salaries for work done and interest charged on drawings.

The Partnership Act is important in the event of a dispute between partners if the dispute should come before a court. The legislation protects all partners, ensures fairness among them and gives direction to magistrates and judges in the event of a dispute that requires resolution.

Advantages and disadvantages

The advantages of forming a partnership are:

- ease of formation – a partnership can be easily formed between two or more persons. All they have to do is agree to form a partnership. Although a written partnership agreement is advisable, a verbal agreement is sufficient to constitute a partnership
- limited rules and regulations – unlike a company, a partnership is not subject to the requirements of the *Corporations Act 2001* (Cwth). The partners are not normally obliged to prepare financial statements in a particular form nor meet any ongoing reporting requirements apart from those that apply to all businesses
- provision of additional capital and expertise – a partnership is often formed to raise more capital than is possible with a sole trader. It may also be formed to bring together the different skills of the partners (for example, an accountant and an engineer)
- possibly reduced income tax liability – there may be income tax advantages in forming a partnership since it is not a separate legal entity. The partnership itself is not taxed, as is the case for a company (the individual partners pay income tax on their share of partnership profits) but there may be advantages, especially for family businesses, in splitting the firm's income for tax purposes
- shared workload, risks and losses – since the partnership has more than one owner, the partners are able to take holidays and sick leave and share the tasks that need to be performed. In addition the financial and business risks and losses are shared.

Accounting and Finance: 2A   ISBN 9780170182041   Cengage Learning Australia

The disadvantages of partnerships include:

- limited life – a partnership can end at any time through, for example, the death of a partner, withdrawal of a partner, bankruptcy of a partner, incapacity of a partner or admission of a new partner. However, the end of the partnership does not signify the end of the partnership business: it may continue under a new partnership for many years
- unlimited liability – each partner is personally liable for all debts of the partnership. This liability is not limited by the partner's share of the equity: if there are two equal partners in a business that becomes insolvent and one of the two has no personal assets to meet their share of the debts, the other partner may be obliged to pay them all. Large partnerships normally purchase professional indemnity insurance because of this risk and structure aspects of their business into proprietary companies (e.g. the building and office section of the business)
- mutual agency – as each partner is an agent of the partnership, they have the authority to enter into contracts on behalf of the partnership provided such contracts are within the scope of normal business operations. The other partners cannot subsequently repudiate such decisions simply because they would not have agreed with them. The effect of this can be mitigated by limiting partners' powers through provisions in the partnership agreement
- sharing of profits – the partners must share the business profits.

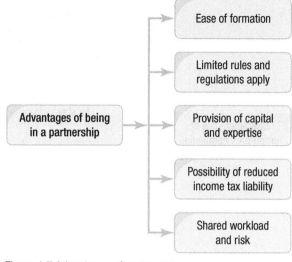

Figure 1.7 Advantages of partnerships

Figure 1.8 Disadvantages of partnerships

Key Concept 1.3

Partnership

A partnership is an unincorporated business owned by two or more partners with a common view to make a profit.

Companies

Characteristics

A company is sometimes referred to as an 'artificial person'. It is an incorporated body created by law and exists, in law, just like an individual. This is described as being *a legal entity*. A company, as defined under the Corporations Act, is a separate legal entity distinct from its owners (usually described as *shareholders*), unlike partnerships and sole traders, which have no legal existence separate from their owners.

Company debts incurred in the normal course of business are those of the company. Although the company has unlimited liability, the liability of the owners is limited, usually to the amount, if any, that they have committed to contribute as capital but which is not yet paid. In the case of unpaid debts it is the company that is sued rather than the owner. The fact that the owners might also be the managers (directors) and the employees is irrelevant.

There are many types of companies. In this textbook we are only concerned with small proprietary companies limited by shares. The other major types of limited

Accounting and Finance: 2A   ISBN 9780170182041   Cengage Learning Australia

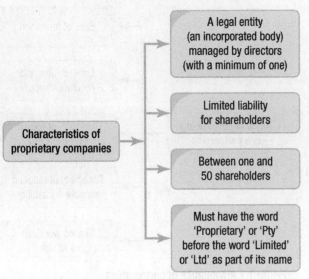

Figure 1.9 Characteristics of proprietary companies

liability companies – large proprietary companies and public companies – will not be considered in this textbook.

Proprietary companies

A proprietary company, sometimes called a private company, must have a minimum of one shareholder up to a maximum of 50 shareholders. It must have the word 'Proprietary' or 'Pty' before the word 'Limited' or 'Ltd' as part of its name. All business documentation must include Pty Ltd and the ACN (Australian Company Number) after the company name. Proprietary companies are often family companies. They have fewer legal formalities than public companies and they are unable to approach the general public to raise money.

Legal considerations

The Corporations Act controls the formation and operation of proprietary companies. Companies are relatively easy to form with a process involving the Australian Securities and Investments Commission (ASIC) Form 201 and a fee less than $1000.

Download Form 201 from the ASIC website and complete it as an exercise.

ASIC must be informed of the names of company officials (directors), the place of business and office hours of each proprietary company. ASIC provides supervision of all companies in Australia, the extent of such supervision being relative to the size of the operation.

All companies require a set of rules to operate. These rules (the constitution) protect the interests of the company, the shareholders and the directors, setting out the rights and obligations of each. The constitution also prescribes how the company will be formed, operated and, if necessary, liquidated.

Small proprietary companies

A small proprietary company, as outlined in the Corporations Act, is one that meets at least two of the following criteria:
- annual sales of less than $25 million
- assets of less than $12.5 million
- fewer than 50 employees.

A small proprietary company does not generally have to prepare audited financial statements. All proprietary companies that do not meet the above criteria are categorised as large proprietary companies and are required to lodge audited financial statements with ASIC unless granted an exemption. At this stage of your accounting and finance course you do not have to deal with large proprietary companies.

A small proprietary company is legally required to complete an annual return to ASIC to confirm its solvency (ability to meet its financial commitments) and identify the current directors. An annual fee (currently $200) must be paid to ASIC.

Companies legislation in Australia is very important for the effective and efficient operation of the capital markets. The Corporations Act protects the rights of investors and lenders and sets out the responsibilities and obligations of directors and other appointed officers of a company. Without such legislation, individuals and businesses

Accounting and Finance 2A   ISBN 9780170182041   Cengage Learning Australia

would be less likely to invest in or lend to companies. However, this sort of protection is not so necessary for small proprietary companies, which are essentially just small businesses that happen to be incorporated with few, if any, significant external stakeholders. Therefore, the legislative controls placed on small proprietary companies are not onerous.

Advantages and disadvantages

The advantages of the company form of organisation are:

- separate legal entity – unlike sole traders and partnerships, a company is a separate legal entity. Therefore, it can, in its own name, buy or sell property, sue or be sued, enter into contracts, hire and dismiss employees, be responsible for its debts and pay tax
- limited liability – shareholders are liable only for what they have contributed or agreed to contribute to the business (i.e. the value of their shares)
- more capital – a company has the potential to raise substantial amounts of capital, which is not possible for sole traders or partnerships (up to 50 for a small proprietary company)
- ease of transfer of ownership – shareholders can buy and sell shares without affecting the operations of the company and thereby easily transfer some or all of their interest in the business
- no mutual agency – shareholders cannot enter into contracts that would bind the company. This responsibility is delegated to the directors, who have the authority to make all business decisions
- professional management – there is a separation of ownership (the shareholders) and control (the directors), which theoretically enables a company to obtain the best management expertise. In reality, in the case of most small proprietary companies, the directors and shareholders are the same people
- continuous existence – a company has an indefinite life and does not cease to exist each time a shareholder sells shares, dies or goes bankrupt.

Disadvantages of the company structure include:

- highly regulated – a company is subject to more government intervention in the form of rules and regulations. This is particularly true for public companies and, to a lesser extent, for large proprietary companies. Small proprietary companies are required only to complete a solvency document each year and to notify ASIC of changes in the company's directorship and such details as its registered office or normal place of business
- separation of ownership and control – this can be an advantage or a disadvantage. Managers might have personal incentives to make decisions that are not in the best interests of all shareholders. The Corporations Act contains certain provisions that are intended to discourage managers from behaving in this manner. As noted above, separation of management and control is more apparent than real in most small proprietary companies
- cost – although the expense involved in setting up a small proprietary company and meeting the ongoing legislative requirements are not great, they are nonetheless greater than for a sole trader or partnership, which bears no such costs.

Figure 1.10 Advantages of companies

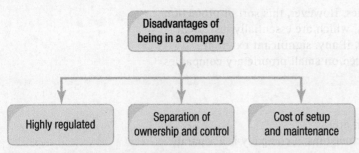

Figure 1.11 Disadvantages of companies

Other considerations when contemplating the formation of a company include:

- taxation – a company is a separate legal entity and it is required to pay tax based on its profits at a fixed rate (currently 30 per cent) while the profits of unincorporated businesses are taxed in the hands of their owners as personal income on a progressive scale. Whether this is an advantage or a disadvantage will depend on the personal circumstances of the owners, but it is certainly a factor that should be borne in mind

- limited liability – while limited liability is generally an advantage, it may restrict its borrowing options because lenders may be wary of making loans to a business whose owners are insulated from the consequences of default. In that case the directors and/or shareholders may be required to give a personal guarantee to secure the company's obligations under the loan.

 Key Concept 1.4

Company

A company is an incorporated body registered under the *Corporations Act 2001*. It has a legal existence separate from its owners and is subject to legal regulation administered by ASIC.

REALITY CHECK 1.1

Bodie and Doyle have at last taken their friends' advice and decided to turn their casual weekend building work into a full-time business. Bodie is a carpenter and Doyle is a bricklayer, but neither knows anything about finance or accounting and their only advertising to date has been word-of-mouth from their many satisfied customers.

They have decided to call their business The Professionals Inc and initially plan to operate out of a small warehouse unit that belongs to a mate of Doyle's in Kewdale. They are optimistic of generating a turnover in excess of $200 000 in their first year. There are a few matters they need to sort out before they embark on their new enterprise. These include:

- form of business structure – should they set up a partnership or should they form a company?
- Legal requirements – what formalities do they need to go through?

Commentary

Obviously, because there are two of them, the choice of business structure is between a partnership and a company. The advantage of the latter is that they would enjoy limited liability (i.e. their personal assets will not be on the line if the business gets into financial trouble). They can also enter into contracts (e.g. the lease agreement for their warehouse unit) in their name of the business rather than their own names and, if the firm has vehicles, these can also be owned by the business rather than by one or other of the partners.

The downside of incorporation is the costs of setting up and running the company, though these are not very great for a small proprietary company, especially when spread over the likely life of the business. The taxation aspect may also be relevant – will they pay more tax as a company than they would as individual partners? This is a matter on which they should seek expert professional advice. Subject to the taxation aspect, it is probably worth forming a company.

As to the legal requirements, there are none if they decide to form a partnership, although they would be well advised to draw up a partnership agreement to avoid future arguments and misunderstandings and to override any unwanted provisions of the Partnership Act. This is another area in which professional advice would be desirable. If they incorporate, they will need to undergo the formal process laid down by the Corporations Act and send in the requisite form, with the prescribed fee, to ASIC. They

Accounting and Finance 2A   ISBN 9780170182041   Cengage Learning Australia

will need to decide whether to accept the internal rules for running companies that are contained within the Act or whether to draw up their own rules in a company constitution. Whichever business structure they adopt, they will need to register their chosen business name with the relevant state authority and they will also need to obtain an Australian Business Number and register for GST (covered later in this chapter).

ACCOUNTING ASSUMPTIONS

There are a number of assumptions and principles that underlie all the procedures involved in business financial management and these need to be understood before we go on to consider the procedures themselves.

The accounting entity assumption

When a business is created it can be identified as an operation apart from the owner or owners (partners or shareholders). For accounting purposes, a business is viewed as one entity and the owner as a separate entity. The business activities of the business are recorded separately from those of the owner. This is the *accounting entity assumption*, which is sometimes called the entity assumption or business entity assumption.

Accountants view the business in relation to the owner. Whether or not the business is a legal entity (i.e. an incorporated body registered under law), it will always be an accounting entity. This perspective of two entities has generated the notion that a transaction within the business ultimately only occurs to benefit the owner. A gain made by the business is in fact a gain made for the owner while a loss made within the business ultimately reduces the value of the owner's interest.

 Key Concept 1.5

Accounting entity assumption

The accounting entity assumption is that the business entity is viewed as being separate from the owner(s) and the business records are kept separate from the records of the owner.

Principle of double entry

The origins of a double-entry recording process emerged in the Italian Renaissance period and it is claimed that around 1458 Luca Pacioli contributed documentation of a logical model to record the financial relationship between a business and its owner. Thankfully computers have removed the need for demanding manual recording processes, though the underlying double entry principles remain.

In its simplest form, this principle reflects the fact that when an owner contributes value to a business, in return the business 'owes' the owner an amount equal to what was contributed (i.e. business assets = business obligations). This model can be extended to include contributions made by other third parties (e.g. lenders).

This relationship can be shown in what is called the 'accounting equation' as follows:

$$A \text{ (assets)} = L \text{ (liabilities)}$$

This is usually refined by distinguishing between the business's obligations to the owner and to outsiders, as follows:

$$A \text{ (assets)} = L \text{ (liabilities to outsiders)} + E \text{ (equity, i.e. liability to owner)}$$

 Key Concept 1.6

The accounting equation

The accounting equation expresses the relationship between a firm's assets and the sources from which these have been funded and can be shown as:

$$A \text{ (assets)} = L \text{ (debts to outsiders)} + E \text{ (debts to the owner)}$$

From this it can be seen that every transaction has a double effect. An increase (or decrease) in assets can only occur with a corresponding increase (or decrease) in liabilities or equity. For example, if a bank lends the business $10000, the assets (cash) will increase by that amount and so will the liabilities (debt to the bank). If an owner withdraws inventory worth $500 from the business for their personal use, the assets (stock) will go down by that amount, as will the equity (what the firm owes the owner).

This principle also applies to transactions within the accounting equation's classifications, particularly when one asset is exchanged for another. For example, if the firm buys a new computer for $1500 cash, this will increase one asset (computers) by $1500 and reduce another (cash) by the same amount. If a debtor pays the business $400 he owes, this will increase one asset (cash) and reduce another (accounts receivable) by $400.

In every case the transaction has two parts which will equal each other and leave the accounting equation in balance. Later in this chapter we will see how the system is applied in practice to record the effect of financial transactions on a business.

Key Concept 1.7

Principle of double entry

The principle of double entry is that every transaction has a two-fold effect, each part affecting one or more of the elements of the accounting equation in such a way that it remains in balance.

The accounting period assumption

Owners are interested in the business results. It is common practice to regularly report the results at particular time periods, such as monthly or yearly. Regular reporting permits the owners and other interested stakeholders to compare the results from one period to the next and make controlling decisions to improve performance. In order to do this, the continuous life of a business must be divided into equal time intervals, described as accounting periods. Within these periods the earned income and the associated expenses for the period are recognised.

In Australia the financial year – and therefore the annual accounting period – is often aligned with the taxation year, which runs from 1 July to 30 June the following year. Some businesses have their financial year running from 1 January to 31 December each year. For management purposes, shorter accounting periods, such as quarters (three months) or months, are frequently adopted.

Key Concept 1.8

Accounting period assumption

The accounting period assumption is that the operating life of a business can be divided into equal, arbitrary time intervals for reporting purposes.

The going-concern assumption

Financial reports are normally prepared on the assumption that an entity (business) is a going concern (i.e. that it will continue to operate successfully for the foreseeable future). Hence it is assumed that the entity has neither the intention nor the need to liquidate (close down) or limit the scale of its operations. All the assets in the business exist to help generate the profit and their value is the future economic benefit the business expects to obtain from them, usually the original cost less any part of that written off as an expense (see Chapter 8 regarding depreciation of assets). They are not valued at what they might sell for if the firm was obliged to sell them (liquidation value) since it is assumed that this is not going to happen. Of course, if a business is failing, the going-concern assumption may no longer apply and assets will be valued at liquidation value, usually giving a far lower total balance for assets and hence lower equity.

Accounting and Finance 2A   ISBN 9780170182041   Cengage Learning Australia

Key Concept 1.9

Going-concern assumption

The going-concern assumption is that the life of the business will continue in operation for the foreseeable future and this will be reflected in the asset values in the balance sheet.

The accrual accounting assumption

Most business financial reports are prepared on the *accrual basis of accounting*. Under this basis, the effects of transactions and other events are recognised when they occur and not when cash or its cash equivalent is received or paid. They are recorded in the accounting records and reported in the financial reports of the periods to which they relate.

An example of accrual accounting could be a worker's wages. A worker can complete a task in one month and be paid in the following month. The expense of the wages is recorded and reported in the first month and related to the earned revenue to calculate the profit for that month. It is not taken as an expense in the second month when it is paid.

A second example is the use of a machine over many years in a business. This creates the need to allocate a proportion of the machine cost per period (through a depreciation accounting process, see Chapter 8), not just a single expense when the machine was purchased.

The alternative to accrual accounting is *cash accounting* where revenue and expense are recognised only when the cash is actually received or paid. This basis is only suitable for very small businesses whose transactions are invariably on a cash (rather than a credit) basis. The Framework for the preparation and presentation of financial reports (discussed in more detail later) envisages the use of accrual accounting.

Key Concept 1.10

Accrual basis assumption

The accrual basis assumption is that income and expense are recognised when they take place – income when it is earned (i.e. the point of sale or provision of service) and expense when it is incurred (i.e. used or consumed) – not necessarily when the payments are made or received.

The monetary assumption

Accountants assume that the currency (i.e. the Australian dollar) is a recognised form of exchange of value and events expressed in money terms provide a useful base to understand decisions of economic importance. Thus financial reports will not include items that cannot be expressed in money terms. There is a move, in the case of public company reports, to include information on social and environmental issues that could have a bearing on a company's performance but until the impacts (negative or positive) of these issues can be expressed in monetary terms they will remain as additional notes to the accounts rather than in the body of the financial reports themselves.

The monetary assumption is important as it assists users to understand the financial information presented to them and also makes it possible for comparisons to be made between businesses and different periods.

Key Concept 1.11

Monetary assumption

The monetary assumption is that measurement of the elements of financial statements and their reporting shall be in terms of money values (i.e. the currency of the country in which the report is presented) and only items capable of being expressed in monetary terms are included in financial reports.

Accounting and Finance: 2A   ISBN 9780170182041   Cengage Learning Australia

Historical cost

There are a number of ways of expressing the value of assets. These include:
- what the asset cost to purchase (historical cost)
- what the asset would be worth if it was sold today (market or net realisable value)
- what the asset is worth to the business (future economic benefit).

The latter two bases of valuation, while they may be more helpful in some circumstances, share the drawback that they are dependent on estimate or opinion rather than verifiable fact. The historical cost method, however, values assets (and other expenditures) at what they originally cost – of which there is factual, documentary evidence in the form of the source document for the payment (tax invoice). Consequently, assets will normally be valued in a business's accounts at what they actually cost when purchased (their historical cost) rather than any estimated current value.

Some assets, such as land, which may gain significantly in value over time, can be the subject of formal revaluation and, in times of high inflation, some large businesses will express their reports in terms of the 'present-day value' of the expenditures. In general, however, reporting will conform to the historical cost principle.

Key Concept 1.12

Historical cost principle

Assets and other expenditures will normally be recorded and reported at their actual, historical cost, as evidenced by the documents used to support the original payment.

ELEMENTS OF FINANCIAL STATEMENTS

Accounting in Australia is guided by a document known as The Framework for the Preparation and Presentation of Financial Statements (called the Framework). The Framework is intended to lay out broad conceptual guidelines within which accounting information can be recorded and reports prepared in such a way that they will be accurate, informative and comparable. Obviously all businesses should be preparing reports on the same basis so that well-informed decisions can be taken – especially those that require the comparison of one business with another. An outline of the purpose and content of the Framework can be found on the CPA Australia website.

The Framework identifies and defines the elements that must be included in financial reports: assets, liabilities, income, expenses and equity (the owner's interest in the business).

www.cpaaustralia.com.au/cps/rde/xbcr/SID-3F57FECB-7978925B/cpa/AASB_fact_sheet_framework_180208.pdf

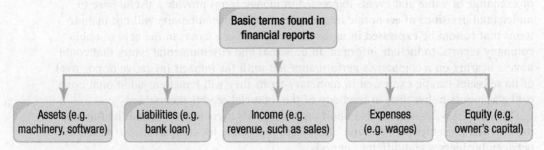

Figure 1.12 Terms in financial reports

The following definitions of assets and liabilities assume that the events will occur and that the assets and liabilities can be accurately measured in dollar terms. For example, the ore in a gold mine is an asset only if it can be mined and sold at a known price; timber in a plantation can be considered an asset if a reasonable estimate can be made of its future selling price; if a firm is sued for damages by an aggrieved customer,

Accounting and Finance: 2A   ISBN 9780170182041   Cengage Learning Australia

the damages only become a liability in accounting terms when the court has ruled in favour of the customer and has set a figure for the damages awarded.

Assets

An asset is defined as a resource controlled by an entity as a result of a past event. A resource is an item that represents a future economic benefit for the business. A list of business assets could include cash, land, machinery, accounts receivable, inventories, artworks, patents and other intellectual property (intangibles). It is assumed that all assets will contribute to the current and future economic benefit of the business by their use or conversion to alternative economic benefits. It is important to note that the item must be the result of a *past* transaction and that the business need only *control* (not own) the item for it to be considered an asset. This enables, for example, a long-term lease to be recorded as an asset.

Key Concept 1.13

Asset

An asset is a resource, embodying a future economic benefit, that is controlled by an entity as a result of a past transaction.

Liabilities

A liability in a business is defined as a present obligation of the entity arising from past events, the settlement of which will result in a future outflow of resources of the business. Common examples of liabilities are loans from a bank or trade creditors (payables) for goods and services provided on credit. Note that the obligation must be a *present* obligation and not a future or extinguished obligation and that it must be the result of a past event.

Key Concept 1.14

Liability

A liability is a present obligation of the entity arising from past events, the settlement of which will result in a future outflow of resources of the business.

Income

Income is expressed as increases in economic benefits during the accounting period as inflows or increases of assets or decreases of liabilities that increase the worth of the owner's investment (equity) other than those inflows relating to contributions by the owner to the business.

Income of a business is described as 'revenue' when the income derives from the normal course of business (e.g. sales of goods in a shop) or fees from performing a service

Accounting and Finance: 2A   ISBN 9780170182041   Cengage Learning Australia

(such as a doctor's consulting fees). Income also includes 'gains', which is income arising from the upward valuation or disposal of non-current assets (i.e. not in the normal course of business). An example of a gain would be the profit on the sale of an investment.

Clearly income is the lifeblood of a business and must exceed expenses if the business is to make a profit and thus increase the net assets of the business and the owner's worth.

Note that capital contributions by the owner, although they would obviously increase equity, are specifically excluded from income.

Examples of income	
Revenue	• Sale of goods (Sales) • Performance of service (Fees) • Interest revenue • Rent revenue • Commission revenue
Gain	• Revaluation • Gain on disposal of asset

Key Concept 1.15

Income

Income is an increase in economic benefits during the accounting period as a result of inflows or increases of assets or decreases of liabilities that increase the worth of the owner's investment (equity) other than those inflows relating to contribution by the owner to the business.

Expenses

An expense is a decrease in the economic benefits of a business during the accounting period in the form of outflows of assets or increases in liabilities that have the effect of reducing the owner's equity other than the owner withdrawing equity. Typical examples of expenses include wages, insurance, advertising, cleaning and depreciation of assets. Expenses can extend to 'losses', such as the theft or deterioration of inventory and the decline in the value of foreign currency holdings or investments.

Once again, reductions in equity as a result of the withdrawal of cash or other resources (drawings) by the owner are specifically excluded from expenses.

Examples of expenses
• Salaries and wages • Electricity • Cost of sales • Insurance • Depreciation • Advertising • Bad debts • Loss on disposal of asset

Accounting and Finance: 2A   ISBN 9780170182041   Cengage Learning Australia

Key Concept 1.16

Expense

An expense is a decrease in economic benefits of a business during the accounting period in the form of outflows of assets or increases in liabilities that have the effect of reducing the owner's equity other than the owner's drawings.

Equity

Equity is the more formal term for the owner's contribution to or interest in the business, often called 'capital'. Equity is described as the residual interest in the assets of the business after deducting all its liabilities (i.e. assets − liabilities = net assets (equity). Equity can obviously increase or decrease as the owner(s) contribute more to a business or withdraw funds (drawings or dividends). However, equity also increases with income and decreases with expense, which will result in a net increase in equity if the business makes a profit and a net decrease if the business makes a loss. This enables us to expand the accounting equation as follows:

$$Assets = Liabilities - (Equity + Income - Expense)$$

Key Concept 1.17

Equity

Equity is the residual interest in assets after the external liabilities have been subtracted.

RECORDING CHANGES – DEBITS AND CREDITS

Having defined the elements of financial reports, we can now turn our attention to the mechanics of recording transactions on a double-entry basis.

We have seen that every financial transaction has a double effect: an increase in an asset may be balanced by an equivalent increase in a liability (e.g. a business buying stock on credit) and an increase in one asset may be balanced by a corresponding decrease in another (e.g. a business buying a vehicle for cash). Accountants use the terms 'debit' and 'credit' to describe the equal and opposite nature of transactions. If we look at the basic accounting equation:

$$A = L + E$$

everything that increases the left-hand side of the equation is described as a debit and everything increasing the right-hand side is a credit. By the same token, of course, anything that decreases assets is a credit and anything decreasing liabilities or equity will be a debit. Assets will normally have a debit value, while liabilities and equity will have a credit value. The equation must remain in balance, so the debits will always equal the credits.

Example 1.1

EXAMPLE:

Josef Sabuni commences his business, Sabuni Office Products, by opening a bank account and depositing $20 000 of his own money into it. Following this initial transaction, the business's accounting equation will look like this:

Assets	=	Liabilities	+	Equity
(Cash at bank) $20 000	=	0	+	(Capital − J Sabuni) $20 000

The item 'Cash at bank' was debited with $20 000 and 'Capital J Sabuni was credited with the same amount.

The business then buys office equipment for $4500 cash. This will require a debit to the new asset 'Office equipment', which has increased and a credit to the asset 'Cash at bank' which has decreased. The new accounting equation looks like this:

Assets	=	Liabilities	+	Equity
Cash at bank $15500	=	0	+	(Capital − J Sabuni) $20000
Office equipment $\dfrac{\$4500}{\$20000}$				$20000

Let us now suppose that the business buys $6000 worth of stock from Supertramp on credit. This creates a new asset (stock), which will be debited with $6000 and a new liability (Supertramp), which will be credited. The new accounting equation will be:

Assets	=	Liabilities	+	Equity
Cash at bank $15500	=	Supertramp = $\dfrac{\$6000}{\$6000}$	+	(Capital − J Sabuni) $20000
Office equipment $4500				$20000
Stock $\dfrac{\$6000}{\$26000}$				

The analysis of these transactions can also be shown in the form of a table, as follows.

Transaction	Items affected	Nature of item A, L or E	+ or −	Debit $	Credit $
Deposit to start business	Cash at bank	A	+	20000	
	Capital	E	+		20000
Buy office equipment	Office equipment	A	+	4500	
	Cash at bank	A	−		4500
Purchase stock on credit	Stock	A	+	6000	
	Supertramp	L	+		6000

This clearly demonstrates that every transaction has both a debit and a credit aspect which must be equal so that the accounting equation remains balanced.

Let us now add income and expenses. Remember income has the effect of increasing equity. Consequently, it has a credit nature. Expense, on the other hand, reduces equity and hence has a debit nature.

Let us assume that the business sells stock for $2800 cash (for simplicity's sake, we will disregard the cost of the stock sold) and pays wages of $750. The first transaction will involve a debit to cash at bank, which is increased by $2800 and a credit to a new item of income called 'sales'. The second transaction will debit an expense item called 'wages' and credit the asset 'cash at bank', which is reduced. We can extend our analysing chart as follows. Expenses are denoted by the letter X.

Transaction	Items affected	Nature of item A, L, E, I or X	+ or −	Debit $	Credit $
Deposit to start business	Cash at bank	A	+	20000	
	Capital	E	+		20000
Buy office equipment	Office equipment	A	+	4500	
	Cash at bank	A	−		4500
Purchase stock on credit	Stock	A	+	6000	
	Supertramp	L	+		6000
Sell stock for cash	Cash at bank	A	+	2800	
	Sales	I	+		2800
Pay wages in cash	Wages	E	+	750	
	Cash at Bank	A	−		750

Accounting and Finance: 2A   ISBN 9780170182041   Cengage Learning Australia

If we were to show the accounting equation for Sabuni Office Products after all these transactions it would look like this:

$$\text{Assets} = \text{Liabilities} + \text{Equity} + (\text{Income} - \text{expenses})$$

Cash at bank $17 550*	$= \text{Supertramp} = \dfrac{\$6\,000}{\$6\,000}$	$+$ (Capital – J Sabuni) $20 000
Office equipment $4 500		$+$ Sales $2 800
Stock $\dfrac{\$6\,000}{\$28\,050}$		$-$ Wages $\dfrac{(\$750)}{\$22\,050}$

*(15 500 + 2 800 − 750)

To summarise, a business entity's assets and Products are said to have a debit nature and its liabilities, equity and income a credit nature. Every transaction has an equivalent debit and credit aspect, so that the accounting equation will always remain in balance. This statement is illustrated in the following table.

Item	Nature	Increase	Decrease
Assets	Debit	Debit	Credit
Liabilities	Credit	Credit	Debit
Equity	Credit	Credit	Debit
Income	Credit	Credit	Debit
Expenses	Debit	Debit	Credit

How the debit/credit convention is used to record information in a business's financial records is covered in detail in Chapter 2.

THE NEED FOR FINANCE

Business proprietors need funds to establish, operate and expand their businesses. These funds may come from internal sources (the owners themselves) – known as equity – or from external sources – known as debt finance (borrowings). The funds may be in the form of cash or access to credit.

Businesses need funds for a variety of purposes, including setting up the business, and for use as working capital and capital expenditure.

Setting up the business

In setting up a business you must take into account the purchase of the assets – plant and equipment, furniture, vehicles, computer system and so on – that the business will need for its operations. If purchasing an existing business, the cost of that business's assets, which could include goodwill, i.e. the value of the firm's reputation, its customer base and its business name.

Working capital

Working capital consists of funds to enable the business to operate from day to day. A merchandising business needs to purchase trading stock before it can be sold. Sales may be on credit so the collection of cash from accounts receivable may occur months after the goods were purchased and paid for. Other expenses (e.g. rent, electricity and wages) have to be paid in cash regularly. Many of them, such as rent and insurance, may have to be paid up front before any revenue is earned. If the firm is newly established, it may be a while before significant cash starts to flow into the business and meanwhile expenses have to be paid. The need for working capital is often underestimated and the lack of adequate working capital is a prime cause of business failure.

Capital expenditure

Capital expenditure is additional capital to fund additional non-current assets. This includes premises from which to operate the business or machinery to expand the business or replace older machinery that has worn out or become obsolete.

SOURCES OF FINANCE

Businesses obtain finance from both internal and external sources. These funds may be needed for different periods of time and are known as short-term, medium-term or long-term finance.

Internal sources

Internal sources of finance are funds provided by the owners, known as equity finance. This includes:

- capital contributed by the owners, including capital introduced by additional owners as partners or, if a company, as shareholders
- retained earnings; after a business has made a profit it usually distributes some of the profit as drawings or dividends, but the undistributed profits are kept within the business and are known as retained earnings.

Capital is usually contributed in the form of cash but it may also be in the form of other non-cash assets such as vehicles or machinery.

The benefits of internal sources of finance are that the money does not have to be paid back, as is the case with loans, nor is there an ongoing cost that must be met in the form of interest. On the other hand, the availability of equity for small businesses is limited: the sole trader has only one owner and, though partnerships and proprietary companies can call on more people (20 and 50 respectively), this is still a limiting factor. Introducing additional owners will dilute the control of the existing owners and reduce their proportional share of the profit.

Relying heavily on equity finance also means that the business is not able to enjoy the benefits of *leverage* or *gearing* – where the owners benefit from the return on the borrowed funds invested, as long as the overall returns remain above the cost of the borrowed funds. This concept will be explored in more detail in Chapter 11.

Internal finance might also be taken to include loans to the business from the owner or owners. Although these have the characteristics of liabilities, they are significantly less risky – it is unlikely that a partner or shareholder will take action against the business if interest or loan repayments have to be deferred when the business is in financial strife.

Internal sources are useful in funding expenditure that is not expected to bring an immediate return, such as the initial establishment of a new business, since they will not need to be repaid and may be content to receive no return in the short term in the expectation of large returns in the long term.

External sources

External sources of finance are funds provided by people or businesses who are not owners of the business. The business will therefore have a liability to pay back the funds and also pay costs to service the loans. For the business these external funds will be

Accounting and Finance: 2A   ISBN 9780170182041   Cengage Learning Australia

shown as liabilities on the balance sheet and the costs shown as financial expenses in the Income statement. There is a wide variety of external sources of finance. The main examples are briefly examined below.

- An *overdraft* is a bank lending agreement under which a business is allowed to make payments in excess of any current 'cash at bank' balance. It is the most common form of temporary finance for business. The purpose of an overdraft is to provide working capital (such as for inventory and creditors), rather than to finance long term non-current assets. Usually the bank sets an overdraft limit (a maximum amount the business can be overdrawn by). The balance of the 'cash at bank' account will go up and down depending on deposits and withdrawals, but must not exceed the overdraft limit. If the cash at bank ledger account is a debit balance ('in the black') it will be shown as an asset; if there is a credit balance ('in the red') it is shown as a liability.

   The benefit of an overdraft is its flexibility – the amount borrowed goes up and down as the funds are needed and the firm is only charged interest on the amount borrowed. On the other hand, banks usually expect the overdraft to be 'fully fluctuating' (i.e. the account should occasionally go into the black) so it is not suitable as a long-term funding source.

- A *bill of exchange* is type of loan where a business borrows money through a bank with the funds provided by one outside investor. It is a written contract for a period of 180 days or less. Accepted bills of exchange have been signed by the bank, which accepts liability to pay out the funds on the due date. The investor provides the net amount, while the borrower must repay the full value of the contract. The difference is the interest earned on the funds borrowed. These are suitable for short-term needs but must be repaid on time and they bear relatively high interest rates.

- A *term loan* is a source of finance from a bank or a finance company that is borrowed for a set period of time and has to be repaid at the end of this term (often a year or number of years). As such, it may be used for relatively long-term funding. These loans should be used to finance the purchase of non-current assets so that the income earned from the asset can help to pay the interest on the loan and to repay the loan amount when it becomes due.

   Loans may be *secured* or *unsecured*. If a loan is secured, it means the borrowers have given the lender security on certain assets. The lender holds the title to certain assets (usually land) so that if the loan is not repaid, the lender can sell the asset to recover their money. One form of secured loan is a mortgage. Since small businesses may be unable to offer any security from within the firm's own assets, it is not uncommon for the owners to have to offer their personal assets (e.g. the family home) as security for business borrowings. From the borrower's viewpoint, an unsecured loan is preferable, since they will not be placing their own or the firm's assets in direct jeopardy. However, as the risk to the lender is higher for an unsecured loan, the rate of interest charged tends to be higher than for a secured loan.

- *Lease finance* is an agreement to rent plant and equipment, usually for a fixed period of time. The business has control and use of the asset but legally does not own the asset. At the end of the lease period, the asset is returned to the lessor or an amount is negotiated to buy the asset. Leasing is very suitable for the funding of assets such as vehicles and equipment, although it can also be used for land and buildings. This form of financing has the benefit that the firm can have the use of the assets without having to fund their purchase. On the other hand, the lease payments must be kept up, even in hard times and the firm does not have the right to sell the assets within the lease period nor, in the case of buildings, benefit from any increase in value over time.

- *Trade credit* – when a business buys on credit and is given a period of time to pay (perhaps as much as one or two months), it is effectively using the supplier's funds to help finance the business. If the supplier does not charge interest on the amounts owed, which is often the case, this effectively amounts to an interest-free short-term loan. However, this is only a very short-term means of providing working capital and firms should beware of extending the time of repayment. Not only may the supplier start charging high interest on amounts owing, but they might also threaten to cut off supply until arrears are paid, which could worsen what is probably already a bad situation.

- *Factoring* is a process where a business sells its debts to a finance company for an amount less than the full value and receives cash immediately. The finance company then collects the full amount owing from the debtors over a period of time. The difference in value is the finance company's profit on the exercise. The firm has the benefit of freeing up the funds otherwise tied up in accounts receivable, which can be used more productively elsewhere and also does not have the cost and aggravation of following up slow-paying debtors. The disadvantage is the commission that has to be paid to the finance company.
- *Credit cards* may be used to pay for some expenses and supplies. Credit cards have the benefit of convenience but they are a very expensive form of short-term finance; if the credit card balance is not paid off within the interest-free period. Interest rates on unpaid credit card balances are usually more than twice the rate applicable to term loans.

The sources of finance outlined above are equally available to all small businesses, no matter what their organisational structure, though obviously partnerships and proprietary companies have a potentially greater supply of equity finance because they can have a larger number of owners. Public companies may approach the general public for funds, which gives them access to a huge source of finance. However, they are outside the scope of this book.

Humpty and Dumpty are going into a business partnership, which they are calling Eggcellent Enterprises, to set up and run a chicken farm in the outer Perth metropolitan area producing eggs for the Western Australian market. They have purchased the necessary land out of their own resources at a cost of $500 000.

They estimate that they will require an additional $800 000 to construct or buy the sheds, equipment and vehicles that are needed. It will be four months before they sell their first eggs, during which time they must pay wages, power and increasing feed bills for the growing chickens as well as other expenses such as insurance and shire rates. These are expected to amount to $10 000 in the first month, rising to $20 000 by month four, giving a total working capital requirement of about $60 000.

Humpty has several rich relatives, including one, Anna Kingsman, who made a fortune out of the mining boom and has a lot of spare cash at the moment. The partners both own their own homes, although both of them have bank home loans (coincidentally with the same bank) secured by a mortgage and each still owes about half the market value of the homes. Their contributions to the cost of the land used up virtually all their own resources.

The partners need to plan how they are going to finance their new business.

Commentary

The business needs long-term finance (to purchase the fixed assets) and short-term finance (to fund the working capital). For the former, it would be feasible to enter into a lease arrangement with a bank or finance company for the land and buildings. However, the partners would like to be able to profit from what they see as the likely long-term increase in the value of the property as the built-up area of the city expands. The best option, therefore, would be a term loan (perhaps five to ten years) from the bank. The firm is in the fortunate position of being able to offer security in the form of the buildings and the land on which they stand and, if this is considered inadequate, could up-stamp the existing mortgages on the partners' homes. It is unlikely that the bank will be prepared to lend the whole amount needed, but the shortfall could be met by an unsecured loan from Anna Kingsman, although the interest rate would need to be a bit higher to make it attractive to her. Kingsman might be interested in an equity contribution (i.e. becoming a partner in the enterprise herself), but Humpty and Dumpty would prefer not to have to share the benefits of what they expect to be a very profitable venture.

As to the long-term finance needs, the firm can obtain some funding through the credit offered by the feed supplier, who is prepared to give two months' interest-free terms to attract the firm's business. The remainder will be provided by a bank overdraft, which, given that the bank will already have security in respect of its other loan, should not be a problem. Factoring is obviously not an option until the firm starts selling eggs, but may perhaps become so as time goes on.

As a side issue, what benefits do you think the partners might obtain from incorporating their business as a proprietary limited company?

FINANCIAL INSTITUTIONS' LENDING DECISIONS

Lenders earn income (interest and fees) by lending money. However, they take a commercial risk that the principal of the loan and all interest owing will be paid on time. Their essential concerns are two-fold:

- security – How safe is our investment? Will the firm be able to make its payments of interest and repayment on the loan? If the business fails, will we get our money back?
- return – Is the return we will receive consistent with the risk we are being asked to take? How does it compare with returns from alternative forms of investment?

As you can see, assessment of risk is fundamental to both these questions. There is generally a direct relationship between risk and return – the higher the perceived risk, the greater the return is likely to be. As we have noted above, unsecured loans are likely to bear a higher rate of interest than secured loans, simply because they are riskier – when a firm goes bankrupt, secured creditors may have some hope of recovering their money, unsecured creditors are very unlikely to do so. In the case of a large, well-established business, such as Wesfarmers or BHP Billiton, the lending risk is relatively low. The same is certainly not true of the average small business, given the statistics that show that 70 per cent of small businesses fail, for one reason or another, within five years of starting up.

Lenders, therefore, will carefully evaluate a number of risk factors before approving finance. These factors include collateral, liquidity, history, guarantors, interest rate available and future business.

Collateral

Can the borrower provide assets that can be used as security for the loan? If there are any amounts unpaid at the end of the loan period, or the borrower defaults on payments during the term of the loan, these assets can be sold and the proceeds used to recover the amounts owing. Any surplus from the sale of the pledged assets is returned to the borrower.

Liquidity

Does the business have adequate cash flow to be able to pay the interest and other fees at the regular due dates? This requires scrutiny of the firm's other short-term obligations as well as the expected cash inflows.

History

Lenders will investigate the credit history of the business (and the owners). This includes a record of previous loans, credit card repayments and court cases (particularly any involving claims for money). They will also look at how long the business and the owner(s) have been operating and the business's previous profitability, working capital and gearing. They will make an assessment of the industry the borrower operates in and the general state of the economy.

Guarantors

Guarantors are people other than the borrower who are prepared to guarantee that the borrower can pay interest and loan principal when due. If the borrower defaults (does not repay any amounts due) then the lender will require the guarantors to make the necessary repayments. If the borrower is a limited company, whose owners therefore do not have liability for the firm's debts, the lender may well require guarantees from the directors and/or shareholders, especially if the company does not have significant assets against which the loan may be secured.

Interest rate available

The lender must judge whether the interest rate that can be charged is sufficiently attractive to make the investment worthwhile, when compared with alternative investments. For instance, if the interest rate that a business borrower can afford is no greater than that which the lender can obtain in the (generally much safer) home loan market, the lender may be reluctant to make the business loan.

Future business

A bank lender will want to make a judgement on the likelihood of the borrower's business going from strength to strength and being able to provide the bank with significant business opportunities in the future. This will be a problematic process, but the long-term benefits might be immense for the lender. Today's struggling young entrepreneur looking for a $20000 loan to help him set up his little IT business could be tomorrow's Bill Gates!

The lender decision

The lender then makes a judgement, based on all these factors, about whether to lend and, if so, at what price. The higher the risk, the higher the rate of interest that will be charged and the more conditions that will need to be met before the loan will be granted. For example, a business that has just started with minimal capital, no significant assets and no profit history will find it harder and more expensive to get a loan than a business that can offer land as security, has been making profits for many years and has strong liquidity.

REALITY CHECK 1.3

Simone Simple is an accountant with a large accounting firm in Perth. She is an experienced and highly respected professional who has worked in a variety of accounting fields in the ten years or so since she qualified. She has decided that she wants to go into business on her own in her home town of Geraldton. Unfortunately, she has very few financial resources of her own, having been involved in a disastrous property deal a couple of years back, which ended up in the courts and cost her all her savings. She lives in rental accommodation and will continue to do so in Geraldton, although she is hoping to find a property that could serve as both residence and office. She is hopeful of being able to exploit her family contacts in the area and, in fact, has already signed up several potential clients. Simone has estimated that the cost of establishing her business, including purchasing furniture and equipment, computers and software and expenses such as rent and insurance payable up front, will be approximately $50000. She has approached the local branch of the A-to-Z Bank for a loan of this amount. How do you think the manager of the bank would assess this request?

Accounting and Finance 2A   ISBN 9780170182041   Cengage Learning Australia

Commentary

From the bank's viewpoint, the main problem with this loan is the complete absence of collateral. Simone has no significant assets at the moment to offer as security, although no doubt some of the $50 000 will be spent on things such as computers and furniture, which would have some resale value in the event of default. There is also the matter of the property deal that went wrong, which the bank would probably want to know a bit more about. Was it Simone's fault or was it just bad luck or fraudulent behaviour on someone else's part?

On the positive side, Simone has shown herself to be a very competent practitioner in the field in which she will be working. She already has a reputation and contacts in the region, which should enable her to establish her business relatively quickly. We can also assume that, as an accountant, she will have produced detailed budgets to demonstrate the firm's future cash flows and its capacity to meet its loan obligations. Geraldton is an area that is likely to grow substantially in the future, with a number of industrial projects planned and it could well be that Simone's business will grow with it.

The bank, of course, does not have unlimited funds to lend and Simone's application will need to be weighed up against other applications that have been submitted at this time. However, on balance, provided the bank is satisfied with the financial projections that Simone will have prepared, it is likely that they will look favourably on her application, though they might ask her if she is able to provide a guarantor for the loan (e.g. a family member) to make up for the lack of collateral.

GOODS AND SERVICES TAX

In order to be able to provide the community with the services it demands, governments have to raise taxes from the community. Much of this tax consists of taxes on income – personal income tax and company tax – and businesses have some obligations in this regard, which we shall consider in Chapter 5. However, much government revenue comes from taxes on expenditure – what are generally known as *sales taxes*. In Australia most of the various sales taxes have now been combined into a single sales tax called the *Goods and Services Tax (GST)*. This applies at a flat rate of 10 per cent on value to the vast majority of goods and services produced and consumed in this country. Those purchasing goods and services are required to pay to the provider of the product a tax of 10 per cent of the value of the product. For example, if you buy a pair of shoes from K-Mart worth $50, you will actually have to pay K-Mart $55, the extra $5 being the GST on the purchase. It is common for displayed prices to be inclusive of GST (i.e. in the example above, the displayed price would probably have been '$55 inc. GST'). The business itself will pay GST on goods and services it purchases in the course of its business. In our example, if K-Mart had purchased the shoes from a factory in Adelaide for $25 excluding GST, they would have had to pay $2.50 in GST to the vendor.

Exemptions

Some goods and services are either exempt from GST or are deemed to be 'input taxed', which comes to almost the same thing. Examples include:
- exemptions
  - most basic foodstuffs
  - certain medical supplies, medicines and medical equipment
  - certain educational supplies and services
  - some childcare and supplies to retirement villages and the disabled
- input taxed
  - residential rent
  - financial supplies (e.g. lending money and trading in securities).

The main difference between exemption and input-taxed status is that providers of input-taxed services are not entitled to claim GST they may have paid on goods or services purchased to provide the input-taxed product (see below under 'GST collections and outlays').

GST is also not included in the payment of wages and salaries.

Registering for GST

Every business with an annual turnover (gross value of income received) greater than $75000 is required to register for GST. Businesses with an annual turnover lower than $75000 may register for GST if they wish. At the time of application for registration they must also apply for an Australian Business Number (ABN) if they do not already have one. The ABN is used to identify the business for GST purposes.

GST collections and outlays

Businesses are required to add GST to the value of all goods and services they provide and to record the amount of GST they receive. These amounts are termed *GST collections*. They should also record the amount of GST paid on the purchase of goods and services and the purchase of business assets. These amounts are called *GST outlays*. The difference between the two must be remitted regularly to the Australian Taxation Office (ATO). Most small businesses do this on a quarterly basis. Businesses with an annual turnover in excess of $20 million must report and remit monthly and smaller businesses may elect to do this if they wish, but it is safe to assume that few do. Businesses that have voluntarily registered for GST and certain other businesses with the permission of the ATO may report annually.

It should be noted that the businesses themselves are not actually paying the GST, the burden of which falls on the eventual customer. The business is effectively merely acting as an agent for the government in collecting the tax and remitting it to the ATO.

Example 1.2

EXAMPLE: Poodles is a fashion house selling clothing to the smart set in Perth. Its results for the March quarter were:

Sales (excluding GST)	$289000
Purchases of taxable goods and services (including GST)	$110000
Purchase of new computer system (including GST)	$4400

What is the firm's GST payable to the ATO for the quarter?

Collections: 10% × 289000	= $28900
Outlays: 110000 / 11	= ($10000)
4400 / 11	= ($400)
Net payable to the ATO	$18500

We will deal with the accounting for GST in Chapter 2.

Documentation

Businesses that make sales of goods or services that are subject to GST must provide their customer with an invoice or receipt that contains certain specified information, notably the value of the goods or services provided and the GST charged. These documents, normally called *tax invoices*, are evidence of GST collections. They must also ensure that they obtain from the suppliers of taxable goods and services they purchase tax invoices

Accounting and Finance 2A   ISBN 9780170182041   Cengage Learning Australia

for those purchases, which provide evidence of GST outlays. They will then, usually quarterly, complete a report to the ATO called a *Business Activity Statement (BAS)*, part of which relates to GST. In this part they will state the collections and outlays for the period and show the net amount that they are remitting to the ATO. It is possible for outlays to exceed collections (e.g. for a supplier of tax-exempt products who has paid GST on purchases or where there have been unusually large asset purchases in a period). In that case the ATO will refund the amount of GST effectively overpaid. More detail on the BAS is included in Chapter 3.

You can find out more about the GST requirements for small businesses by visiting the ATO website.

www.ato.gov.au/businesses/
content.asp?doc=/
content/20724.htm

ETHICS

Before concluding, we will refer briefly to a non-financial factor that can have a significant influence on business. It is fair to say that the two dominant factors governing business financial operations are the wish to maximise profit and the need to comply with the law of the land. Often these factors conflict: the business owner may wish to boost the firm's profits by not taking out employer's liability insurance (workers' compensation), especially if the employees are engaged in very low-risk activities, such as normal office work, but the law says that employer's liability insurance is compulsory. Most people would accept, however, that there is a third factor – that of 'ethics'. Ethics may be defined as a set of moral principles or rules of conduct. You could also call ethical behaviour 'doing the right thing'. Sometimes ethical standards are supported by the law and sometimes not. The Christian 'Ten Commandments', for example, state 'you must not steal' (also a legal requirement) and 'you must not covet your neighbour's belongings' (not a legal requirement).

Whether businesses behave ethically will depend partly on whether the owners or managers believe that you should do the right thing as a matter of principle, but also partly on commercial considerations. If a firm is seen to be treating its employees, customers or the general community unfairly, this may harm its reputation or jeopardise the loyalty of employees or the customers, which may have a detrimental effect on its profitability (if not immediately, then some time in the future). We will examine these issues in more detail in later chapters.

Test your knowledge

1 Explain the difference between merchandising, service and manufacturing businesses and give an example of each.

2 Distinguish between a sole trader, a partnership and a limited company.

3 What are the advantages of an incorporated business?

4 Explain the concept of limited liability.

5 What are the legal requirements for a partnership?

6 What is a partnership agreement and what provisions might it contain?

7 What are the legal requirements for a small proprietary company?

8 Define and briefly explain the following accounting assumptions or principles:
   a accounting entity
   b monetary assumption
   c accounting period
   d historical cost
   e going concern.

9   What is the difference between cash and accrual accounting?

10 Explain the principle of double entry accounting.

11 Identify and briefly define the five essential elements of financial reports stated in the Framework.

12 Distinguish between revenue and gains, giving examples of each.

13 Outline the obligations of a business in relation to GST.

14 Identify and compare the main sources of finance available to small business.

15 What factors are likely to influence the decision of a prospective lender on whether to lend money to a small business? How might the lender seek to protect their investment?

16 What is meant by 'ethics' in a business context?

Test your understanding

Topic guide
- Business types: 1.1
- Business organisational structures: 1.2, 1.23, 1.24
- Accounting principles and assumptions: 1.3, 1.4, 1.7, 1.8
- Elements of financial reports: 1.5–1.8
- Accounting equation: 1.9–1.13
- Double entry: 1.14–1.18
- GST: 1.19–1.21
- Sources of finance: 1.22–1.24
- Factors in lending decisions: 1.23, 1.24

1.1   Complete the following table by indicating with a tick what type of business each is.

Business	Merchandising	Service	Manufacturing
Video rental store			
Electronics store			
Cinema			
Gold mine			
Wheat/sheep farm			
Petrol station			
Architect			
Restaurant			
Brickworks			
Newsagent			
Piggery			
Butcher			

1.2   Complete the following table by indicating what types of organisational structure might be suitable for the each of businesses listed? (You can pick more than one type for some businesses.)

Business	Sole trader	Partnership	Proprietary company	Public company
Medical practice				
Iron ore mine				
National retail chain				
Smallgoods manufacturer				
Hairstylist				

Panelbeater				
Vineyard				
Dairy farm				

1.3 The following sentences about accounting assumptions and principles have been jumbled. Rewrite them by matching the descriptions in italics to the correct terms.

a The accounting entity assumption *records transactions when they occur, not necessarily when cash is paid or received.*

b The accounting period assumption *avoids assets being recorded at current market prices.*

c The going concern assumption *focuses on the owner's personal affairs being separated from the business's financial records.*

d The accrual basis of accounting *divides the continuous life of the business into equal time periods.*

e The monetary assumption *assumes the business will continue operating indefinitely.*

f Historical cost accounting *requires that financial reports are confined to items that can be expressed in dollars and cents.*

1.4 For each of the following situations, state which accounting assumption or principle is being illustrated and whether it is being complied with or breached. (There may be more than one assumption involved!)

a Rio Tinto operates in many countries and trades in many different currencies. Its annual report shows its results in terms of Australian dollars.

b Miracle Motors produces its financial reports at the end of the financial year on 30 June and once in between, usually in November, December or January, when the owner has time to do it.

c H Angels has included his motorcycle as a business asset so that he can write off its costs as a business expense. The motorcycle is not used in the business.

d Ming Vases sells many of its products on credit. These sales are recorded when they are made, although the cash may not be received from the debtors for several weeks.

e At the end of each year, Tran's Trucking makes an estimate of what it would get for each of its trucks if it sold them and re-values them accordingly.

1.5 The following sentences about the elements of financial reports have been jumbled. Rewrite them by matching the descriptions in italics to the correct terms.

a An asset is *an inflow of resources resulting in an increase in equity other than capital contributed by the owner.*

b A liability is *an outflow of resources resulting in a decrease in equity other than withdrawals by the owner.*

c Income is *the owner's interest in the business.*

d An expense is *a debt that the entity owes to outsiders.*

e Equity is *a resource with future economic benefits controlled by the entity.*

1.6 For each of the items listed below, state whether it is an asset, a liability, income, an expense or equity for the business:

a fees earned by the business

b rent paid

c an account receivable

d interest earned

e sales

f bank overdraft

g capital contributed by the owner

h credit card balance

i office wages

j salespersons' commissions

Accounting and Finance: 2A   ISBN 9780170182041   Cengage Learning Australia

k   owner's drawings
l   an unpaid bill for electricity
m   office furniture.

1.7   Carey Denmark owns and operates a small florist business as a sole trader called Carey's Florist at the local shopping strip in South Perth. She began operations about three months ago on 1 July 2010 and the following is a sample of some of the events that have taken place during that time:

- She began the business by opening a bank account in the name Carey's Florist, depositing $30000 as capital.
- She signed an agreement on 1 July 2010 to rent a shop for a period of three years. She paid six months rent in advance at that time.
- A supplier of WA local native flowers supplied $1000 worth of flowers on 5 July 2010. Carey received the invoice on 5 July but did not pay the supplier until 15 July 2010.
- She signed a loan agreement with the local bank on 1 August borrowing $20000. A repayment of $300 plus interest of $40 is due each month.
- She purchased $18000 worth of fixtures and fittings on 2 August 2010 for cash.
- She sold flowers worth $200 in relation to a funeral, sending an invoice on 3 August 2010 but did not receive the cash until 20 August 2010.
- She employed one staff member on 1 September 2010 on a wage of $550 per week.
- She signed an agreement on 1 September 2010 with the local advertising agency to advertise the business, agreeing to the production of flyers, brochures and newspaper advertisements in the local newspaper. This will cost $4000 and begin in two months time.
- She paid an electricity bill of $300 for July and August 2010 on 20 September 2010.

Required
a   For each of the above items explain whether they represent an asset, liability, expense, income or equity item, giving reasons for your answer.
b   Where appropriate, explain the accounting assumption(s) that has/have been followed.

1.8   Tom Harley owns and operates a small men's clothing suit hire and retail business, Cats Clothing, at the local shopping centre in Fremantle. The business has been in operation for three years and the following is a sample of some of the events that have taken place during that time:

- Tom decided on 1 April 2010 to contribute a further $10000 to the business.
- He purchased inventory worth $3000 on 5 April, receiving an invoice at this time and paid the amount owing on 14 April.
- He went into overdraft to the extent of $2000 on 15 April 2010.
- He purchased $25000 (invoice cost price) worth of equipment on 30 April 2010 and paid for these items at the same time.
- He sold clothing worth $900 for cash on 3 May 2010.
- He paid $1200 cash on 10 May 2010 to employees, being their wages for the past two weeks.
- He received an order on 1 June 2010 for the hire of suits for a wedding that would take place in July 2010. The customers paid a deposit of $150 on 8 June 2010 to secure the hire arrangements.
- He paid the telephone bill of $410 for April and May 2010 on 12 June 2010.
- Tom withdrew $800 cash from the business for personal use. At the same time he informed the bookkeeper to record $900 for a holiday he had paid for from his own personal bank account. The bookkeeper informed him that this transaction did not need to be recorded in the business records.
- The business bookkeeper prepared the end of year financial statements on 30 June 2010 to determine the business profit. This included determining depreciation on the business assets.

Required
a   For each of the above items explain whether they represent an asset, liability, expense, income or equity item and give reasons for your answer.
b   Where appropriate, explain the accounting assumption(s) that has/have been followed.

Accounting and Finance: 2A   ISBN 9780170182041   Cengage Learning Australia

1.9 For each of the cases below determine the missing figure.

Case	Total assets $	Total liabilities $	Equity $
A	520000	268000	?
B	?	212000	365000
C	689000	?	567200
D	687950	235600	?

1.10 For each of the cases below determine the missing figure.

Case	Total assets $	Total expenses $	Total liabilities $	Equity $	Total income $
A	235600	42100	89500	?	102000
B	?	36500	75600	356420	98600
C	365800	?	81200	209500	112000
D	425000	99560	?	302000	105200
E	654200	206500	104000	406500	?

1.11 Show how each of the following transactions will affect the accounting equation for Hannah's Bananas.
- Hannah opened her business by contributing $30000 and equipment worth $5000.
- The firm bought bananas (stock) worth $3000 for cash.
- The firm received a loan of $8000 from the bank.
- The business purchased a vehicle from Midstream Motors on credit for $25000.
- Hannah withdrew $500 cash from the business for personal use.
- The firm paid Midstream Motors $5000.

1.12 The following are the financial items for Scott Traders as at 30 June 2010:

Accounts receivable	$30000
Bank overdraft	$15000
Capital	?
Fixture and fittings	$70000
Machinery	$220000
Loan payable, due 30/9/15	$50000
Inventory	$25000
Office equipment	$24000
Accounts payable	$32000

Required
Show the accounting equation as at 30 June 2010.

1.13 As at 1 June 2010 Kim's Traders had:

Assets	$500000
Liabilities	$200000
Equity	?

The following are the transactions for Kim's Traders for the month of June:
- Sold inventory for cash $3000.
- Paid $110 to advertise in a local newspaper.
- Sold inventory on credit for $7700.
- Paid wages to a sales assistant $500.
- Purchased inventory on credit worth $14000.
- Paid for the inventory purchased on credit.
- Paid electricity bill of $550.

Accounting and Finance: 2A   ISBN 9780170182041   Cengage Learning Australia

Required

Prepare a new accounting equation after each transaction.

1.14 For each of the items listed, state whether it is of a debit or a credit nature.

Item	Debit	Credit
Delivery vehicle		
P Rose (a debtor)		
Bank overdraft		
Stock of stationery		
Owner's capital		
V Urse (a creditor)		
Unpaid wages		
Goodwill		
Cash in the till		
Office furniture		

1.15 For each of the following transactions, draw up a table to show which item would be debited and which credited.

Transaction	Item to debit	Item to credit
Made a cash sale		
Paid a creditor		
Purchased a truck on credit		
Owner withdrew stock		
Debtor paid his account		
Owner contributed cash		
Purchased stock on credit		
Paid rent		
Received electricity bill (not yet paid)		
Repaid bank loan		

1.16 Enter the following transactions into a table with these headings:

Transaction	Items affected	Nature of item A, L, E, I or X	+ or −	Debit $	Credit $

- Paid annual insurance premium $3200.
- Owner took $250 worth of stock for own use.
- Purchased stock worth $4100 from A Trader on credit.
- Bought a new printer for the office for $300 cash.
- Owner donated two office chairs worth $100 each.
- Made cash sales of $2750.
- Purchased stock for $900 cash.
- Paid wages of $1250.
- Credit sale of $800 to B Carefull.
- Paid A Trader what he was owed ($4100).

1.17 The following financial transactions relate to Sandy Traders for the month of August.
- Owner invested $203 000 cash into the business.
- Purchased $26 200 worth of fixtures and fittings on credit.
- Purchased inventory on credit for $18 000.

Accounting and Finance: 2A   ISBN 9780170182041   Cengage Learning Australia

- Paid $896 to advertise in a local newspaper.
- Sold inventory for cash $7700. The cost of the inventory had been $3100.
- Paid wages to a sales assistant $1020.
- Sold inventory on credit for $9150. The cost of the inventory had been $3120.
- Paid for the fixtures and fittings purchased on 1 August.
- Paid electricity bill of $987.
- Owner withdrew $800 from the business bank account to purchase a television for his house.
- Received the money owing from the debtor for a sale on 13 August.

Required

Prepare a table with the following headings to analyse the above transactions.

Date	Transaction	Items affected	Nature of item A, L, E, I or X	+ or −	Debit $	Credit $

1.18 The following is a summary of the transactions of Stu Chew's business for the month of August. All transactions are exclusive of GST.

Purchase of goods and services	$56 000
Purchase of fixed assets	$20 000
Sales	$131 000

Required

a   Do you think the business would be registered for GST? Explain your answer.

b   On the assumption that it is registered:

   i   Calculate GST outlays for the month.

   ii   Calculate GST collections for the month.

   iii   Calculate the GST payable to the ATO for the month of August.

1.19 From the following transactions calculate the business's GST liability to the ATO.

- Purchased stock on credit for $6820 inclusive of GST.
- Sold a vehicle that was surplus to requirements for $2000 plus GST.
- Cash sales of $3400 plus GST.
- Credit sales of $5610 inclusive of GST.
- Purchased a new filing cabinet for $594 including GST.
- Purchased stock for $1100 cash inclusive of GST.

What are the business's obligations to the ATO with regard to the GST liability that you have calculated?

1.20 The following is a list of transactions for Fatt Tackie Tyres for the month of May. None of the figures includes GST.

Cash sales made	$241 000
Credit sales made	$124 000
Stock purchased	$163 000
Insurance premium paid	$12 400
Owner's drawings	$4 000
Electricity paid	$1 300
Wages paid	$33 600
Repairs to office computer	$400

Required

a   Calculate the GST collections, the GST outlays and the GST payable for the month.

b   If there are any items on the list for which you have not calculated GST, explain the reasons for this.

1.21 For each of the following expenditures, indicate which source(s) of funds would be appropriate (there might be more than one in some cases).

Item	Equity	Loan	Overdraft	Supplier credit	Lease	Factoring	Credit card
Purchase of vehicle							
Purchase of land							
Temporary increase in working capital							
Increase in stock							
Payment of unexpected expenses							
Replacement of old plant							
Make tax payment							
Purchase another business							

1.22 Harriet Vanda, aged 40, years has been operating the Easy Panelbeaters business in Welshpool. The business has a good track record, liquidity has not been a problem and the business has made approximately $75000 profit each year. It produces regular financial reports on an accrual basis.

Harriet now wishes to establish another panelbeating business in Myaree but to do so needs an injection of funds. Anne Young, a friend, has expressed interest in joining the business as a partner. She is willing to contribute $120000 to the business. Anne has recently completed studies in business management. She has suggested that they might also consider incorporating the business.

To establish this new business outlet in Myaree, new assets (such as equipment, computers, delivery van, furniture and fittings and fixtures) will be required. In addition, funds will be needed for working capital items (such as material supplies, prepaid rent and other outgoings) while the new branch is getting established. The total cost of this is estimated to be $190000. Harriet could borrow much of this against the equity in the family home although her husband is not too keen about this risk. The family home is valued at $480000 but they have a bank mortgage on which they still owe $170000. Harriet has about $40000 saved, which she could use to help set up the new operation.

a   Outline and evaluate the options available to Harriet in financing her new venture.
b   If Harriet were to approach the bank for a loan, what factors would be in her favour and what might discourage the bank from lending?
c   What are the possible benefits and drawbacks, from Harriet's point of view, of entering into a partnership with Anne? If she did, what would you recommend to ensure that the business proceeds in a trouble-free manner?
d   What would be the advantages of setting up a company as Anne has suggested and, if they did, what sort of company would they set up?

1.23 Two friends, Noel Pember and Gail Wallace, both 26 years old, have decided to enter into a fast food business by buying an existing fast food outlet, a burger shop in Trigg, WA, which they hope to expand. Neither of them has any accounting training nor have they ever owned their own business.

Both Gail and Noel had been previously working in the tourism industry. Gail has worked for only two employers since leaving TAFE about six years ago after studying tourism. Noel has not done any study and has had nine employers in the tourism and hospitality industries in the past six years. This was due to personality conflicts with fellow employees and disagreements with employers.

Accounting and Finance 2A   ISBN 9780170182041   Cengage Learning Australia

Gail owns a house valued at $320000, on which there is a mortgage of $280000. She also owns a small car valued at $7000 and has saved $30000 over the past six years.

Noel has only $1500 in the bank due to some poor investment decisions in shares and an expensive standard of living. This financial crisis had also resulted in him defaulting on a personal loan for furniture and electronic whitegoods he had purchased for his rental flat. His parents agreed to provide him with a small loan to get himself out of this situation. He still owes his parents $5000.

Noel and Gail plan to expand and improve the business through the replacement of the business equipment and the establishment of a new product line. The equipment will cost $80000 and the new product line $20000 in working capital. To purchase the business and fund this expansion the owners would have to borrow $300000. They have approached their local bank's commercial lending manager about borrowing this amount.

Required

a   What factors will the bank take into consideration in assessing Neil and Gail's application?
b   What other information would the bank require before making a decision? What conditions might the bank impose on them before lending them the money?
c   Do you think that the bank would lend them the money? Explain your answer.
d   What other sources of funds might there be for the equipment and the working capital required for the business expansion and new product line?
e   What type of business structure would you suggest for Noel and Gail and why?

Investigation

1   Access the website of the Australian Securities Exchange. Select a public company, such as Commonwealth Bank of Australia, locate its annual report and answer the following questions:
a   What is the business's accounting period?
b   Is the business a retail, service or manufacturing type of business?
c   Who are the major shareholders?
d   What types of assets does the business have?
e   What sort of liabilities does the company have?
f   What is the value of the equity of the business?
g   What are the major types of revenue for the business?
h   What are some of the expenses the business has?
i   Were any of the assets de-valued or re-valued this year?

2   Prepare a document with the following questions (modify the questions or add to them as appropriate), making space for answers and then visit your local shopping centre to interview the owner or manager of one business (pre-arrange a visit) or interview a business operator you may know.
a   What type of business structure do you have?
b   If you are a proprietary company is the business a small or large proprietary company?
c   If you are a partnership how many partners does the business have?
d   Does the partnership have a formal agreement?
e   Would you regard your business as a retail, service or manufacturing business?
f   What is the business's accounting period?
g   What types of assets does the business have?
h   What types of liabilities does the business have?
i   What types of revenue does the business generate?
j   What types of expenses does the business incur?
k   Do you use the accrual or cash basis for reporting GST?

3   Go to the websites of two of the major banks operating in Western Australia (ANZ, BankWest, Commonwealth Bank, National Australia Bank or Westpac) and investigate the

Accounting and Finance: 2A   ISBN 9780170182041   Cengage Learning Australia

loan facilities they provide for small businesses. Produce a report comparing the two banks as a source of finance. Your report should include:

- types of finance available
- costs in fees, interest, etc. including details on current interest rates
- the amounts that can be borrowed for each form of borrowing
- the time for which the funds can be borrowed
- security required
- other conditions applied to borrowing.

If you were a small business owner, which of the two banks would you be more inclined to approach and what would you use their different types of finance for?

Essay

1   'A small proprietary company is the best type of business structure for any small retail business.' Discuss this comment, giving consideration to the following aspects:
- the characteristics of a proprietary company compared to those of a sole trader and a partnership
- the ease or otherwise of forming a proprietary company
- the advantages and disadvantages of a small proprietary company compared to a partnership and sole trader.

2   You are establishing a business to manufacture and sell solar power generators for the Australian market. This is going to require a great deal more money than you personally possess. Outline the alternative sources of finance likely to be available to you and indicate how these sources might be used to minimise your finance costs. Assuming that you will need to borrow money, what factors would you wish to emphasise in order to persuade the potential lenders to approve your application?

Ethics case study

Edgar runs a small engineering firm that employs about a dozen people, many of whom have worked for him for a number of years. The firm has been hit hard by the recession, which has reduced the demand for its products. Edgar sits down at the beginning of December with his accountant to plan their reaction to the crisis. The accountant tells him that he needs to fire at least half his workers. They will be entitled to one week's notice and most of them have accumulated leave entitlements. Edgar seems to have two broad alternatives:
- immediately dismiss those workers he no longer needs, paying them the minimum required by law
- inform his workforce that, unless things improve, some of them will lose their jobs. In the meantime, they must take all their leave entitlements and a decision on redundancies will be taken in the new year.

The accountant points out that the first alternative is the cheaper option for a number of reasons, including lower employer's liability insurance premiums and probably less wages paid.

What do you think Edgar should do? Are there any other possible courses of action? Some of the things you might want to consider include:
- Does Edgar owe workers who have served him well for several years anything over and above the minimum prescribed by law?
- Christmas is coming up – traditionally a time of high expenditure for families and not a good time to lose your job.
- If Edgar warns all the workers that they might lose their jobs, the more capable ones might use the time to find other jobs, meaning that he will be left with the less valuable employees.
- Should Edgar be concerned about his reputation as a good employer? Will this affect him when the economy recovers and he has to hire new staff?

Accounting and Finance: 2A   ISBN 9780170182041   Cengage Learning Australia

Chapter 2

MANUAL PROCESSING OF FINANCIAL TRANSACTIONS

What You Will Learn

After studying this chapter you should be able to:

1 Explain the accounting cycle, from source documents to financial reports
2 Outline the principles of the perpetual inventory system and compare it with the physical or periodic system
3 Compare and evaluate the weighted average and first-in, first-out inventory costing methods
4 Explain the role of journals in the accounting process
5 Carry out the manual processing of financial transactions for a small business on a double entry and accrual basis

through the General journal, including posting from journal to ledger accounts. Transactions to be recorded will include:

- entries to commence business
- cash and credit transactions
- purchase and sale of inventory using the perpetual inventory method
- withdrawals of cash and inventory by the owner
- correction of errors
- accounting for the GST

6 Balance ledger accounts and take out a Trial balance

Introduction

Accounting may be defined as the process of providing decision-makers with financial information that will enable them to make economic decisions in relation to some entity. An *economic decision* is one that relates to the allocation of scarce resources. Such decisions might be taken by an individual or a family; by businesses of various types and structures (sole traders, partnerships, companies, etc.); by not-for-profit organisations, such as clubs, associations and charities and by the various arms of government and the organisations and departments that operate under their control.

In this book we concentrate on accounting for businesses, with an emphasis on small business. However, the essential elements of accounting are the same whatever entity they are being applied to. They may be summarised as follows:

- recording financial transactions as they occur
- transferring these initial records to a form of storage where data can be secured, summarised and easily accessed
- using the data stored to produce informative reports that can be read, analysed and interpreted to assist in the decision-making process
- making decisions that will affect future financial transactions.

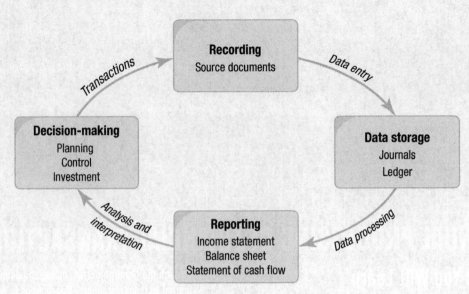

Figure 2.1 Processing of financial transactions

The first two elements of accounting – recording and data storage – are sometimes described as *bookkeeping*. Much of this is done automatically with computers these days, as is some of the reporting (see Chapters 6 and 10). However, in order to better understand the accounting process, it is useful to learn how it is done manually (a method employed in the past by most small businesses and which is still, at least to some extent, used by many such businesses today).

In this chapter we examine the recording and storage of financial data. Processing and reporting are covered in Chapters 3 and 7 to 9; analysis and interpretation are covered in Chapter 11.

Key Concept 2.1

Accounting

Accounting is the process of providing decision-makers with financial information to enable them to make economic decisions about an entity. This process includes the identification, recording, storage and processing of financial information and its use in decision-making.

SOURCE DOCUMENTS

Source documents are the initial written (printed) record of financial transactions. They fulfil two main purposes:

1 They are the source of the data that is recorded in the firm's accounting system.
2 They provide evidence of the legitimacy of the transactions, enabling managers and those responsible for checking their work to establish that the transactions actually did take place and were properly authorised.

There is a wide range of types of source documents for various kinds of transaction.

Accounting and Finance 2A   ISBN 9780170182041   Cengage Learning Australia

Cash transactions

Payments

Payments are normally made either by cheque or by electronic funds transfer.

A cheque is a written instruction to the bank on a prescribed form to pay a specified sum out of a specified bank account to a particular person (the payee). The cheque itself is given or sent to the payee and a stub or butt is retained in the chequebook by the payer as evidence of the payment. Business cheques must usually be signed by two authorised signatories to minimise the chance of fraudulent or incorrect payments (see Chapter 4). The source document in this case is the cheque stub or butt.

Electronic funds transfers are normally supported by a voucher indicating that the payment has been properly authorised and this, together with the tax invoice issued by the payee at time of payment, comprise the source documents for this sort of payment.

In either case, the source document will show the date, the payee, the amount and the purpose of the payment. Cheques and payment vouchers are numbered for control purposes.

Sometimes amounts may be debited or credited directly to the firm's bank account. These include debits for interest paid on the account and bank fees or charges and credits for interest earned or payments from customers by direct funds transfer. The firm usually becomes aware of these only when reading the statement of account, in which case the bank statement itself is a source document for those transactions. Statements of account are sent out periodically by the bank or accessed online.

Receipts

When payments are received, a receipt will be issued to the payer acknowledging the payment. This receipt will be completed in duplicate, the original being handed to the payer, while the duplicate is retained by the firm as its source document for the transaction. Retail firms process the vast majority of their sales through one or more cash registers. These produce, for each sale, a tax invoice similar to that referred to under 'Payments' above. It is called a *tax invoice* because it provides the recipient with details of goods and services tax (GST) included in the payment as required by law. (GST is dealt with in detail later in this chapter.) The original tax invoice is given to the customer while a copy is retained by the business. In addition to this, each cash register can produce, at the end of the day, a cash register summary (CRS) that lists and summarises the sales made through that register during the day, which must be reconciled with the cash balance in the register and the copies of the tax invoices.

Date: 30 April 2010

Payee: Landlord Pty Ltd

Purpose: Rent

This cheque: $600.00

001458

TAX INVOICE
Sue's Shirt Supplies
8 Main Street Malaga 8255
ABN 10 111 222 333 4

05/05/10	15.35	Ref.ADB3469
60 t-shirts @ $6.50		$234.00
Total (incl. GST)		$234.00
Paid		$234.00
Total includes GST of		$21.27
Change		$0.00
Total includes GST of		$21.27

NORTHBANK

Account of: GOFERIT TRADING

CHEQUE ACCOUNT STATEMENT
BSB number: 444-555
Account number: 230460
Period ending: 31 May 10

Date	Particulars	Debit	Credit	Balance
01 May 10	Opening balance			657.35
01 May 10	Electronic withdrawal fee	0.80		656.55
01 May 10	Maintenance fee	7.00		649.55
01 May 10	Credit interest		0.10	649.65
02 May 10	Polygon Motors – inv. A0643		276.40	926.05
02 May 10	Cheque 001458	600.00		326.05
03 May 10	Deposit		479.20	805.25

Figure 2.2 Examples of accounting source documents

GOFERIT TRADING

CASH RECEIPT   No. **0056**

Date: 5 May 2010

Received from: Polygon Motors

The sum of: $387.50

Including GST:

Being for: Payment of account

Figure 2.3 Example of a cash receipt

GOFERIT TRADING

266 East Street
Midland 6056

TAX INVOICE No. A0657

Date: 1 May 2010

Order no. 617

Sold to: Polygon Motors
99 West Street
Hamilton Hill

Quantity	Item	Unit price	Total	GST	Total payable
2	Gondrils	$25.60	$51.20	$5.12	$56.32
13	Hagaboks	$11.20	$145.60	$14 56	$160.16
			$196.80	$19.68	$216.48

Terms: Net 14 days
BSB 444-555 Account No. 230460

Figure 2.4 Example of a tax invoice

Credit transactions

The source document for both credit sales and credit purchases is the invoice issued by the vendor of a product to the purchaser. This is usually described as a *tax invoice* because it also details the GST included in the purchase or sale amount. The original invoice is given to the purchaser and they use it as the source document for their credit purchase. The duplicate invoice is retained by the vendor and is used by them as the source document for their credit sale.

The duplicate copy of the invoice in Figure 2.4 will be used by Goferit Trading as the source document for the sale, while the original invoice will be used by Polygon Motors as the source document for the purchase. Note that in addition to the details of this particular transaction, the invoice also contains information for the purchaser about the expected terms of payment (in this case, within 14 days) and details of the vendor's bank account to enable the purchaser to make a direct electronic funds transfer. (See Chapter 6 for more information on e-commerce.) The invoice also contains the number of the order to which this invoice relates (see below) and the GST component (see later in this chapter).

There are two other documents often associated with credit sales, which, although not strictly source documents, are important. These are:

- the order – this is an instruction from the would-be purchaser to the vendor of a good or service requesting the delivery of specified goods or provision of a particular service
- the delivery note – this accompanies the delivery of goods ordered as notification of delivery.

The purchasing firm should check the delivery note against both the order and the actual goods delivered to ensure that they have received what they asked for and what the vendor claims to have provided. Later, when the invoice is received, this too will be checked against the order to make sure all is correct. Often a copy of the invoice will accompany the goods, which removes the need for a delivery note.

🔒 Key Concept 2.2

Source documents

Source documents are the primary sources of data regarding financial transactions, including cheque stubs, receipts, tax invoices, invoices and bank statements.

Accounting and Finance: 2A   ISBN 9780170182041   Cengage Learning Australia

LEDGER ACCOUNTS

Before going on to consider in detail the different types of transaction and how they may conveniently be recorded by a firm, it will be helpful to outline the method used to store this information in a way that enables it to be accessed easily (e.g. for the purpose of preparing reports). For each item the owners or managers of a business want to keep a record for, there will be an *account*. This is a chronological record of all the transactions that affect that item. All the firm's accounts together are known as the *ledger*.

A ledger account must record, for every transaction that affects an item, the following information:

- its date
- its nature
- its dollar value
- its effect on the item (i.e. whether it has resulted in an increase or a decrease in value).

It is also necessary to be able to say, after each transaction, what the current value of the item is. This figure is known as the *balance*.

 Key Concept 2.3

Account

A chronological record of all the transactions affecting a particular item. The accounts together are known as the ledger.

Chart of accounts

One of the first things a business must decide is exactly what items they will need an account for. These will be drawn up in a systematically arranged list known as a *chart of accounts*. Charts of accounts are usually arranged so that groups of like accounts are listed together; it will normally have a numbering system that reinforces this classification. Numbering will also facilitate access to the accounts in a computerised system.

Example 2.1

EXAMPLE: P Wrench is going into business as a plumber and has decided to utilise a double entry accounting system. His firm will have a number of different assets for which he wants to keep separate accounts, as well as several expense items. His chart of accounts might look something like this:

Account number	Account name
Current assets (Accounts 100–149)	
101	Cash in hand
105	Cash at bank
110	Stock of materials
120	Accounts receivable (amounts owing by customers)
Non-current assets (Accounts 150–199)	
150	Tools and equipment
155	Vehicles
160	Computer system
Current liabilities (Accounts 200–249)	
201	Trade creditors
205	Credit card
210	Bank loan
220	Accrued expenses

Non-current liabilities (Accounts 250–299)	
250	Mortgage
Equity (Accounts 300–399)	
300	Capital
310	Owner's drawings
320	Retained earnings
Expenses (Accounts 400–499)	
401	Wages
410	Materials used
420	Motor vehicle expenses
430	Insurance
440	Telephone costs
450	Interest expense
460	Sundry office expenses
Income (Accounts 500–599)	
501	Fees revenue
510	Sale of materials

Note that the different categories of assets have similar numbering (e.g. assets are all 100 numbers, liabilities are all 200 numbers and so on). The distinction between 'current' and 'non-current' assets and liabilities will be dealt with later (see Chapters 3 and 9). Also note that, in allocating numbers, there are gaps left for insertion of accounts later on. For example, if Wrench wanted, at a later date, to distinguish between jobs in houses and those in commercial properties, he could rename Account 501 'Fees revenue – domestic' and open a new Account 502 'Fees revenue – commercial'.

Key Concept 2.4

Chart of accounts

A chart of accounts is a systematically arranged list of all the financial accounts in an entity's ledger.

Types of ledger account

In the previous chapter you were introduced to the concept of 'double entry' – the idea that every financial transaction has both a positive and negative aspect. For example, the purchase of stock for cash will have a positive effect on one asset (stock or inventory) and a negative effect on another asset (cash), the repayment of a loan will have a positive effect of reducing a liability (loan) and a negative effect of reducing an asset (cash). From this it follows that every transaction will lead to an entry being made in at least two accounts, which will be either 'debited' or 'credited' in such a way that the debits equal the credits and the accounting equation (representing the balance between assets, liabilities and owner's equity) remains in balance. As you learned in the previous chapter, increases in assets or expenses and decreases in liabilities or owners' equity are recorded as debits, while increases in liabilities or owners' equity, as well as income and decreases in assets, are recorded as credits.

There are two forms of ledger account in common use. The first of these is known as the *T-form account* and is illustrated below.

Dr			Account title		Cr
Date	Particulars	$	Date	Particulars	$

Accounting and Finance: 2A   ISBN 9780170182041   Cengage Learning Australia

All details of the debits to the account are recorded on the left-hand side of the account and all details of the credits are recorded on the right. On each side there is a column to record the date, the identity of the other account(s) of which this entry is part and the amount of the transaction.

Example 2.2

EXAMPLE:

Ava Mango is setting up in business as a greengrocer. On 1 May she opened a bank account for the business with a deposit of $30 000 of her own money and on 2 May she purchased, for cash, fittings and furniture for the shop worth $4 360. She will at this stage open three ledger accounts, one for Cash at bank, one for Capital and one for Fittings and furniture. It may be helpful to use an analysing chart to break the transactions down into their components. As you become more familiar with the process and confident in identifying the debits and credits in transactions, this part of the recording can be bypassed.

An analysis of the transactions is as follows:

Date	Transaction	Account to debit	Account to credit	$
1 May	Deposit of cash into bank	Cash at bank	Capital	30 000
2 May	Purchase fittings and furniture	Fittings and furniture	Cash at bank	4 360

These transactions can now be entered into ledger accounts.

Dr			Cash at bank			Cr
Date	Particulars	$	Date	Particulars		$
1 May	Capital	30 000	2 May	Fittings and furniture		4 360

Dr						Cr
Date	Particulars	$	Date	Particulars		$
			1 May	Cash at bank		30 000

Dr						Cr
Date	Particulars	$	Date	Particulars		$
2 May	Cash at bank	4 360				

To obtain the balance of each account at any time it is necessary to add up all the debit entries, add up all the credit entries and take the smaller total from the greater. In this example, two of the accounts have only a single entry and the third one has one on each side. The balances of the accounts after these two transactions are therefore as follows:

Cash at bank (30 000 – 4360)	$25 640 Dr (Debit)
Capital	$30 000 Cr (Credit)
Fittings and furniture	$4 360 Dr (Debit)

The other type of ledger account is called the three-column account. It looks like this:

	Account title			
Date	Particulars	Debit $	Credit $	Balance $ Dr or Cr

For both debit and credit entries, the date and the particulars (i.e. the other account involved) will be entered into the first two columns and the amount of the transaction is

Accounting and Finance: 2A   ISBN 9780170182041   Cengage Learning Australia

then entered into either the debit or the credit column, depending on whether it is a debit or a credit for this particular account. The final column records the running total of the balance of the account, recalculated after each transaction.

Example 2.3

The same transactions detailed in Example 2.2 on the previous page could be entered in three-column ledger accounts as follows:

Cash at bank				
Date	Particulars	Debit $	Credit $	Balance $ Dr or Cr
1 May	Capital	30 000		30 000 Dr
2 May	Fittings and furniture		4 360	25 640 Dr

Capital				
Date	Particulars	Debit $	Credit $	Balance $ Dr or Cr
1 May	Cash at bank		30 000	30 000 Cr

Fittings and furniture				
Date	Particulars	Debit $	Credit $	Balance $ Dr or Cr
2 May	Cash at bank	4 360		4 360 Dr

The three-column ledger account has some advantages over the T-form ledger account. These include that:
- the layout is simpler and more straightforward
- the balance in the account can be read instantly without the need for a time-consuming arithmetic process
- it is used by most computer accounting systems in their reports (for example, see the bank statement in Figure 2.2 on page 39.

While the use of either form of account will continue to be perfectly acceptable, from here on we employ the three-column form unless specified otherwise.

JOURNALS

It would be possible for business financial transactions to be entered into the ledger accounts directly from the source documents. However, particularly with a manual system (such as we are currently examining), this has some drawbacks:
- the large amount of detail that needs to be entered directly into the ledger
- the lack of an easily accessible chronological record of transactions
- the necessity to permit all those entering financial data to have access to the firm's ledger. With a manual system there is the inconvenience of having a number of people wishing to use the ledger at the same time. Even with a computerised system, where a number of people may simultaneously access the same database, there is still the problem of allowing a wide range of people to read everything in the ledger. There may be sensitive information that the firm would not necessarily wish to make available to data-entry personnel.

For these reasons, most businesses employing a manual system enter the data from source documents into *journals* (literally 'daily records'). For cash transactions there may be a single journal called a *cash book* (which has sections dealing with both payments and receipts) or there may be two separate journals, called *cash receipts journal* and *cash payments journal*. Credit transactions relating to the purchase and sale of inventories may

Accounting and Finance: 2A   ISBN 9780170182041   Cengage Learning Australia

be recorded in a *purchases journal* and a *sales journal*. Businesses with a large number of credit transactions that give rise to numerous sales and purchase returns (see later in this chapter) may have separate journals for these. All these journals may be known collectively as *special journals*. The journals are sometimes called the *books of original entry*.

With the increasing prevalence of computerised systems that can, at the touch of a button, produce lists of transactions sorted according to date, type or any other recorded criteria, fewer businesses now use special journals and many enter all their transactions into a single General journal. Firms with special journals would still, in any case, have a General journal to accommodate transactions that do not qualify for one of the special journals. In this textbook, all transactions will be entered through the General journal.

Key Concept 2.5

Journal

A journal is a chronological record into which data is entered before posting it into the ledger. It is known as the *book of original entry*.

Example 2.4

EXAMPLE: The layout of the General journal is shown below, with the transactions from Example 2.2 entered into it.

General journal			
Date	**Accounts to debit or credit**	**Dr**	**Cr**
1 May	Cash at bank	30 000	
	Capital		30 000
	(Cash deposit to start business)		
2 May	Fittings and furniture	4 360	
	Cash at bank		4 360
	(Purchase of asset)		

Note that the debit and credit aspects of each transaction are stated separately. For clarity of understanding, the title of the account to be debited is stated first and the title of any account to be credited is indented slightly. After each transaction there is a brief description (called a '*narration*'), which explains what the transaction is about. In many cases, such as the ones shown above, this is fairly clear anyway from the titles of the accounts involved, but that will not always be the case. The narration will also include reference to the source document for each transaction, by stating the cheque, invoice or receipt number or other source document (such as the bank statement).

Apart from all cash and credit transactions, the General journal may be used to record a variety of other transactions, including:

- withdrawal or contribution by the owner of resources other than cash (e.g. if the owner contributes her vehicle to the business, or if she takes some inventory for her own use)
- write-off of bad debts – if the amount owing by a trade debtor is deemed to be irrecoverable (e.g. because the debtor has gone bankrupt) it needs to be written out of the firm's accounts, reducing both the accounts receivable and the profit
- correction of errors (e.g. if it turns out that the wrong amount has been entered or if the wrong account has been debited or credited)
- balance day adjustments (see Chapter 7)
- closing entries (see Chapter 3).

Periodically (perhaps once a week or once a month) the data will be entered from the journal into the ledger accounts. This process is known as *posting to the ledger*.

Discounts allowed or received

Many businesses who sell on credit will offer their customers a discount for prompt payment to encourage these customers to pay their bills without delay. These discounts need to be recorded at the same time as the payment or receipt is recorded, then debited or credited to ledger accounts entitled 'Discount allowed' (expense) or 'Discount received' (revenue).

Example 2.5

EXAMPLE:

One of the firm's customers, J James, has an outstanding account of $650. It is the firm's policy that trade debtors who pay their accounts within one week of the invoice will be allowed a 2% discount.

On 4 March 2010, J James pays her account. This is within the one-week limit. On the same day, the firm pays a supplier with whom it has an account, W Earp Ltd, the balance owing to them of $1400 less a discount for prompt payment (W Earp not being quite so generous) of 1%. These transactions would be recorded in the journal and ledger accounts as follows:

Date	Accounts to debit or credit	Dr $	Cr $
4 March	Cash at bank	637	
	Discount allowed	13	
	J James, account receivable		650
	(Receipt less 2% discount for prompt payment)		
4 March	W Earp Ltd, account payable	1400	
	Cash at bank		1386
	Discount received		14
	(Payment less 1% discount for prompt payment)		

General journal (table title)

Ledger

Cash at bank

Date	Particulars	Debit $	Credit $	Balance $ Dr or Cr
4 March	J James	637		637 Dr
4 March	W Earp Ltd		1386	749 Cr

J James

Date	Particulars	Debit $	Credit $	Balance $ Dr or Cr
4 March	Balance			650 Dr
4 March	Cash at bank		637	13 Dr
	Discount allowed		13	–

Discount allowed

Date	Particulars	Debit $	Credit $	Balance $ Dr or Cr
4 March	J James	13		13 Dr

W Earp Ltd

Date	Particulars	Debit $	Credit $	Balance $ Dr or Cr
4 March	Balance			1400 Cr
4 March	Cash at bank	1386		14 Cr
	Discount received	14		–

Accounting and Finance 2A   ISBN 9780170182041   Cengage Learning Australia

Discount received				
Date	Particulars	Debit $	Credit $	Balance $ Dr or Cr
4 March	W Earp Ltd		14	14 Cr

Bad debts

There will inevitably be occasions when a firm has to accept that some or all of an amount owing to it by a credit customer is not going to be paid. This is despite the fact that firms will normally take steps to prevent it (by carefully checking the creditworthiness of customers and immediately following up credit customers who do not pay within the time permitted). In these circumstances the firm must take steps to cancel the revenue that the original sale represented and eliminate the asset comprising the debt that is now worthless. This process is known as *writing off a bad debt*. The entry required is:

Debit   Bad debts (expense account)
Credit   Account receivable with the amount that is now considered to be irrecoverable.

Example 2.6

EXAMPLE:

B Dodgy Pty Ltd is an account receivable of Trusty Traders, owing them $1000. On 15 May Trusty Traders receives a letter from lawyers representing B Dodgy advising them that the company has gone into liquidation (i.e. corporate bankruptcy) and it is expected that its creditors will only be paid 10 cents in every dollar they are owed. Consequently Trusty Traders will have to write off the remainder of the amount owing to them as a bad debt.

Step 1: Calculate the bad debt = 90 cents per $1 × 1000 = $900

Step 2: Make out the journal entry

General journal			
Date	Accounts to debit or credit	Dr $	Cr $
15 May	Bad debts	900	
	B Dodgy Pty Ltd		900
	(90 cents/dollar written off as bad debt)		

Step 3: Post to the ledger.

Ledger				
Bad debts				
Date	Particulars	Debit $	Credit $	Balance $ Dr or Cr
15 May	B Dodgy Pty Ltd	900		900 Dr
B Dodgy Pty Ltd				
Date	Particulars	Debit $	Credit $	Balance $ Dr or Cr
15 May	Balance			1000 Dr
	Bad debts		900	100 Dr

At this stage it will be helpful to show a comprehensive example, tracing a number of transactions from the source documents to the journal and then posting them to the ledger.

Example 2.7

S Blanco has decided to set up a double entry accounting system for his business Fullback Enterprises with effect from 1 September. On that date his business had the following assets and liabilities:

	$
Cash at bank	8600
Inventory	13500
Harry Nordeky (account receivable)	200
J Rives (account receivable)	1120
Vehicle	18800

During the first week of September the following transactions took place:

Date	Transaction
2 September	Paid rent (expense) $450, cheque 057. J Rives paid part of her account $500, receipt B143. She was allowed a discount of 1% for prompt payment. Purchased inventory worth $2200 from PD Princes, invoice 095.
3 September	S Blanco contributed a computer to the business. This is valued at $2000. Sold goods on credit to P Villepreux for $900, invoice 222.
4 September	S Blanco withdrew $300 cash for his own use, cheque 058. Received information that Harry Nordeky has been declared bankrupt. His debt must be written off as bad.
5 September	Paid PD Princes $1500 on account, cheque 059. The firm received a discount of 2% for prompt payment. S Blanco withdrew inventory worth $270 for his own use. Sold goods worth $1850 for cash (cash register summary).
6 September	Bought office furniture from Berbizier Supplies for $1900, of which a 10% deposit was paid in cash (cheque 060); the remainder being payable in 30 days (inv. C2)

The accounting for sales of inventory will be dealt with in some detail later in this chapter. For the purpose of this exercise we will simply debit purchases of inventory to the 'Inventory' account and credit sales of goods to a 'Sales' account.

Before starting to process the data, it will be necessary to calculate S Blanco's capital at the start of the period, since he has not specifically included this in his list of opening balances. Based on the accounting equation Owners' equity = Assets – Liabilities, S Blanco's equity may be calculated as follows:

$$\text{Assets } 8600 + 13500 + 200 + 1120 + 18800 - \text{Liabilities } 0 = 42220$$

The transactions are analysed.

ANALYSING CHART

Date	Transaction	Account to debit	Account to credit	$
1 Sept	Opening balances	Cash at bank		8600
		Inventory		13500
		Harry Nordeky		200
		J Rives		1120
		Vehicle		18800
			Capital	42220
2 Sept	Rent (cheque 057)	Rent	Cash at bank	450
2 Sept	J Rives payment (receipt B143)	Cash at bank	J Rives	495
		Discount allowed	J Rives	5
2 Sept	Purchased inventory (invoice 095)	Inventory	PD Princes	2200
3 Sept	Owner contributes computer	Computer	Capital	2000
3 Sept	Sale to P Villepreux (invoice 222)	P Villepreux	Sales	900
4 Sept	Owner's drawings (cheque 058)	Drawings	Cash at bank	300
4 Sept	Write off bad debt	Bad debts	Harry Nordeky	200

Accounting and Finance: 2A   ISBN 9780170182041   Cengage Learning Australia

5 Sept	Paid PD Princes (cheque 059)	PD Princes	Cash at bank	1470
		PD Princes	Discount received	30
5 Sept	Owner withdrew inventory	Drawings	Inventory	270
5 Sept	Cash sales (Cash register summary)	Cash at bank	Sales	1850
6 Sept	Bought office furniture (cheque 060)	Office furniture	Cash at bank	190
	Debt to Berbizier Supplies	Office furniture	Berbizier Supplies	1710

Note that the owner's withdrawals of cash and inventory are debited to a separate account called 'Drawings' rather than to 'Capital'. This will enable the owner to show the capital contributed separately from any drawings made, which would usually be regarded as a withdrawal of the profit the business has made for the owner.

The transactions are entered in the journal.

General journal			
Date	**Accounts to debit or credit**	**Dr $**	**Cr $**
1 Sept	Cash at bank	8600	
	Inventory	13500	
	Harry Nordeky	200	
	J Rives	1120	
	Vehicle	18800	
	Capital		42220
	(Balances to open accounts)		
2 Sept	Rent	450	
	Cash at bank		450
	(Payment of rent chq. 057)		
2 Sept	Cash at bank	495	
	Discount allowed	5	
	J Rives		500
	(Payment on account, rec. B143)		
2 Sept	Inventory	2200	
	PD Princes		2200
	(Purchase on credit, inv. 095)		
3 Sept	Computer	2000	
	Capital		2000
	(Owner contributed asset)		
3 Sept	P Villepreux	900	
	Sales		900
	(Credit sale, inv. 222)		
4 Sept	Drawings	300	
	Cash at bank		300
	(Owner's cash drawings, chq. 058)		
4 Sept	Bad debts	200	
	Harry Nordeky		200
	(account receivable written off)		
5 Sept	PD Princes	1500	
	Cash at bank		1470
	Discount received		30
	(Payment on account, chq. 059)		

Accounting and Finance: 2A   ISBN 9780170182041   Cengage Learning Australia

5 Sept	Drawings	270	
	Inventory		270
	(Taken for own use)		
5 Sept	Cash at bank	1850	
	Sales		1850
	(Cash register summary)		
6 Sept	Office furniture	1900	
	Cash at bank		190
	Berblzier Supplies		1710
	(Asset purchased, chq. 060 and inv. 22)		

Finally the transactions are posted from the journal to the ledger.

Ledger				
Cash at bank				
Date	Particulars	Debit $	Credit $	Balance $ Dr or Cr
1 Sept	Capital	8600		8600 Dr
2 Sept	Rent		450	8150 Dr
4 Sept	J Rives	495		8645 Dr
5 Sept	Drawings		300	8345 Dr
5 Sept	PD Princes		1470	6875 Dr
6 Sept	Sales	1850		8725 Dr
	Office furniture		190	8535 Dr

Inventory				
Date	Particulars	Debit $	Credit $	Balance $ Dr or Cr
1 Sept	Capital	13500		13500 Dr
2 Sept	PD Princes	2200		15700 Dr
5 Sept	Drawings		270	15430 Dr

J Rives				
Date	Particulars	Debit $	Credit $	Balance $ Dr or Cr
1 Sept	Capital	1120		1120 Dr
2 Sept	Cash at bank		495	625 Dr
	Discount allowed		5	620 Dr

Vehicle				
Date	Particulars	Debit $	Credit $	Balance $ Dr or Cr
1 Sept	Capital	18800		18800 Dr

Capital				
Date	Particulars	Debit $	Credit $	Balance $ Dr or Cr
1 Sept	Cash at bank		8600	8600 Cr
	Inventory		13500	22100 Cr
	Harry Nordeky		200	22300 Cr
	J Rives		1120	23420 Cr
	Vehicle		18800	42220 Cr
3 Sept	Computer		2000	44220 Cr

Accounting and Finance: 2A   ISBN 9780170182041   Cengage Learning Australia

Rent

Date	Particulars	Debit $	Credit $	Balance $ Dr or Cr
2 Sept	Cash at bank	450		450 Dr

PD Princes

Date	Particulars	Debit $	Credit $	Balance $ Dr or Cr
2 Sept	Inventory		2200	2200 Cr
2 Sept	Cash at bank	1470		730 Cr
	Discount received	30		700 Cr

Computer

Date	Particulars	Debit $	Credit $	Balance $ Dr or Cr
3 Sept	Capital	2000		2000 Dr

P Villepreux

Date	Particulars	Debit $	Credit $	Balance $ Dr or Cr
3 Sept	Sales	900		900 Dr

Sales

Date	Particulars	Debit $	Credit $	Balance $ Dr or Cr
3 Sept	P Villepreux		900	900 Cr
5 Sept	Cash at bank		1850	2750 Cr

Drawings

Date	Particulars	Debit $	Credit $	Balance $ Dr or Cr
4 Sept	Cash at bank	300		300 Dr
5 Sept	Inventory	270		570 Dr

Harry Nordeky

Date	Particulars	Debit $	Credit $	Balance $ Dr or Cr
1 Sept	Capital	200		200 Dr
4 Sept	Bad debts		200	–

Bad debts

Date	Particulars	Debit $	Credit $	Balance $ Dr or Cr
4 Sept	Harry Nordeky	200		200 Dr

Office furniture

Date	Particulars	Debit $	Credit $	Balance $ Dr or Cr
6 Sept	Cash at bank	190		190 Dr
	Berbizier Supplies	1710		1900 Dr

Berbizier Supplies

Date	Particulars	Debit $	Credit $	Balance $ Dr or Cr
6 Sept	Office furniture		1710	1710 Cr

Discount allowed				
Date	Particulars	Debit $	Credit $	Balance $ Dr or Cr
4 Sept	J Rives	5		5 Dr

Discount received				
Date	Particulars	Debit $	Credit $	Balance $ Dr or Cr
5 Sept	PD Princes		30	30 Cr

Accrual accounting

In Chapter 1 we introduced the concept of *accrual accounting* – the idea that a financial transaction should be recorded when it is recognised as having taken effect, regardless of when the transfer of cash represented by that transaction occurs. For example, the firm may receive an account from Synergy for electricity supplied during June that will be paid sometime in July. Though the payment of the bill takes place in July, it must be recognised as an expense in June and recorded as such. Consequently, for each such transaction there will be two records: once when its effect is recognised and again when a cash payment takes place.

Similarly, when the firm pays its annual insurance premium for the next 12 months and part of this period falls in the following financial year, the expense of the premium must be divided proportionately between the two financial years to which it relates.

This principle can also be seen in the treatment of credit sales and purchases. In the example above, the sale of goods to P Villepreux is recorded as a sale when the invoice is issued and the sale takes effect, creating revenue in the sales account and a corresponding asset in the form of an account receivable in the name of P Villepreux. Later, when Villepreux pays his account, this will also be recorded as the loss of one asset (debt from P Villepreux) and the gain of another (Cash).

The application of the accrual accounting principle necessitates what are known as *balance day adjustments*. These are dealt with in detail in Chapter 7.

TRIAL BALANCE

Once all the data has been posted to the ledger accounts at the end of the accounting period – whether this is at the end of each month or the end of the financial year – it is customary to produce a list of all the ledger balances at that date. This is called a *Trial balance*. This serves two main purposes:

1 By listing and totalling separately all the debit and all the credit balances in the ledger, it will check, to some extent (see below) that the data entry has been done correctly. Clearly the debit entries (and hence the resultant debit balances) must equal the credit entries (and the resultant credit balances) and if they do not an error must have been made.

2 The balances listed in the Trial balance can conveniently be used in the preparation of the firm's financial statements for the period.

If the firm has been using the three-column form of ledger account, the balance of each account will have already been calculated and can simply be transferred to the Trial balance. If T-form accounts have been used, it will be necessary in many cases to calculate the account balance. This will then be written (usually in pencil) on the appropriate side of the account. This process is known as *footing the accounts*.

As an example, here is the 'Cash at bank' account for Fullback Enterprises in Example 2.7 up to 6 September, footed at that date.

Accounting and Finance: 2A   ISBN 9780170182041   Cengage Learning Australia

Dr	Cash at bank				Cr
Date	**Particulars**	**$**	**Date**	**Particulars**	**$**
1 Sept	Capital	8600	2 Sept	Rent	450
2 Sept	J Rives	495	4 Sept	Drawings	300
5 Sept	Sales	1850	5 Sept	PD Princes	1470
		8535	6 Sept	Office furniture	190

The sum of the credits (450 + 300 + 1470 + 190 = 2410) is taken from the sum of the debits (8600 + 495 + 1850 = 10945) and the resultant balance of $8535 is written on the debit side to show that the debits exceed the credits by that amount.

The accounts will now be listed with the balance for each shown in the debit or credit column (as the case may be). If an account had no balance in it at that particular date (e.g. the account of a debtor who had paid off all she owed), it would simply be omitted. This account when 'balanced' will be shown as follows.

Dr	Cash at bank				Cr
Date	**Particulars**	**$**	**Date**	**Particulars**	**$**
1 Sept	Capital	8600	2 Sept	Rent	450
2 Sept	J Rives	495	4 Sept	Drawings	300
5 Sept	Sales	1850	5 Sept	PD Princes	1470
			6 Sept	Office furniture	190
				Balance carried down	8535
		10945			10945
7 Sept	Balance brought down	8535			

Using the balances shown in the ledger for Fullback Enterprises above, the Trial balance of the firm at 6 September would be as follows:

Fullback Enterprises
Trial balance as at 6 September 20XX

	Dr $	Cr $
Cash at bank	8535	
Inventory	15430	
J Rives	620	
Vehicle	18800	
Capital		44220
Rent	450	
PD Princes		700
Computer	2000	
P Villepreux	900	
Sales		2750
Drawings	570	
Bad debts	200	
Office furniture	1900	
Berbizier Supplies		1710
Discount allowed	5	
Discount received		30
	49410	49410

Note that although the firm had an account for Harry Nordeky, at the date of the Trial balance this had no balance in it, so it has been omitted.

Accounting and Finance: 2A   ISBN 9780170182041   Cengage Learning Australia

Once all the balances have been written in, the two columns can be totalled and if, as is the case in this example, they are the same, this is *prima facie* (at first appearance) evidence that the recording process has been accurate. If the two columns are not equal, there is clearly an error and the following procedure is suggested for locating it:

1   Calculate the difference between the two balances and see if this difference corresponds with a transaction or an account balance that might have been mistakenly left out. Check figures that are equal to one half of the difference as this might indicate that a balance has been entered into the wrong column or that one part of a transaction has been wrongly debited or credited (e.g. if PD Princes in the example above had been entered in the debit column instead of the credit column, the difference between the balances would have been $1400, i.e. 2 × the balance of $700).
2   Check that all account balances have been transferred to the Trial balance.
3   Check that balances of the accounts have been correctly calculated.
4   Check that all transactions have been posted correctly from the journal.
5   Check that the journal itself has been correctly entered.

Useful though the Trial balance is, it needs to be recognised that it will not reveal all recording errors. Errors not revealed by a Trial balance include:

*   the same incorrect amount entered into both sides of the ledger
*   amounts entered into the wrong sides of both accounts (e.g. Account A debited instead of credited and Account B credited instead of debited)
*   the wrong account debited and/or credited
*   transactions omitted altogether
*   transactions duplicated (i.e. mistakenly entered twice)
*   compensating errors – where one mistake is exactly cancelled out by another mistake of the same amount in the other direction. (This happens more often than you might think!)

 Key Concept 2.6

Trial balance

A trial balance is a listing, in separate debit and credit columns, of all the account balances in an entity's ledger on a particular date. If the sum of the credits is equal to the sum of the debits, this is an indication – though not an infallible one – that the recording process has been accurate.

ACCOUNTING FOR INVENTORY

For the large number of businesses that are *trading* or *merchandising* businesses (i.e. they earn their revenue by selling physical products at a profit), the cost of what they are selling – their *stock* or *inventory* – is their most significant expense. This inventory is a vitally important asset that must be carefully managed.

The term *inventory* usually means the stock of goods purchased for resale. However, manufacturing businesses have inventories (raw materials, work in process and finished goods awaiting sale) and even service businesses may apply the term to the value of service contracts only partially completed during the accounting period. In this textbook, however, we will only consider the inventory of merchandising firms.

Accounting for inventory has two main purposes:

1   to accurately determine the cost of goods sold, which will be offset as an expense within an accounting period against the revenue earned by selling those goods
2   to place an accurate value on the stock of unsold goods held by the firm at any time.

Australian Accounting Standard AASB 102 deals with the accounting for inventories and, although its terms are not necessarily legally binding on most small businesses, they do provide useful guidelines and definitions with which most businesses do comply.

Accounting and Finance: 2A   ISBN 9780170182041   Cengage Learning Australia

Cost of inventories

In terms of AASB 102, this includes – as well as the purchase cost – all other costs involved in bringing the inventories to the point at which they can be sold. This might include customs duty and the costs (freight, transit insurance, etc.) required to transport the goods from the supplier's premises to the merchandising firm's warehouse or shop. These costs (often called *freight inwards*) may be allocated to the cost of inventory. However, it may be difficult to allocate the freight on a consignment of inventory between the various stock items in the consignment, in which case they will be added to the cost of sales when preparing financial statements. This is the approach adopted in this book (see Chapters 3 and 9).

Example 2.8

EXAMPLE:

Shafto's Shoes has imported 60 assorted pairs of ladies' shoes from a factory in Taipei. The price paid to the supplier was $26 per pair, freight and insurance on the consignment amounted to $68 and customs duty at a rate of 15% of purchase price was paid. The total cost of these items of inventory would be as follows:

Purchase price (26 × 60)	$1560
Customs duty @ 15%	$234
Freight and insurance	$68
Total cost	$1862

Note that the amount paid for inventories purchased from an Australian supplier would include GST, unless the item is from one of the categories that are exempt (such as basic foodstuffs or certain medical equipment or medicines). However, the GST paid will be recorded separately and the amount recorded as inventory cost will be net of GST. For example, if Shafto's had bought its shoes for the same price from a factory in Victoria, it would not have had to pay customs duty, but the vendor would have added 10% to the price for GST. The amount paid to the supplier would therefore have been $1560 + $156 = $1716. The amount recorded as the value of the inventory, however, would have been $1560, plus any other costs, such as transport, involved in getting the goods to Shafto's Shoes' shop.

Valuing inventory

For the purpose of valuing the inventory held at any time, AASB 102 requires that it be valued at *the lower of cost or net realisable value*. 'Net realisable value' means the amount the firm might reasonably expect to receive from the sale of the inventory in the normal course of business, less any costs associated with the sale. For the majority of firms most of the time the value of inventory will remain above the cost of its purchase. However, there will be occasions when the net realisable value falls below cost, requiring inventory to be revalued downwards. This could arise through:

- deterioration in the condition of the inventory
- technological or commercial factors.

Example 2.9

EXAMPLE:

There is a stockfeed firm in the outer Perth metropolitan area. Among other products, it sells bales of hay to local racehorse owners, agistment businesses and equestrian centres. The hay was purchased from farms at a cost of $4 a bale (including delivery) and it is sold to customers at $8 a bale. One of the sheds on the premises, containing 500 bales of hay, had part of its roof ripped off by a severe thunderstorm and rain got in and soaked the hay. It was no longer able to be sold as feed. The owner of the business believes she will be able to sell the hay for stock bedding or garden mulch at a price of $3 per bale. However, this would require the hay to be laid out to dry and then restacked, which is estimated to cost $200 in wages.

Value of inventory at cost (500 × 4)	$2 000
Value of inventory at net realisable value (500 × 3)	$1 500
Less Cost of disposal	$200
	$1 300

Valued at the lower of cost and net realisable value, the hay would need to be valued at $1300 instead of $2000. The loss of value would be treated as an expense during the period in which the revaluation took place.

Example 2.10

Trenditogs, a clothing store for the young and fashionable, has miscalculated its purchases of summer clothing. It is now almost the end of summer and the store needs to focus on winter gear, but they still have in stock 15 summer dresses that they do not expect to be able to sell at the usual price at this time of year. As they cannot afford to keep the dresses until next summer season (by which time the style and/or colours will probably be out of fashion), the manager decides to sell them at below cost price in order to get rid of them. As an additional incentive, purchasers will be given a voucher for two movie tickets for each dress they buy. The cost of these to the firm will be $5 each. The dresses cost $150 each and the sale price will be $120 each.

Value of inventory at cost (15 × 150)	$2 250
Value of inventory at net realisable value (15 × 120)	$1 800
Less Cost of disposal (30 tickets × 5)	$150
	$1 650

Again, the dresses would need to be revalued to $1650, being the lower of cost and net realisable value.

 Key Concept 2.7

Cost of inventory

The cost of inventory includes the purchase cost and all other costs required to get the inventory into a position from which it can be sold. Inventory must be shown in the accounts at the lower of cost and net realisable value.

Methods of determining cost of sales

There are two main methods of determining the cost of goods sold by a merchandising firm. These are:
- physical or periodic method
- perpetual method.

Physical (periodic) method

The physical (periodic) method does not attempt to identify the cost of goods sold at the time of sale. The cost of purchases during an accounting period is debited to a 'Purchases' expense account and no changes are made to the inventory account during the period. At the end of each period, a physical count of the goods in stock, a *stocktake*, is done to measure the value of inventory at that time. The cost of sales can then be calculated as follows:

	Opening stock (determined by stocktake at the end of the previous period)
Plus	Cost of purchases (debited to purchases account during the period)
=	Value of goods available for sale
Less	Closing stock (determined by stocktake at the end of the period)
=	Cost of goods sold

Accounting and Finance: 2A   ISBN 9780170182041   Cengage Learning Australia

The physical method has the advantage of being simple and straightforward. It is cheap to install and operate in that it does not require the purchase of computer systems which, although much cheaper than they were, may still represent a significant cost for a small business. It may also be the only practicable method where it is difficult to determine easily the cost of sales as the sales are made.

On the other hand, the physical method has the disadvantage that an accurate profit statement cannot be produced without a stocktake – a fairly laborious, costly and inconvenient process. The fact that it must be done for the whole stock at the end of the financial year which, for some businesses, may be a very busy trading time, can seriously disrupt the firm's operations. The firm may need to be closed for the stocktake, or it may need to be done after hours, with consequent extra labour costs.

In the absence of a stocktake, profit determination will require an estimate to be made of the value of goods in stock. This is not necessarily a major drawback for a small business if the owner is knowledgeable and experienced and able to make quite an accurate estimate of the value of stock on hand. A more serious deficiency of the system is that it is very difficult to identify and therefore to do anything about losses of stock. These may be due to shoplifting by customers, fraud or theft by employees, dishonesty by suppliers or merely recording errors (e.g. mistakes in recording the quantity of a consignment received). Stock losses from these causes are often collectively known as *shrinkage* and, under the periodic system, are impossible to measure. From a physical stocktake we know what *is* there, but we do not know what *should* be there.

Key Concept 2.8

Physical (periodic) inventory system

Using this system, the cost of sales is determined by adding opening inventory (determined by a physical stocktake) to purchases (debited as incurred during the year) and deducting closing inventory (determined by a physical stocktake).

Perpetual method

The perpetual method requires the cost of the goods sold to be transferred out of the inventory account into a *cost of sales expense* account at the time they are sold. The cost of goods purchased is debited to the inventory account at the time of purchase. Both the inventory account and the cost of sales account are therefore being perpetually updated (hence the name of the method).

Stocktakes are still carried out, for the purpose of checking what is actually on the shelves against what the records state is there, but they can be done at any time convenient to the firm, rather than having to be done at the end of an accounting period. Stocktakes may also be done at short notice to further discourage theft by staff.

The cost of sales under the perpetual system is simply determined by taking the balance of the cost of sales account at the end of the period concerned.

The main reason that the perpetual system was not widely used in the past was a practical one. The necessity of identifying and transferring the cost of goods sold whenever a sale was made rendered the method impossibly laborious for any business other than one selling a relatively few units of inventory. A used-car firm selling a dozen cars a week could perhaps afford to sit down and make the journal entries necessary to transfer their cost from 'Inventory' to 'Cost of sales'. A supermarket, selling hundreds or even thousands of different products every day, clearly could not. This has all changed over the past 20 years or so with the introduction of effective and affordable computer systems. By the use of barcoding, stock items can be identified and their cost transferred automatically at the point of sale at the same time as the sale price is registered, so that even quite small businesses are able to adopt the perpetual inventory method which, apart from the advantages already mentioned, offers much greater control and efficiency. It is expected that this trend towards the use of the perpetual system will continue and consequently the perpetual system is the one which will be used in this book.

Accounting and Finance 2A   ISBN 9780170182041   Cengage Learning Australia

Key Concept 2.9

Perpetual inventory system

Using this system, the inventory account is perpetually updated, being debited with purchases of inventory as they are made and credited with the cost of goods sold, which is transferred (debited) to a cost of sales account at the time of the sale. The cost of goods sold is the balance in the cost of sales account at the end of the period.

The main features of the physical and perpetual inventory systems

	Perpetual system	Physical system
Costs	For most businesses it will require expenditure on computer hardware and software and on staff training	Minimal establishment costs
Treatment of stock purchases	Debited to Cost of sales expense account	Debited to Purchases expense account
Treatment of stock sales	Sales proceeds credited to Sales account, cost of stock sold transferred from Inventory to Cost of sales	Sales proceeds credited to Sales account, no change made to Inventory
Determination of cost of sales	Can be derived at any time from the balance in the Cost of sales account	Requires a physical stocktake: Cost of sales = opening inventory + purchases − closing inventory
Determination of inventory levels	Can be derived at any time from the balance in the Inventory account	Can only be determined accurately by a stocktake or may be roughly estimated by management
Purpose of stocktake	Check actual stock levels against records to identify shrinkage	Determine stock levels for the purpose of calculating cost of sales
Timing of stocktake	May be done at any time convenient to the business. May be done on a departmental basis and at short notice	Needs to be done at the end of the financial period
Ease of gross profit determination	Gross profit may be determined at any time by deducting the Cost of sales balance from the Sales balance	Accurate determination of gross profit requires a stocktake

Inventory costing methods

Before going on to show the accounting entries to deal with inventory, we will briefly consider the question of inventory costing (i.e. exactly what cost will be transferred from Inventory to Cost of sales when a sale is made). The cost of the item sold may be easy to identify (e.g. the cost of a particular car or piece of machinery may be known). In a sense this type of product is a unique and separate stock item. For most products, however, this is not the case – one can of beans looks very much like another and they will all have the same barcode. If, as often happens, the items in stock were purchased at different prices, the question arises: which price should be used as the cost of sale when some of these items are sold? The two most commonly-used methods of stock costing are *First in, First out (FIFO)* and *Weighted average*.

Under the FIFO method, it is assumed that the inventory sold at any time will be the inventory that was first purchased and the cost of sales to be transferred out of the inventory account will be the cost of those 'oldest' units in stock. Under the weighted average system the total cost of inventory at any time is divided by the number of units in stock at that time to get an average unit cost and the amount transferred to the Cost of sales account will be the number of units sold × average cost.

Accounting and Finance: 2A   ISBN 9780170182041   Cengage Learning Australia

Example 2.11

EXAMPLE:

Grinnings is a hardware store selling a variety of tools, materials and building equipment. One of its stock items is a 2-litre can of Scottish Paint interior gloss enamel. On 1 August it had 26 cans of this paint in stock. Of these, three had been purchased on 15 July at a cost of $18.90 each, five had been purchased on 22 July, also at $18.90 each and 18 on 29 July at a cost of $21.40 each.

On 1 August the firm sold three cans of this paint. What would the cost of sale and the value of the remaining inventory be on both the FIFO and weighted average bases?

COST OF SALE – FIFO

On the first in, first out assumption, the cans sold would be taken to be those purchased on 15 July. Cost of sales is therefore $3 \times 18.90 = \$56.70$. The value of the remaining inventory is $(5 \times 18.90) + (18 \times 21.40) = \$479.70$.

COST OF SALE – WEIGHTED AVERAGE

At 1 August the total value of the inventory is $(8 \times 18.90) + (18 \times 21.40) = \$536.40$. Dividing this by 26 gives an average unit cost of $20.63, which would provide a cost of sale for those three cans (3×20.63) of $61.89 and a remaining inventory after the sale $(536.40 - 61.89)$ of $474.51.

Which method should be used? In the short term, where stock prices are rising – as was the case in our example and is usually true of most manufactured products – the weighted average will result in a higher cost of sales and hence a lower profit and lower income tax liability. If stock prices are falling, as may happen with some agricultural or horticultural products on a seasonal basis and with products such as petrol, which responds to fluctuations in world markets, FIFO might give a higher short-term cost of sales. In the long run, of course, it makes no difference: the same total cost will be allocated as an expense and any short-term differences will, in the end, cancel each other out. The choice of inventory costing methods will come down to which seems easier and therefore cheaper to apply, considering the nature of the firm's products and its recording system.

Accounting entries for the perpetual inventory system

When goods are sold by a firm using the perpetual inventory system, there are essentially three elements that need recording:

- purchase of inventory
- proceeds of the sale
- cost of the sale.

The recording of inventory purchases will be as follows:

Debit	Inventory
Credit	Cash at bank (for a cash purchase) or Account payable (for a credit purchase) with the cost of the goods purchased

The recording of the sale of the inventory will be as follows:

Debit	Cash at bank (for a cash sale) or Account receivable (for a credit sale)
Credit	Sales with the proceeds of the sale

The recording of the cost of sale will be as follows:

Debit	Cost of sales (expense)
Credit	Inventory with the cost of the goods sold

Example 2.11 continued

Using some of the information above (the sale and the latest of the purchases), we can show how these would be recorded in the journal and ledger of Grinnings.

It is assumed that Grinnings uses the FIFO inventory method so that the cost of sales was $56.70, that inventory is purchased from Paint Supplies Ltd on credit and that sales, at $35 per can, are made for cash. We will also assume that the firm keeps a separate inventory account for this particular stock item and that the balances in the ledger before these transactions are as follows:

Sales	$789 400.00 Cr
Cash at bank	$23 580.00 Dr
Cost of sales	$315 700.00 Dr
Inventory of SP gloss enamel 2-litre cans	$151.20 Dr

Example 2.12

General journal			
Date	**Accounts to debit or credit**	**Dr**	**Cr**
29 July	Inventory	385.20	
	Paint supplies		385.20
	(Purchased 18 cans of paint at $21.40 each, inv. D782)		
1 August	Cash at bank	105.00	
	Sales		105 00
	(3 cans of paint sold for cash at $35 each – CRS)		
1 August	Cost of sales	56.70	
	Inventory		56.70
	(Cost $18.90 each of 3 cans of paint sold)		

The transactions are posted from the journal to the ledger.

Ledger				
Cash at bank				
Date	**Particulars**	**Debit** $	**Credit** $	**Balance** $ Dr or Cr
29 July	Balance			23 580.00 Dr
1 Aug	Sales	105.00		23 685.00 Dr
Inventory of SP gloss enamel, 2-litre cans				
Date	**Particulars**	**Debit** $	**Credit** $	**Balance** $ Dr or Cr
29 July	Balance			151.20 Dr
29 July	Paint Supplies Ltd	385.20		536.40 Dr
1 Aug	Cost of sales		56.70	479.70 Dr
Cost of sales				
Date	**Particulars**	**Debit** $	**Credit** $	**Balance** $ Dr or Cr
29 July	Balance			315 700.00 Dr
1 Aug	Inventory	56.70		315 756.70 Dr
Paint Supplies Ltd				
Date	**Particulars**	**Debit** $	**Credit** $	**Balance** $ Dr or Cr
29 July	Inventory		385.20	385.20 Cr

Accounting and Finance: 2A   ISBN 9780170182041   Cengage Learning Australia

Sales				
Date	Particulars	Debit $	Credit $	Balance $ Dr or Cr
1 Aug	Balance			789 400.00 Cr
	Cash at bank		105.00	789 505.00 Cr

Sales and purchase returns

It sometimes happens that goods purchased are found to be deficient in some respect. They may be the wrong size, they may be faulty or they may have been damaged in transit between the vendor's and the purchaser's premises. Under these circumstances either the goods will be returned by the purchaser or the purchaser may agree to retain the goods in consideration for a discount or allowance off the purchase price. The source document for this kind of transaction is called an *adjustment note*; the original is issued to the purchaser, the duplicate copy is retained by the vendor. This transaction, from the viewpoint of the vendor, is a *sales return or allowance* and will have the effect of reducing revenue through a sales returns expense account, normally shown as a deduction from the value of sales and reducing the accounts receivable asset. Where the goods sold have been taken back into stock, the transfer of the cost of those goods made at the time of sale must obviously be reversed to correct both the inventory balance and the cost of sales expense. In the case of sales allowances, as opposed to returns, this last journal entry is not needed. From the purchaser's viewpoint this event is a *purchase return or allowance* and the purchaser will need to record the value of the goods returned (or discount allowed) as a reduction in both inventory asset and the liability to the supplier. Under the perpetual inventory system, the purchase returns will be directly credited to inventory rather than recorded in a separate account. The journal entries may be summarised as follows:

Sales returns
Debit	Sales returns
Credit	Account receivable
Debit	Inventory
Credit	Cost of sales (with cost of goods returned)

Purchase returns
Debit	Account payable
Credit	Inventory

Example 2.13

EXAMPLE: Winsome Loosome has the following balances in its ledger at 30 June.

Inventory	$31 600
Ari Lee (account receivable)	$880
S Herman (account payable)	$500

On 2 July, Lee returns goods that he had purchased for $200 but which turned out to be the wrong colour. The firm agrees to issue him with an Adjustment note no. C46 for this amount. The cost of the goods sold was $110.

On the same day, S Herman provides the firm with an Adjustment note no. 0092 for $100 being an allowance for damage to goods purchased earlier on credit.

The journal entries and the ledger accounts for the debtor and creditor will be as follows:

General journal

Date	Accounts to debit or credit	Dr	Cr
2 July	Sales returns	200	
	Ari Lee (account receivable)		200
	(Goods returned, Adjustment note C46)		
	Inventory	110	
	Cost of sales		110
	(Cost of goods returned, Adjustment note C46)		
2 July	S Herman (account payable)	100	
	Inventory		100
	(Allowance on damaged goods, Adjustment note 0092)		

Ledger

Ari Lee

Date	Particulars	Debit $	Credit $	Balance $ Dr or Cr
30 June	Balance			880 Dr
2 July	Sales returns		200	680 Dr

Sales returns

Date	Particulars	Debit $	Credit $	Balance $ Dr or Cr
2 July	Ari Lee	200		200 Dr

S Herman

Date	Particulars	Debit $	Credit $	Balance $ Dr or Cr
30 June	Balance			500 Cr
2 July	Inventory	100		400 Cr

Inventory

Date	Particulars	Debit $	Credit $	Balance $ Dr or Cr
30 June	Balance			31 600 Dr
2 July	S Herman		100	31 500 Dr

ACCOUNTING FOR GST

The above examples have disregarded the goods and services tax (GST). In the previous chapter you learned about the GST, the *ad valorem* (in proportion to the value) sales tax that applies to most products traded in Australia. To recap, the majority of businesses, except very small ones, are required to register for GST and to charge the tax on their products, although certain items (such as basic foods, some medicines and health products and most educational supplies) are free of GST. By the same token, purchases by businesses of most goods and services will have GST added to the cost of the product purchased. In their Business Activity Statement (BAS), usually submitted to the Australian Taxation Office (ATO) by small- to medium-sized businesses on a quarterly basis, firms must show *GST collected* (i.e. GST added to the sale price of products sold to customers) and *GST outlays* (i.e. GST paid when purchasing inventories or other business assets). The difference between the two represents the amount that must be remitted by the firm to the ATO or, less commonly, refunded by the ATO where the firm's outlays have exceeded its collections.

Accounting and Finance 2A   ISBN 9780170182041   Cengage Learning Australia

In transactions that contain a GST element, this will be separately identified (see the examples of source documents given at the start of this chapter) and both GST outlays and collections will be recorded in two ledger accounts *GST outlays* and *GST collected*. The balances in these accounts will then be transferred to a ledger account, usually called *GST clearing*. The balance in this account at any time represents the amount owing to (or by) the ATO. As it is usually the case that the firm owes tax to the ATO, this account is typically shown in the balance sheet as 'GST payable' in the Current liabilities section. Should it happen that the firm's outlays had exceeded collections in a period, the account balance would be included in Current assets under the heading 'GST refundable'.

EXAMPLE:

Example 2.14

Billy the Kidd, a small firm selling fodder and equipment to goat farmers, has the following transactions during the week.

1 August	Purchased stock from BG Gruff for $1320, including $120 GST (inv. 234)
3 August	Sold stock for cash for $2915 including $265 GST (cash register summary)

The cost of the goods sold was $1400. The balances in Billy the Kidd's ledger before these transactions were as follows:

Sales	$39 500 Cr
Cost of sales	$19 600 Dr
Inventory	$73 800 Dr
Cash at bank	$11 400 Dr
GST clearing	$2 100 Cr

REQUIRED

Enter these transactions, including the transfer of the cost of sales, into the journal and the ledger.

General journal			
Date	**Accounts to debit or credit**	**Dr**	**Cr**
1 Aug	Inventory	1 200	
	GST outlays	120	
	BG Gruff		1 320
	(Purchased, invoice 234)		
3 Aug	Cash at bank	2915	
	Sales		2 650
	GST collected		265
	(Cash sales – CRS)		
	Cost of sales	1 400	
	Inventory		1 400
	(Transfer cost of goods sold)		

Ledger				
Cash at bank				
Date	**Particulars**	**Debit $**	**Credit $**	**Balance $ Dr or Cr**
1 Aug	Balance			11 400 Dr
3 Aug	Sales	2650		14050 Dr
	GST collected	265		14315 Dr

Inventory

Date	Particulars	Debit $	Credit $	Balance $ Dr or Cr
1 Aug	Balance			73 800 Dr
1 Aug	BG Gruff	1 200		75 000 Dr
3 Aug	Cost of sales		1 400	73 600 Dr

Cost of sales

Date	Particulars	Debit $	Credit $	Balance $ Dr or Cr
1 Aug	Balance			19 600 Dr
3 Aug	Inventory			21 000 Dr

BG Gruff

Date	Particulars	Debit $	Credit $	Balance $ Dr or Cr
1 Aug	Inventory		1 200	1 200 Cr
	GST outlays		120	1 320 Cr

GST clearing

Date	Particulars	Debit $	Credit $	Balance $ Dr or Cr
1 Aug	Balance			2 100 Cr

Sales

Date	Particulars	Debit $	Credit $	Balance $ Dr or Cr
1 Aug	Balance			39 500 Cr
3 Aug	Cash at bank		2 650	42 150 Cr

GST outlays

Date	Particulars	Debit $	Credit $	Balance $ Dr or Cr
1 Aug	BG Gruff	120		120 Dr

GST collected

Date	Particulars	Debit $	Credit $	Balance $ Dr or Cr
3 Aug	Cash at bank		265	265 Cr

At the end of the month (or the quarter, as the case may be) the balances in the GST outlays and GST collected accounts will be transferred to the GST clearing account. The effect on that account (assuming no further transactions occur) would be as follows:

GST clearing

Date	Particulars	Debit $	Credit $	Balance $ Dr or Cr
1 Aug	Balance			2 100 Cr
31 Aug	GST outlays	120		1 980 Cr
	GST collected		265	2 245 Cr

The balance in this account will be cleared at the end of the reporting period when the balance is paid to (or received from) the ATO.

Accounting and Finance: 2A   ISBN 9780170182041   Cengage Learning Australia

Firms are permitted to account for GST on a cash basis (recognising the GST component when the cash is actually paid or received) or on an accrual basis (recognising GST when the related transactions occur, regardless of when cash changes hands). For a firm working on an accrual basis in all other respects, it makes sense to account for GST on the same basis and that is the assumption we shall make in this textbook.

Other consequences of including GST

The inclusion of a GST component will affect virtually all transactions a business makes as well as the sales income and purchase of stock illustrated in Example 2.13. These would include:
- purchase of other goods and services (excluding wages, which are exempt)
- sales and purchase returns
- discounts allowed and received
- purchase and sale of non-current assets
- withdrawal of stock by the owner.

Transactions creating a new GST outlay or collection

In essence, the treatment of all these transactions is the same as far as GST is concerned. The expense, asset or income account involved will be debited or credited with the amount of the transaction *excluding* GST. The GST outlays or GST collection account, as the case may be, will be debited or credited with the amount of GST. Cash, debtor or creditor accounts will be credited or debited with the whole amount, including the GST.

Example 2.15

EXAMPLE:

Purchase of goods or services

Carnaby Fashions has received a bill for electricity for the past two months for $313.50, including $28.50 GST. The bill is paid on 13 June using cheque number 678.

General journal				
Date	Accounts to debit or credit		Dr	Cr
13 June	Electricity expense		285.00	
	GST outlays		28 50	
	Bank			313.50
	(Paid bill for April–May cheque 678)			

Ledger				
Electricity				
Date	Particulars	Debit $	Credit $	Balance $ Dr or Cr
13 June	Bank			285.00 Dr
GST outlays				
Date	Particulars	Debit $	Credit $	Balance $ Dr or Cr
13 June	Bank	28.50		28.50 Dr

Accounting and Finance: 2A   ISBN 9780170182041   Cengage Learning Australia

Bank			
Date	Particulars	Debit $	Credit $	Balance $ Dr or Cr
June 13	Electricity		285.00	285.50 Cr
	GST outlays		28.50	313.50 Cr

Purchase or sale of non-current asset

Carnaby Fashions sold its trouser-creasing machine on 3 July for $150 cash plus GST. On the same day it bought an electronic inside-leg measurer on credit from Tailor Supplies for $300, exclusive of GST.

General journal			
Date	Accounts to debit or credit	Dr	Cr
3 July	Bank	165	
	GST collected ($150 × 10%)		15
	Proceeds of sale of machine		150
	(Sales of trouser-creasing machine for cash)		
3 July	Inside-leg measurer	300	
	GST outlays ($300 × 10%)	30	
	Tailor supplies		330
	(Purchase of new asset on credit)		

Ledger			
Bank			
Date	Particulars	Debit $	Credit $	Balance $ Dr or Cr
3 July	GST collected	15		15 Dr
	Proceeds of sale	150		165 Dr
GST collected			
Date	Particulars	Debit $	Credit $	Balance $ Dr or Cr
3 July	Bank		15	15 Cr
Proceeds of sale			
Date	Particulars	Debit $	Credit $	Balance $ Dr or Cr
3 July	Bank		150	150 Cr
Inside-leg-measurer			
Date	Particulars	Debit $	Credit $	Balance $ Dr or Cr
3 July	Tailor supplies	300		300 Dr
GST outlays			
Date	Particulars	Debit $	Credit $	Balance $ Dr or Cr
3 July	Tailor supplies	30		30 Dr
Tailor supplies			
Date	Particulars	Debit $	Credit $	Balance $ Dr or Cr
3 July	Inside-leg measurer		300	300 Cr
	GST outlays		30	330 Cr

Accounting and Finance: 2A   ISBN 9780170182041   Cengage Learning Australia

Withdrawal of stock by owner

On15 August, the owner of Carnaby Fashions took out of stock for his own use a floral waistcoat, which had an inventory cost of $85 and an original cost of $93.50 (GST inclusive) when purchased. GST will need to be reversed and the full GST inclusive cost charged to Drawings. GST outlay will therefore be credited and the Drawings debited with the GST inclusive amount.

General journal			
Date	Accounts to debit or credit	Dr	Cr
15 August	Drawings	93.50	
	Inventory		85 00
	GST outlay ($85 × 10%)		8.50
	(Floral waistcoat taken for own use)		

Ledger

Drawings

Date	Particulars	Debit $	Credit $	Balance $ Dr or Cr
15 Aug	Inventory	85.00		85.00 Dr
	GST outlay	8.50		93.50 Dr

Inventory

Date	Particulars	Debit $	Credit $	Balance $ Dr or Cr
15 Aug	Drawings		85.00	85.00 Cr

GST outlay

Date	Particulars	Debit $	Credit $	Balance $ Dr or Cr
15 Aug	Drawings		8.50	8.50 Cr

In the examples given above, the transaction amounts have been given exclusive of GST and in each case GST has been calculated by multiplying the relevant figure by ten per cent. If amounts are stated to be *inclusive* of GST, the tax component can be calculated by dividing the given amount by 11. For example, if a business buys an office desk for $616 GST inclusive, the GST calculation is 616/11 = $56.

To check this:

Cost without GST	560
GST @ 10%	56
Cost including GST	616

Transactions modifying previous GST outlays or collections

Sales or purchase returns and discounts allowed or received have the effect of cancelling or modifying previously recorded transactions. Since these transactions usually involve GST, the GST effect of the change must also be recorded. Essentially this will have the effect of reversing the original entry, as the following examples will show. Compare them with the entries for purchases and sales in Example 2.13.

Example 2.16

EXAMPLE:

Purchase and sales returns

Minimouse Traders returned some stock, which was the wrong colour, to the supplier, Pluto Wholesalers. The stock had cost $360, exclusive of GST. Pluto issued an Adjustment note C45 to this effect on 3 September 2009. On the same day Minimouse Traders also issued an

Adjustment note 024 to one of its customers, D Duck, for an allowance of $200 (GST exclusive) in respect of some goods that had been damaged in transit.

The first stage is to calculate the GST element of the two transactions, which are:

Purchase returns: $360 × 10% = $36

Sales returns: $200 × 10% = $20

General journal			
Date	Accounts to debit or credit	Dr	Cr
3 Sept	Pluto Wholesalers	396	
	GST outlays		36
	Inventory		360
	(Purchase returns, Adjustment note C45)		
3 Sept	Sales returns	200	
	GST collected	20	
	D Duck		220
	(Sales returns, Adjustment note 024)		

In the following ledger accounts, opening balances have been assumed for Pluto Wholesalers, GST outlays, Inventory, D Duck, and GST collected.

Ledger				
Pluto Wholesalers				
Date	Particulars	Debit $	Credit $	Balance $ Dr or Cr
1 Sept	Balance			3200 Cr
3 Sept	GST outlays	36		3164 Cr
	Inventory	360		2804 Cr
GST outlays				
Date	Particulars	Debit $	Credit $	Balance $ Dr or Cr
3 Sept	Balance			1900 Dr
	Pluto Wholesalers		36	1864 Dr
Inventory				
Date	Particulars	Debit $	Credit $	Balance $ Dr or Cr
1 Sept	Balance			24000 Dr
3 Sept	Pluto Wholesalers		360	23640 Dr
D Duck				
Date	Particulars	Debit $	Credit $	Balance $ Dr or Cr
1 Sept	Balance			1200 Dr
3 Sept	Sales returns		200	1000 Dr
	GST collected		20	980 Dr
GST collected				
Date	Particulars	Debit $	Credit $	Balance $ Dr or Cr
3 Sept	Balance			4250 Cr
	D Duck	20		4230 Cr
Sales returns				
Date	Particulars	Debit $	Credit $	Balance $ Dr or Cr
3 Sept	D Duck	200		200 Dr

Accounting and Finance: 2A   ISBN 9780170182041   Cengage Learning Australia

Discounts allowed and received

As an incentive to customers to pay their bills promptly, many businesses offer a discount for payments within a certain period (such as seven days). The firm itself may well take advantage of such discounts, which will have the effect of reducing the amounts payable and receivable and will also therefore affect the GST outlays and collections.

Let us suppose that on 4 September the firm pays the amount owing to Pluto Wholesalers and thereby gains a 2.5% discount and D Duck also pays promptly to earn a 2% discount. The calculations are as follows:

Discount received $2804.00 \times 2.5\% = \$70.10$ so cash paid is $2733.90

GST component of discount $= 70.10/11 = \$6.37$ so that net discount is $63.73

Discount allowed $980 \times 2\% = \$19.60$ so cash received is $960.40

GST component of discount $= 19.60/11 = \$1.78$ so that net discount is $17.82

We have assumed an opening Bank balance of $3000.

General journal			
Date	Accounts to debit or credit	Dr	Cr
4 Sept	Pluto Wholesalers	2804.00	
	Bank		2733.90
	Discount received		63.73
	GST outlays		6.37
	(Payment of account earning 2.5% discount)		
4 Sept	Bank	960.40	
	Discount allowed	17.82	
	GST collected	1.78	
	D Duck		980.00
	(Receipt from debtor earning 2% discount)		

Ledger				
Pluto Wholesalers				
Date	Particulars	Debit $	Credit $	Balance $ Dr or Cr
3 Sept	Balance			2804.00 Cr
4 Sept	Bank	2733.90		70.10 Cr
	Discount received	63.73		6.37 Cr
	GST outlays	6.37		–
GST outlays				
Date	Particulars	Debit $	Credit $	Balance $ Dr or Cr
3 Sept	Balance			1864.00 Dr
4 Sept	Pluto Wholesalers		6.37	1857.63 Dr
Bank				
Date	Particulars	Debit $	Credit $	Balance $ Dr or Cr
3 Sept	Balance			3000.00 Dr
4 Sept	Pluto Wholesalers			266.10 Dr
	D Duck	960.40	2733.90	1226.50 Dr

D Duck			
Date	Particulars	Debit $	Credit $	Balance $ Dr or Cr
3 Sept	Balance			980.00 Dr
4 Sept	Bank		960.40	19.60 Dr
	Discount allowed		17.82	1.78 Dr
	GST collected		1.78	–

GST collected			
Date	Particulars	Debit $	Credit $	Balance $ Dr or Cr
3 Sept	Balance			4230.00 Cr
4 Sept	D Duck	1.78		4228.22 Cr

Discount received			
Date	Particulars	Debit $	Credit $	Balance $ Dr or Cr
4 Sept	Pluto Wholesalers		63.73	63.73 Cr

Discount allowed			
Date	Particulars	Debit $	Credit $	Balance $ Dr or Cr
4 Sept	D Duck	17.82		17.82 Dr

Test your knowledge

1 What is the purpose of accounting?

2 Outline the accounting cycle.

3 List the main accounting source documents and the type of transaction for which each one is a source.

4 What is meant by 'double entry'?

5 What is a ledger account? What are the two main ways of setting out a ledger account?

6 What is a Chart of accounts and what is its purpose?

7 What is a journal and what is its purpose?

8 Explain 'accrual accounting'.

9 What is a Trial balance and what is its purpose?

10 What recording errors will *not* be disclosed by a Trial balance?

11 What needs to be included in the cost of inventories for a merchandising firm?

12 Explain how inventory must be valued in terms of AASB 102?

13 Outline the physical (periodic) method of accounting for inventory. What advantages does it have over the perpetual method?

14 Outline the perpetual method of accounting for inventory. What advantages does it have over the physical (periodic) method?

15 Outline the difference between the weighted average and first in, first out methods of inventory costing.

16 What accounting records does a firm need to keep in relation to the GST?

Accounting and Finance: 2A   ISBN 9780170182041   Cengage Learning Australia

Test your understanding

Topic guide

- Source documents: 2.1, 2.2
- Chart of accounts: 2.3, 2.4
- Transaction analysis: 2.5, 2.6
- Transaction analysis and journal: 2.7, 2.8, 2.9, 2.10
- Transaction analysis, journal, ledger: 2.11, 2.12
- Journal and ledger (no transaction analysis): 2.13, 2.16, 2.17
- Ledger only (including GST): 2.14, 2.15
- Trial balance (given balances): 2.18–2.20
- Journal, ledger, Trial balance: 2.21–2.23
- Journal, ledger Trial balance (inventory): 2.24
- Journal, ledger, Trial balance (inventory and GST): 2.25–2.28

2.1 What do you think would be the source documents for the following business transactions?

Transaction	Source document(s)
a Bought stock on credit from a wholesaler	
b Paid an outstanding account payable	
c Paid bank fees and charges	
d Sold stock to customers for cash through the cash register	
e Sold stock to customers who paid by credit card	
f Received a payment from an account receivable	
g Paid electricity bill online	
h Provided service to a customer, payable within 30 days	
i Received a payment from a customer by direct credit online	
j Owner drew cash out of the business bank account for personal use	

2.2 What kind of transaction might be represented by the following source documents? (In some cases there might be more than one kind.)

Source document	Transaction(s)
a Bank statement	
b Duplicate invoice	
c Tax invoice	
d Cheque stub	
e ATM receipt	
f Receipt	
g Original invoice	

2.3 You are purchasing a business that runs a shop selling health foods in a Perth suburban shopping centre. You have decided to set up a double entry accounting system. Draw up an appropriate chart of accounts for the business.

2.4 After years of working as an electrician for other people, you have decided to go into business on your own, providing electrical services to individuals and businesses in a small country town. You expect to employ at least a couple of other electricians and possibly an apprentice. You have decided to set up a double entry accounting system. Draw up an appropriate chart of accounts for the business.

2.5 M Giteau established his hairdressing business on 1 July 2010 when he paid $12000 into the business bank account. During the next week the firm carried out the following additional transactions.
- Purchased shop fittings and equipment on credit worth $28000.
- Purchased stock (hair dyes, gel and other products) for $1340 cash.
- Obtained a loan of $25000 from the bank.
- Signed a lease on the business premises and paid the first three months' rent of $4500.
- Paid the annual insurance premium of $2900.

Enter these transactions in an analysing chart with the following headings:

Type of source document	Account to be debited	Account to be credited	$

2.6 Goodasgold Jewellers had the following transactions during the first week of May 2010:
1 May   Purchased inventory on credit from Ring Supplies worth $8700
2 May   Owner took a ring worth $250 out of stock to give her loved one
3 May   Sold jewellery for $4300 cash
4 May   Paid shop assistant's wages $620
5 May   Lady Godiva paid her account of $550
6 May   The owner contributed a computer to the business valued at $2300

Enter these transactions in an analysing chart with the following headings:

Date	Type of source document	Account to be debited	Account to be credited	$

2.7 Grytpype Plumbers had the following transactions during January:
2 Jan   Purchased plumbing materials on credit from Sellers & Co. for $1980, including GST
7 Jan   Was paid fees for a plumbing job worth $800 plus GST
10 Jan   Bought a welder on credit from Milligan Pty Ltd for $1430, including GST
12 Jan   Owner took some plumbing materials that had cost $300 net of GST for his own use
15 Jan   Paid telephone bill of $240 plus GST

Enter these transactions in an analysing chart with the following headings:

Date	Type of source document	Account to be debited	Account to be credited	$

2.8 B Counter set herself up in business as an accountant on 1 July 2010. She will be using a double entry system for the firm's accounting records. The following transactions occurred in her first week of operation.
1 July   Owner paid $15000 into a bank account in the name of the business. She also contributed to the business her computer worth $1900 and some office furniture valued at $950.
2 July   Owner paid the first month's rent on the premises of $1200 (cheque 001)
3 July   Owner bought $800 office stationery from Le Bureau on credit (invoice C34)
4 July   Owner paid the annual insurance premium to AGIO of $2300 (cheque 002)
5 July   Owner withdrew $500 for her own use (cheque 003)
5 July   Firm bought accounting software at a cost of $1600 from BG Lo-Fi (invoice 678 payable in 14 days)

Enter these transactions into an analysing chart and then into the General journal.

2.9 J Catt has been running a restaurant called Cream for some time on a cash basis.
On 1 January 2010 he decided to convert to an accrual-based double entry system.
On that date the assets and liabilities of the business were:

Cash at bank	$9200
Cash in the till	$400
Kitchen equipment	$18900

Furniture and fittings	$13 000
Food supplies on hand	$2 200
Amount owing to food suppliers	$4 800

Over the next couple of days, the following transactions occurred:

2 January	Cash sales (Cash register summary)	$6 900
	Paid food suppliers on account (cheque 097)	$2 000
3 January	Cash sales (cash register summary)	$5 850
	Purchased food supplies on credit (inv. 999)	$3 400
	Purchased a new microwave oven from Norman Harvey on credit (inv. NH756)	$400

Required
a Enter these transactions into an analysing chart and then into the General journal.
b Explain the difference between a cash and an accrual accounting system.

2.10 Fairplay Sports Supplies is a shop that sells sporting gear to the general public and also does a lot of business with sports clubs throughout Western Australia. During the first week in September the firm had the following transactions:
2 September Upper Yarloop Football Club (an account receivable) returned four guernseys they had bought for $240 plus GST because they were the wrong size
Paid food suppliers on account (cheque 097) $2000
4 September Bittabunji Baseball Club paid their bill of $1100 (including GST) and were allowed a 2% discount for prompt payment
8 September The firm decided to write off a debt of $495 (including GST) owed by Firepower Inc.
11 September The firm sold its old cash register for $100 cash, plus GST
Enter these transactions into an analysing chart and then into the General journal.

2.11 Enter the following transactions into an analysing chart and General journal and then post them to ledger accounts. Disregard the cost of sales and GST.

1 March	N Diamond started his florist business, Cracklin' Roses, by depositing $20 000 of his money into a business bank account
2 March	Paid rent in advance of $800 (cheque 001)
	Purchased fixtures and fittings for cash $4800 (cheque 002)
	Owner contributed a delivery van valued at $15 000
3 March	Purchased stock from Floral Suppliers on credit worth $1800 (inv. 335)
4 March	Sales for cash (CRS) $3200
	N Diamond took $50 worth of roses to give his mum for her birthday
5 March	Sales for cash (CRS) $3950
	Paid Floral Suppliers what they are owed (cheque 003)
	Purchased stock from Floral Suppliers worth $1600 (inv. 398)

2.12 The following transactions relating to Bob's Brickies occurred in the first week of June 2010. The balances in the firm's ledger at that date included:

Bank	$4 320 Dr
Tools and equipment	$11 500 Dr
Motor vehicles	$48 000 Dr
A Punter (account receivable)	$970 Dr
Fees revenue	$439 000 Cr
Wages	$84 500 Dr

Accounting and Finance 2A   ISBN 9780170182041   Cengage Learning Australia

1 June	Received payment from A Punter in full payment of her account (rec. 079)
	Received cash fees of $1650 from a customer (rec. 080)
2 June	Bought petrol on account from High Road BP $80 (inv. B56)
	Bought new wheelbarrow for $190 cash (cheque 0987)
	Received an electricity bill from Synergy for $150 (inv. 098765)
3 June	Received cash fees of $980 (receipt 081)
	Sent invoice 0036 to K Marks for $1330 for work done
4 June	Paid wages $1490 (cheque 0988)
	Owner used a business cheque (0989) to pay his personal insurance premium of $1100
5 June	Cash fees received of $980 (rec. 082)

Required

a Enter the transactions in an analysing chart and then into the General journal.

b Enter the opening balances into ledger accounts.

c Post the transactions from the journal to the ledger accounts.

d Explain your treatment of cheque 0989.

2.13 T Jones set up Delilah Fashions on 1 September 2009. On that day she paid $30000 into a business bank account and obtained a loan of a further $20000 from the bank, repayable over the next four years. The transactions of her business over the first few days of operations were as follows:

2 Sept	Purchased fittings and equipment for the store from Shopfitters Inc. for $18000 (invoice A467)
	Purchased inventory from KokoChannel for $29000 (inv. C46)
3 Sept	Paid customs duty on inventory of $1450 (online receipt 97531)
4 Sept	Cash sales of $3450 (CRS)
	Paid shop rent of $1000 (cheque 0001)
	Owner took skirt worth $80 out of stock for her own use
5 Sept	Paid Shopfitters Inc. $10000 on account (cheque 0002)
	Cash sales of $2890 (CRS)
	Owner withdrew $450 for her own use (cheque 0003)
6 Sept	Returned some inventory worth $400 to KokoChannel (adjustment note K003)

Required

a Enter the transactions (including those that occurred on 1 September) into the journal.

b Post from the journal to the ledger accounts.

c Explain your treatment of the customs duty paid on 3 September.

2.14 Cockatoo Traders had the following balances (among others) in its ledger at 30 June 2009:

Inventory	$32400 Dr
Account receivable – R Budgie	$900 Dr
Account receivable – B Parrot	$1300 Dr
Cash at bank	$8200 Cr
Account payable – Twentyeight Ltd	$3200 Cr
Capital	$60000 Cr

During the first week of the new financial year the business had the following transactions:

1 July	Purchased inventory worth $1700 from Rosella Enterprises (inv. 572)
	Paid the amount owning to Twentyeight Ltd, obtaining a 2% discount for prompt payment (cheque 0067)
2 July	Cash sales of $2950 (CRS)
	Sold goods worth $600 to A Carnaby (invoice 246)
3 July	Owner contributed a computer to the business worth $2500
	Paid telephone bill of $245 (cheque 0068)
5 July	Cash sales of $3100 (CRS)
	A Carnaby paid her bill and received a 3% discount for early payment (receipt 0147)

Required
a   Enter the opening balances in the ledger accounts.
b   Post the transactions to the ledger.
c   Apart from its use by Cockatoo Traders as a source document for its inventory purchases, what function would invoice 572 from Rosella Enterprises have?

2.15 Trout Bros included the following balances in its ledger at 31 December 2009:

Inventory	$41 900 Dr
Account receivable – J Haddock	$2 200 Dr
Account receivable – P Salmon	$1 800 Dr
Cash at bank	$7 100 Dr
Account payable – M Akkerill	$5 500 Cr
GST clearing	$4 700 Cr
Sales	$457 000 Cr

During the first week of January the business had the following transactions:

3 Jan	Purchased inventory worth $3200 plus GST from Carp Company
	Paid M Akkerill the amount owing obtaining a 2% discount for prompt payment
4 Jan	Cash sales of $3900 plus GST
	Sold goods worth $2200 plus GST to R Whiting
5 Jan	Returned goods worth $300 exclusive of GST to Carp Company
	Paid the GST owing at 31/12/09 to the ATO
6 Jan	Cash sales of $4200 plus GST
	R Whiting paid his bill and received a 3% discount for early payment

Required
a   Enter the opening balances in ledger accounts.
b   Post the transactions to the ledger (disregard cost of sales).

2.16 Jo Lyons has been running her business, Big Cat Carpets, for some time on an informal basis, simply sending her chequebooks, receipt books and bank statements to the accountant every month for the production of financial reports. However, the business has been doing well and she is planning a substantial expansion. Her accountant has recommended that she should set up a double-entry accounting system and she has decided to do this with effect from the start of the new financial year on 1 July 2010. At that time her assets are as follows:
- Stock of carpets, at cost $68 900
- Cash at bank $23 500

Accounting and Finance 2A   ISBN 9780170182041   Cengage Learning Australia

- Cash in hand $600
- P Ounce (debtor) $1400
- K Cheetah (debtor) $960

The first days of the new year bring the following transactions:

1 July	Purchase of a computer system, including software, for $3100 cash (cheque 0178)
	Purchase of warehouse for $400 000 from D Veloppa. The firm paid a deposit of $20 000 (cheque 0179) with the balance of the purchase price being payable over the next five years
2 July	Obtained a business loan of $25 000 from the Federated Bank (receipt A678)
	Purchased warehouse furniture and equipment for $9800 cash (cheque 0180)
	Sales of carpets for cash $3600 (CRS)
3 July	P Ounce pointed out that he had mistakenly been debited with an invoice for $250, which represented a carpet actually sold to K Cheetah. Investigations reveal that Ounce is right and a correction will have to be made. Ounce then paid his (amended) amount owing (receipt A679).
4 July	Purchased additional carpets from Ali Baba Carpet Co. at a cost of $8000 (invoice AB198)

Required

a   Enter the opening balances listed and the subsequent transactions into the general journal. Disregard GST and cost of sales.

b   Post from the journal to the ledger, opening whatever accounts may be necessary.

c   Name six other ledger accounts that you think Big Cat Carpets might need at some stage.

2.17   The following transactions occurred in the dental practice of Chopper and Fang during the first week of October 2009:

1 October	Fees charged to customers $1600 via Visa card
	Cash fees $250 (receipt 097)
2 October	Purchased dental supplies worth $450 from Drills'n'Fillings (invoice D457)
	Visa transferred to the firm's bank account the amount charged on 1 October, less 1.5% commission
3 October	Chopper contributed office furniture worth $600
4 October	Cash fees $380 (receipts 098 & 099)
	Fees charged to customers via Visa card $1800
5 October	Paid receptionist's wages $650 (cheque 268)
	Fang withdrew $800 for her own use (cheque 269)
	Visa transferred to the firm's bank account the amount charged on 4 October less 1.5% commission

The firm's ledger on 30 September included the following balances:

Cash	$1 980 Dr
Fees revenue	$92 400
Dental supplies	$350
Commission expense	$1 200
Office furniture	$8 600
Wages	$7 250
Capital – Chopper	$30 000
Capital – Fang	$20 000

Required

a Enter the opening balances listed and the subsequent transactions into the General journal.

b Post from the journal to the ledger, opening whatever accounts may be necessary.

c Given that it costs the firm 1.5% of its revenue, why do you think they would be prepared to allow their clients to pay using Visa card?

2.18 Use the following list of balances at 30 June 2010 to produce a Trial balance for Hoki's Pokeys at that date.

	$
A Bee (account receivable)	1 800 Dr
Bank loan	25 000 Cr
C Dee (account receivable)	3 100 Dr
Capital	45 000 Cr
Cash at bank	11 000 Dr
Cash in hand	200 Dr
Computer system	2 700 Dr
Drawings	2 100 Dr
EF Gee (account payable)	2 200 Cr
Equipment	6 300 Dr
HI Jay (account payable)	900 Cr
Inventory	13 700 Dr
Office furniture	4 200 Dr
Vehicles	28 000 Dr

2.19 The ledger balances for Brunel Engineering Consultants at the end of July 2010 are given below.

Bank loan				
Date	Particulars	Debit $	Credit $	Balance $ Dr or Cr
31 July	Balance			15 000 Cr

Accounts receivable				
Date	Particulars	Debit $	Credit $	Balance $ Dr or Cr
31 July	Balance			21 400 Dr

Advertising expense				
Date	Particulars	Debit $	Credit $	Balance $ Dr or Cr
31 July	Balance			3 400 Dr

Fees				
Date	Particulars	Debit $	Credit $	Balance $ Dr or Cr
31 July	Balance			388 900 Cr

Stock of stationery				
Date	Particulars	Debit $	Credit $	Balance $ Dr or Cr
31 July	Balance			400 Dr

Insurance expense

Date	Particulars	Debit $	Credit $	Balance $ Dr or Cr
31 July	Balance			12 000 Dr

Wages

Date	Particulars	Debit $	Credit $	Balance $ Dr or Cr
31 July	Balance			238 000 Dr

Furniture and equipment

Date	Particulars	Debit $	Credit $	Balance $ Dr or Cr
31 July	Balance			21 600 Dr

Motor vehicles

Date	Particulars	Debit $	Credit $	Balance $ Dr or Cr
31 July	Balance			61 000 Dr

Drawings

Date	Particulars	Debit $	Credit $	Balance $ Dr or Cr
31 July	Balance			66 000 Dr

Capital

Date	Particulars	Debit $	Credit $	Balance $ Dr or Cr
31 July	Balance			30 000 Cr

Rent expense

Date	Particulars	Debit $	Credit $	Balance $ Dr or Cr
31 July	Balance			18 000 Dr

Sundry office expenses

Date	Particulars	Debit $	Credit $	Balance $ Dr or Cr
31 July	Balance			2 800 Dr

Postage and telephone

Date	Particulars	Debit $	Credit $	Balance $ Dr or Cr
31 July	Balance			3 900 Dr

Commission earned

Date	Particulars	Debit $	Credit $	Balance $ Dr or Cr
31 July	Balance			14 600 Cr

Required

a   Draw up a Trial balance for the firm at 31 July 2010.

b   Does the fact that the Trial balance balances mean that all the recording has been done correctly? Explain your answer.

Accounting and Finance 2A   ISBN 9780170182041   Cengage Learning Australia

2.20 Simpson's Homeware has provided you with the following ledger balances at 31 August 2010.

C Marge

Date	Particulars	Debit $	Credit $	Balance $ Dr or Cr
31 Aug	Balance			950 Dr

Leesa Ltd

Date	Particulars	Debit $	Credit $	Balance $ Dr or Cr
31 Aug	Balance			600 Cr

Inventory

Date	Particulars	Debit $	Credit $	Balance $ Dr or Cr
31 Aug	Balance			38 300 Dr

B Art

Date	Particulars	Debit $	Credit $	Balance $ Dr or Cr
31 Aug	Balance			750 Cr

M Aggie

Date	Particulars	Debit $	Credit $	Balance $ Dr or Cr
31 Aug	Balance			1 400 Cr

Salaries and wages

Date	Particulars	Debit $	Credit $	Balance $ Dr or Cr
31 Aug	Balance			298 000 Dr

Office expenses

Date	Particulars	Debit $	Credit $	Balance $ Dr or Cr
31 Aug	Balance			37 000 Dr

Bank loan

Date	Particulars	Debit $	Credit $	Balance $ Dr or Cr
31 Aug	Balance			40 000 Cr

Plant & equipment

Date	Particulars	Debit $	Credit $	Balance $ Dr or Cr
31 Aug	Balance			76 000 Dr

Capital – E Burns

Date	Particulars	Debit $	Credit $	Balance $ Dr or Cr
31 Aug	Balance			70 000 Cr

Insurance

Date	Particulars	Debit $	Credit $	Balance $ Dr or Cr
31 Aug	Balance			17 000 Dr

Accounting and Finance 2A   ISBN 9780170182041   Cengage Learning Australia

Owner's drawings				
Date	Particulars	Debit $	Credit $	Balance $ Dr or Cr
31 Aug	Balance			29 000 Dr

Rent				
Date	Particulars	Debit $	Credit $	Balance $ Dr or Cr
31 Aug	Balance			24 000 Dr

Interest expense				
Date	Particulars	Debit $	Credit $	Balance $ Dr or Cr
31 Aug	Balance			4 800 Dr

Sales commission				
Date	Particulars	Debit $	Credit $	Balance $ Dr or Cr
31 Aug	Balance			5 400 Dr

Discount allowed				
Date	Particulars	Debit $	Credit $	Balance $ Dr or Cr
31 Aug	Balance			1 900 Dr

Discount received				
Date	Particulars	Debit $	Credit $	Balance $ Dr or Cr
31 Aug	Balance			900 Cr

Sales				
Date	Particulars	Debit $	Credit $	Balance $ Dr or Cr
31 Aug	Balance			422 000 Cr

Sales returns				
Date	Particulars	Debit $	Credit $	Balance $ Dr or Cr
31 Aug	Balance			2 100 Dr

Required

a   Use the balances to draw up a Trial balance for the firm at 31 August 2010.

b   If you have entered and added up the balances correctly, you will find that the Trial balance does not balance. Suggest two reasons, based on the information you have been given, why this might be so.

2.21 G Walkabout set up his business, Dreamtours, to run outback safaris to the wild parts of Western Australia on 1 April 2010. He contributed his own 4WD vehicle valued at $40 000, as well as $32 000 in cash. On the same day the business took delivery of two other vehicles, worth a total of $90 000, from Greenmount Toyota. These will need to be paid for in 30 days. During the first week of April the firm had the following transactions:

1 April	Paid registration fees for the vehicles $2400 (cheque 001)
	Obtained a loan from the bank for $80 000, repayable over five years
2 April	Paid insurance premiums on the vehicles $6000 (cheque 002)

Accounting and Finance: 2A   ISBN 9780170182041   Cengage Learning Australia

	Opened an account with the local service station for fuel	
	Owner contributed a computer system worth $3000	
	Paid for advertising $2400 (cheque 003)	
3 April	Received payment for safaris later in the month – $9000 in cash (receipts 001–006) and $12 000 on credit cards (funds transferred into the bank online, net of a 1% commission, tax invoices printed)	
	Filled up vehicles with fuel on credit – $480 (invoice S432)	
4 April	Owner paid his son's school fees out of the business bank account $1200 (cheque 004)	
5 April	Purchased stationery for cash $250 (cheque 005)	
	Paid wages ($900 cheque 006)	

Required

a   Enter the opening balances and subsequent transactions in the General journal. (Disregard GST.)

b   Post from the journal to the ledger.

c   Take out a Trial balance for Dreamtours as at 5 April 2010.

2.22   Petal Stayman owns Floribunda, a business importing flowers to sell to local florists and supermarkets. At 30 September 2010 the firm had the following balances in its ledger:

Accounts payable	$49 800 Cr
Accounts receivable	$52 400 Dr
Bank loan	$200 000 Cr
Buildings, at cost	$360 000 Dr
Capital	$240 000 Cr
Cash at bank	$22 300 Dr
Cash in hand	$100 Dr
Inventory	$26 000 Dr
Plant and equipment	$29 000 Dr

These transactions occurred early in October:

1 Oct	Payment received from accounts receivable owing $4500. They are allowed a discount of 2% for prompt payment (receipts 032–033)
	Paid wages $3200 (cheque 0912)
2 Oct	Cash sales $2200 (receipts 034–036)
	Bank statement received, showing that the bank has charged six-monthly interest of $9000 and bank charges of $65 to the bank account
	Owner took orchids worth $60 out of stock as a present for her grandmother
3 Oct	Received $8000 from accounts receivable (receipts 037–038; they do not qualify for a discount)
	Sent an invoice to accounts receivable for $4800 (invoice A0078)
	Paid accounts payable $8000, earning a discount of 1.5% for prompt payment (cheque 0913)
4 Oct	Owner withdrew $500 cash for her own use (cheque 0914)
	Paid telephone bill $450 cheque 0915

Required

a   Enter the transactions into the General journal. (Disregard GST.)

b   Enter the opening balances into ledger accounts and then post from the journal to the ledger, opening additional accounts where necessary.

c   Take out a Trial balance at 4 October 2010.

d   This firm's inventory is presumably valued at cost. Under what circumstances might it be valued in some other way?

2.23   Muzack is a small store selling videos, DVDs and other musical media in a suburban shopping centre. It conducts some business over the internet, for which payment is invariably made by credit card. Credit card payments are immediately transferred to the firm's bank account, less the 2% commission charged by the credit provider. On 1 January 2010, the firm's ledger has the following balances in it:

Cash at bank	$7 500 Cr
Accounts payable	$12 500 Cr
Inventory	$48 200 Dr
Fixtures and fittings	$17 400 Dr
Sales	$183 000 Cr
Cost of sales	$102 000 Dr
Wages	$24 500 Dr
General expenses	$18 800 Dr
Commission expense	$2 200 Dr
Discount revenue	$900 Cr
Sales returns	$800 Dr
Drawings	$30 000 Dr
Capital	$40 000 Cr

During the first few days of January 2010 the following transactions occurred:

2 Jan	The firm paid the balance owing to accounts payable, less a 2% discount for prompt payment (cheque 0076)
	Cash sales of $1250 (CRS)
	Credit card sales of $2300 (tax invoices)
3 Jan	Owner took DVDs worth $40 out of stock for his own use
	Paid wages $950 (cheque 0077)
	Received an adjustment note (A43) from one of the suppliers for $230, being the net cost of goods incorrectly supplied
	Cash sales of $2450 (CRS)
4 Jan	During the previous month, the owner paid his personal insurance of $580 with a business cheque (0062). The payment was debited to General expenses. This was clearly wrong and needs to be corrected.
	A customer has not received the CDs she ordered and paid for over the internet and wants to cancel the sale. The firm sends her an adjustment note for $55 (no. 024)
	Cash sales of $1800 (CRS)

Required

a   Enter the transactions into the General journal. (Disregard GST.)

b   Enter the opening balances into ledger accounts and then post from the journal to the ledger, opening additional accounts where necessary.

c   Take out a Trial balance at 4 January 2010.

d   What would be the consequence of not correcting the error mentioned above on 4 January?

2.24 Ric Tangle bought The Corner Shop, a small local deli, on 1 March 2010. At that time the business had the following assets and liabilities:

Assets	
Fixtures and fittings	$21 400
Inventory	$31 600
Equipment	$5 200
Cash at bank	$7 100
Liabilities	
EG Stores (account payable)	$16 100

Assuming Ric paid the previous owner exactly what the business was worth to him, how much should he have paid? Ric intends to operate a double-entry accounting system using the perpetual method of accounting for inventory. Over the next few days, the following transactions took place:

2 March	Purchased a computerised accounting and inventory system from IT Extra for $7300, payable in 30 days (invoice C456)
	Owner contributed an additional $10 000 cash (receipt 078)
3 March	Cash sales $1800 (CRS); the cost of these sales was $760
	Paid rent $600 (cheque 001)
	Purchased inventories from EG Stores for $2600 (invoice EG887)
4 March	Returned $200 of goods to EG Stores (damaged in transit) (Adjustment note 015)
	Paid EG Stores for the remainder of the previous day's purchases, earning a 2% discount (cheque 002)
	Cash sales $2900 (CRS); the cost of these sales was $1160
5 March	Ric took four cases of cool drinks costing $30 home for his son's birthday party
	Cash sales $1750 (CRS); the cost of these sales was $700

Required
a   Enter the transactions (including the entries to commence the business) into the General journal. (Disregard GST.)
b   Post from the Journal to the Ledger.
c   Take out a Trial balance as at 5 March 2010.
d   Briefly describe the two alternative methods Ric might have used to determine the cost of the inventory sold for each transaction.

2.25 Enter the transactions contained in the previous question into the Journal and then the Ledger with the addition of GST. In each case, assume that the figure quoted in the original question is *exclusive* of GST.

2.26 Sue Naami owns Surfstuff selling surfboards, swimwear and other beach gear. She uses the perpetual method of accounting for inventory. At the start of November 2009 her ledger had the following balances in it:

Cash at bank	$7 700 Cr
Accounts payable	$12 500 Cr
Shop fittings	$11 300 Dr
Office equipment	$9 800 Dr
Sales	$96 000 Cr
Cost of sales	$32 100 Dr
Office expenses	$18 900 Dr

Wages	$23 200 Dr
Capital	$20 000 Cr
Inventory	$14 900 Dr
Drawings	$26 000 Dr

The firm's transactions for the first days of November were:

1 Nov	Paid advertising $300 (cheque 0069)
	Cash sales $1850 (CRS); the cost of these sales was $620
2 Nov	Purchased surfboards on credit for $2800 (invoice C342)
	Paid wages of $820 (cheque 0070)
	Cash sales $1360 (CRS); the cost of these sales was $450
	Credit card sales $800 (tax invoices); the cost of these sales was $300. The sales proceeds, less 1.5% commission, is paid into the firm's bank account the same day.
3 Nov	Sue's accountant has noticed that a previous payment of $820 for wages was debited to Office expenses instead of Wages
	Cash sales $1760 (CRS); the cost of these sales was $580
	Sue drew out $350 for her own use (cheque 0071)

Required

a Enter the transactions into the General journal.

b Enter the opening balances into ledger accounts and then post from the journal to the ledger, opening additional accounts where necessary.

c Take out a Trial balance at 3 November 2010.

d What special problems do you think Sue's business might have in relation to inventory?

2.27 T Woods is setting up a golf shop that he is calling Caddie Shack. On 10 April 2009 he paid $40000 into a business bank account. He also donated to the business his personal computer valued at $1600. Woods will be using the perpetual inventory system. Over the next few days the following transactions occurred:

10 April	Signed a lease on shop premises, paying three months rent in advance of $3300 (cheque 001), including $300 GST
	Purchased shop fittings for cash $4620 (cheque 002), including $420 GST
	Purchased inventory from Fairway Supplies worth $9900, including $900 GST (invoice F759)
11 April	Paid insurance premium of $1980 (cheque 003), including GST $180
	Sold stock for $3575 cash, including $325 GST; the cost of the stock was $1900
	Woods took a box of golf balls worth $30 out of stock for his own use
12 April	Cash sales of $2640 (GST $240); cost of stock sold was $1130
	Paid wages $350 (cheque 004)
	Owner paid his personal golf club subscription of $800 using business cheque 005
	Sold a set of clubs worth $2200 (including GST $200) to G Norman on credit (invoice A0001); the cost of the set was $850

Required

a Enter the transactions (including the opening entries) into the General journal.

b Post from the journal to the ledger.

c Take out a Trial balance at 12 April 2009.

Accounting and Finance: 2A   ISBN 9780170182041   Cengage Learning Australia

d   The balance in the GST clearing account of most businesses is usually a credit one, indicating a debt from the firm to the ATO. Why is that not currently the case with Caddie Shack?

2.28 Pam's Pets sells a wide range of pet foods, aquariums, cages and other equipment to pet owners in the eastern suburbs of Perth. The business also sells quite a lot of stock to country customers who order via the internet and pay by credit card. It accounts for inventory by the perpetual system. At the beginning of the new financial year, on 1 July 2010, the firm's assets and liabilities are as follows:

Assets	
Cash in hand	$200
Cash at bank	$16400
Inventory	$42300
Shop furniture and fittings	$13600
Computer system	$4500
Liabilities	
Accounts payable	$15000
GST payable	$2000
Bank loan	$20000

During the first week of July the following transactions occur:

1 July	Cash sales (CRS) $3960 (including GST $360); cost of sales was $1620
	Paid GST owing at 30 June to the ATO (cheque 914)
	Paid an account payable owed $5600, earning a 1% discount (cheque 915)
2 July	Credit card sales of $1100 plus 10% GST. The credit card company charges 1% commission on the value of the sales (excluding GST); the cost of these sales was $480
	Cash sales (CRS) $3410 (including GST $310); cost of sales $1400
3 July	Pam withdrew $700 cash (cheque 916). She also took a sack of guinea pig pellets worth $20 for her son, who has unusual tastes in food
	Cash sales (CRS) $3080 (including GST $280); cost of sales $1250
4 July	Pam returned to the supplier some goods that were unsatisfactory and received an adjustment note no. C448 for $460 (plus GST $46)
	Purchased goods worth $5390 (including GST $490) from a supplier (invoice 00997)
	Cash sales (CRS) $2860 (including GST $260); cost of sales $1170
5 July	Credit card sales of $900 plus 10% GST, less the usual 1% commission on the value of the sales (excluding GST); cost of sales was $405
	Cash sales (CRS) $3575 (including GST $325); cost of sales $1465

Required
a   Enter the transactions into the General journal. Where necessary, round figures off to the nearest whole dollar.
b   Enter the opening balances (including capital) into ledger accounts and then post from the journal to the ledger, opening additional accounts where necessary.
c   Take out a Trial balance at 5 July 2010.
d   Why do you think it is likely that the firm uses a computerised accounting system?

Accounting and Finance 2A   ISBN 9780170182041   Cengage Learning Australia

Investigation

(This task could be done as an individual or group project.)

Carry out a survey of a small retail business to which you have access. This could be a business run by family members or friends or one in your neighbourhood that is willing to help you. Ask the following questions:

- What sort of products does the business sell?
- What kind of inventory system does it operate?
- How does the business value and cost inventory?
- What sort of accounting system does the business operate?
- What are its source documents?
- What accounts does the business have (i.e. chart of accounts)?

The results of your survey should be presented in the form of a written or electronic report. In your report, you should state whether you think the firm's accounting systems are appropriate and why. Identify any improvements you think could be made.

Essay

You are setting up your own small retail business. Outline the accounting system that you will need to set up to control your business. In your explanation you should cover the following aspects:

- recording and storage of information
- inventory system.

Ethics case study

Your friend Freddy Foxe runs a small landscaping business, Vixen Vistas, doing garden renovations, driveways and other small earthmoving tasks for individual and local government authorities. The shires and councils always give him written orders and require formal tax invoices, showing GST included in the price. However, some of the jobs he does for individuals are paid for in cash without any supporting documentation. This way, he does not need to add GST and can charge a lower price for the job. He argues that nobody is getting hurt and, in fact it is good for the customer as they are getting a better price and good for him because it reduces the amount of paperwork he has to do.

Discuss whether you think Freddy's practice is ethical.

Accounting and Finance 2A   ISBN 9780170182041   Cengage Learning Australia

Chapter 3
FINANCIAL REPORTING FOR SMALL BUSINESS

What You Will Learn

After studying this chapter you should be able to:

1 Explain the importance of financial statements in determining the performance, financial position and liquidity of a small business

2 Review the definitions of the essential elements of financial statements (asset, liability, income, expense, equity) and outline the criteria for recognition of each

3 Explain the concept of closing entries to determine profit at the end of an accounting period and carry out the closing journal entries for simple profit determination

4 Prepare an Income statement for a small business run as a sole trader

5 Prepare a Statement of financial position (Balance sheet) for a small business run as a sole trader

6 Prepare a Business Activity Statement (BAS) for GST for a small business run as a sole trader

Introduction

The owners and managers of any business (for very small businesses, such as sole traders, the owner and the manager is often the same person) have three broad questions:

- How profitable is the business? How much money is it earning for me in absolute dollar terms as well as in relation to the size of the business and my investment in it?
- How secure or stable is the business? How likely is it that my investment will be safe in the medium- to long-term?
- What is the business's liquidity position? Is it going to generate the cash needed to pay its debts when they must be paid?

  Obviously these questions are interrelated: if the business is not profitable, this may lead to a lack of resources, particularly cash, which may jeopardise the firm's capacity to pay its debts and therefore to survive into the future. The three broad questions will also, of course, give rise to other questions. If profitability is unsatisfactory, why? What could be done to improve the situation? If liquidity and/or security are less than acceptable, what has caused this position and how can it be rectified?

REPORTS OF PAST FINANCIAL PERFORMANCE

Information about a firm's past performance and financial position will not be the only considerations when making economic decisions about its future. Conditions in the market in which it operates, the general economic situation and the owner's future aspirations and needs will all have their influence. There is also obviously a problem in relying on reports of past events (which is generally what financial statements are) to guide future action. However, because we cannot obtain reliable forecasts of future performance, we must make the best possible use of the information we have, despite its shortcomings. In the absence of an accurate crystal ball, reports of past financial performance are the most valuable guide available to the owner or manager in pursuit of what is generally assumed to be the aim of business, namely maximising profit in the long term.

In this book, therefore, we shall be focusing on the production and use of financial statements by the managers and owners of small businesses, beginning in this chapter with the production of a simple Income statement and Statement of financial position (balance sheet) for a small business organised as a sole trader.

REALITY CHECK 3.1

Dum and Dee are a husband and wife who own a medium-sized farm producing wheat, canola and sheep. Dum manages the financial records, which he sends off to the accountant from time to time so that she can produce reports and also, at the end of the financial year, do their tax return. Dee doesn't get to see any financial reports nor does she participate in decision-making about farm policy and future directions. She has complained about this, but Dum points out that he is the trained agriculturalist and so he needs to make the decisions. He decides what is best for them both and the whole family benefits.

Do you agree with Dum's position? What do you think he should do?

ELEMENTS OF FINANCIAL REPORTS

There are two basic financial statements that all businesses produce. These are:

* *Income statement* (also called *Profit and loss statement or P&L*) – this sets out, for a particular period of time, the *income* earned by the business, the *expenses* incurred in earning that revenue and the resultant *profit or loss* for the period (if income exceeds expense, there is a profit; if expense is greater than income, there is a loss). Such a report will be produced at least once a year and most businesses would produce one every quarter (three months) or every month. It will be helpful in answering questions relating to profitability.

* *Statement of financial position* (also called *Balance sheet*) – this sets out the details of the *assets* owned and the *liabilities* owed by the business at the end the period (i.e. the end of the year, the quarter or the month) and consequently the value of the owner's investment in the business, the *owner's equity*, at that point in time. It is used to assess the firm's stability and liquidity.

Although these two reports are invariably produced at the same time, they do have different focuses. The Income statement is a period report (i.e. it records the events of the selected period of time). An analogy might be of a video taken of a particular lesson. The Statement of financial position is a moment-in-time report (i.e. it records the position at a certain point in time, normally at the end of the selected period). An analogy might be of a still photograph taken at the end of the lesson.

Accounting and Finance 2A   ISBN 9780170182041   Cengage Learning Australia

Incidentally, the terminology in relation to these reports has changed over recent years and will no doubt change again in the future. In this textbook we will use the names of the reports, Income statement and Statement of financial position, currently employed in accounting standards and other official documents. However, there would be nothing to prevent individual businesses using the old terminology to describe their reports.

Income statement

Strictly speaking, the Income statement deals with income, not just revenue, which, as defined in the Framework (see Chapter 1), is just one element of income – the other being *gains*. Revenue is income arising in the normal course of operations – sales, fees, commissions, interest, etc. – while gains refers to income arising from the sale or revaluation of non-current assets. In this textbook we confine ourselves to revenue.

As you will recall from Chapter 1, income is defined as an increase in future economic benefits during a period, by way of increased assets or decreased liabilities, leading to an increase in equity other than contributions of capital by the owner(s). As income has the effect of increasing equity, it is treated (as equity is) as a 'credit' type of transaction.

Firms may have a number of sources of revenue that they wish to account for separately. For a merchandising firm, there may simply be one 'Sales' account. Or the firm may wish to record 'Credit sales' and 'Cash sales' separately. Or it may want to have distinct accounts for different categories of sales. For example, a hardware store may want to have one account for sales of tools, one for sales of timber, one for sales of garden products and so on. A service business may just have one revenue account 'Fees', or they may wish to distinguish between different categories of work (e.g. an accountant might have separate revenue accounts for 'Audit', 'Financial accounting', 'Tax returns', 'Financial advice' and so on). Types of revenue other than sales may also have their own accounts, such as Interest on surplus funds invested, Commission earned on sales as an agent and Rent revenue from the leasing of surplus office space.

Expenses are defined as decreases in future economic benefits during a period by way of decreased assets or increased liabilities leading to a decrease in equity other than by withdrawals of resources by the owner or owners. Most businesses would have a greater number of expense accounts than revenue accounts. A merchandising business will have a cost of sales account (perhaps more than one, if it wishes to track the contributions of different types of inventory) and a wide range of other expenses that it will wish to record, including rent, insurance, wages and salaries, communication expenses, vehicle expenses, office stationery, electricity, interest and fees. The list of expenses for a service business will include many of the same accounts, although obviously they will not need a 'cost of sales' account.

An important consideration to determine is when revenue and expenses will be recognised (i.e. considered to have occurred and brought into the accounts). The two essential criteria are 'probability' and 'reliability of measurement' – in other words, the probability that the increase or decrease in economic benefit has occurred and whether it can be reliably expressed in terms of dollars and cents. It can be seen from this that it is not necessary for a physical transfer of resources to have occurred for an expense or revenue to be recognised. Once a good or service has been provided and a legal obligation to pay a defined amount arises, the transaction should be entered into the financial records of both the provider and the purchaser as, respectively, revenue and expense.

REALITY CHECK 3.2

Sadie Cleaners provides cleaning services for offices in Perth. They have sent an invoice to one of their clients, Gogo Insurance Company, for $1760 for cleaning services provided during the month of May. Although this amount is unlikely to be received until some time in June, it will be recorded as revenue by Sadie in May because the service was provided then and, consequently, it is *probable* (in fact, certain) that a *measurable* ($1760) increase in economic benefit has occurred at that time (in the form of an increase in accounts receivable by that amount). When the payment is eventually made, there is no change in the overall assets of the firm (and hence the equity), merely the exchange of one asset (account receivable) for another of the same value (cash). By the same token, Gogo Insurance Company will record the transaction as an expense because a measurable increase in liabilities can be said to have probably occurred (increase in accounts payable).

If Sadie Cleaners tendered (i.e. made an offer to supply) for cleaning services to another firm in the same building at, say, $2000 per month for the next three months, when should this be recognised as revenue?

The final part of the Income statement, the so-called 'bottom line', is the result of deducting the sum of all the expenses from the total revenue and gains. This represents the amount by which equity has increased (profit) or decreased (loss) during the period.

Key Concept 3.1

Income statement

An Income statement is a financial statement for a specified period of time setting out the income and expense occurred by the business during that period and the resultant profit or loss for the period.

Statement of financial position

As previously mentioned, the Statement of financial position sets out the financial position of the business at a particular date, usually the last day of the financial period to which the corresponding Income statement refers. It will show the firm's assets and liabilities and, using the accounting equation of *Owner's equity = Assets − Liabilities*, the owner's interest in the business.

As you will recall from Chapter 1, an asset is a resource embodying future economic benefits, controlled (though not necessarily legally owned) by the business as a result of a past event. Businesses will have a variety of assets ranging from physically tangible ones (such as furniture, buildings, vehicles and office equipment) to more ephemeral ones (such as bank accounts and amounts owing by credit customers, i.e. accounts receivable). The basic criteria for the recognition of an asset are the same as those for revenue and expense (i.e. probability and ability to be 'reliably measured'). Once it can be stated that an item embodying future economic benefits with a definable dollar value has come within the firm's control, it should be recognised as a business asset.

Remember, a liability is a present obligation that will result in an outflow of future economic benefits. Note that the liability must be 'present' (i.e. exist as an obligation at the time of the report). An obligation that might arise in the future (such as a guarantee of a loan taken out by a third party) is not considered to be 'present' and will not be shown as a liability. Liability accounts are usually less numerous than asset accounts and might include the bank account if it is in overdraft, amounts owing to suppliers (accounts payable) and loans from banks or other financial institutions. A liability will be recognised once it is probable that the obligation has arisen and can be quantified in dollar terms.

The third element of the firm's financial position, the owner's equity, may be defined as the residual interest in the assets of the business after deducting all the liabilities. It does not require specific recognition criteria since it merely depends on recognition of the other two elements.

Example 3.1

EXAMPLE:
Tran's Transport was set up on 1 September when Tran deposited $50000 in a business bank account and contributed his personal vehicle worth $25000 to the business. At the same time, he purchased another vehicle costing $30000 from Vin's Vans, paying $10000 deposit, the remainder being on credit terms. Both the cash ($40000 left in the account) and

Accounting and Finance: 2A   ISBN 9780170182041   Cengage Learning Australia

the vehicles ($55000) are resources controlled by the business, having a defined value and future economic benefits for the business. They will therefore be recognised as assets on 1 September. The $20000 owing to Vin's Vans is a quantifiable present obligation that will, in due course, result in an outflow of economic benefits of that amount from the business. It will therefore be recognised as a liability on 1 September. Tran's capital (owner's equity) is the difference between the assets ($95000) and liabilities ($20000), i.e. $75000. Or, put another way, the $50000 cash plus vehicle of $25000.

This may be summarised as follows:

Assets	
Cash	$40000
Vehicles	$55000
	$95000
Liabilities	
Loan from Vin's Vans	$20000
Equity	
Capital: Tran	$75000
Total liabilities and equity	$95000

Note that if (as many business owners do) Tran were to go to the bank and arrange an overdraft facility of, say, $20000 (i.e. the capacity to withdraw funds from the bank account over and above any amounts deposited up to a maximum of $20000) to deal with future temporary cash shortages, this would not constitute a liability until such time as the facility were to be used. Even then, it would only become a liability to the extent of the actual money overdrawn. For example, if the firm went $3500 into overdraft, the liability at that point would be the amount actually owing i.e. $3500, not the potential limit of the overdraft of $20000.

Key Concept 3.2

Statement of financial position

A Statement of financial position is a financial statement as at a certain date setting out the assets and liabilities of the business at that date and the resultant equity, or owner's interest, in the business.

PROFIT DETERMINATION AND CLOSING ENTRIES

The process of *profit determination* consists of:
* identifying the revenue and expenses for a particular period
* aggregating these to work out the profit or loss
* recording that profit or loss as an increase or decrease in the owner's equity.

As far as the first part of this process is concerned, revenue earned and expenses incurred during the period will have been posted to the various ledger accounts so that the balances in these accounts, assuming they started at zero – which they would have (see below) – will represent the revenue and expenses for the period. These balances can then be transferred to one or more profit-determining accounts. Transferring the balances from revenue and expense accounts achieves two things:
* the profit or loss for the period is calculated
* the revenue and expense accounts are returned to a zero balance, ready to begin recording the transactions for the next accounting period.

The final balance in the profit-determining account will represent the profit (credit balance) or loss (debit balance) for the period. This balance will then be transferred to an account in the owner's equity section (either the capital account or a separate account called *Retained profit account* or *Current account*), which will have the effect of recognising the increase or decrease in equity that has resulted from the firm's trading operations for the period.

The profit-determining account, normally called Profit and loss summary account, is a temporary working account that exists only for the purpose of aggregating the revenue and expenses for the period before transferring the resultant profit or loss to owner's equity. It will clearly have no opening or closing balance. Merchandising businesses used to have an additional intermediate profit-determining account called the Trading account to determine the gross profit, which was then transferred to the Profit and loss summary. However, this practice is not now widely used and will not be employed in this book.

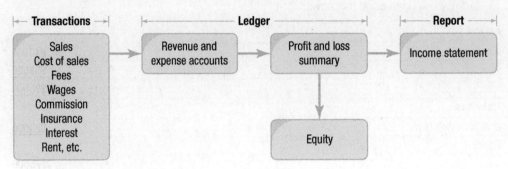

Figure 3.1 The profit-determining process

The transference of ending balances from the revenue and expense accounts to the profit-determining account and the transfer from Profit and loss summary to Equity (Capital or Current account) is achieved by entries made in the General journal. These are termed *Closing entries*.

Key Concept 3.3

Closing entries

Closing entries are the journal entries used to transfer balances from revenue and expense accounts to the profit-determining account at the end of the financial period.

Example 3.2

EXAMPLE:

B Baggins' business, Hobbit Hardware, had the following balances in its ledger at the end of the financial year on 30 June 2010.

Sales				
Date	Particulars	Debit $	Credit $	Balance $ Dr or Cr
30 June	Balance			328 000 Cr

Sales returns				
Date	Particulars	Debit $	Credit $	Balance $ Dr or Cr
30 June	Balance			2 000 Dr

Cost of sales				
Date	Particulars	Debit $	Credit $	Balance $ Dr or Cr
30 June	Balance			134 000 Dr

Freight inwards				
Date	Particulars	Debit $	Credit $	Balance $ Dr or Cr
30 June	Balance			8 000 Dr

Interest revenue				
Date	Particulars	Debit $	Credit $	Balance $ Dr or Cr
30 June	Balance			1 900 Cr

Wages				
Date	**Particulars**	**Debit $**	**Credit $**	**Balance $ Dr or Cr**
30 June	Balance			86000 Dr

Insurance				
Date	**Particulars**	**Debit $**	**Credit $**	**Balance $ Dr or Cr**
30 June	Balance			13000 Dr

Rent				
Date	**Particulars**	**Debit $**	**Credit $**	**Balance $ Dr or Cr**
30 June	Balance			12000 Dr

Sundry expenses				
Date	**Particulars**	**Debit $**	**Credit $**	**Balance $ Dr or Cr**
30 June	Balance			43000 Dr

These balances will be transferred through the General journal to the profit-determining account. In the case of credit balances (revenue), the entry will be:

Debit: Revenue account

Credit: Profit-determining account.

In the case of debit balances (expenses) the entry will be:

Debit: Profit-determining account

Credit: Expense account.

Freight inwards is usually recorded separately as shown on page 92 and not initially recorded as part of the Cost of Sales. However when closing the revenue and expense accounts at balance day the amount of Freight inwards is transferred to the Cost of Sales account as follows:

Debit: Cost of Sales

Credit: Freight inwards.

Multiple debits or credits may be done in a single journal entry, as follows:

General journal			
Date	**Accounts to debit or credit**	**Dr**	**Cr**
30 June	Sales	328000	
	Interest revenue	1900	
	Profit and loss summary		329900
	(Closing entries)		
	Cost of sales	8000	
	Freight inwards		8000
	(Closing entry)		
	Profit and loss summary	298000	
	Cost of sales		142000
	Sales returns		2000
	Wages		86000
	Insurance		13000
	Rent		12000
	Sundry expenses		43000
	(Closing entries)		

These entries can now be posted to the ledger.

These entries can now be posted to the ledger.

Sales

Date	Particulars	Debit $	Credit $	Balance $ Dr or Cr
30 June	Balance			328 000 Cr
	Profit and loss summary	328 000		–

Sales returns

Date	Particulars	Debit $	Credit $	Balance $ Dr or Cr
30 June	Balance			2000 Dr
	Profit and loss summary		2000	–

Cost of sales

Date	Particulars	Debit $	Credit $	Balance $ Dr or Cr
30 June	Balance			134 000 Dr
	Freight inwards	8000		142 000 Dr
	Profit and loss summary		142 000	–

Freight inwards

Date	Particulars	Debit $	Credit $	Balance $ Dr or Cr
30 June	Balance			8000 Dr
	Cost of sales		8000	–

Interest revenue

Date	Particulars	Debit $	Credit $	Balance $ Dr or Cr
30 June	Balance			1900 Cr
	Profit and loss summary	1900		–

Wages

Date	Particulars	Debit $	Credit $	Balance $ Dr or Cr
30 June	Balance			86 000 Dr
	Profit and loss summary		86 000	–

Insurance

Date	Particulars	Debit $	Credit $	Balance $ Dr or Cr
30 June	Balance			13 000 Dr
	Profit and loss summary		13 000	–

Rent

Date	Particulars	Debit $	Credit $	Balance $ Dr or Cr
30 June	Balance			12 000 Dr
	Profit and loss summary		12 000	–

Sundry expenses

Date	Particulars	Debit $	Credit $	Balance $ Dr or Cr
30 June	Balance			43 000 Dr
	Profit and loss summary		43 000	–

Accounting and Finance 2A   ISBN 9780170182041   Cengage Learning Australia

Profit and loss summary				
Date	Particulars	Debit $	Credit $	Balance $ Dr or Cr
30 June	Sales		328000	328000 Cr
	Sales returns	2000		326000 Cr
	Cost of sales	142000		184000 Cr
	Interest revenue		1900	185900 Cr
	Wages	86000		99900 Cr
	Insurance	13000		86900 Cr
	Rent	12000		74900 Cr
	Sundry expenses	43000		31900 Cr

The revenue and expense accounts now have nil balances and are ready to record the transactions for the next accounting period. The balance in the Profit and loss summary account is the profit for the year, which can now be transferred to the Capital account as follows. A previous balance in the Capital account of $80000 has been assumed. If the owner maintains a separate Retained profits account to indicate the extent to which his or her equity consists of profit retained within the business, as opposed to capital contributed, then the Profit and loss summary account would be closed off to Retained profits rather than Capital.

General journal			
Date	Accounts to debit or credit	Dr	Cr
30 June	Profit and loss summary	31900	
	Capital (or Retained profits)		31900
	(Transfer profit for the year)		

Finally, these entries will be posted to the ledger, concluding the profit-determining process for that year.

Profit and loss summary				
Date	Particulars	Debit $	Credit $	Balance $ Dr or Cr
30 June	Sales		328000	328000 Cr
	Sales returns	2000		326000 Cr
	Cost of sales	142000		184000 Cr
	Interest revenue		1900	185900 Cr
	Wages	86000		99900 Cr
	Insurance	13000		86900 Cr
30 June	Rent	12000		74900 Cr
	Sundry expenses	43000		31900 Cr
	Capital	31900		–

Capital (or Retained profits)				
Date	Account debited/Credited	Debit $	Credit $	Balance $ Dr or Cr
30 June	Balance			80000 Cr
	Profit and loss summary		31900	111900 Cr

Had there been a debit balance in the Profit and loss summary account after the revenue and expense accounts were closed off, this would represent a loss for the year. This would still be transferred to Capital, but the journal entry would be as follows:

Debit: Capital

Credit: Profit and loss summary

with the loss for the year.

Apart from the entries used to transfer income and expense balances at the end of the financial period, there is one other closing entry that may be entered in the journal. This occurs when it is desired to transfer the balance in a Drawings account either to the Capital account or to the Retained profits account. This closing entry would be:

Debit: Capital (or Retained profit)
Credit: Drawings
with the balance in the Drawings account.

A final Trial balance can now be drawn up if desired, containing only the asset and liability accounts (which are not affected by the closing entries) and the owner's equity accounts (Capital and Retained profits).

PREPARATION OF FINANCIAL REPORTS

Income statement

The Income statement (or Profit and loss statement, as it is also sometimes called) is essentially a presentation in statement form of the information contained in the profit-determining account. Its purpose is to enable the reader to see:

- what profit or loss the firm made over the period
- what its main sources of income were and how much each contributed
- what the expenses were and how much each cost the business.

These figures can then be related to the size of the business and the owner's investment and compared with other similar businesses, the firm's performance in previous years and budgets (financial estimates) in order to make judgements about the firm's performance. Areas of weakness can be identified so that measures can be taken to improve profitability in the future. (The matter of the analysis of financial reports will be dealt with in more detail in Chapter 11.)

The Income statement may be prepared by transcribing the figures from the profit-determining account or even from the income and expense accounts prior to the closing entries. However, it is usually more convenient to obtain the necessary information from the Trial balance, which will have been taken out prior to closing off the accounts.

EXAMPLE:

Example 3.3

This example uses the balances contained in Example 3.2 above.

Hobbit Hardware
Trial balance for the year ended 30 June 2010 (extract)

	Dr $	Cr $
Sales		328 000
Sales returns	2 000	
Cost of sales	142 000	
Interest revenue		1 900
Wages	86 000	
Insurance	13 000	
Rent	12 000	
Sundry expenses	43 000	

Accounting and Finance: 2A   ISBN 9780170182041   Cengage Learning Australia

Hobbit Hardware
Income statement for the year ended 30 June 2010

	$	$
Sales		328000
Less Sales returns		2000
Net sales		326000
Less Cost of sales		142000
Gross profit		184000
Add Other operating revenue: Interest		1900
Total income		185900
Less Operating expenses		
Wages	86000	
Insurance	13000	
Rent	12000	
Sundry expenses	43000	
Total expenses		154000
Profit		31900

Note that, like all financial statements, this one has a heading informing the reader:
- the name of the business
- the type of statement
- the date or time period to which it refers.

Sales returns could simply be debited to the Sales account to give a net figure. However, it is helpful to the manager to know the quantity of returns in relation to sales since, if they are too high, this may indicate problems in the selling system. The same would have applied to Purchase returns if there had been any. They would have been shown as a deduction from the Cost of sales.

The Operating expenses are offset in a different column for greater ease of reading. The Income statement for a service business is the same except that there is no need to calculate the Gross profit.

An example using data for a service business is given below.

Example 3.4

EXAMPLE: Paula's Panelbeaters has provided you with the following excerpt of the trial balance at the end of the financial year on 30 June 2010. You are required to produce an Income statement for the business for that year.

Paula's Panelbeaters
Trial balance for the year ended 30 June 2010 (extract)

	Dr $	Cr $
Commission revenue		9600
Electricity	12300	
Fees		624500
General office expenses	4500	
Interest expense	8000	
Materials used	98000	
Rent of premises	36000	
Wages	396000	

Paula's Panelbeaters
Income statement for the year ended 30 June 2010

Revenue	$	$
Fees		624500
Commission revenue		9600
Total income		634100
Less Operating expenses		
Electricity	12300	
General office expenses	4500	
Interest expense	8000	
Materials used	98000	
Rent of premises	36000	
Wages	396000	
Total expenses		554800
Profit		79300

This amount of $79300 will be transferred from the Profit and loss summary to the Capital (or Retained profits) account.

The only difference between this statement and the one for a merchandising business is the absence of a section calculating the gross profit. The expenses in this example are stated in a single list. It is common for expenses to be *classified* or grouped on a functional or departmental basis to provide useful information on the performance of various aspects of the business. (This will be dealt with in more detail in Chapter 9.)

Statement of financial position

While the Statement of financial position does have a role in assisting the evaluation of a firm's profitability (as we shall see in Chapter 11) its main purpose is to enable the owner and manager to assess the firm's stability and liquidity, i.e. to establish how likely it is that the firm will survive and be able to pay its debts on time. The statement:
- lists and classifies (see below) the firm's assets
- lists and classifies the firm's liabilities
- quantifies the owner's investment in the business.

By comparing assets and liabilities, especially the current assets and current liabilities, the firm's viability can be judged and trends identified by comparison with previous accounting periods. The value of the owner's investment can be seen as well as the manner in which the firm has been financed (i.e. by capital contributed by the owner or through borrowings); an aspect of the firm's financial position that has implications both for its stability and its profitability in terms of the return on the owner's investment.

For the time being, we will just consider the construction of the Statement of financial position. There are several ways of setting out the statement, of which the two most common are the account form and the narrative form.

The account form

Statement of financial position of XYZ as at 30 June 20XX

Assets		Liabilities	
		Equity	
Total assets		Total liabilities and equity	

Accounting and Finance: 2A   ISBN 9780170182041   Cengage Learning Australia

Obviously the two sides of the statement must add up to the same figure (i.e. must balance). This format focuses on the manner in which the assets of the business have been funded and corresponds to the $A = L + OE$ form of the accounting equation.

The narrative form

Statement of financial position of XYZ as at 30 June 20XX

Equity			
	Total equity		
Assets			
Less			
Liabilities			
	Net assets		

Again, Total equity must equal Net assets. This format focuses on the owner's equity and corresponds to the $OE = A - L$ form of the accounting equation. The narrative format may also be presented as:

Assets			
Less			
Liabilities			
	Net assets		
Equity			
	Total equity		

which still focuses on Equity, or as:

Assets			
	Total assets		
Liabilities			
Add			
Equity			
	Total liabilities and equity		

which, like the Account form layout shown opposite, focuses on how the assets have been funded. Either format is acceptable, although in this textbook we use the narrative form.

The Statement is usually *classified* by dividing the assets and the liabilities into *Current* and *Non-current*.

'Current assets' are those that are cash or are expected to be used up or converted into cash in the normal course of business within 12 months of the date of the statement. This would include cash holdings, short-term cash deposits, accounts receivable, inventory, stock of supplies (such as stationery) and prepaid expenses and accrued revenue (see Chapter 7). Any asset that is not a current asset is a non-current asset. This includes land, buildings, furniture, equipment, vehicles and long-term investments.

'Current liabilities' are debts that need to be paid within 12 months in the normal course of business, such as a bank overdraft, accounts payable, GST payable, short-term loans and accrued expenses and revenue received in advance (see Chapter 7). Non-current liabilities are those due to be paid after 12 months, such as long-term loans.

Equity may simply be shown as the closing balance in the owner's Capital account. However, it is not uncommon for small businesses to include in the statement a brief schedule showing how the equity has changed over the accounting period.

Capital at start of year	$xxxx
Add (less): Profit (Loss) for the year	$xxx
	$xxxx
Add Capital contributed	$xxx
Less Drawings	($xxx)
Capital at end of year	$xxxx

The Statement of financial position could be prepared directly from the ledger accounts, but it is more usual and certainly a great deal more convenient to do so from the Trial balance.

Example 3.5

EXAMPLE:

The Trial balance of Trev's Tyres after the determination of profit for the year ended 31 December 2009 was as follows:

Account	Debit $	Credit $
Accounts payable		33 200
Accounts receivable	16 300	
Capital		70 000
Cash at bank		6 700
Cash deposit (3 months)	10 000	
Cash in hand	500	
Drawings	30 000	
GST payable		4 800
Inventory	105 000	
Mortgage loan (repayable 2013)		100 000
Office furniture	9 000	
Profit and loss summary (profit for the year)		55 000
Stock of workshop materials	2 400	
Vehicle	28 000	
Workshop plant and equipment	68 500	
	269 700	269 700

The figures in the debit column are all assets with the exception of Drawings, which is a negative equity account, while those in the credit column consist of liabilities and equity. These figures can now be entered in the statement.

Accounting and Finance: 2A   ISBN 9780170182041   Cengage Learning Australia

Trev's Tyres
Statement of financial position as at 31 December 2009

	$
Equity	
Capital at start of year	70000
Add Profit for the year	55000
	125000
Less Drawings	30000
Capital at end of year	95000
Represented by:	
Current assets	
Cash in hand	500
Cash deposit	10000
Stock of workshop materials	2400
Accounts receivable	16300
Inventory	105000
Total current assets	134200
Non-current assets	
Office furniture	9000
Vehicle	28000
Workshop plant and equipment	68500
Total non-current assets	105500
Total assets	239700
Less	
Current liabilities	
Bank overdraft	6700
GST payable	4800
Accounts payable	33200
Total current liabilities	44700
Non-current liabilities	
Mortgage loan	100000
Total non-current liabilities	100000
Total liabilities	144700
Net assets	95000

The Cash at bank balance is a credit, which indicates that it is an overdraft and must be shown as a current liability. If it were a debit balance, it would be included in current assets.

The mortgage loan is shown as a non-current liability on the grounds that it is due for repayment in more than 12 months from the date of the statement. In reality, such loans are usually repayable in regular monthly or annual instalments. If that is the case, then a distinction might be drawn between that part of the loan that must be repaid in the next 12 months and the part that is repayable after the next 12 months.

Suppose, for example, that Trev's Tyres' loan was repayable by equal instalments over the four years to 2013. One quarter of the $100000 would be repayable within a year and the remainder after one year. Consequently $25000 would appear as a current liability and $75000 as a non-current liability.

The Net assets is the value of the total assets less the total liabilities (i.e. $239700 − 144700 = $95000). This must equal the value of the owner's equity.

Now let's look at a comprehensive example that requires the production of both reports.

Accounting and Finance: 2A   ISBN 9780170182041   Cengage Learning Australia

Example 3.6

EXAMPLE:

A Herring is the proprietor of Samaki, a business selling fish from a shop in a suburban shopping centre and also supplying seafood products to Perth hotels and restaurants. At the end of the last financial year, on 30 June 2010, the following Trial balance was taken from the firm's ledger.

Trial balance as at 30 June 2010

	Dr $	Cr $
Accounts payable		12 200
Accounts receivable	19 500	
Bank loan (repayable in equal amounts 2011–15)		60 000
Capital – A Herring		60 000
Cash at bank	18 600	
Cash in hand	400	
Cost of sales	458 900	
Delivery van expenses	2 800	
Delivery van	29 000	
Discount allowed	1 800	
Discount received		4 900
Drawings	50 000	
Electricity	3 600	
Insurance	6 300	
Interest expense	5 400	
Inventory	11 400	
Office furniture and equipment	7 400	
Refrigerators and coolrooms	123 000	
Sales returns	2 200	
Sales		843 000
Shop rent	15 600	
Sundry expenses	36 200	
Wages	188 000	
	980 100	980 100

The first step will be to identify the balances that will be included in the Income statement (i.e. the expenses and revenue). The trial balance is reproduced below with these highlighted.

Trial balance as at 30 June 2010

	Dr $	Cr $
Accounts payable		12 200
Accounts receivable	19 500	
Bank loan (repayable in equal amounts 2011–15)		60 000
Capital – A Herring		60 000
Cash at bank	18 600	
Cash in hand	400	
Cost of sales	447 900	
Delivery van expenses	2 800	
Delivery van	29 000	
Discount allowed	1 800	

Accounting and Finance: 2A   ISBN 9780170182041   Cengage Learning Australia

Discount received		4900
Drawings	50000	
Electricity	3600	
Freight inwards	11000	
Insurance	6300	
Interest expense	5400	
Inventory	11400	
Office furniture and equipment	7400	
Refrigerators and coolrooms	123000	
Sales returns	2200	
Sales		843000
Shop rent	15600	
Sundry expenses	36200	
Wages	188000	
	980100	980100

The Income statement will be drawn up using the highlighted items. As they are transcribed from the Trial balance to the Income statement, you should mark off each item to ensure that nothing is omitted.

Samaki
Income statement for the year ended 30 June 2010

	$	$
Sales		843000
Less Sales returns		2200
Net sales		840800
Less Cost of sales		458900
Gross profit		381900
Add Other operating revenue: Discount received		4900
Total income		386800
Less Operating expenses		
Delivery van expenses	2800	
Discount allowed	1800	
Electricity	3600	
Insurance	6300	
Interest expense	5400	
Shop rent	15600	
Sundry expenses	36200	
Wages	188000	
Total expenses		259700
Profit		127100

We can now look at a revised Trial balance from which have been eliminated the revenue and expense accounts, which are summarised in the Profit and loss summary account, the ending balance of which is the profit for the year.

Accounting and Finance 2A ISBN 9780170182041 Cengage Learning Australia

Trial balance as at 30 June 2010 (after profit determination)

	Dr $	Cr $
Accounts payable		12200
Accounts receivable	19500	
Bank loan (repayable in equal amounts 2011–15)		60000
Capital – A Herring		60000
Cash at bank	18600	
Cash in hand	400	
Delivery van	29000	
Drawings	50000	
Inventory	11400	
Office furniture and equipment	7400	
Refrigerators and coolrooms	123000	
P&L summary (profit for the year)		127100
	259300	259300

These balances can then be used to prepare the Statement of financial position as follows. Since the loan is repayable in equal instalments over the next five years, we will show one-fifth of the loan ($12000) as a current liability and the remainder ($48000) as a non-current liability.

Statement of financial position as at 30 June 2010

	$
Equity	
Capital at start of year	60000
Add Profit for the year	127100
	187100
Less Drawings	50000
Capital at end of year	137100
Represented by:	
Current assets	
Cash in hand	400
Cash at bank	18600
Accounts receivable	19500
Inventory	11400
Total current assets	49900
Non-current assets	
Office furniture and equipment	7400
Delivery van	29000
Refrigerators and coolrooms	123000
Total non-current assets	159400
Total assets	209300
Less	
Current liabilities	
Bank loan	12000
Accounts payable	12200
Total current liabilities	24200

Accounting and Finance: 2A   ISBN 9780170182041   Cengage Learning Australia

Non-current liabilities	
Bank loan	48000
Total non-current liabilities	48000
Total liabilities	72200
Net assets	137100

Business Activity Statement

As you will recall from your study of Chapters 1 and 2, nearly all businesses in Australia are required to charge GST on the price of goods and services they sell and then remit to the ATO the GST collected, less any GST paid on goods, services or assets purchased. As part of their obligations under GST legislation, firms need to provide the ATO with a report outlining the details of GST collections and outlays called a Business Activity Statement (BAS). The BAS, which most firms complete on a quarterly basis, will also give details of other taxation matters such *Pay as You Go* personal income tax deducted from employees' pay (PAYG) and Fringe benefits tax (FBT). We will confine ourselves to the section in the BAS relating to GST.

GST may be accounted for on either a cash or a non-cash (accrual) basis. A business that already keeps its accounts on an accrual basis will naturally record GST collected or paid in the same way and that is the assumption we will make in this chapter. Businesses may report and pay GST monthly, quarterly or annually. Businesses have an option to pay an estimated amount of GST quarterly and submit a detailed report annually, at which time any discrepancy between instalments paid and actual GST liability will be adjusted.

Option 1: Calculate GST and report quarterly

Total sales **G1** $

Does the amount shown at G1 include GST? (indicate with **X**) ☐ Yes ☐ No

Export sales **G2** $

Other GST-free sales **G3** $

Capital purchases **G10** $

Non-capital purchases **G11** $

Report GST on sales at 1A and GST on purchases at 1B in the summary section

Summary section

GST on sales **1A** $

GST on purchases **1B** $

Your payment or refund amount **9** $

Figure 3.2 The section of the BAS relating to GST

This form has been copied from the ATO's 'Instructions for businesses: Goods and services tax – how to complete your activity statement', www.ato.gov.au/content/downloads/bus42132nat7392062009.pdf.

Notes

- Firms that are unwilling or unable to record separately the GST from every transaction may calculate their GST outlays and collections on a quarterly basis using a calculation sheet provided for that purpose.
- Firms that have been accounting for GST throughout their operating activities will clearly need to reconcile the amounts they have been recording in the GST clearing account with the amounts that can be calculated by dividing gross sales (or purchases) by 11.
- Certain transactions, including some export sales, sales of basic foods and some educational and medical products are exempted from GST. In addition, some products (notably financial supplies and certain provisions of residential property) are deemed by the law to be 'input taxed' and are similarly exempt from additional GST in the hands of the provider. For simplicity's sake, we will assume in this chapter that all sales and purchases, except foods, attract GST.

- 'Non-capital purchases' includes the purchase of inventory, services and other products used in the firm's operating activities.
- Payment of GST due must be made by a set date after the end of the quarter and may be made by cheque or electronic funds transfer. The BAS itself can also be submitted electronically or by post.

EXAMPLE:

Example 3.7

Lammermoor Textiles reports quarterly for GST. Its results for the first quarter of the financial year ended 30 September 2010 are as follows:

Sales (net of GST)	$286 000
Purchases of inventory and other operating consumables (net of GST)	$127 000
Purchase of capital items (net of GST)	$12 000
GST clearing (debits $13 900, credits $28 600)	$14 700

The BAS report for the quarter relating to GST will be as shown below.

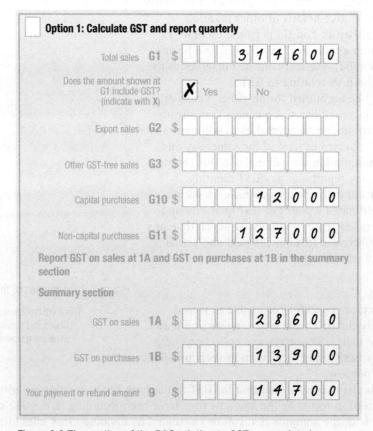

Figure 3.3 The section of the BAS relating to GST – completed

Accounting and Finance: 2A   ISBN 9780170182041   Cengage Learning Australia

Test your knowledge

1   What are the main information needs of the owner or manager of a small business?

2   What factors, other than past financial performance and position, may influence an owner's or manager's decisions in relation to a business?

3   Define the two main elements of an Income statement.

4   Define 'profit'.

5   Define the three main elements of a Statement of financial position.

6   Outline the difference between a merchandising and a trading business.

7   What is an overdraft? To what extent is it a liability?

8   What are the three steps in profit determination?

9   What are 'closing entries' and what is their purpose?

10 What is a 'profit-determining account'?

11 What does the Income statement tell its reader?

12 What does the Statement of financial position tell its reader?

13 What information needs to be contained in the heading of a financial statement?

14 How are Statements of financial position usually classified?

15 What is a firm's reporting obligation with regard to the GST?

Test your understanding

Topic guide
- Definition of elements of financial reports: 3.1
- Recognition of elements: 3.2, 3.3
- Closing entries, journal only: 3.4–3.7
- Closing entries, journal and ledger: 3.8–3.9
- Income statements: 3.10–3.13
- Statements of Financial Position: 3.14–3.17
- Both statements: 3.18–3.21
- BAS reports: 3.22–3.23

3.1   The following is an alphabetical list of accounts in a firm's ledger.
Accounting fees
Accounts payable
Accounts receivable
Capital
Cash at bank
Cash in hand
Commission earned
Cost of sales
Discount allowed
Discount received
Drawings
Freight inwards
Furniture and fittings
GST clearing

Insurance
Interest expense
Interest revenue
Inventory
Long-term loan from bank
Office expenses
Postage and stationery
Rates and taxes
Rent
Sales
Sales returns
Stock of stationery
Telephone
Vehicle running costs
Vehicles
Wages and salaries

Rearrange them into a chart of accounts under these category headings:
Equity
Income
Expense
Current assets
Non-current assets
Current liabilities
Non-current liabilities

3.2 For each of the following transactions, state whether they give rise to an asset, a liability, an expense or revenue and, in each case, when these elements would be recognised.

a The firm sends M McGregor an invoice for $800 for stock sold on 12 May.

b M McGregor pays his bill on 16 May.

c The firm pays wages on 15 May.

d The firm calculates that sales commission of $1670 is due to its sales staff for their sales in the month of April. It is paid with their wages on 15 May.

e The firm receives an invoice from T Gloucester for $3200 for inventory supplied.

f The firm signs an agreement on 24 May with an advertising agency for advertisements to be placed in the media during June, July and August at a cost of $1200 per month.

g The firm pays Gloucester what they owe him on 29 May earning a 2% discount for prompt payment.

3.3 For each of the following transactions, state whether they give rise to an asset, a liability, an expense or revenue and, in each case, when these elements would be recognised.

a The firm orders a new workshop machine worth $4600 from Plant Supplies on 6 August. It is expected that the machine will be delivered in early September.

b The owner uses a business cheque on 8 August to buy his daughter a car costing $8000.

c On 10 August the owner arranges an overdraft with the bank with a limit of $10000.

d The firm buys a new truck on August 15 from Midstream Semis for $60000, paying a deposit of $10000, the remainder being payable within 30 days.

e The firm makes an electronic transfer to the bank on August 20 of $1100 of which $1000 is a loan repayment and $100 is for interest.

f The owner contributes some office chairs worth $250 on 24 August.

3.4 Show the entries needed to close the following ledger balances to the profit-determining account at the end of the financial year on 30 June 2010.

Accounting and Finance: 2A   ISBN 9780170182041   Cengage Learning Australia

Cost of sales	$139 000 Dr
Electricity	$6 100 Dr
Rent	$12 000 Dr
Sales	$286 000 Cr
Sundry office expenses	$25 000 Dr
Wages	$46 000 Dr

3.5 Show the entries needed to close the following ledger balances to the profit-determining account at the end of the financial year on 31 December 2009.

Fees	$426 800 Cr
Interest revenue	$1 250 Cr
Wages and salaries	$298 000 Dr
Discount allowed	$6 000 Dr
Insurance	$26 000 Dr
Repairs and maintenance	$9 200 Dr
General office expenses	$19 600 Dr

3.6 The following is an extract from the Trial balance for TG Winkle & Sons at the end of the last financial year on 30 June 2010.

Trial balance as at 30 June 2010 (extract)

	Dr $	Cr $
Accounting fees	2 500	
Advertising	3 800	
Bank charges	300	
Cost of sales	256 000	
Freight inwards	7 000	
Interest earned		900
Sales returns	1 600	
Sales		492 000
Sales-persons' commission	24 600	
Shop rent		36 000
Sundry office expenses	22 100	
Wages and salaries	103 000	

Required

a Explain the purpose of the Closing entries done at the end of the accounting period.

b Show the closing entries in the General journal required for TG Winkle & Sons at 30 June 2010.

3.7 Benjamin & Bunny Accountants has provided you with the following extract from its Trial balance at 30 June 2010.

Trial balance as at 30 June 2010 (extract)

	Dr $	Cr $
Fees		791 000
Office wages	147 000	
Accountants' salaries	626 000	

Insurance	23400	
Office rent	48000	
Postage and telephone	3100	
Vehicle expenses	11200	
Rent revenue (office sub-let)		12000
Training costs	5600	
Repairs and maintenance	9700	
General office expenses	4800	

Required

Show the General journal entries required to close the accounts for Benjamin & Bunny Accountants at 30 June 2010, including transferring the profit or loss to capital.

3.8 Wong World Traders has provided you with the following extract from its Trial balance at the end of the first quarter of the financial year on 30 September 2010. The firm produces accounts on a quarterly basis.

Trial balance as at 30 September 2010 (extract)

	Dr $	Cr $
Capital		98000
Commission earned		2850
Cost of sales	106500	
Discount allowed	3100	
General office expenses	6425	
Insurance	5325	
Interest expense	4725	
Office wages	41250	
Discount revenue		1125
Rates and taxes	750	
Repairs and maintenance	4325	
Sales returns	950	
Sales salaries	44000	
Sales		237250

Required

a   Show the General journal entries required to close the accounts for Wong World Traders at 30 September 2010, including transferring the profit or loss to capital.

b   Enter the balances above into ledger accounts and then post the journal entries to the ledger.

c   Why do you think it is important for a firm of this type to be able to identify its gross profit?

3.9 Poppy's Petcare provides a mobile grooming, washing and 'peticure' service for pets in a large WA regional town. (Its slogan is 'You love 'em, we'll look after 'em'.) At the end of the last financial year on 30 June 2010, the following balances appeared in the ledger.

Accounting and Finance: 2A   ISBN 9780170182041   Cengage Learning Australia

Trial balance as at 30 June 2010 (extract)

	Dr $	Cr $
Accounting fees	1 800	
Capital		42 000
Cost of pet products	2 800	
Fees		297 000
Insurance	12 000	
Office expenses	3 500	
Petrol, oil and lubricants	16 700	
Repairs to cleaning equipment	1 700	
Sales of pet products		6 800
Telephone	3 600	
Vehicle repairs and maintenance	11 200	
Wages	184 000	

Required

a   Show the General journal entries required to close the accounts for Poppy's Petcare at 30 June 2010, including transferring the profit or loss to capital.

b   Enter the balances above into ledger accounts and then post the journal entries to the ledger.

c   Poppy's Petcare also sells merchandise. Would you treat it as a service or a merchandising business for accounting purposes? Explain your answer.

3.10   Use the information contained in the following extract from a Trial balance to produce an Income statement for the business concerned for the year ended 30 June 2010.

Grimm's Grocery
Trial balance as at 30 June 2010 (extract)

	Dr $	Cr $
Cost of sales	263 900	
Discount received		2 800
Electricity	11 200	
General office expenses	19 300	
Insurance	32 000	
Interest expense	5 600	
Office wages and salaries	97 000	
Sales wages	146 000	
Sales		672 000
Shop rent	18 000	
Stationery	800	

3.11   Wally, the owner of Wally's Wares, has provided you with the following extract from its Trial balance at the end of the first half year on 31 December 2010.

Trial balance as at 31 December 2010 (extract)

	Dr $	Cr $
Bad debts	2 500	
Cost of sales	202 500	

Discount allowed	3250	
Discount received		2050
General office expenses	36700	
Insurance	29000	
Interest earned		1400
Rent	12000	
Sales returns	6000	
Sales		453000
Stationery expense	150	
Vehicle running costs	9250	
Wages and salaries	168000	

Required

a Prepare an Income statement for Wally's Wares for the six months ended 31 December 2010.

b In what ways would Wally make use of this Statement?

3.12 Eve's Electrical Services prepares financial reports on a quarterly basis. At the end of the third quarter of the financial year, on 31 March 2010, the business had the following balances in its ledger.

Trial balance as at 31 March 2010 (extract)

	Dr $	Cr $
Accounting fees	400	
Commission earned		3200
Electrician's wages	21000	
Equipment rental	1250	
Fees		98000
Insurance	5200	
Interest expense	800	
Materials used	2700	
Office wages	13000	
Postage and stationery	150	
Sundry office expenses	600	
Vehicle expenses	6100	

Required

Prepare an Income statement for Eve's Electrical Services for the three months ended 31 March 2010.

3.13 Kormoran Enterprises (proprietor H Sydney) has taken out a Trial balance at the end of the financial year on 30 June 2010, of which an extract is given below.

Trial balance as at 30 June 2010 (extract)

	Dr $	Cr $
Advertising	9800	
Cost of sales	359300	
Discount allowed	1300	

	Dr	Cr
Discount received		700
General office expenses	9700	
Insurance	23600	
Interest expense	11800	
Office wages	164000	
Property taxes and rates	24000	
Rent revenue		12000
Repairs and maintenance	18500	
Sales returns	4600	
Sales wages	221000	
Sales		896500
Transport costs	12400	

Required

a   Prepare an Income statement for Kormoran Enterprises for the year ended 30 June 2010.

b   What effect does the profit or loss have on the owner's investment in the business? What could H Sydney measure the profit against in order to judge whether or not it is satisfactory?

3.14   Grimm's Grocery has prepared the following Trial balance after the ledger accounts had been closed off to determine profit for the year at 30 June 2010. You are asked to prepare a classified Statement of financial position for the firm at that date. What is the benefit of classifying this statement?

Trial balance as at 30 June 2010

	Dr $	Cr $
Accounts payable		16000
Capital – B Grimm		40000
Cash at bank	36600	
Cash in hand	200	
Computer system	2800	
Drawings	72000	
GST payable	3200	
Inventory	44500	
Mortgage loan (repayable 2012)		40000
Profit and loss summary		81000
Shop furniture and fittings	16900	
Stock of stationery	800	
	177000	177000

3.15   Below is the Trial balance of the ledger of Wally's Wares after the determination of profit at 31 December 2010.

Trial balance as at 31 December 2010

	Dr $	Cr $
Accounts payable		23500
Accounts receivable	16700	
Capital – Wally		120000
Cash at bank	10600	

Cash in hand	500	
Drawings	30 000	
Furniture and equipment	15 000	
GST payable		2 200
Inventory	18 000	
Profit and loss summary	12 900	
Short-term deposit	20 000	
Vehicle	22 000	
	145 700	145 700

Required

a Prepare a classified Statement of financial position for Wally's Wares as at 31 December 2010.

b Explain your classification of 'GST payable' and 'Short-term deposit'.

3.16 After the closing entries at the end of March 2010, the Trial balance for Eve's Electrical Services was as follows:

Trial balance as at 31 March 2010

	Dr $	Cr $
Accounts payable		1 350
Accounts receivable	3 800	
Bank loan (2013)		25 000
Capital – Eve		30 000
Cash at bank	16 800	
Computer	4 000	
Drawings	15 250	
GST clearing	4 200	
Profit and loss summary		50 000
Stock of materials	1 400	
Tools and equipment	18 900	
Vehicles	42 000	
	106 350	106 350

Required

Prepare a classified Statement of financial position for Eve's Electrical Services as at 31 March 2010.

3.17 Kormoran Enterprises has provided you with its post-profit-determination Trial balance at 30 June 2010, as follows:

Trial balance as at 30 June 2010

	Dr $	Cr $
Accounts payable		38 000
Accounts receivable	45 900	
Building	325 000	
Capital – H Sydney		250 000
Cash at bank		34 000
Cash in hand	500	
Drawings	40 000	
GST payable		5 700

Accounting and Finance: 2A   ISBN 9780170182041   Cengage Learning Australia

Inventory	33700	
Land	200000	
Mortgage loan		300000
Office furniture	3200	
Plant and equipment	28000	
Profit and loss summary		149200
Stock of cleaning materials	1600	
	776900	776900

Additional information

The mortgage loan is repayable over the next five years in equal instalments. The first of these instalments is due in April 2011.

Required

a Prepare a classified Statement of financial position for Kormoran Enterprises as at 30 June 2010.

b Under what circumstances could any of the Plant and equipment be classified as a Current asset?

3.18 Greenhills Pharmacy is a shop in a Perth suburban shopping centre. At the end of the last financial year on 30 June, the following Trial balance was taken of the accounts in the firm's ledger.

Trial balance as at 30 June 2010

	Dr $	Cr $
Accounts payable		29000
Bank loan (2012)		20000
Capital – G Hills		23000
Cash at bank	12000	
Cash in hand	400	
Cleaning expenses	2400	
Commission revenue		4600
Computer system	5500	
Cost of sales	563500	
Drawings	50000	
Freight inwards	12500	
Furniture and fittings	13500	
GST clearing	2100	
Interest	1800	
Inventory	48000	
Postage and telephone	2300	
Power	5600	
Rent	36000	
Sales		832000
Wages	153000	
	908600	908600

Required

a Prepare an Income statement for Greenhills Pharmacy for the year ended 30 June 2010.

b Prepare a Statement of financial position for Greenhills Pharmacy as at 30 June 2010.

c In what way do you think the Income statement could be made more useful to the owner?

Accounting and Finance: 2A   ISBN 9780170182041   Cengage Learning Australia

3.19 Betty Bunn runs a small bakery, Well Bread. Betty produces financial statements every quarter and her firm's balances at the end of the first quarter of the year, on 30 September 2010, are as follows.

Trial balance as at 30 September 2010

	Dr $	Cr $
Accounting fees	1500	
Accounts payable		8900
Capital – B Bunn		30000
Cash at bank		8500
Cash in hand	300	
Cash register	1600	
Cost of sales	79900	
Discount received		1300
Drawings	24000	
Electricity	10000	
Fixtures and fittings	44000	
Insurance	6000	
Interest expense	1200	
Inventory	2200	
Long-term loan (2013)		20000
Sales returns	1000	
Sales		142000
Shop rent	10000	
Short-term loan		10000
Wages	39000	
	220700	220700

Required

a Prepare an Income statement for Well Bread for the quarter ended 30 September 2010.

b Prepare a Statement of financial position for Well Bread as at 30 September 2010.

c On the evidence of these statements, what problems does this business appear to have and what do you think the owner could do about them?

3.20 Vids R Us is a store renting DVDs and video games. At the end of its financial year on 31 December 2009, the following Trial balance was produced.

Trial balance as at 31 December 2009

	Dr $	Cr $
Accounts payable		5500
Advertising	9000	
Bank loan (Nov. 2011)		10000
Capital – Hiram Cheep		30000
Cash at bank	11500	
Cash in hand	200	
Cost of replacement DVDs and games	18900	
Discount received		1300
Drawings	25000	
Electricity	8000	
Equipment	9800	

	Dr $	Cr $
Fixtures and fittings	33000	
GST payable		6700
Insurance	43000	
Interest expense	5000	
Rent	24000	
Rental fees		495000
Sale of old DVDs and games		9100
Vehicle costs	1200	
Vehicle	23000	
Videos and DVDs for hire	21000	
Wages	325000	
	557600	557600

Required

a   Prepare an Income statement for Vids R Us for the year ended 31 December 2009.

b   Prepare a Statement of financial position for Vids R Us as at 31 December 2009.

3.21   Mean Machinery sells plant and equipment to the mining industry. At the end of the last financial year on 30 June 2010, the balances in the firm's ledger were as follows:

Trial balance as at 30 June 2010

	Dr $	Cr $
Accounts payable		124000
Accounts receivable	153000	
Capital – FE Loader		360000
Cash at bank	28000	
Cost of sales	322000	
Discount allowed	9000	
Discount received		15000
Drawings	55000	
General administration expenses	38000	
GST payable		8000
Insurance	39000	
Interest	32000	
Inventory	300000	
Land and buildings	400000	
Mortgage loan		400000
Office salaries and wages	102000	
Rates and taxes	7000	
Rental revenue		18000
Repairs and maintenance	29000	
Sales		915000
Sales commission	12000	
Sales returns	18000	
Sales salaries	222000	
Vehicle expenses	9000	
Vehicles	65000	
	1840000	1840000

Additional information

- The business leases part of the offices at its depot to a small engineering firm.
- The mortgage loan is repayable in equal instalments over the next ten years.

Required

a   Prepare an Income statement for Mean Machinery for the year ended 30 June 2010.

b   Prepare a Statement of financial position for Mean Machinery as at 30 June 2010.

3.22 Mpishi's Tours calculates and pays GST on a quarterly basis. Its financial results for the second quarter of the year, the three months to 31 December 2010, included the following amounts, all net of GST:

Sales	$223 000
Non-capital purchases	$98 000
Capital purchases	$52 000

All the firm's sales and the purchases stated above are subject to GST.

Required

Show how the GST section of the BAS report for Mpishi's Tours would appear for the quarter ended 31 December 2010.

3.23 Kim's Klothing has the following (summarised) ledger accounts at the end of the first quarter of the current financial year, 30 September 2010.

Sales				
Date	Account debited/Credited	Debit $	Credit $	Balance $ Dr or Cr
30 Sept	Cash at bank and Accounts receivable		196 000	196 000 Cr
Cost of sales				
Date	Account debited/Credited	Debit $	Credit $	Balance $ Dr or Cr
30 Sept	Cash at bank and Accounts payable	84 000		84 000 Dr
Plant and equipment				
Date	Account debited/Credited	Debit $	Credit $	Balance $ Dr or Cr
30 June	Balance			160 000 Dr
31 Aug	Cash at bank	32 000		192 000 Dr

All the firm's sales and purchases are subject to GST. Apart from the purchase of the Plant and equipment on 31 August, there were no capital purchases during the quarter.

Required

a   Show a summary of the GST clearing ledger account at 30 September 2010.

b   Show how the GST section of the BAS report for Kim's Klothing would appear for the quarter ended 30 September 2010.

Investigation

(This task could be done as an individual or group project.)

Investigate several (perhaps two or three) small businesses to which you have access (local business, family firms, etc.) and determine for each:

- what financial reports they produce
- how frequently these are produced
- what use is made of the information contained in the reports.

Accounting and Finance 2A   ISBN 9780170182041   Cengage Learning Australia

Draw up a summary of the data you have obtained and make a comparison of the different businesses as far as their production and usage of financial reports is concerned. If there are significant differences, explain why you think this is the case. Which business do you think is making best use of the financial reports?

Essay

1   Discuss the value of the Income statement and the Statement of financial position in assisting the owner of a small business. If you were the owner of such a business, how often do you think you would produce such reports? Explain your answer.

2   Give a detailed outline of the process of identifying and reporting the trading operations of a business in order to assess its profitability. How do you think this process might be aided with the use of computer technology?

Ethics case study

B Potter is the proprietor of Puddleduck Enterprises. She is planning a significant expansion of her firm's business operations. To help finance this she is applying for a loan of $200000 from the Rabbit Community Bank. As part of their process of deciding whether Potter's business is profitable and secure, the bank has asked for recent Income statements and the latest Statement of financial position. When preparing the latter report, Potter's accountant sees that her liabilities include a loan from her great aunt Jemima for $50000, which is due to be repaid in 11 months' time. Potter has instructed him to show it as a 'non-current liability' in the Statement of financial position, arguing that it almost is and that, anyway, the lender is family, so that it hardly qualifies as a liability at all.

a   What do you think of Potter's reasoning?

b   Why might the way Aunt Jemima's loan is classified make a difference?

c   What do you think the accountant ought to do?

Chapter 4
CONTROLLING THE BUSINESS

What You Will Learn

After studying this chapter you should be able to:
1. Explain the nature of internal control
2. Distinguish between administrative and accounting controls
3. Explain the importance of internal control
4. Explain the principles of internal control
5. Explain the application of internal control principles to the managing of cash, inventory, accounts receivable, accounts payable and non-current assets
6. Explain the factors to be considered when supplying credit to customers
7. Examine the limitations of internal control

Introduction

This chapter will examine the importance of internal control to the successful operation of a business. There are a number of principles of internal control that a business should follow. These principles include: segregation of duties; establishing responsibility; use of physical, mechanical and electronic devices; maintenance of adequate documentation, verification and authorisation and employment of competent and reliable staff.

In this chapter these principles will be examined and applied in the areas of the management of cash, accounts receivable, inventory, accounts payable and non-current assets. An integral part of the success of internal control is the audit function — both internal and external audits. Internal control procedures, like all systems, have their weaknesses and the cost of establishing good internal control should not outweigh the benefits of such procedures. This is particularly so in regard to small business.

THE NATURE OF INTERNAL CONTROL

Internal control represents the procedures and processes in place within a business designed to ensure effective and efficient operations and achievement of the business's objectives. Those charged with the responsibility for the presentation and preparation of financial reports must ensure that the business's reports are reliable and relevant. These reports must represent a true and fair view of the entity's financial results. This information is to be presented to its stakeholders and is the basis for their decision-making. Reliable information is that which is free from material error and bias. It faithfully represents that which it purports to represent or could reasonably be expected to represent. To maximise the chance of business success – and therefore the wealth of the owners – a business must operate in an efficient and effective way. Compliance with relevant laws and regulations is also a responsibility of the business's owners and managers.

Key Concept 4.1

Internal control

Internal control is the procedures, policies, processes and systems in place within a business that ensure that its operations are effective and efficient, the financial records and reports are reliable and the objectives are achieved

IMPORTANCE OF INTERNAL CONTROL

Internal control is vital to the operation of a business; if not done correctly it can lead to the collapse of the business.

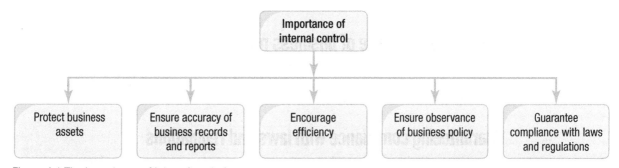

Figure 4.1 The importance of internal control

Protecting business assets

A business's assets are highly valuable to its operation. They are the means by which it earns income and cashflow. It is important that accounts receivable are not too high and that credit is supplied only to good customers otherwise the result can be excessive bad debts. Accounts receivable should be collected rapidly as cashflow is vital to business operation.

Inventory is a large investment for a business and it is easily subject to theft, deterioration and waste. Carrying insufficient inventory can result in loss of customers and carrying too much inventory is an excessive cost that a business can ill afford to maintain. It is important that inventory levels are appropriate to meet customer demand.

Non-current assets are usually a large part of the total assets of a business. If such a large investment goes wrong it can lead to the end of the business. The business relies on these assets to generate income and cashflow. Non-current assets are also subject to theft, deterioration and loss and therefore need to be secured, insured and monitored carefully.

Cash is very important to a business because it directly affects the liquidity position of the business. Cash is often the target of theft and can be easily mishandled so it needs to be carefully secured and supervised.

Ensuring the accuracy of business records and reports

Internal control is also important in ensuring that the business records and reports are accurate and free from bias. These records and reports are relied on by internal and external users for the purposes of decision-making. Managers must review performance, forecast the future, allocate scarce resources, manage the assets and liabilities and be accountable to external users. External users will make decisions, such as whether to invest or lend to the business, and will use its reports to evaluate and monitor its performance.

Encouraging efficiency

Business success depends on efficiency and effectiveness of operation. The establishment of internal controls includes analysis and review of business operations. In this process the objectives of efficiency and effectiveness of the use of business resources are paramount.

Ensuring observance of business policy

Business policy is important so that employees have clear direction on key issues. This ensures that consistency is achieved in decision-making and the application of laws, regulations, methods and procedures.

Guaranteeing compliance with laws and regulations

Compliance with laws and regulations is absolutely necessary for any business to continue to operate and to avoid prosecution by government authorities. Businesses are subject to many laws and regulations, such as GST and PAYE compliance, equal opportunity and anti-discrimination laws, local government health and safety requirements and accounting standards. Internal control systems help to ensure that these laws and regulations are adhered to.

 Key Concept 4.2

Importance of internal control
- Protect business assets
- Ensure the accuracy of business records and reports
- Encourage efficiency
- Ensure observance of business policy
- Guarantee compliance with laws and regulations

Accounting and Finance: 2A   ISBN 9780170182041   Cengage Learning Australia

ADMINISTRATIVE AND ACCOUNTING CONTROLS

Internal controls may be divided into two categories: administrative controls and accounting controls.

Administrative controls

Administrative controls refer to those procedures and systems that a business puts in place to ensure its efficient and effective operation and compliance with its set policies. The principles of internal control to do with the segregation of duties, establishing lines of responsibility, employment of competent and reliable staff and establishing authorisation processes relate closely with administrative controls. Examples of administrative controls include: controls necessary to ensure the good quality of the products the business produces, the budgeting and performance reporting system, code of conduct for employees, the credit policy and policies for the recruitment of staff.

Accounting controls

Accounting controls are the measures and systems set up to protect the business assets and ensure that its records and reports are accurate. The principles of internal control closely related with accounting controls cover ensuring there is appropriate security of assets and records, that suitable verification and checking processes are in place, that mechanical and electronic devices are installed and that adequate records and documentation systems are in place. Examples of accounting controls include the engraving of all business assets (for identification in case of theft), periodic inspection of assets, the monthly bank reconciliation, the monthly completion of Trial balance completed each month and the security of access to the business's computer system.

PRINCIPLES OF INTERNAL CONTROL

Certain principles are essential for there to be effective internal control of business operations.

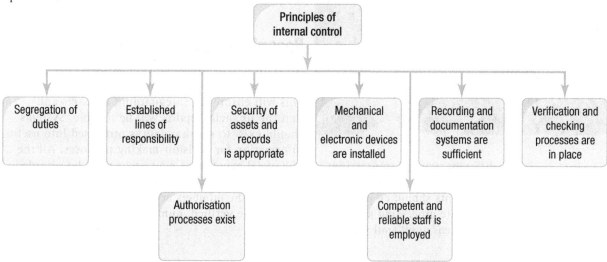

Figure 4.2 Principles of internal control

Segregation of duties

The segregation of duties is a basic element of a good internal control system. The various tasks, activities and functions of a business should be divided up so that no one person has complete control over them. This feature reduces the likelihood of fraud and increases the probability of accurate accounting records. The more staff that are involved in the various parts of a system the better.

Established lines of responsibility

An organisational structure that has clear lines of responsibility is essential for effective internal control. The various tasks and functions for the successful operation of the business must be determined and these then assigned to the positions in the business. In this way staff know what they are expected to do, have been given the appropriate authority to carry out these tasks and know exactly what they are accountable for. This will lead to less confusion and overlapping of tasks, which promotes efficiency.

Security of assets and records

The assets and records of the business are very important to its operation and success and they are usually very valuable. These assets can be the target of thieves and embezzlers and thus need to be protected. Assets are used to generate cashflow and income streams and are therefore vital to the business.

Mechanical and electronic devices

To ensure the security of assets and the accuracy of record-keeping, mechanical and electronic devices can be installed that can take the 'human element' out of the process.

Records and documentation

All transactions, financial events, assets and liabilities must be documented and/or recorded. This will ensure the safeguarding of assets and that the financial reports will be reliable. Systems should exist to see that data is processed into useful information for decision-making purposes. All the different types of transactions and financial events that may occur must be recorded on documents. These documents should cover both routine and non-routine items. All documents should be pre-numbered and all the numbers accounted for. In the case of electronic processing all transactions must be verified, numbered and accounted for and a clear audit trail shown.

Verification and checking processes

To ensure that accounting records are correct, external or internal verification of these records should take place where possible. In addition, processes should be in place that enable the independent checking of information from the accounting system.

Accounting and Finance 2A   ISBN 9780170182041   Cengage Learning Australia

Authorisation processes

Transactions and financial events must be authorised by an appropriate person in the management structure. The authorisation must be in line with the established business policy. The authority given to a staff member must be clearly determined and set out in a procedures manual or job description document.

Competent and reliable staff

All internal control systems rely on the employment of capable and honest staff. The process for employing staff should be set out in appropriate policy documents and include such activities as checking references and qualifications. Staff should be appropriately trained, supervised, evaluated and rewarded. A culture of adhering to high ethical standards, honesty and integrity must be established through mentoring by managers and owners, appropriate performance indicators and a code of conduct.

 Key Concept 4.3

Principles of internal control
- Segregation of duties
- Established lines of responsibility
- Appropriate security of assets and records
- Installation of mechanical and electronic devices
- Adequate records and documentation systems
- Suitable verification and checking processes
- Established authorisation processes
- Employment of competent and reliable staff

APPLICATION OF INTERNAL CONTROL PRINCIPLES

We shall now consider the application of internal control principles to the areas of cash, accounts receivable, inventory, accounts payable and non-current assets. There are too many examples of specific internal controls in these areas to cover them all in this textbook. We shall therefore only give an outline of those that can be applied. Before we consider these areas in detail there are some aspects of internal control that we can deal with first as there is no real difference in their application to each of the areas.

Rotation of duties

The rotation of duties involves changing the duties of employees around periodically. This practice makes it difficult for any employee to cover up any errors or fraud. This policy applies to all areas of operation in the control of cash, inventory, accounts receivable, accounts payable and non-current assets. For example, it should be common practice to rotate those involved in duties related to such areas as handling cash, petty cash or inventory. It should also be ensured that those who handle cash take their annual leave; errors and theft are more likely to be uncovered at that time. These concepts apply to all areas, including inventory and non-current assets.

Employing competent and reliable staff

This principle applies in all areas of operation in the control of cash, inventory, accounts receivable, accounts payable and non-current assets. In the case of a small business it is very important to employ reliable and honest staff as it is often very difficult to rotate or segregate duties and a sole trader must rely on some staff to do a number of tasks.

Subsidiary ledgers

A subsidiary ledger is a separate ledger record from the General ledger. The subsidiary ledger contains all the details pertaining to a specific group of accounts and this detail is summarised in the General ledger in a control account. When using a computerised accounting package this concept is automatically applied in the areas of accounts receivable, accounts payable, inventory and non-current assets.

Internal control and electronic systems

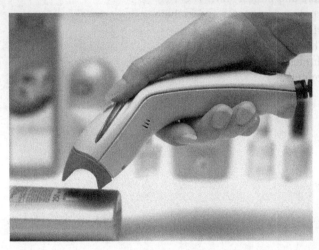

Most processing of financial transactions is done using electronic devices, such as electronic cash registers, computerised accounting systems, barcode scanners and EFTPOS. Your order at a restaurant can be taken electronically, many customers now use credit cards to make payments, businesses make payments via the internet, some customers make payments online and all stock is electronically tagged so as to make for easy processing at the checkout. All these electronic devices are designed to improve internal control. This means that there is less human involvement and therefore potentially fewer errors can occur. However, humans are still involved in the process and thus there is still a need for internal control. The usual principles of internal control must still apply.

For example, separation of duties is still important – the person who controls the computerised accounting program should not be the person who receives cash or writes cheques or approves invoices for payment. Computerised accounting and other electronic processing systems can be established with protocols so that access to certain parts of the system can be restricted. For example, the tasks of issuing sales invoices, receiving cash, writing cheques, making deposits and recording invoices can all be segregated and restricted so that no one person has access to all areas. In addition, computerised accounting systems are usually able to be set up so that past transactions cannot be changed and alterations only made through a General journal entry, enabling subsequent independent audit.

Of major importance for internal control in these computerised accounting systems is the audit trail. The audit trail is a listing of all entries made in the computerised accounting system. It cannot be altered.

Verification and checking of data entered is still important, authorisation processes are still necessary and security is still vital.

Security processes are becoming more and more electronic with the use of security cameras and security sensors as we enter and leave a store. This again is all part of internal control. In Chapter 6 we will learn a lot more about the security issues associated with electronic processing.

Internal audit

Many medium and large businesses employ internal auditors and where this occurs they are a key component of internal control. The role of the internal auditor is to

Accounting and Finance: 2A   ISBN 9780170182041   Cengage Learning Australia
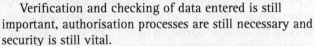

conduct an ongoing investigation, monitoring and review of the internal control systems in place within the business. They check that procedures and policies are being adhered to, check for errors and deficiencies and see that they are corrected, test for possible fraudulent activity and make recommendations for improved policies and procedures.

CASH MANAGEMENT AND CONTROL

An adequate supply of cash (liquidity) is vital to the success and survival of the business. Cash is an asset that can easily be misappropriated, it is involved in most business dealings and its correct management is critical to the survival of the business.

A business needs to ensure that it does not have too much excess cash or too little cash. Excess cash means a business resource is not being profitably used to maximise the rate of return and too little cash can mean that it is not able to pay its debts as they fall due.

Monitoring cash

Separation of duties

It is important to segregate the duties of bookkeeper, cashier, petty cashier and administration staff where possible. The administrative staff will often be involved in tasks such as opening the mail, depositing cash at the bank, approving invoices for payment, purchasing goods and services and preparing the bank reconciliation. The business manager or owner should sign cheques.

Examples of cash handling tasks that should be segregated among different employees

- Recording cash transactions
- Receiving cash
- Opening the mail
- Approving tax invoices
- Purchasing goods and services
- Signing cheques
- Depositing cash at the bank

By separating such tasks we reduce the possibility of those involved in the handling of cash from engaging in such actions as:
- making cheques out to themselves and covering this up by creating false invoices which they have approved or by altering records
- stealing cash or cheques received and altering records to cover up the theft
- making errors that go undetected.

Authorisation processes

The following are examples of tasks related to handling cash that require an approval process:
- all tax invoices, statements of account or other payment vouchers to be paid should be approved prior to payment. This should involve:
  - confirmation of the receipt of the goods or services
  - once approved, the tax invoice, statements of account or other payment voucher should be stamped to ensure that it is not paid twice
- all payments using electronic funds transfers or credit cards should be approved by the business manager or owner
- cheques should require the signatures of two people, of whom one should be the business manager or owner.

Accounting and Finance 2A   ISBN 9780170182041   Cengage Learning Australia

Recording and documentation systems

The following are examples of recording and documentation systems related to handling cash that should be in place:

- Cash budgets and cash budget performance reports should be prepared each month and analysed and monitored to see that the business has sufficient cashflow.
- All cash received should be documented (using pre-numbered forms) immediately so that there is a record of the receipt and to make it more difficult to steal. This may be on a receipt document, through a cash register or on a sales tax invoice. Cheques received through the daily mail should be recorded immediately and the information sent straight away to the appropriate employee who makes the accounting entries.
- All money received should be banked intact daily. This means that no money is taken from the cash received to make any payments and that cash is not left on the premises overnight. The cash received will then match the documented evidence of the receipt. The passage of all cash through a bank account will provide independent documented evidence of all transactions.
- All payments should be made by cheque, electronic funds transfer or credit card as this leaves a paper or audit trail as proof of payment and makes it difficult to steal cash as no coins and notes are involved.
- A separate petty cash fund should be used for those small payments that need to be made in cash.

Petty cash fund

The petty cash fund is a small amount of money that can be used to make trivial payments for items such as postage, stationery or tea and biscuits for the office. The amount of the petty cash fund will vary from business to business depending upon the size and nature of the business. The amount in the fund always has an upper limit, which is the petty cash imprest or advance. A limit should be set on the size of the amount of money that can be paid from the petty cash fund.

This fund is controlled by a petty cashier and all payments from the fund must be accompanied by an approved petty cash voucher. Appropriate source documents, such as a tax invoice or cash register receipt should accompany all petty cash vouchers. All transactions affecting the petty cash fund must be recorded in a petty cash record.

When the amount left in the fund reaches a certain point the petty cashier will prepare the required documents and apply for further funds to bring the amount in the fund up to the set limit. This is called a petty cash reimbursement. Reimbursement of the petty cash fund should be approved by the business manager or owner. The person in control of the petty cash fund should be the only employee who has access to the fund. They should not have access to other sources of cash nor be responsible for the writing of cheques or maintaining accounting records. The money should be stored in a locked cabinet or tin and checked regularly by the business manager or owner.

Verification and checking processes

Verification and checking processes that should be in place and are related to handling cash include:

- credit card signatures and expiry dates are checked for all receipts from customers paying by credit card
- all cheques for payment are checked against an approved tax invoice, statement of account or other payment voucher
- the daily mail is opened by two people
- all cash received, including that received through the cash register, to the cash register tapes or other documentary proof of receipt is reconciled daily
- all cancelled cheques or receipts are accounted for
- bank reconciliations are carried out each month.

Accounting and Finance: 2A   ISBN 9780170182041   Cengage Learning Australia

Bank reconciliation

The cash and cheque receipts deposited can be checked against an independent record: the bank statement from the bank. This requires the business's bank account records and details to be compared to the bank's record: the bank statement. The records may differ for such reasons as deposits in transit, unpresented cheques, dishonoured cheques, bank fees, direct debits, interest and errors. This checking process is called a bank reconciliation.

To show how the business's bank records reconcile with the bank statement a bank reconciliation statement is prepared. This process should be carried out each month. It should be carried out by someone not responsible for cash receipts and payments or the accounts records.

Established lines of responsibility

Tasks relating to the handling of cash require someone to be given the appropriate responsibility for doing them or overseeing that they are done. These tasks include:

- signing of cheques
- opening the mail
- preparing the monthly bank reconciliation statement
- depositing cash into the bank.

Security of assets and records

Security measures that should be undertaken in regards to cash include:

- limit access to cash registers
- store blank cheques, cancelled cheques and cancelled receipts in the safe
- use cash registers to receipt all cash received, EFTPOS receipts and credit card receipts
- use a night safe to deposit money at the end of the day
- install CCTV over cash registers
- use a safe to store all cash kept on the premises
- employ security guards to protect cash.

REALITY CHECK 4.1

Bookkeeper stole $235 000 to feed poker machine addiction
by Victor Violante, Legal Affairs Reporter

A 53-year-old Canberra woman stole almost $235 000 over three years from her employer to fund her poker machine addiction, an ACT court heard yesterday.

Joanne Whitford-Smith was bookkeeper and accounts manager for the family-owned Fyshwick tile company, R West Tiles, between 2001 and 2005.

After gaining the trust of her employer, who entrusted her with complete control of the business's finances, she stole $234 989 between October 2002 and July 2005 through fraudulent cheques and unauthorised electronic fund transfers to her account.

Her breach of trust has pushed the business to the brink of bankruptcy. Owner Roy West, who started the company almost 50 years ago, told *The Canberra Times* yesterday he had put the Gladstone Street building for sale in an effort to save the business.

Mr West said the figure was only a fraction of what Whitford-Smith was believed to have stolen from the company, as a 12-month police investigation could not account for all the missing money.

"We were turning over a lot of work, but nobody, no matter how big you are, can take losses that big," he said.

"In the last four weeks she worked with us she stole $27 500 through electronic fund transfers. I'm 74, nearly 75 and broke as a bastard."

She appeared in the ACT Supreme Court yesterday for sentencing proceedings, having pleaded guilty to five theft charges encompassing 115 fraudulent transactions. She has been in custody since her arrest in February and has no prior criminal record.

The court heard that Whitford-Smith moved to Canberra from Victoria in 2000 and started working in October 2001 at R West Tiles as their bookkeeper and office manager, responsible for the monthly reconciliation of the company's bank statements and the payment of invoices and wages.

In January 2002 she was added as a signatory to the bank account, allowing her to sign company cheques without the need for a second signature. She was also given authority to establish an electronic banking account. In September 2005 she resigned.

Source: *The Canberra Times*, 18 July 2008, www.canberratimes.com.au/news/local/news/general/bookkeeper-stole-235000-to-feed-poker-machine-addiction/844647.aspx.

Commentary

This article highlights the importance of internal control. A lack of internal control can, in some cases, lead to the bankruptcy of a business. For any business, selecting reliable and honest staff is vital to the success of internal control processes – particularly small businesses that are unable, due to cost constraints, to employ the required number of employees to set up the checking mechanisms that larger businesses can do.

In this case the lack of internal control extended to the bookkeeper having unchecked access to bank accounts, ability to sign cheques without a second signatory, being given unsupervised responsibility for paying invoices and wages and carrying out monthly reconciliations even though she had access to both the accounting records and bank accounts. This enabled her to make fraudulent transactions to attempt to cover up the money stolen.

 Discuss with your teacher what internal control procedures should have been in place to make such embezzlement more difficult.

INVENTORY MANAGEMENT AND CONTROL

Inventories are important to any merchandising, service or manufacturing business because a large amount of money is invested in them and they have a large impact on profit determination. The cost of maintaining inventory is high so we need to consider how to keep this cost to a minimum. Inventories may be subject to:
- theft
- physical deterioration
- obsolescence – this can occur through products reaching their use by date, customers' preferences changing or new and better products coming onto the market.

The last two factors above make it vital that the business's inventory turnover is as high as possible.

To meet customer demand it is important to maintain the right level of inventory. Too much inventory can result in a higher risk of deterioration and obsolescence. Maintaining too little inventory could lead to running out of stock and not being able to meet customer demand and losing sales.

Accounting and Finance: 2A   ISBN 9780170182041   Cengage Learning Australia

Monitoring inventory

Separation of duties

It is important to segregate the duties of bookkeeper, inventory storeperson, purchasing officer, cashier and administration staff where possible. The administrative staff will often be involved in tasks such as approving invoices for payment. The business manager or owner should be responsible for approving suppliers or determining which inventory is no longer required. Where possible, the role of inventory storeperson should be split so that the duties of receiving, issuing and storing inventory are segregated. In many small businesses, of course, such segregation is impractical.

Examples of inventory management tasks that should be segregated among different employees

- Approval of suppliers
- Physical stocktaking of inventory
- Purchasing inventories and supplies
- Approving tax invoices for payment
- Custody of inventories and supplies
- Recording inventory

The above tasks should be separated to reduce the possibility that employees involved in the management of inventories can:
- approve the purchase of inventories for personal use and falsify the records to cover this up
- steal inventories and cover it up by altering the records
- make errors that go undetected.

Authorisation processes

Tasks related to the management of inventory that require an approval process include:
- approving of inventory suppliers – businesses should obtain competitive prices for all items they purchase
- purchasing inventory
- approving of tax invoices for payment
- requisitioning inventory from storage for sale in the shop
- writing off inventory no longer needed.

Recording and documentation systems

The following recording and documentation systems related to inventory management should be in place:
- purchase order forms (pre-numbered) – required before the purchase is made
- sales order forms (pre-numbered) – required for all sales of inventory
- goods received notes and delivery dockets – required for all receipts of inventory
- requisition forms or goods issued notes or delivery dockets – required for all inventories issued from the store
- perpetual inventory system (if possible)
- an inventory management system.

Inventory management system

A business should have in place inventory management systems based on the perpetual inventory method of keeping a record of all inventory purchased and sold. This also requires the determination of a reorder point and a reorder quantity for each inventory item, taking into account the lead time required for the inventory to be received.

A reorder point is the predetermined level to which the inventory may fall to before reordering is necessary. A reorder quantity is the predetermined quantity of inventory to be ordered once the reorder point has been reached. The lead-time for inventory is the time it takes for the inventory to be received or ready for sale from the time it was ordered.

A system that is set up in this way will minimise the likelihood of overstocking or understocking and therefore reduce the loss of potential sales and keep storage and opportunity costs to a minimum.

A person in authority should be responsible for the determination of reorder points and reorder quantities of inventories as well as monitoring the turnover of inventory. This will include the investigation of slow-moving items. It is important for a business to turn over its inventory as quickly as possible to ensure that stock does not become damaged or outdated and to minimise storage costs.

An inventory management record – sometimes called a stock card – is a record of

all details pertaining to a stock item, including the movement into and out of the business (retail outlet or warehouse). It will show the number, location, description, quantity and value of the items moving in or out of the business as well as the reorder point and reorder quantity.

Verification and checking processes

Inventory management verification and checking processes that should be in place

- Inspection of goods received and comparison with delivery docket and order form
- Comparison of inventory records with the General ledger inventory account
- Regular stocktakes

Stocktaking

A stocktake is a physical count of all inventories and comparison with the inventory records and General ledger inventory account balance. At least one stocktake should be undertaken each year. All differences should be investigated and resolved.

Established lines of responsibility

Specific responsibility should be allocated for the following tasks:
- issuing/dispatching inventory from storage
- storing inventory
- stocktaking
- monitoring inventory levels.

Security of assets and records

The following are examples of security measures that should be undertaken in regards to inventory:
- all inventory is electronically tagged or barcoded for identification
- security cameras and/or guards are used to protect and monitor inventory warehouses and retail outlets to reduce the incidence of burglary, shoplifting and pilfering

Accounting and Finance: 2A   ISBN 9780170182041   Cengage Learning Australia

- where appropriate, valuable inventory is locked away, bars are fitted on windows and alarms are installed at warehouses and retail outlets
- adequate insurance is maintained
- access to inventory warehouses is restricted to appropriate personnel.

Woolworths defend security after shoplifting job uncovered

Woolworths has defended its security systems after police arrested two men over a major shoplifting operation in Sydney.

Police were patrolling the inner-city suburb of Alexandria just before 6:00pm (AEDT) last Saturday when they noticed two men looking suspicious in Euston Road.

A search and subsequent questioning led police to a warehouse where police say they found cosmetics worth millions of dollars stacked in boxes, some of it stolen from Woolworths.

Police also searched a luxury home in Rose Bay where they say they also found thousands of other stolen products, which filled every room.

It is alleged the men hired people to steal from Woolworths, Coles and other shops and on-sold the goods at markets.

Police believe the operation, which is thought to be the biggest of its type ever uncovered in Australia, has been going on for about 10 years.

Darin Croft from Woolworths says the retail chain has been working with police for two years.

'There's various methods that professional thieves use to steal from our stores, the methods I'm not prepared to go into for obvious reasons,' he said.

'But we work hard at deterring theft in our stores and we work hard with our suppliers in attaching security devices to our stock. In this case it helped us to identify stock and recover that stock.'

Source: ABC News website, 30 January 2009, www.abc.net.au/news/stories/2009/01/30/2478884.htm.

Commentary

The theft of inventory – whether through shoplifting or pilfering – is very costly to a business. It is vital to make use of store security guards, cameras, inspection of the bags of customers and employees and ensure that stock is electronically tagged where possible.

What other processes have you noticed in place at your local shops to safeguard the store's stock?

ACCOUNTS RECEIVABLE MANAGEMENT AND CONTROL

The provision of credit is convenient to many customers and it is vital to the operation of many businesses so that they can increase their sales and thus their profitability. However, this provision of credit comes at a cost. These costs include the:

- cost of financing accounts receivable
- possibility of bad debts
- slow receipt of cash from the debtor (this is an opportunity cost in that the business is not able to use this money until it is received)
- cost of administering accounts receivable, which includes
    - employing staff to control the provision of credit
    - following up on delinquent debtors
    - providing discounts for prompt payment.

The aforementioned costs can affect the liquidity of the business; they need to be considered against the benefits to be obtained. It is very important that accounts receivable are well controlled.

If accounts receivable are too low it may indicate that the business credit policy is too strict, which may mean loss of customers and sales. If, however, accounts receivable are too high then this may indicate that the credit policy and procedures of the business are too lenient and not effective. The latter can lead to losses and reduced profitability.

Supplying credit to customers and credit management

Before supplying credit to customers they must be approved as creditworthy. This is important because the business does not wish to approve credit to someone who cannot repay the amount owed. The business does not want to incur bad debts (or at least wants to reduce the likelihood of this occurring). It is important therefore for businesses to develop a credit policy.

Credit policy

A credit policy is the conditions under which a business will provide credit to its customers. This credit policy should incorporate some of the following aspects:
- the terms of credit provision, such as the credit limit, when payment is expected, when discounts are given and when interest is charged on overdue accounts
- credit analysis, including such aspects as the requirement for collateral, security and guarantees, when credit is extended or not extended and differentiating between good and bad debtors; this may involve obtaining external information such as a credit rating or bank details
- collection of the amount owing, including what happens in the event of the debt not being paid on time and means of debt recovery.

When considering whether to supply credit to a customer the business must consider the customer's background, including such as aspects their credit history, employment history and assets. Therefore financial and non-financial information must be requested on a credit application form from the customer before credit is extended to them.

Credit application

A credit application form will ask for information such as:
- financial information
  - current and previous debts
  - current earnings and expenses – and in the case of a business, details of its financial statements
  - assets and other collateral or security – and in the case of a business, its financial statements
  - current and previous employment details showing the salary or wage earned in the case of an individual
- non-financial information
  - name and address
  - Australian Business Number (ABN) where appropriate
  - references.

Credit rating

The business may obtain a credit rating report for a potential customer from a credit rating agency. These agencies are an external third party that gathers data on the credit history of businesses and individuals. Based on this information a credit rating is provided that gives the business some idea as to whether the customer (business or individual) will repay the debt. These credit ratings are usually given as a symbol or alphabetical or numerical rating according to some kind of scale.

Accounting and Finance: 2A   ISBN 9780170182041   Cengage Learning Australia

Credit history

A business investigating a credit application will request details on the credit history of the potential customer as it tells them how well the person has been in the past in repaying their debts. This gives the business an idea as to how they may perform in the future. Questions about the assets and liabilities of the potential customer will give the business an idea as to whether the net worth of the person is sufficient to enable them to repay the debt should there be a problem in the future.

Employment history

Details on employment history are important to the business as it provides them with some idea as to the potential customer's ability to meet the repayments on a regular basis in the future.

Other factors to be considered

In some instances a business may request a deposit from the potential customer. The purpose of this is to determine how serious the individual is about purchasing the product or service and assists the business to cover any initial costs. It is also advisable in some instances for the business to provide a written quote for the product or service to be supplied on credit. References should be checked before approving credit.

Monitoring accounts receivable

Once credit has been provided to customers it is very important for the business to monitor its accounts receivable. This can be done through the use of an aged Trial balance. Under this method debtors are categorised according to how long the debt has been overdue for payment. Debtors that are shown to have been outstanding beyond the acceptable period are then followed up. This may involve phone calls, reminder notices and letters, or even placing the debt in the hands of a lawyer or debt collection agency. If it is considered that the debt will not be received then it must be written off as a bad debt.

Separation of duties

It is important to segregate the duties of bookkeeper, credit manager, accounts receivable clerk, cashier and sales assistants. The business manager or owner should approve the writing off of bad debts.

Examples of accounts receivable tasks that should be segregated among different employees

- Approving credit to customers
- Recording in the General ledger
- Receiving cash
- Approving the writing off of bad debts
- Controlling the Accounts receivable records
- Selling goods (issuing tax invoices)

By separating the above tasks we reduce the possibility of the accounts receivable staff engaging in such actions as:

- setting up bogus customers, selling goods and services to them and then writing these off as a bad debt
- receiving cash from a debtor, stealing the money and altering account records to cover this up
- making errors that go undetected.

Accounting and Finance 2A   ISBN 9780170182041   Cengage Learning Australia

Authorisation processes

The following are examples of tasks related to the accounts receivable function that require an approval process:

- granting credit to customers should be approved by a credit manager
- writing off bad debts needs to be approved by the business manager or owner
- making credit adjustments for returned goods or non-delivery of services should be done by the business manager or owner
- cash refunds to customers need to be approved by a senior person, such as the business manager or owner.

Recording and documentation systems

The following are examples of recording and documentation systems related to the accounts receivable function that should be in place:

- credit and collection policy
- accounts receivable subsidiary ledger
- credit application forms
- sales tax invoices, which should be recorded promptly
- statement of accounts, which should be issued each month
- aged accounts receivable Trial balance report, which should be prepared each month and overdue accounts followed up
- credit notes for all adjustments (use pre-numbered forms).

Verification and checking processes

The following are examples of verification and checking processes related to the accounts receivable that should be in place:

- review of accounts receivable balances each month
- reconciliation of accounts receivable subsidiary ledger with the General ledger control account
- follow up of credit references and verification of credit ratings.

Established lines of responsibility

The following are examples of accounts receivable functions for which appropriate lines of responsibility need to be established:

- approving credit
- checking credit ratings
- approving the write-off of bad debts
- approving credit adjustments and refunds
- controlling the accounts receivable ledger.

ACCOUNTS PAYABLE MANAGEMENT AND CONTROL

Control of accounts payable is important in the prevention of fraud and vital to the effective working capital management of any business. A business must manage its accounts payable so that it can ensure that its cash outflow is equal to or lower than its cash inflow and thus maintain its liquidity. When considering who and when to pay, a business will take into account the availability of cash against the possibility of disruption to the supply if payments are delayed. The continuous and uninterrupted supply of goods and services to the business is vital in its day-to-day operations.

Paying invoices on time will improve a business's relationship with its suppliers, which is important to enable the business to take full advantage of the credit terms offered and maintain the supply of credit. In addition, suppliers often provide other benefits, such as advice on new products, and this assists in meeting consumer demands.

Accounting and Finance: 2A   ISBN 9780170182041   Cengage Learning Australia

If the accounts payable is too low then it may be that the business is not taking sufficient advantage of the terms of credit. Paying creditors earlier than necessary may adversely and unnecessarily affect the firm's liquidity position. If the accounts payable is too high this may indicate that the business does not have enough cash to pay its debts and the supplier may be reluctant to continue doing business with them.

Monitoring accounts payable

Separation of duties

It is important to segregate the duties of bookkeeper, accounts payable clerk, purchasing officer, inventory storeperson and administration officers. The business manager or owner should approve suppliers and any adjustments and sign cheques. The administration officers would normally check and approve invoices for payment.

Examples of accounts payable tasks that should be segregated among different employees

- Checking and approving invoices for payment
- Controlling inventory
- Making payments by cheque
- Ordering goods and services
- Approving of suppliers
- Controlling the accounts payable subsidiary ledger
- Recording in the General ledger
- Making adjustments

By separating the above tasks we reduce the possibility of the accounts payable staff engaging in such actions as:
- preparing false invoices to make payments to themselves and covering this up by being able to approve invoices for payment
- ordering and receiving goods or services for themselves and then covering this up by approving invoices for payment and altering inventory records
- making errors that go undetected.

Authorisation processes

Tasks related to the accounts payable function that require an approval process include the following:
- The ordering of all goods should be approved by a specified person and limits to their authority set so that the larger the order the more senior the authoriser must be.
- All new suppliers must be approved by a senior person before any goods or services are acquired. It is preferable to have at least two suppliers for each type of product or service so that if one supplier is unable to supply the item then the other can do so.
- All invoices should be approved by someone (who has been given an upper limit to the amount they can approve) before payment is made. Invoices over this set limit will require approval by a more senior person.

Recording and documentation systems

The following are examples of recording and documentation systems relating to the accounts payable function:
- budgets prepared to predict any cashflow problems
- accounts payable subsidiary ledger is maintained
- reports are prepared to ensure that deadlines for receiving discounts and payment of accounts are made on time. Taking advantage of discounts can save money and

improve liquidity. Paying accounts on time is important for relationships with suppliers and the reputation of the business. Continuation of credit facilities with suppliers is important

- detailed reports are prepared when goods are received and ordered and payments are made to suppliers to allow monitoring of transactions and services received related to each supplier.

Verification and checking processes

Verification and checking processes related to the accounts payable function that should be in place include:

- before being paid each tax invoice (purchase) is checked to ensure that
  - calculations, quantities and pricing are accurate
  - it corresponds with the order form and goods or services receipts note
  - the invoice is an original and not a copy or fax
  - details are as per the approved list (supplier's name, ABN, address and other details)
- once approved invoices are stamped as evidence that they have been properly processed
- the approved supplier list is reviewed on a regular basis
- monthly account statements are compared with ledger account balances
- the accounts payable subsidiary ledger is reconciled with the General ledger control account.

Established lines of responsibility

The following are examples of accounts payable functions for which appropriate lines of responsibility need to be established:

- keeping in touch with suppliers so that a positive relationship is developed
- reviewing all purchases each month
- controlling the accounts payable ledger.

REALITY CHECK 4.3

Pregnant, 25 and in jail for fiddling with the books
by Glenis Green

They treated her like she was one of their own, but for three years their trusted office manager was stripping their company of almost $400000.

Fiona Maxine Fenech spent the money buying land in Gympie, 160km north of Brisbane, as well as buying horses to indulge her passion for endurance riding, plus shopping, gifts and gambling.

Now, just 25 and newly pregnant, she is behind bars where she will give birth well before the 2010 parole date comes around in her five-and-a-half-year sentence handed down in Gympie District Court last week.

However she is not getting any sympathy from Waterfall Feedlot Pty Ltd owner Robert Maudsley and his family who took her into their home, trained her into her first real job and had trusted her without question.

On Friday, two days after Fenech, from Kilkivan, had pleaded guilty to one count of fraud as an employee and another count of fraud which happened just after she left her job, Mr Maudsley and his son John were still shaking their heads.

'We trusted her 100 per cent and this is what happens,' said Mr Maudsley, who has operated the feedlot between Tansey and Goomeri, inland from Gympie, for the past 23 years.

'We treated her like a member of the family so it hurts a bit,' he said. 'And it made it pretty tough for us for a while with the Australian dollar going so high and the feed prices.'

Accounting and Finance 2A   ISBN 9780170182041   Cengage Learning Australia

Mr Maudsley said Fenech had worked for them for seven years after she had brief jobs at Coles and Nolan's Meatworks.

However the court heard that in October 2004 she hit on a scheme to feather her own nest by disguising transactions from the company's account into her own using false invoices claiming to have made payments to creditors – such as grain suppliers.

With about 9000 head of cattle in Waterfall at any one time – many on consignment – the feed bill was usually large and varying.

At first the amounts were in the hundreds of dollars but as Fenech got bolder they got bigger and more frequent – 38 transactions in all.

Eventually a $53 100.61 transaction on May 31 last year, just days after she left the job to be with a boyfriend in New South Wales, brought her undone.

'She'd given three weeks' notice, but she left earlier before she did the bank reconciliations otherwise we might never have known – she made a mistake,' Mr Maudsley said.

'She was a greedy little lady.' The total amount stolen was $394 258 and the court heard this week that Fenech, from Kilkivan, had repaid $176 000 of this from property she had sold.

Mr Maudsley said neither he nor his family had received so much as a 'sorry' from Fenech and his mission now was to try to recover the outstanding stolen $218 000.

He said he had now put systems in place to ensure such a betrayal could never happen again and warned other business owners about being too trusting.

Sentencing a tearful Fenech this week, Judge John Robertson said she would now end up having a child in prison 'which is a shocking thing for any mother'.

Source: *Courier Mail*, 30 June 2008, www.news.com.au/couriermail/ story/0,23739,23941457-3102,00.html.

Commentary

This article illustrates the importance of employing honest and reliable staff and not giving too much responsibility to one individual staff member. When using an electronic payment system it is still very important that all invoices be approved before payment by someone other than the person making the payment. In addition, two people must make the payment even in a computerised accounting system. It is important to make use of passwords and codes when using a computerised accounting system and to ensure that tasks are segregated with access to other areas of the system restricted.

NON-CURRENT ASSET MANAGEMENT AND CONTROL

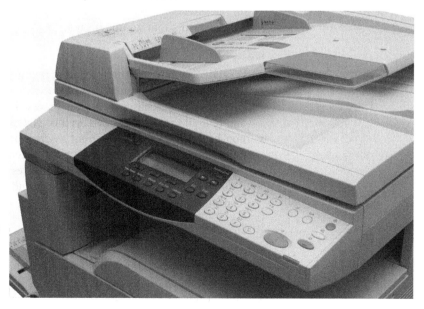

Non-current assets are important to a business because there is a high risk attached to them. They usually comprise a large proportion of the firm's assets. Often the business has to raise large amounts of external finance to purchase its non-current assets. Therefore, it is important that the non-current asset generates enough cash flow to repay the borrowed money and provide a good rate of return to the owners.

Non-current assets are usually expected to be utilised for a long period of time and will be expected to generate cash flows over a long period of time.

Once a non-current asset is purchased it is difficult to reverse the decision unless the business is prepared to sustain a loss on the transaction.

If the non-current assets of a business are insufficient the business may not be able to grow and achieve its goals – and sales may suffer. If investment in non-current assets is excessive then they are likely to be relatively unproductive resulting in a lower return on investment and possibly an inability of the business to repay any borrowed funds, as cash flow will be lower than is required.

Monitoring non-current assets

Separation of duties

It is important to segregate the duties of bookkeeper, assets clerk and those charged with responsibility for control and custody of individual non-current assets. The business manager or owner should take responsibility for approving the purchase or disposal of non-current assets, periodically checking non-current assets and making the final approval of invoices for payment in the case of the purchase of an asset. Administrative staff should carry out the task of checking invoices before payment.

Examples of non-current assets tasks that should be segregated among different employees

- Approval of the purchase and disposal of non-current assets
- Preparation of non-current asset registers
- Preparation of General ledger records
- Custody of non-current assets
- Checking of tax invoices before payment
- Payment for the purchase of non-current assets
- Periodic checking of non-current assets

By separating the above tasks we reduce the possibility of the staff engaging in such actions as:

- approving the purchase of non-current assets for their own benefit through the purchase of fictitious non-current assets from a fictitious supplier (who is, in fact, the employee) and covering this up by approving the invoice, making payment and then carrying out the periodic physical check on the asset
- stealing non-current assets and then covering this up by being able to alter non-current asset registers and General ledger records and carrying out the periodic physical check on the asset
- making errors that go undetected.

Authorisation processes

Tasks related to non-current assets that require an approval process include:

- purchase of non-current assets – procedures must be in place to ensure that all non-current asset purchases have been assessed as to their costs and benefits to the business and that all the options have been considered
- non-business use of non-current assets – procedures must be in place to prevent unauthorised use of a business's non-current assets
- disposal of non-current assets – procedures must be in place to ensure that the asset is in fact no longer of use to the business and that the best possible price is obtained for its disposal.

Recording and documentation systems

Recording and documentation systems relating to non-current assets include:

- insurance record-keeping systems
- legal documentation systems
- non-current asset registers.

Accounting and Finance: 2A   ISBN 9780170182041   Cengage Learning Australia

Non-current asset register

This is a separate record of all the details pertaining to the non-current asset from its acquisition through to its disposal.

What should be included in a non-current asset register

- Identification number
- Manufacturers and other registration serial numbers
- Date of purchase
- Supplier and manufacturer
- Original cost
- Type/make/model
- Insurance
- Location
- Depreciation method and rate and taxation rate of depreciation
- Estimated life
- Estimated residual value
- Repairs and maintenance history
- Depreciation details
- Disposal details

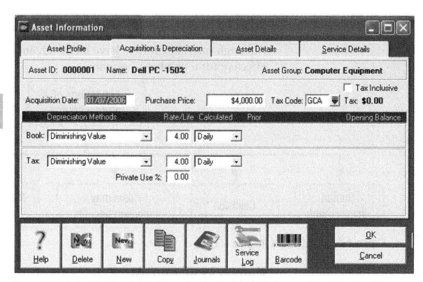

Figure 4.3 Extract of the MYOB non-current asset register section showing the Acquisition and Depreciation tab. The other three tabs show further details about assets.

Verification and checking processes

Non-current asset verification and checking processes that should be in place include:

- periodic physical checking of all non-current assets, including sighting of legal documents, such as proof of ownership, and comparison to details on non-current asset registers
- periodic reconciling of the non-current asset register with the General ledger
- annual checking of the insurance policy on each asset.

Established lines of responsibility

Appropriate lines of responsibility for non-current assets need to be established, including:

- approval of non-current asset purchases – this should be done by a senior person (such as the business manager or owner) and preferably involve two or more people
- approval the disposal of non-current assets – this should require the approval of the business manager or owner to prevent the unauthorised sale of assets for personal gain
- preparation of and maintenance of the non-current asset registers
- custody of each non-current asset
- periodic physical checking of non-current assets.

Security of assets and records

Security measures for non-current assets should include the following:

- all non-current assets are engraved or tagged or barcoded with the business name and identification number
- legal documents associated with non-current assets are locked away or placed in a fireproof safe
- security cameras and/or guards are used to protect and monitor business assets
- non-current assets are adequately maintained and insured
- alarms are installed on the business premises.

Accounting and Finance 2A   ISBN 9780170182041   Cengage Learning Australia

LIMITATIONS OF INTERNAL CONTROL

Although internal controls have many advantages, the systems in place will not always be effective for a number of reasons.

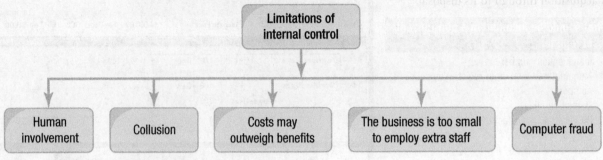

Figure 4.4 Limitations of internal control

Human involvement

The internal control systems will only be as effective as the personnel involved. Some individuals will find ways around internal control procedures – this is when errors or fraud may occur. When employees are careless, negligent, apathetic or suffer from fatigue the internal control systems can be ineffective.

Collusion

Collusion is when two or more people conspire as one to commit a fraud. Internal control systems are usually only designed, through the segregation of duties, to prevent one individual from perpetrating a fraud on their own.

Costs may outweigh benefits

In some instances the cost of introducing an internal control procedure may outweigh the benefits to be achieved. When introducing control measures the business must consider the cost as well as the impact on staff, customers and business operations. For example, to completely prevent the possibility of a cashier from making errors or stealing money it would be necessary to establish a very onerous process of checking and re-checking entries as well as security searches and checks of the staff involved. This would be very costly and also an imposition on the staff that could lead to poor morale and problems with staff-relations. A cheaper option – albeit less effective – is to install cameras over the cashier area and to use these cameras if fraud is suspected.

Business is too small to employ extra staff

The size of the business will also determine whether some internal control procedures will be implemented. The cost of implementing ideal internal control systems may be too high for a small business. In addition, in a small business the number of employees is much less than that of a larger business and so it may not be possible to segregate some duties or feasible to rotate some tasks. In the case of a small business the owner will need to do a lot of the checking, authorising, verifying and monitoring of procedures.

Computer fraud

Most businesses now make use of computer accounting systems. Because this process often only involves one person, segregation of duties and checking procedures is more difficult to implement. The individuals who input data and operate the computer system often do so without supervision and therefore it is difficult to detect any fraud they may commit.

Accounting and Finance: 2A   ISBN 9780170182041   Cengage Learning Australia

Test your knowledge

1 Define internal control.

2 Describe the internal control principle of segregation of duties and outline its purpose.

3 Explain the control characteristics of establishing an organisational structure with obvious lines of responsibility and describe its purpose.

4 Describe why internal control is important.

5 Distinguish between accounting controls and administrative controls.

6 Explain the internal control principle of establishing verification and checking processes and describe its purpose.

7 State your understanding of the internal control principle that a business should have appropriate authorisation processes in place and describe its purpose.

8 Why is internal control over cash important?

9 How is a monthly bank reconciliation useful to a business in controlling its cash and cash records?

10 What is a petty cash imprest system and how does it improve internal control over cash?

11 What is the purpose of developing a credit policy?

12 How does checking the credit history, employment history and assets of the potential customer reduce the possibility of bad debts?

13 Why is internal control of accounts receivable important?

14 Why is internal control of inventory important?

15 What factors may reduce the benefits of internal control for a business?

16 Why is internal control of accounts payable important?

17 Why is internal control of non-current assets important?

Test your understanding

Topic guide
- Internal control of cash: 4.1–4.6
- Internal control of inventory: 4.7–4.13
- Internal control of accounts receivable: 4.14–4.20
- Internal control of accounts payable: 4.21–4.25
- Internal control of non-current assets: 4.26–4.30

4.1 In each of the following cases identify the principle of internal control that has been adhered to:
   a cheques are signed by two people
   b cash received is banked daily
   c monthly bank reconciliation is conducted
   d all payments, except small amounts, are made by cheque
   e checking and approving invoices for payment is not done by the person who signs cheques
   f only one person has control and access to the petty cash fund
   g cash, surplus to that needed in the cash register, is locked in the safe.

4.2 The owner of McKay's Jewellers has found that over the past year the business cash performance report and profit report both seem not to reflect the business's actual results and that the business cash balance is in decline. The owner has also discovered that payments are being made from the cash takings. How would banking all cash intact daily assist in making the financial results more accurate and detect if cash is being stolen?

4.3 At DVD Ezy Stores the business owner is concerned that the daily cash deposits are down compared to the same time last year and yet sales seem to be up on the previous year. The business has a small number of staff and therefore the business bookkeeper is also one of the shop assistants. How is this arrangement not good from the perspective of internal control and what could the owner do about it?

4.4 Liberty Home Fashions is a small business that employs 18 people. The company owner has asked an external auditor to review the firm's accounting and administration procedures and they have identified the following practices that are of concern to them:
- The mail is opened each day by the business bookkeeper.
- All staff have access to the petty cash tin.
- Cheques are signed by one manager only.
- All staff have access to the cash register.

Suggest what improvements need to be made to the internal control procedures, how these will benefit the business and why.

4.5 Freo Travel Agency allows one of its travel consultants, who collects and issues receipts for cash, to also prepare the monthly bank reconciliation. The owner, Alice Docker, is very concerned that the business cash balance is declining although the business seems to have lots of clients.

Further enquiries reveal that cash registers are monitored by camera, a petty cash imprest system controlled by one of the clerical staff is used and that all cheques are signed by the two owners. In addition, it is noted that the mail is opened by the travel consultant who collects and receipts money through the cash register.

What are the drawbacks of these arrangements with regard to internal control and what could the owner do to improve them? What aspects of internal control are appropriate and why?

4.6 Donnybrook Winery is a small business that employs 19 staff at its premises in the south-west of Western Australia. An accounting consultant was contracted to review the business operations concerning the handling of cash. The process includes the following:
- All cheques are signed by the two directors.
- Tax invoices for payment are checked by the same person who manages the materials inventory store.
- Tax invoices are stamped approved once the checking process has been completed.
- Purchasing of goods and services is performed by the bookkeeper.
- A designated petty cashier has been chosen who is a clerical officer in the business.
- Sales dockets (tax invoices) issued are pre-numbered and their sequence is checked each month.
- Blank cheques are kept in an open drawer in the office area.
- Excess cash is kept in one of the office table drawers.
- Staff have been instructed to check the signatures, expiry date and credit limits on all sales made by credit card.

How effective are the firm's internal control measures? What do you think could be improved?

4.7 In each of the following cases identify the principle of internal control that has been adhered to:
a The purchasing of goods and services is not done by the person in charge of the inventory store.

Accounting and Finance: 2A   ISBN 9780170182041   Cengage Learning Australia

    b   A designated officer is given the task of monitoring inventory levels.

    c   All inventory is barcoded.

    d   The business only purchases from its approved supplier list.

    e   Adequate insurance has been maintained.

    f   Stocktaking is done at least once a year.

    g   Purchase order forms are in use.

4.8   Howard Fine Gifts Stores maintains an inventory warehouse in Canning Vale. The manager of the warehouse also has the task of purchasing all the stock required. Why is this arrangement unsatisfactory from the perspective of internal control and how could it be improved?

4.9   Beasley Gourmet Foods uses the perpetual inventory system as part of its computerised accounting package. However, complaints from customers have indicated that some stock sold is past its use by date or not available and it often appears that what is recorded as the stock balance is not reflected on the store shelves. How can the owner use the computerised accounting package and a physical stocktake to try to overcome the problems indicated?

4.10 West Coast Shoe Fashions is a small business where the bookkeeper also does some purchasing and receiving of goods into the store. The owner is concerned about the unexplained loss of stock over the past year. How is this arrangement not good from the perspective of internal control and what could the owner do about it?

4.11 Joondalup Electronic Products has been reviewed by a public accountant and the following areas were highlighted as being of concern:
*   The bookkeeper also receives money from the sale of products to customers.
*   A sales assistant has the authority to make adjustments to accounts for returns of inventory from customers.
*   The General ledger record is not reconciled with the subsidiary inventory records.
*   Access to the inventory store is not restricted to authorised personnel.

      Why would the above be of concern and what improvements should be made to the internal control procedures? Outline how these would benefit the business.

4.12 The owner of the Hills Nursery Farm is concerned about the current business position as the profitability and cash amounts seem to be deteriorating for no apparent reason. An investigation reveals that tax invoices for payment are approved by the person who makes the original order and this same person also receives all the goods into the nursery.

      The investigation shows that a stocktake is done each year, that the main store area is monitored by cameras and that all stock is electronically tagged. In addition, sales tax invoices are numbered and accounted for, goods sold are checked against the customer's original order form and only the owner can approve suppliers. Only one bookkeeper is employed and this person reconciles the General ledger and stock records each month.

      Briefly discuss the arrangements the firm has in place for the internal control of inventory, indicating and explaining strengths and weaknesses. What could be done to improve this control?

4.13 Denmark Cottage Products is a small business with 17 staff members making jams, jellies, body lotions, candles and fragrances. A review was recently conducted of its business operations concerning inventory management. Their current process includes the following:
*   A stocktake is done every year.
*   Delivery dockets are used for all goods transported to customers.
*   Goods received are not checked against the original order form.
*   Goods received are not inspected.
*   Tax invoices are checked against the goods received report before being paid.
*   Security cameras are not used in the inventory store.
*   Sales dockets for goods sold are pre-numbered.
*   The pre-numbered sales dockets are not accounted for.

Indicate which of the aforementioned procedures is a weakness in internal control, then explain why this is the case and what could be done to improve the situation.

4.14 In each of the following cases identify the principle of internal control that has been adhered to:
a The approving of credit adjustments is assigned to the business manager.
b The approving of bad debts to be written off is done by the business manager and not done by the bookkeeper.
c The accounts receivable subsidiary ledger is reconciled with the General ledger control account each month.
d The provision of credit to customers is approved.
e A Statement of account is issued each month.

4.15 Glass Products Myaree employs a business manager who has responsibility for granting credit to customers, selling goods and issuing tax invoices, writing off bad debts, making adjustments for goods returned, checking the accounts receivable aged Trial balance and following up on overdue accounts. How is this arrangement not good from the perspective of internal control and what should the owner of the business do about it?

4.16 Wendy's Chocolates of Perth is a small business where the accounts receivable officer also carries out the function of cashier. The owner is concerned about the unexplained loss of cash over the past year. How is this arrangement not good from the perspective of internal control and what could the owner do about it? What special controls are needed if the business is small and cannot employ two people to perform these duties?

4.17 Morrison's Patisseries' accounts receivable balance over the past year has been increasing and a number of customers have complained about errors on their monthly statement of account. This has been embarrassing for the owner, Jim Morrison. Enquiries reveal that the business has a credit policy that is administered by the owner and this requires that all customers are approved by him. The owner also monitors all debtor balances each month.

Currently there is no subsidiary ledger for accounts receivable, tax invoices are not checked against order forms from customers, delivery notes for goods issued are not checked back against order forms and tax invoices are not stamped once approved. One of the administration clerks is supposed to follow up with those debtors who are behind in their payments. Bad debts can only be written off with the approval of the owner.

Briefly discuss the arrangements the firm has in place for the internal control of accounts receivable, indicating and explaining strengths and weaknesses. What could be done to improve this control?

4.18 Kats Outdoor Camping of Midland sells all its products on credit and over the past year bad debts have been increasing. The credit policy is administered by the senior administration clerk, but it only requires her to ask if the customer is employed and how much they earn each year. A discount is given for prompt payment of accounts and a written quote is given for all jobs undertaken. Although written letters are sent to overdue debtors, these are only sent after the account has been outstanding for three months. A tax invoice is issued after the job is done but to save on costs no statement of account is issued at the end of each month. What improvements to the credit policy, credit collection policy and other internal controls would you suggest to reduce the incidence of bad debts?

4.19 Rockingham Surfboard Manufacturers has requested a review of its accounts receivable procedures, which are as follows:
• The duties of accounts receivable are rotated with accounts payable and inventory management every three years.
• Bad debt write-offs are approved by the bookkeeper.
• All customers requesting credit are approved by the business manager.

Accounting and Finance: 2A   ISBN 9780170182041   Cengage Learning Australia

- The business does not use a credit application form for new customers seeking credit.
- Credit adjustments and cash refunds to debtors are approved by the business manager.
- Sales tax invoices are checked against order forms and stamped approved before payment is made.
- The owner checks the accounts receivable overdue account balances each month.
- The cashier also follows up with debtors who are overdue, receives the cash and makes entries in the accounts receivable subsidiary ledger.
- The General ledger control account is not reconciled with the accounts receivable subsidiary ledger.

  Indicate which of the above procedures is a weakness in internal control and then explain why and how this can be overcome.

4.20 Jenson Fashion Clothing Makers sells its products to retailers and through its factory outlet. All goods are sold on credit, but a recent review of its accounts receivables indicates that the level has been increasing steadily over the past year and that the cash position of the business has declined.

At present the business does not have a strict credit policy with approvals being made based on the potential customers' interviews over lunch with the business manager. Discounts for prompt payment are not offered to debtors, there has been an increase in bad debts during the past year and the length of time for debtors to repay has gone from an average of 45 days to 68 days.

One of the administration clerks checks the sales tax invoices against the goods delivery dockets and customer order forms for products sold. Statements of accounts are issued monthly and include all pre-numbered sales tax invoices.

At present the business owner must approve all bad debts written off, cash refunds to customers and adjustments to any account due to product refunds. In some cases the business manager may request a deposit bond from a customer who is unknown to him and he will, on occasion, give a quote for items made to special order. The owner of the business checks account balances each month and then requests a junior clerk to follow up overdue debtors by telephone. However, this does not affect subsequent sales made to that customer. The junior clerk is instructed not to place too much pressure on customers for fear of offending them and losing their patronage.

Required
a   Comment on the credit policy of the business, indicating what changes should be made.
b   Which aspects of the internal control over accounts receivable are appropriate?
c   How could the business improve its credit collection procedures?

4.21 In each of the following cases in relation to accounts payable identify the principle of internal control that has been adhered to:
a   Comparison of monthly account statements with ledger account balances.
b   Assigning one person to keep in touch with suppliers so that a positive relationship is developed.
c   The person who receives goods into the store should not also be ordering goods.
d   Detailed reports should be prepared on the ordering of goods, receiving of goods and payments made to suppliers so that there is a monitoring of the transactions.
e   Ordering of all goods should be approved by a person in authority.

4.22 Success Pizzas is a small business that has employed one person to perform the tasks usually divided between a bookkeeper and an accounts payable clerk. Why should these roles normally be kept separate? What special controls are needed in the case of Success Pizzas to ensure good internal control in this situation?

4.23 Sinatra's Men's Boutique's system of internal control allows for any staff member to purchase goods from suppliers. Tax invoices for payment are not checked nor stamped once paid. How is this arrangement not good from the perspective of internal control and what should the owner of the business do about it?

4.24 Claremont Top Gifts' system of operation allows its sales staff to order goods and receive goods into the retail shop. One of the sales assistants is also given the task of checking purchase order forms against tax invoices received but no check is made against the delivery docket of goods received and no inspection is made of the goods received by the sales staff. The business manager approves all suppliers after vetting them and ensures that the business has two suppliers for each stock item.

The bookkeeper manages the General ledger control accounts and the assistant bookkeeper controls the subsidiary ledger for accounts payable. They reconcile the records at the end of each month. The assistant bookkeeper checks all the monthly account statements received against the cheque payments made and the tax invoices received.

Briefly discuss the arrangements the firm has in place for the internal control of accounts payable, indicating and explaining strengths and weaknesses. What could be done to improve this control?

4.25 Janey's Café has asked for a review of its business operation procedures and the following is noted:
- All suppliers are approved by the owner.
- Goods received are checked against the order form.
- Tax invoices are compared with order forms and goods received reports.
- The business only has one supplier for each item of inventory.
- The bookkeeper is also the main purchasing officer and receives the goods into the store.
- No reporting is in place to ensure that deadlines for receiving discounts and payment of accounts are made on time.
- Adjustments for obsolete stock written off are approved by the bookkeeper.
- The General ledger control account for accounts payable is reconciled with the accounts payable subsidiary ledger.

Indicate which of the above procedures are weaknesses in internal control. Explain why and how they can be overcome.

4.26 In each of the following cases identify the principle of internal control that has been adhered to:
a   Non-current asset registers are used.
b   Approving the purchase of non-current assets is not done by the person who makes the payments for their purchase.
c   All non-current assets are engraved, tagged or barcoded with the business name and an identification number.
d   Periodic physical checking of all non-current assets is made and comparison to details on non-current asset registers is checked.
e   The raising of finance for non-current assets purchases is approved by a person in a senior position.
f   One person is given the task of approving of the disposal of non-current assets.

4.27 Mandurah Burgers is a small business that allows its bookkeeper to approve the purchase of assets, receive new non-current assets, approve invoices for payment as well as pay for assets. Why is this arrangement not good from the perspective of internal control?

4.28 Grant's Bookshop has employed an administration officer who is given the responsibility of maintaining the asset register and receiving cash as well as approving the disposal of non-current assets and then making the necessary arrangements for their sale or scrapping. Why would this arrangement not be a good internal control procedure? For a small business with perhaps only one or two employees, what special arrangements need to be made to control the disposal of non-current assets?

Accounting and Finance: 2A   ISBN 9780170182041   Cengage Learning Australia

4.29 West Art Prints operates with a limited number of five staff in its office administration area. At present the control of non-current assets is given to one of the clerks. This person has responsibility for ensuring that all new assets are engraved, that alarms are installed and that access to the warehouse area is restricted. The purchase of new non-current assets is authorised by the owner but then all other duties are handed over to the clerk concerned. This allows the clerk to purchase all the required assets, approve the tax invoices for payment, write off and dispose of non-current assets, receive the asset as well as manage the non-current asset registers.

What are the weaknesses in internal control in the above office arrangement? What improvements would you suggest, given that it is a small business?

4.30 Shinny Panel Beaters is a small business employing 15 staff at its Cannington premises of which five people work in the office area. The office is busy and many of the staff perform multiple duties. The usual arrangement is for the bookkeeper to control the General ledger for non-current assets. However, reconciliation of the balances each month with the non-current asset register is performed by the clerk who is responsible for the non-current asset registers. The bookkeeper has also been given the duties of recording and managing investment documents and securing all important legal documents, which are kept in the office safe, and also purchasing all new non-current assets. The bookkeeper also checks all the tax invoices for payment. The office clerk who manages the non-current assets maintains the non-current asset registers, physically checks the assets once a year, approves the disposal of assets and makes the necessary arrangements as well as acting as the business cashier.

What are the weaknesses in internal control in the above office arrangement? What improvements would you suggest given that it is a small business?

Investigation

1 Search on the internet to find two insurance companies and investigate the types of products they offer businesses to protect them from losses in the event of a failure of internal control. List these products and give a description of each. Do they provide any advice on business security? If so, give a brief overview of the advice they give.

2 Using the internet find two retail businesses that supply credit to their customers and locate the credit application form. What information do they require?

3 Visit two businesses at your local shopping centre. Observe, identify and record based on the table below, giving a short description of the internal control procedures that you see in operation. You may see more than one in each or any one category.

Internal control principle	Business name: Internal control procedure	Business name: Internal control procedure
Separation of duties		
Authorisation required		
Security measures in use		
Electronic devices in use		
Recording and documentation required		
Verification and checking processes		

Essay

'It is vital to the success of a small business that it implements all the principles of good internal control to their fullest extent'.

Discuss this statement, including in your answer the following:

- a definition of internal control
- an examination of the principles of internal control
- a description of the aims and objectives of internal control
- a description of the limitations of internal control
- a discussion of the costs of implementing internal control
- the difficulties that a small business has in implementing internal control.

Ethics case study

Tim Hardwick is the assistant accountant for a small business that is a wholesaler providing beauty products to retailers. His business employs 19 people at its warehouse in Canning Vale. The business is managed by Alan Hooper, who reports to the owners, who are the directors of the business called Magnific Pty Ltd. There are three directors: Alice Hooper (the Chairperson of the Board), Marion Hooper and William Hooper. Alice owns 40 per cent of the company and Marion and William own 30 per cent each.

Tim has conducted a review of the internal controls over the ordering, receiving, dispatching, recording and payment of inventory at the business. He was asked to undertake this review by the board of directors, but he was told to first report his findings to the business manager, Alan Hooper, a relative of the directors. In the review he has found that there is a need for the following changes to be made to improve internal control:

- security cameras should be installed
- a security guard should be employed at the warehouse gate to check all vehicles leaving the premises
- inventory write-offs must be approved by a senior clerk and not a junior warehouse clerk
- ordering of goods must not be made by a clerk who receives and dispatches goods
- special discounts to retailers must only be approved by the company directors.

He has presented his report to the business manager, Alan Hooper, and been told that all aspects of the report are to be reviewed for their cost of implementation. However, Alan has told Tim that his report is to be rewritten leaving out the comments on special discounts and the ordering of goods by the clerk. Alan has said that the approval requirement for special discounts to retailers is not to be taken any further and that there is no need to change the current set-up where some goods are being ordered by the clerk who receives and dispatches goods. Alan has informed Tim that he is in line to become the new company accountant. During the investigation Tim discovered that Alan had been approving the special discounts. These special discounts are costing $3 000 per month in reduced income. Tim also discovered that Alan had given approval for the clerk who receives and dispatches goods to also order goods and that the clerk is Alan's son.

- Who are the stakeholders in this case?
- Explain what the ethical problem is for Tim.
- What are the consequences for Tim if he does nothing about the issue of the special discounts?
- What alternatives are available to Tim?
- What would you suggest that Tim do in this case?

Accounting and Finance: 2A   ISBN 9780170182041   Cengage Learning Australia

Chapter 5

BUSINESS IN THE COMMUNITY

What You Will Learn

After studying this chapter you should be able to:

1 Describe the social, environmental and ethical responsibilities of a business towards the community in which it operates
2 Outline the ways in which a firm can make a positive contribution to resource conservation and the costs and benefits of this behaviour
3 Outline the ways in which a firm can interact with its local community (e.g. sponsorship of community groups, sporting bodies, etc.) and the costs and benefits of this sort of involvement
4 Explain how a firm may behave ethically in relation to its taxation responsibilities

Introduction

This chapter will examine the ways a business interacts with its community and responds to the accounting and finance issues involved. Community includes lenders, investors, employees and governments, as well as the general public in the business's locality.

This relationship between a business and its community can involve social, environmental and ethical issues. The issue of taxation responsibility has always been an important part of successful business operation. Moreover climate change and environmental damage have placed demands on businesses to make alterations to their business operations, such as resource conservation, and these changes have a cost. Furthermore businesses may be expected to give more to their local communities through the support of local charities and sporting or cultural groups.

These activities have benefits to the business but they come at a cost. This chapter will examine the role that small businesses can play in their community and the effect that the various environmental and social pressures can have.

ETHICS IN BUSINESS

In Chapter 1 you were introduced to the concept of *ethical behaviour* (i.e. acting in accordance with a set of moral principles, which may or may not be reflected in the requirements of the law). As noted, ethical constraints may often go beyond legal regulations. For example, the industrial award governing working conditions may specify a period of notice in the event of redundancy that is the same for all employees. Ethical considerations may suggest that long-serving employees ought to get a longer period of notice of dismissal. There may be occasions when there is a direct conflict between ethical and statutory requirements but in a business context this is very rare.

Large firms, especially public companies, need to consider ethical aspects of their dealings with those who have (or might have) an investment in the business. Small businesses (such as sole traders, partnerships and small proprietary companies, which are the focus of our study in this book) only need to consider that in relation to finance institutions and others from whom they might borrow. Consequently, the groups with whom the firm may deal can be summarised as:

- lenders, such as banks and other financial institutions and other members
- suppliers, customers and others with whom the firm may have business dealings
- employees
- co-owners (in the case of partnerships and small proprietary companies).

We will also consider, separately, the way the firm's activities might impact on the general community and how this may influence the way it behaves.

The firm and its lenders

There are two aspects of a firm's dealings with its lenders that need attention in this context. They are:

- the provision of information to the lender at the time the decision is taken to lend
- compliance during the term of the loan with the conditions under which it was made.

Banks and other financial institutions will normally specify what information they require to enable them to decide whether or not to lend. This would probably include past Income statements and balance sheets as well as budgets showing that the firm will be able to meet future interest payments and repay the loan when it is due.

There will always be a temptation on the part of the would-be borrower to do some 'creative accounting' to make the firm's present or future performance look better than it really was or will be. Unless it is a very large loan, the bank may not be willing or able to carry out the investigation needed to verify the information it has been given and it is even less likely that this will be done if the lender is a friend or family member.

Ethical standards require that a borrower provides complete and truthful disclosure of all relevant information, even if this may reduce the likelihood of the loan being approved.

EXAMPLE:

Example 5.1

Sonia owns a business, Triple-Ess, which owns a recording studio and other music processing facilities in Perth. The business has been struggling somewhat in recent years, but Sonia is hopeful of getting a long-term contract from a well-known music producer, which should improve things a lot. To be able to do this, she needs to re-equip her studio at a cost of $50000, which she is proposing to borrow from her bank. At the moment, the firm's only significant liability, apart from a small bank overdraft, is a loan of $20000 from her godfather, I Munnybaggs.

In putting together the budget that will accompany her application to the bank, Sonia is showing the payments under the contract with the music producer as assured, whereas, in fact, the contract is yet to be signed. Also in the balance sheet she is producing, she has left out her godfather's loan on the grounds that it is a family matter and therefore does not need to be included. She accepts that what she has done is technically wrong, but says that, with the

Accounting and Finance: 2A   ISBN 9780170182041   Cengage Learning Australia

expansion, her business will go from strength to strength so that the interests of the lender will be protected and anyway, no-one will ever know.

Commentary

While it may be true that, if all goes well, no-one will be any the wiser, the fact is that Sonia would be obtaining a loan under false pretences. This is ethically wrong. From a practical viewpoint, if things do go bad in the future and her misrepresentations come to light – as they well may – it could have serious repercussions for her and her business. For example, she may find it very difficult to borrow in the future and, if she earns a reputation as a person inclined to 'sharp practice' she might find people reluctant to deal with her. On balance, the truth is not only right, but probably commercially preferable, at least in the long term.

When a loan has been agreed to, there will invariably be conditions with which the borrower must comply for as long as it is outstanding. These will include the interest rate on the loan and when interest payments must be made, as well as the terms of repayment of the sum borrowed. If the loan has been used for the purchase of non-current assets, the lender may also require that these be insured against loss or damage for their full value. These terms, set out in the loan agreement, may be seen as the minimum requirement. There may, however, be additional obligations with which the borrower should comply, on both ethical and practical grounds.

Example 5.2

EXAMPLE:

Charlie's Chicken Factory has been financed in part by two loans, one from his bank and another from Charlie's Uncle Fester. Repayments on both loans are due at the end of the year in a couple of months time and at this stage it seems unlikely that the firm, which has been hit by the economic downturn, will have the cash available to make them. Charlie is an optimist, however, and believes that things will turn around before then. If they do not, he will go to the bank and seek an extension of time and/or some temporary funding. As for Uncle Fester, Charlie feels that his repayment can simply be delayed if necessary: he thinks Uncle Fester is extremely rich and is unlikely to notice a missing $10000.

Commentary

There are both ethical and practical reasons for doing something immediately about the expected future shortfall. From an ethical standpoint, it could be argued that both lenders are entitled to be kept informed about changes in the firm's circumstances that might endanger their investment. From a practical point of view, if the expected cash shortfall occurs, Charlie will presumably need to borrow from someone and both the bank and Uncle Fester will be much more receptive to an approach from the firm now, accompanied by a budget that shows that they might need money in a couple of months' time, than a last-minute appeal when it becomes obvious that disaster has struck. Charlie's reputation as a sound financial manager will also be at stake. His proposed treatment of Uncle Fester's loan repayment is clearly unethical. Fester is entitled to be treated like any other lender, despite his family connection. In any case, Charlie may well be wrong about Uncle Fester not noticing that he has not been repaid: rich people do not generally get that way by being careless over collecting their debts!

The firm and those it deals with

The most important group that any business deals with outside the firm itself is undoubtedly its customers. It is upon their willingness to buy the firm's products that the profitability and survival of the firm depends. Legislation will, to some extent, ensure that customers are treated fairly, through, for example, laws against misleading advertising, proper labelling of foodstuffs and so on. However, there is much that the firm can do, over and above what is required by law, to ensure that at all times the customer is given a fair go. In the long term, this is almost invariably in the firm's best commercial interests. The most effective form of advertising – especially for a small

Accounting and Finance 2A   ISBN 9780170182041   Cengage Learning Australia

business – is word of mouth. Not only will satisfied customers purchase goods or services from the firm in future, but they will spread the word among their friends and associates, which will encourage them also to give the firm their custom.

The reverse will be the case with customers who feel they have been unfairly treated: not only will they not be back, but they may discourage others.

The same is true to a lesser extent with regular suppliers and others with whom the firm deals, such as government agencies. A reputation for honesty and doing the right thing may prove invaluable when favours are called for and sympathetic treatment is needed. For example, if there is a temporary shortage of some supplies, all other things being equal, the supplier will be inclined to favour those who have in the past 'done the right thing' by keeping the supplier informed of changes in demand, paying their bills on time and so on.

Example 5.3

EXAMPLE:

Jane Farmer lives on a cattle station in the Kimberleys. She visits Perth every few months to do some shopping and visit the dentist or doctor. On one of her visits she bought an electric food mixer. This came with a 12-month warranty. Eleven months after she bought it, it stopped working. On her next visit to Perth a couple of months later, she took it along to the supplier, Fizzbang Electrical, to get a replacement under warranty. It was pointed out to her that in fact the warranty period had expired a month before so that technically she had no claim. However, when she explained the situation to the store manager, he authorised a replacement to be given to her.

Commentary

The store had no legal obligation to meet Jane's claim. However, the spirit of the warranty (that the machine should be replaced if it did not keep working for at least 12 months) would be complied with by meeting her claim, even though, by the letter of the law, the warranty had expired. The benefit for the firm, apart from the satisfaction of doing 'the right thing', is that Jane will feel well disposed towards them and will be inclined to give the firm her business in the future and encourage others to do the same. This will tend to override her dissatisfaction at the quality of a product which broke less than 12 months after purchase!

The firm and its employees

In addition to customers, the other group of people vital to a firm's success are its employees. Very small firms may employ very few people and in most small businesses the owners comprise a significant portion of the workforce. However, even a firm with just a handful of employees can benefit from treating them fairly and, indeed, the influence of a particular employee's level of satisfaction with his employer on a firm's success may be a lot greater in a firm with few employees than in one with a massive workforce.

Industrial legislation lays down minimum standards for employees' conditions of service, such as pay, overtime rates, leave (annual, long-service, maternity/paternity, sick) and hours of work. Many employers will provide benefits in excess of these, while others will seek ways of cutting short-term costs to a minimum, especially when they are dealing with workers who may be less well-informed and more vulnerable, such as immigrant workers on temporary working visas. If it is acting ethically, a firm will not seek to exploit such vulnerability. Owners and managers should treat workers exactly as they would wish to be treated in a similar situation. The other practices firms ought to employ, where possible, is to keep employees informed about the firm's progress and future prospects. Its capacity to do this may be limited in some cases by the need for commercial confidentiality, but this is probably less important than is often stated.

Again, apart from the nice warm feeling imparted by having done the right thing, treating employees fairly and honestly can have direct economic benefits. Employees who

Accounting and Finance: 2A   ISBN 9780170182041   Cengage Learning Australia

feel valued will be better disposed towards their employer and motivated to strive for the success of the enterprise. Dissatisfied workers will be inclined to do the bare minimum and make no extra efforts on behalf of the firm.

Example 5.4

EXAMPLE:

Felicity's Furniture is a small manufacturing business making quality wooden furniture in its factory in Malaga, a suburb of Perth. The firm has been operating for nearly 20 years and some of the workforce of around 25 people have been with the firm most or all of that time. The firm has been very successful in the past, but the economic downturn has hit its markets severely and the Income statement for the last three months showed a loss.

Felicity is confident that her business will be able to bounce back in time, but in the short to medium term the firm is going to have to cut back on production and reduce costs to survive. After preliminary discussions with her three managers, Felicity calls a meeting of all employees. At this meeting employees are:

a   told of the firm's current financial position and the cut-backs that are needed

b   asked whether they will agree to a 10 per cent salary reduction. (The senior managers have already accepted this and Felicity has undertaken to reduce her drawings by 10 per cent.) The previous wage levels will be restored as soon as the firm's profitability allows it

c   encouraged to take any outstanding annual or long-service leave

d   told that people who resign or retire in the normal course of events over coming months will only be replaced if their job is absolutely essential

e   told that if they wish to take leave without pay they may do so, with a guarantee that their job will be kept open for them when they return

f   asked for any comments or suggestions they may have to help deal with the firm's problems.

Commentary

While Felicity's employees will no doubt be unhappy with the sacrifices they are being asked to make, the chances are that most of them will be willing to accept them for the greater good of all. They are likely to identify with the business and to feel that those who run the business care about them. They will feel good that they have been kept informed and given a chance to have their say. Most of them will probably share Felicity's optimism about the firm's long-term future and be prepared to stick with it.

From Felicity's point of view, she will know that she has a loyal and dedicated workforce on whom she can rely in the tough times that lie ahead and also that, when the economic recovery does occur, she will be able to take swift advantage of it, having a trained and motivated labour force who can immediately pick up the slack.

The firm and its owners

In the case of most small businesses – however they are structured – the owners are personally closely involved in the day-to-day running of the firm. There will be times, though, when one or more of the owners is not so involved and those who are managing the business will need to remember their responsibilities towards these 'remote owners'. Like investors in a public company, they are entitled to be informed about the profitability and viability of the business and to be consulted when decisions are going to be made that will affect their investment.

Example 5.5

EXAMPLE:

Jane and Bob run a firm selling tyres, alloy wheels and other motor accessories under the trading name Tyres of Strength. Their business was originally set up as a small proprietary company with Jane and Bob as the two equal shareholders. Needing more capital, however, they approached their rich Auntie Lucretia for a loan. She was happy to invest but would only do so as a shareholder, which they agreed to. She now owns 20 per cent of the shares in the company; the remainder is divided equally between Jane and Bob. Jane and Bob work in the firm and pay themselves generous salaries. They see profit reports printed out every month from the firm's computerised accounting system and they make all the decisions about future directions of the company. Lucretia is not included in the decision-making process and the only reports she gets to see are the summarised statements produced for the taxation department at the end of the year. She gets her proportion of the dividends (shares of the profit distributed to the shareholders). Jane and Bob can ensure that they do not really miss out on much profit by increasing the level of their salary payments.

Commentary

Although nothing that they have done is actually illegal, there is little doubt that Jane and Bob have acted unfairly as far as Auntie Lucretia is concerned. While it could be argued that, since they are the majority owners of the business, their will is always going to prevail in the end and also that Lucretia only has herself to blame for getting into this situation, it would seem fair to keep her informed and consult her whenever possible on major decisions. By manipulating the profit through their salary payments and so depriving Lucretia of her fair share, most people would say they are acting unethically.

The idea of keeping part-owners informed can be extended to the need to be honest with potential investors when an owner may be seeking to sell their business. They are entitled to be given complete and truthful information and if they are not, then the vendor is acting unethically and perhaps even fraudulently.

EXAMPLE:

Example 5.6

Mario and Maria own a coffee shop, which they are proposing to sell. They have a buyer, Omar, and Mario has put together some extremely optimistic financial projections to increase the price Omar is prepared to pay. However, Omar (who was obviously not born yesterday) wants to work in the shop for a couple of weeks to see if Mario's projections for the business are realistic. Mario and Maria have agreed to this proposal. They have a large number of friends and relatives living in the area and they strongly encourage them to visit the coffee shop during the two weeks to boost the takings. Omar is duly impressed and the deal is closed.

Commentary

Mario and Maria have evidently manipulated the performance of their business in order to obtain from Omar a higher price than he would otherwise have paid. They have acted dishonestly and unethically and if Omar were to discover the truth he would certainly be entitled to repudiate the deal.

 Key Concept 5.1

Ethical behaviour

Ethical behaviour is where a firm behaves towards its employees, customers and other business associates in accordance with a moral code of conduct in which it acts fairly, honestly and with integrity at all times.

RESOURCE CONSERVATION AND THE ENVIRONMENT

The environment is quite a loose term that may include the built and natural surroundings in the immediate vicinity of the firm, the region or state in which it operates or even the world as a whole. It may also be taken to describe the structure of the society where the firm operates, the market in which it competes or the industry of which it is a part. In this section we will confine ourselves to consideration of the firm's interaction with the built or natural environment.

Firms impact on their environment in two ways, through their:
1 inputs – the resources they consume to produce the goods or services they sell
2 outputs – the goods and services produced, including packaging and transport, and the by-products of the production process in terms of noise, air or water pollution, etc.

Accounting and Finance: 2A   ISBN 9780170182041   Cengage Learning Australia

In addition, most businesses have an indirect effect on their environment. For example, any Australian business that requires customers to visit their premises to buy their product will generate road traffic, with the accompanying air and noise pollution and will require paved areas for parking. The presence of a club or licensed tavern in a street may lead to gatherings of rowdy drunks late at night who cause a nuisance to passers-by and local residents. Many of these indirect effects are the subject of regulation by various levels of government. For example, shire or city councils generally do not permit businesses to be operated in residential areas because of their likely effect on the lives of other residents and licensed premises are required to meet strict conditions in consideration for being granted their license, many of which are designed to minimise the indirect effects of the business on its environment.

Example 5.7

EXAMPLE:

Dawn has been running her dance school in the local hall. However, she would like to use a large shed on her property in a Perth hills suburb instead. This will save her quite a bit of money as well as being a lot more convenient for her. The school runs for a couple of hours four evenings a week with two different classes, each with 15–20 children in it.

Dawn has spoken to all her neighbours who say they have no objection, but she has been told that she will need to get the permission of her local council. What do you think they are likely to say?

Commentary

Local authorities do not, as a rule, permit businesses to operate in areas that are zoned under the regulations for residential use, though they can make exceptions (e.g. an architect or an IT consultant who does most of their work on the net who wish to work from home). They may consider that Dawn's proposed business will have an unacceptable impact on the surrounding residents – there will inevitably be significant music noise for a couple of hours each evening that the school operates and there will also be a large increase in traffic resulting from 15–20 parents dropping off and picking up their children for two sessions each night.

Although Dawn has apparently got the agreement of her immediate neighbours, some of them may be unhappy about the proposal but do not want to say so to her face. Others may become unhappy once they see the amount of disruption it entails. Furthermore people who buy a neighbouring house in the future may not be prepared to put up with the inconvenience of living next door to a dance school.

The impact of Dawn's business on its environment may be relatively slight, but it will probably be enough in this particular situation to prevent her from getting permission to establish it there. Back to the local hall, Dawn!

It is in the management of their direct inputs and outputs that businesses can have a greater effect on resource conservation and the environment.

Managing inputs

Apart from materials built into the inventory purchased, firms buy a large number of goods and services that have resource usage and environmental implications. These include electricity, fuel, water and raw materials.

Electricity

The means of electricity generation generally used in Western Australia are major contributors to air pollution and, specifically, carbon emissions, as well as using up non-renewable resources (oil, gas and coal). Anything that the firm can do to reduce its demand for publicly-provided power will therefore be of benefit to the community at large. Individuals may be able to obtain their power from alternative sources, such as wind generators and solar panels, though most businesses will not be able to do this. If alternative sources are available, businesses will usually expect them to be economically competitive, which is often problematic. What all businesses can do is make a conscious effort to avoid waste – use long-life low-wattage lighting, use air-conditioning and heating only when necessary and ensure that lights and appliances are not left on unnecessarily. Apart from the benefits for the environment, this will result in lower costs to the business.

Fuel

Particularly important for transport businesses and firms having a large fleet of motor vehicles, the opportunities for reduced fuel usage are numerous. These would include avoidance of wastage (including reduction of unnecessary journeys and regular maintenance of vehicles to ensure maximum fuel efficiency), conversion of vehicles to cheaper and/or less-polluting fuels (such as LPG) and, once the technology makes them economic, use of alternative types of engines (e.g. hybrid cars or hydrogen powered units).

Water

For most firms, especially small retailers, the use of our most precious resource, water, is not very significant. Firms that do use a lot of water, however – either as part of a manufacturing process or to maintain extensive landscaping around business premises – should do what they can to limit water usage by such things as recycling water where possible, ensuring irrigation programmes are capable of modification when it rains and using native flora in landscaping that has a lower demand for water. The benefits of all these measures will include lower costs for the business.

Raw materials for manufacture

Manufacturing firms may use a variety of unprocessed or semi-processed materials in the production of their products. It has always been in a firm's best interest economically to make best use of these inputs and avoid wastage. Growing consciousness of the need for resource conservation has added a new urgency to this requirement.

Example 5.8

EXAMPLE:

Walt's Woodworks owns and operates a small sawmill in the south-west of Western Australia. It buys logs from local plantations and converts them into sawn timber of various types and sizes, which it sells to hardware stores and retail timber merchants. It also sells a small amount of sawn timber direct to customers who come to the mill. It has two trucks to deliver its product to customers in the region. The machines in the mill, some of which are extremely noisy, are driven by electricity. The waste products of the process – sawdust and the odd bits of timber known as 'mill ends' – are stored in the yard. Some of the timber is treated against termites by being soaked in a very strong and poisonous chemical. Although the mill is a few kilometres from the nearest town, there have been several houses built nearby over the past few years.

Walt is very concerned about resource conservation and the impact his business may be having on the environment. Among the measures he has taken are:

- Sound-proof cladding has been installed on the walls of the buildings housing the noisier machines. These are never used at weekends.
- Trees have been planted around the property to screen the buildings and reduce visual pollution, as well as to help deaden the machinery noise.
- Both trucks are regularly maintained and have been converted to run on LPG.
- Sawdust and mill ends are bagged and distributed to garden centres for sale to the public.
- The storage tanks for the anti-termite chemical and the tanks in which the treated timber is soaked are located in a separate shed with concrete floors and a protective drainage system so that any spills will not find their way into the soil and the groundwater.

Accounting and Finance 2A   ISBN 9780170182041   Cengage Learning Australia

Commentary

Walt has evidently recognised that a business of this sort can have a significant impact on its environment and has taken some sensible measures to minimise this.

Managing outputs

Perhaps the most obvious way in which retail firms can manage their outputs relates to the packaging of their products. There is no doubt that, in our society, a huge amount of resources is devoted to packaging: the boxes, cartons, moulded plastic and other containers in which products are sold. Often these are part of the process of promotion of the product, making it eye-catching and attractive to potential buyers. Apart from the usage (some would say waste) of resources in packaging, much of the packaging material is difficult to recycle and therefore inevitably adds to the pollution load through having to be disposed of in landfill sites.

The influence of a small retailer on the packaging of the products it sells may be quite small and its need to provide customers with what they demand usually takes precedence. However, there is evidence that customers are becoming increasingly aware of the drawbacks of excessive packaging and some retailers are discovering there is a market for products with less packaging. A recent development has been the move away from disposable plastic shopping bags. Many businesses give customers bags with the firm's name on them as a form of advertising. These are usually strong enough to be reused. Thin plastic carry bags are not so readily reusable and are also difficult to recycle. They can lead to significant pollution, especially in rivers and the ocean where they can pose a threat to wildlife. Many businesses seek to minimise the use of such bags by encouraging the use of reusable cloth bags (which can be purchased quite cheaply) or by imposing a penalty on the use of plastic bags. Some businesses are dispensing with the use of plastic bags altogether.

Other ways that a firm can manage its outputs will depend on the nature of its business. A transport business should ensure that its vehicles are fuel efficient, well-maintained and not overloaded; a firm producing or selling potentially hazardous chemicals should ensure that they are properly packaged, stored and transported and appropriate safety measures are taken; bars and hotels should attempt to encourage responsible consumption of alcohol. Many of these measures are covered to some extent by legislation, but compliance with this is often difficult to enforce and there is always room for firms that wish to act ethically to ensure that the spirit, as well as the letter, of the regulations are observed.

REALITY CHECK 5.1

Businesses and sustainability

Many large businesses have specific policies or strategies in relation to their usage of resources and the impact of their operations on the natural environment. Some business examples and their URLs are given below.

Woolworths is a company that owns a large number of stores throughout Australia selling groceries and general household products.

http://crreport08.woolworthslimited.com.au/environment.php
www.packagingcovenant.org.au/documents/File/AP_Woolworths_07_10.pdf

Marks & Spencer is a British company that has stores all over the UK selling mainly groceries and clothing.

http://corporate.marksandspencer.com/howwedobusiness/our_policies/sustainable_raw_materials/

Walmart is an American organisation with a large chain of stores in the USA and some other countries.

http://walmartstores.com/Sustainability/

While sustainability policies will vary from one business to another, there are likely to be common themes in the following areas.

Reducing greenhouse gases:
- purchasing power supplies from renewable energy sources
- economies in electricity use – energy-saving lighting, reducing power wastage
- use of hybrid vehicles
- working towards being 'carbon neutral' (i.e. funding the planting of trees to offset carbon production as a result of the firm's operations).

Recycling:
- use of recycled materials in products and packaging
- reusing packaging and other materials.

Encouraging environmentally sensitive production:
- purchasing products or raw materials from energy-efficient and environmentally conservative sources
- not promoting products that encourage wastage of resources.

Reducing production of damaging waste products:
- reducing amount of disposable packaging
- phasing out use of disposable plastic bags.

Economies in water usage:
- minimising water usage and eliminating waste
- recycling water where possible
- installing rainwater collection tanks.

Commentary

Although the businesses mentioned above are huge organisations, very different to the sort of small business we are dealing with in this book, the challenges they face in relation to their use of resources and impact on the environment are not essentially different. Some of their responses to these challenges may also be applicable to a smaller business.

THE FIRM AND THE COMMUNITY

These days most stores don't identify as closely with their local community as used to be the case. However, outside big city centres, and especially in country towns, it is still often the case that businesses, particularly retail stores, can play an important role in the life of the community. There are several ways that a firm can be involved with the community in which it operates: as an employer, a sponsor of local activities and a donor to charity.

As an employer

It is likely (in a country town, inevitable) that firms employ people who live nearby. This can provide a strong link between a firm and its local community and in this situation it is even more important that the firm treats its employees ethically. The firm may also be able to provide traineeships or apprenticeships to local young people, as well as work experience for school students and assistance with school projects. The cost of such assistance is usually not great and is probably more than outweighed by the goodwill (and hence future custom) generated.

Accounting and Finance: 2A   ISBN 9780170182041   Cengage Learning Australia

As a sponsor of local activities

Many firms donate cash or products to support sporting or cultural groups within the community where they operate. This sort of expenditure can be justified economically as a form of advertising – the firm's name on the team's guernsey, a mention in the concert programme or a free promotion in the tour booklet. While it is unlikely that this sort of advertising will generate sufficient extra sales directly to cover its cost, it is thought that the long-term benefit in terms of goodwill and therefore customer loyalty justifies it.

As a donor to charity

A firm may contribute to local charities (such as a bushfire appeal or a fund to raise money for the family of a local policeman killed on duty). In truth such donations are really being made by the business's owner since the donation will simply reduce the profits of the business going to the owner. However, putting donations to charity through the business rather than the owner making a personal donation will have the benefit of placing the business as a whole in a good light in the eyes of the community. There is also a possibility that donations that might not otherwise be tax deductible could be regarded as a promotional expense when made by the business (rather than the owner personally), which would have a tax benefit for the owner.

Example 5.9

EXAMPLE:

Sukie's Superstore is a grocery and general store in the small country town of Mukinuppin. Sukie and her husband provide most of the labour, but they have one permanent employee, a long-time resident of the town, and also employ several local high-school students as casual workers on Thursday evenings (for late-night shopping) and weekends.

The firm sponsors the town girls' netball team (the Mukinuppin Marauders) and also donates a prize for citizenship at the District High School. They are always happy to have collection boxes for local charities on the counter in the shop and sell raffle tickets to support such causes. They are happy to sell local produce in the way of fruit, vegetables and homemade preserves. They have a large pinboard just outside the shop on which people can put notices ('Free kittens', 'Lost dog', 'Music lessons available', etc.) and posters advertising coming events.

They also have a sign in the shop that says 'We will not serve school children during school hours unless they are accompanied by a parent or teacher'. This is intended to discourage truancy. They have a 'suggestions' box on the counter inviting comment from customers about the shop and its stock although, to tell the truth, such comments are usually made verbally to Sukie or her husband.

Commentary

The firm has clearly made a considerable effort to integrate with the town community and build customer loyalty. This obviously has benefits for the community, but it also has important practical advantages for the business. Small stores like this one find it difficult to compete with supermarkets and large specialty shops in Perth or bigger regional centres, which are usually able to offer greater variety at lower prices. Sukie's Superstore must aim to generate loyalty in the local community, which, together with the greater convenience, will encourage customers to do their shopping in the small store.

THE FIRM AS A TAXPAYER

Taxes are fees charged to individuals or other entities within the community, which are used by the various levels of government to fund the provision of community services. Businesses have a number of obligations in relation to tax. These include:
* payroll tax
* income tax

Accounting and Finance: 2A   ISBN 9780170182041   Cengage Learning Australia

- goods and services tax (GST)
- personal income tax payable by employees (PAYG)
- fringe benefits tax (FBT)
- local government rates.
  Firms also have obligations in relation to statutory superannuation.

Payroll tax

In Western Australia, businesses with a gross salaries or wages bill of more than $62500 per month ($750000 per annum) are required to pay a tax to the State Government, currently 5.5 per cent of the gross wages. A lot of small businesses fall below this threshold so do not need to worry about it. For those that are liable, the tax is 'self-assessable' – in other words, the taxpayer will calculate the amount owing and remit it with the requisite form to the Office of State Revenue monthly, quarterly or annually.

Income tax

Unless a business is incorporated (a company) it does not pay income tax. However, the firm's profit or loss must be included by the owners in their personal income tax return, so in any case the business must keep records of income and expenses sufficient to enable profit to be calculated. If the business is a company, it will complete a company income tax return and submit it to the Australian Taxation Office (ATO), which will issue an assessment. If it is not a company, the owners will complete their own personal tax returns on which they will be assessed by the ATO.

Goods and services tax (GST)

The basis of the GST and its accounting implications have been dealt with in some detail in Chapters 1, 2 and 3. Nearly all small businesses are required to account for GST paid on purchases (outlays) and charged on sales (collections) and to remit the difference between the two with regular returns to the ATO.

Employees' personal income tax

Firms that employ workers are required to make appropriate deductions for personal income tax from the payments they make to their employees. This tax withheld is reported to the ATO on the firm's Business Activity Statement (BAS; see Chapters 1 and 2) and paid to the ATO together with any amounts owing for GST and FBT. This system is known as *Pay As You Go* (PAYG). The firm will give each employee a statement of their pay for each period (week, fortnight or month) showing how much tax has been deducted.

AJ Worka: Summary of pay for 14 days to 3 December 2009

	$
Gross pay	2400.00
Income tax	(600.00)
Net pay	1800.00

The $600, together with the tax deducted from all the other employees, will be remitted to the ATO in due course by the employer.

Fringe benefits tax (FBT)

Fringe benefits are benefits provided by an employer to its workers other than cash payments. For example, if the employer provides a car that the employee can use for private transport, free or subsidised housing and free or discounted products (e.g. a chocolate factory allowing

Accounting and Finance: 2A   ISBN 9780170182041   Cengage Learning Australia

its workers to take a certain amount of chocolates home for free), these are called 'fringe benefits'. They used to be taxable in the hands of the employee (i.e. they were supposed to include the value of fringe benefits in their own personal income tax return) but this requirement was so widely evaded and difficult to police that legislation was brought in placing the onus of valuing and paying FBT on the employer. Any business that provides its workers with fringe benefits (not all small businesses do) must keep records of the value of benefits provided. The tax on these benefits is usually at the highest personal tax rate (currently 46.5%). Reporting of FBT to the ATO is done on the BAS.

Local government rates

Firms that rent their premises will not normally be responsible for rates on the property. However, if the business owns the building it operates out of, it will need to pay annual rates to the shire, town or city council (as well as fees for garbage removal and sewerage). These rates are determined by the council based on the size and usage of the property and the business doesn't need to keep any special records – all they need to do in relation to rates is pay the bill when it is due.

SUMMARY

In general the firm's obligations in relation to taxation are the same as those of any taxpayer. They must:
- maintain the records necessary for tax to be assessed
- disclose to the relevant authorities all the information necessary to enable a correct assessment to be made of the tax due
- pay the tax due by the prescribed date.

Failure to meet these obligations can result in significant penalties for the firm. For example, late payment of taxes can lead to punitive interest and other financial penalties. Tax evasion (illegal avoidance of taxes by concealing or misrepresenting information) can result in fines for the business and/or its owners – and even prison sentences. Al Capone, the notorious Chicago gangster, was jailed in 1931– not for extortion, robbery or murder (all of which he doubtless committed) but for tax evasion!

There is also a moral issue. If we assume that a certain amount of tax is needed for the government to provide the services that the community demands and if some people and organisations within the community pay less tax than they should, the taxation burden on the rest of the community will be greater and/or taxation rates will need to be set at a higher level than they would otherwise have been. The ethical thing to do is to pay the amount of tax that you should.

Having said this, it is an accepted principle that people are entitled to arrange their affairs in such a way, within the law, that it minimises their liability for tax. For example, a family business may be structured as a partnership so that the taxable income from the business can be split between the family members. Under a '*progressive*' tax system such as we have in Australia, where the marginal rate of tax on individual income increases as income increases, splitting the income in this way will result in less tax being paid overall.

Example 5.10

EXAMPLE:

Sky and Sarah own Masterton Electronics selling iPods, DVD players, mobile phones and a wide range of other electronic gadgetry. The business is actually owned by a trust company, which enables the profits to be allocated (before tax is deducted) to Sky and Sarah and their two children, Mindy and Nathan, thereby reducing the tax payable.

The family members quite often take items out of stock for their own use or for presents and they don't usually bother to record these in the firm's books. They show up eventually as stock losses, which have the effect of reducing taxable profit.

Masterton Electronics has a van that is used to collect stock and make deliveries. Their senior employee, the store manager, is allowed to take the van home and use it after hours and over the weekend. All the costs relating to the van are charged to the firm's expense accounts and these amount to about $6000 per year. Probably half of the annual kilometres are travelled by the store manager on private business, but he does not pay any of the costs. Sky and Sarah do not include any of the vehicle costs as a fringe benefit, arguing that they are quite trivial in the great scheme of things and that no-one is ever going to know.

Consider and comment on the extent to which the owners of this firm are meeting their taxation obligations.

Commentary

The arrangement that Sky and Sarah have made to structure their family business to minimise their liability for income tax is a sensible and legitimate exercise that they are perfectly entitled to do, both in law and in equity.

However, their practice of recording drawings of stock as an expense is incorrect from an accounting point of view and is certainly contrary to the requirements of the taxation laws. It is the sort of action that will probably never come to light, but it is dishonest and illegal.

The same can be said of their treatment of the costs of the vehicle provided to their employee. The proportion of the costs that can be attributed to private use should be identified and fringe benefits tax should be paid on it. Not to do so, even if undetected, is breaking the law.

Superannuation guarantee payments

In 1992, the Federal Government, concerned about its capacity to meet the future burden of age pensions for an increasingly elderly population, introduced the Superannuation Guarantee Scheme. Under this scheme employers are required to pay a specified percentage (currently nine per cent) of the gross earnings of every employee between the ages of 18 and 69, whether full-time, part-time or casual, who earns more than $450 in any calendar month, into an approved superannuation fund or retirement savings account. The employee has the right to nominate his or her preferred superannuation scheme if they wish. The intention is that people will be enabled to build up a fund to support them in their retirement, so that they will not be dependent on the government pension. The employer has the right to make additional payments into the employee's superannuation fund and the employee may also make additional payments into superannuation.

What the employing firm has to do in relation to the Superannuation Guarantee is:
- keep records of the amount of superannuation payment for each employee and how this was calculated
- offer all employees, within 28 days of commencing to work for the firm, a choice of superannuation fund (on a standard form, a copy of which is retained by the employer as evidence that the employee has been given this choice)
- make superannuation contributions into the specified fund(s) within 28 days of the end of each quarter.

The superannuation guarantee payment is an additional burden on the firm – effectively the labour cost is nine per cent more than the gross salaries and wages of the employees, a fact that needs to be remembered when planning to employ more staff. If the new staff member is hired on a salary of $60000 per annum, the actual cost to the firm will be $60000 + 9% = $65400.

Tax avoidance and tax evasion

Taxation is a cost to the business and its owners that will reduce the profit available to the owners. Clearly the owners will have an incentive to minimise this cost. This can be achieved legally by *tax avoidance* or illegally by *tax evasion*.

Accounting and Finance: 2A   ISBN 9780170182041   Cengage Learning Australia

Taxation avoidance is the reduction of taxation liability within the taxation laws. It may be possible, for example, to structure a business in such a way as to reduce the tax payable or to make the most of allowable tax deductions. It is important in these situations to ensure that full disclosure of relevant information is made to the relevant taxation authority.

Taxation evasion is the deliberate attempt by a business or individual to evade paying tax by illegal methods. This usually involves the business or person concealing or falsifying the details that are forwarded to the relevant taxation authority. This may involve deliberately understating income or overstating expenses or deductions. Tax evasion is a crime and can result in fines or imprisonment. As taxation law is often very complicated, it is highly recommended that a business seeks the advice of an expert in the field, such as a taxation accountant or financial advisor, to ensure that taxation laws are being complied with.

Test your knowledge

1   Define ethics.

2   List the groups with which a firm may interact in the course of business.

3   Give an example of *ethical* and *unethical* behaviour in relation to each of the groups identified in question 2.

4   Explain, with examples, why ethical behaviour may be in a firm's best economic interests.

5   Outline the ways in which a firm may harm the environment and, in each case, explain how that harm may be minimised.

6   What can a firm do to promote resource conservation?

7   In what ways can a firm become involved with the community in which it operates? What is the benefit to the business of such involvement?

8   Outline a firm's responsibilities in respect of the collection of taxes on behalf of the ATO.

9   Outline a firm's responsibilities in relation to income tax payable on its own profits.

10 Outline a firm's responsibilities in relation to statutory superannuation.

Test your understanding

Topic guide
- Ethical dealing with lenders, customers, employees: 5.1–5.3
- Resource conservation and environmental concerns: 5.4–5.8
- Community involvement: 5.9–5.10
- Taxation responsibilities: 5.11–5.12

5.1   As part of his application for a business loan from the bank, the owner of Hotspot Night Club, Ivan Ripov, had to fill in a form giving details of his past financial dealings. One of the questions he had to answer was 'Have you ever been declared bankrupt?' to which he wrote 'No'. In fact, about ten years earlier, a company of which he was part owner and director went bust and was wound up (formally terminated) as insolvent (unable to pay its debts). Do you think that the bank would consider this information relevant? Why? Comment on Ivan's actions. What do you think he should have done?

5.2   Mary Canary runs a store, Cheep & Cheerful, selling cut-price goods of all sorts. One of her lines is a toy dump truck, made overseas, which sells for $10. Mary knows, because she gave one to her own nephew as a present, that the toy is of poor quality – the wheels fall off after a very short period of use and the dump mechanism does not work properly. However, she argues that people do not expect to get quality goods if they shop at that sort of store, so she continues to stock the item, which is very popular. What do you think of Mary's attitude from both an ethical and an economic standpoint? What do you think she ought to have done?

5.3 Bert Berger, owner of a fast food establishment called Bert's Burgers, employs young people to work in his restaurant. Under the terms of the industrial award that sets minimum working conditions for his industry, workers are considered to be adults when they turn 18 and are then entitled to a much higher rate of pay. Consequently, Bert only employs people aged 15 to 17 and when any of his workers turns 18 years of age they are sacked. Do you think Bert is entitled to do this? Is it fair on the workers concerned, given that everyone who works for him knows about the practice? What do you think he should do?

5.4 M Pressario is proposing to run a rock concert in the grounds of a vineyard he owns in the Swan Valley. You are the official working for the local government authority who has to approve his application for a permit for the event. List and explain the conditions you might place on the grant of such a permit.

5.5 Beans & Leaves is a business importing foodstuffs from overseas (mainly coffee and tea), which they repackage for the local market. Nearly all of these products come from developing countries in Africa or South America. Some come with a 'fair trade' warranty (i.e. a guarantee by the supplier that the growers of the product received a fair price for their crop). Some do not carry any such guarantee. These tend to be quite a bit cheaper.
a   What are the ethical arguments in favour of purchasing the 'free trade' products?
b   What can the firm do to act in an ethical manner but still maximise its profits?

5.6 You are the owner of a small intensive piggery sited in a country shire close to the Perth metropolitan area. The waste from the piggery is flushed out down concrete channels to a series of effluent ponds in which it settles and digests before being recycled as irrigation water. There is a creek in the valley below the farm which is used by other farms downstream for stock watering and irrigation. During a severe rainstorm recently, the large amount of rainwater flooding into the first effluent pond caused a breach in its wall, which led to the release of several thousand litres of untreated effluent into the stream.
a   What are the likely effects of this accident?
b   What do you think you should do about it, now and in the future?

5.7 The proprietor of Deb's Deli has decided to do her bit for the environment by banning plastic shopping bags in her shop. Customers who want bags can either bring their own, use old cardboard boxes that the deli has available (from stock purchased) or buy a cloth bag, which the shop sells at the very affordable price of $1 each.
a   What might be the environmental benefits of what Deb is proposing?
b   Is it likely to have an effect (positive or negative) on the shop's business?

Deb has read in the newspaper that the energy usage in producing each of the cloth bags is about ten times that required to make a plastic bag.
c   In light of this do you think Deb should go ahead with her proposal? Explain your answer.

5.8 Re-read the sustainability policy features in Reality Check 5.1. Your shop is a small neighbourhood hardware store. Draw up a statement of sustainability policies that you think would be suitable for a business like yours.

5.9 You are opening a music shop in a shopping mall in one of Perth's outer suburbs. You will be working in the shop yourself but are going to need to hire other workers on a full- or

Accounting and Finance: 2A   ISBN 9780170182041   Cengage Learning Australia

part-time basis. In terms of employment opportunities *only*, what could you do to identify your business with the local community and what might be the benefits for your business of doing so?

5.10 Do you think small businesses have an obligation to support charities and local community organisations? Do you think that there can be commercial advantages in them doing so?

5.11 Mandy's Manic Music sells music CDs, DVDs and other forms of recorded music from a shop in a large mall. The business employs a number of workers, both full-time and casual. The store manager gets, as part of her salary package, the use of a car, the expenses of which are borne by the firm. The business is not incorporated. (Mandy runs it as a sole trader.)

State and briefly explain the firm's obligations in relation to income tax, GST and FBT. What records does it need to keep, and to whom and when must reports be submitted?

5.12 Jack Hammer owns and runs a landscaping firm. Most of his clients are large companies or local government authorities and all transactions with them are properly invoiced and recorded in the firm's accounts. However, the firm also often does small jobs for individuals and Jack usually just pockets the cash payments without issuing invoices or receipts. This way he is able to offer his clients a better price.

a What effect will his treatment of these private jobs have on the firm's and Jack's personal tax liability (income tax and GST)?

b Comment on the legality of Jack's actions.

c Is Jack's behaviour ethical? Explain your answer.

Investigation

(These tasks could be done as an individual or group project.)

www.ato.gov.au

1 Visit the website of the Australian Taxation Office and go to its business web page. Locate the information it provides on compliance issues and, in particular, tax planning and schemes and tax evasion and crime. Using this information choose one aspect to clearly explain, using real-world examples, the difference between tax evasion and avoidance. Give some indication of the penalties involved and any other ethical issues that you believe should also be considered.

2 Visit the website of the state government organisations that have responsibility for assisting small business (e.g. the WA Small Business Development Corporation and NSW Department of State and Regional Development) and locate information they provide on business sustainability.

Select a business at your local shopping centre and, using this information on business sustainability, prepare a list of ten actions that you think the business could implement to become more environmentally conservative.

Essay

1 What ethical considerations may govern a firm's dealings with its employees, customers and others with whom it has business dealings? What are the benefits of acting ethically? What are the likely consequences of unethical behaviour? Illustrate your arguments with specific examples.

2 'A business has a duty to the community in general to be conscientious and honest in its collection of taxes on behalf of the government.' Discuss this statement with reference to the specific taxes that a business is required to collect and/or pay.

Ethics case study

Mel Hardball is a long-time business owner who has built up a reputation as a tough and uncompromising entrepreneur. His approach to business can be summarised in the saying 'nice guys finish last'. In his dealings with employees, customers, suppliers and everyone else, he does the minimum required to comply with the law. The same is true of his dealing with the taxation department; he employs a tax adviser to help him minimise his taxation burden. In fact, he is not above a bit of tax evasion if he feels reasonably certain that he can get away with it.

Mel often receives requests for assistance or sponsorship from clubs and schools in his area, but he always knocks these back unless the proposal contains some obvious and immediate advantage for his business.

Comment on Mel's approach to business from an ethical standpoint. Are there any economic disadvantages resulting from the way he does business? Explain your answer.

Accounting and Finance: 2A   ISBN 9780170182041   Cengage Learning Australia

Chapter 6

E-COMMERCE

What You Will Learn

After studying this chapter you should be able to:

1 Explain the nature of electronic processing in small businesses
2 Outline the benefits of electronic processing for small businesses
3 Discuss the risks of electronic processing for small business
4 Explain what is meant by EFTPOS
5 Explain how small businesses use electronic payment systems
6 Explain how small businesses use online banking
7 Explain how small businesses use direct debit

Introduction

Businesses' primary objective is to increase their owners' investment (total equity) by using their assets as efficiently as possible to make profits. Management will use any method that helps to increase profit by increasing income and decreasing expenses. Even not-for-profit business still need to operate at maximum efficiency to achieve their goals.

All business entities need adequate liquidity for financial survival so they will try and improve their cashflow. To do this they aim to increase and speed up cash inflow while restricting cash outflow. The managers must evaluate each system they use to ensure that the benefits are greater than the costs involved in operating that system.

The term *e-commerce* is not specific; it usually relates to the electronic trading activities of goods and services by business. This includes electronic payment for goods and services.

The term *e-business* is somewhat wider, usually referring to all forms of electronic data transmission relating to business activities.

E-COMMERCE

E-commerce can be transacted between any two entities. It can be entirely electronic, such as direct debit banking transfers for payment of amounts owing, but much e-commerce still requires physical activities. For example, purchasing may be done online, but the goods purchased must be physically delivered.

The various forms of e-commerce involve accounting transactions using computers and other forms of electronic data transmission. Previously all internet connections had to be made by connecting hard-wired landlines, but with the availability of wireless technology and smart phones, many types of e-commerce can now be transacted from anywhere.

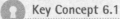

Key Concept 6.1

E-commerce

E-commerce (short for electronic commerce) refers to business activities that are transacted through electronic devices, such as computers, internet and other data transmission systems.

Benefits of e-commerce

The benefits of e-commerce are:
- increased sales by making buying easier and more convenient for customers
- increased cash inflow as transactions can be completed and funds received immediately
- greater efficiency as electronic transactions are faster with less risk of human error
- reduction in operating costs by needing less staff for processing and recording transactions
- greater safety for the business and customers by having less cash on the premises
- greater verifiability because transactions are documented by the electronic processing system
- financial safety through being able to identify and communicate to staff information about good customers (such as regular purchasers, large buyers or those with special relationships to the business) and bad customers (such as poor payers or those who are insolvent)
- capacity to trade with customers any time from anywhere in the world.

Risks of e-commerce

Risks of using e-commerce include:
- periodic loss of sales due to failure of the e-commerce systems resulting from hardware or software problems or power failures
- loss of profit due to fraudulent transactions caused by hackers or users of stolen cards
- loss of goodwill if a customer's confidential information is not kept secure and is obtained by people outside the business
- loss of future sales if commercially confidential information is obtained by competitors.

Many of these risks are common to all forms of e-business; they are outlined in more detail in the following section.

Accounting and Finance: 2B   ISBN 9780170182041   Cengage Learning Australia

E-BUSINESS

These days almost every business uses electronic devices in some form, at some stage of their business activities – not just for accounting purposes. This usage may include:

- using computers to assist with production of their goods or services
- using computers to record and monitor inventory transactions and balances
- using computers to assist with sales of goods or services
- using the web as a source of information or research
- using a website as a form of advertising or for information on products or services
- selling product or services on the internet
- communicating with customers via email
- sending invoices or statements via email
- receiving customer payments electronically
- conducting online banking via the internet.

 Key Concept 6.2

E-business

E-business is a term that refers to a wider range of applications than e-commerce. It refers to business activities that use electronic devices to conduct any part of business operations. This may or may not involve the internet. These terms are not standard and as electronic applications increase and change, the definition will change also.

Benefits of e-business

The benefits of e-business include:

- increased business efficiency by use of electronic processing
- capacity to transact business at any time or any day of the week; this is especially valuable if business is conducted with parties in a different time zone (interstate or overseas)
- capacity to transact business that is convenient to the customers (especially outside normal business operating hours)
- reduced expenses for businesses as they can locate in lower rental cost areas (such as industrial areas) if they do not need large retail premises in high rental areas

Risks of e-business

Risks of using e-business include the following:

- Power failure at the trader's business premises will disrupt business operations. Many business premises are totally dependent on an external power supply. If this is disrupted for any reason, the business operations may be impacted in several ways. The physical building environment may be affected (lights, air-conditioning, lifts, escalators, automatic doors, products kept in refrigerated or heated storage areas, alarms and security). The trading system may be affected (computer networks, cash registers, weighing and measuring devices, barcode readers, inventory reporting systems and the accounting system). Some businesses have limited backup electrical supply to maintain minimum essential services for operations. Systems also need to be in place that allow for manual operations until power can be restored.
- Internal electronic failure of operating systems due to hardware problems (such as computer faults or internal network breakdown) or software problems (due to operating or application software breakdown), network management problems, lack of adequate data backups, lack of qualified staff and delays in fixing these types of problems. Businesses may be able to reduce staff numbers by installing electronic systems but they will need to ensure that they have staff who are adequately experienced and trained to operate the systems efficiently.

- There may be corruption of data or loss of commercially sensitive data due to fraudulent actions by unauthorised people. They may obtain this information a number of ways, including fake websites, phishing emails (pretending to be from the business but with the intent of gathering customers' personal data) and unauthorised access to the business's computer systems.
- Websites need to be constantly monitored and updated to ensure all details are relevant and up to date. If not, they can quickly become counter-productive.

EFTPOS

Electronic funds transfer at point of sale (EFTPOS) is a system where businesses, particularly shops, can make sales and receive cash immediately for goods or services sold without the customer having to use actual cash. The shop arranges with their bank to be linked electronically so that the customer can pay by presenting an approved card at the point-

of-sale terminal. These may be debit, credit or bank access cards. Certain identification and other data are stored in an electronic format on the card. Usually the card is scanned by a special machine, which reads the oncard data and the customer provides additional information, usually a personal identification number (PIN). Details on the card and the PIN are checked electronically to ensure it is valid and then this data and the transaction value are transmitted to the bank. The value of the sale is transferred electronically to the business's bank account and deducted from the customer's bank account.

Many merchants have arrangement with banks to allow customers to withdraw actual cash ('cash out') at the same time as a sale is transacted. By providing this extra service they may increase sales by encouraging more customers into the business.

Benefits of using EFTPOS: trader

Benefits of using EFTPOS for the trader or merchant include:
- potential increase in sales as customers who are not carrying sufficient cash can still make purchases
- improved cash inflow by receiving cash immediately from the sale rather than having to set up an accounts receivable ledger account
- reduction in costs as there is no need to set up and operate an accounts receivable ledger system
- reduction in costs by not having to prepare and post end-of-month debtors' statements
- elimination of bad debts, as transactions are immediately refused if the customer does not have sufficient funds in their account
- additional service offered to customers – a (limited) cash withdrawal facility
- increase in safety for the business and the staff as less cash is held on the business premises – less cash from cash sales and also because some cash collected from cash sales is paid out to EFTPOS customers as cash withdrawals
- reduction in cash holdings leads to decreased insurance premiums.

Benefits of EFTPOS: customer

Benefits of using EFTPOS for the customer include:
- capacity to buy goods or services without having to carry large amounts of cash
- ability to make purchases without having to visit a bank or ATM (a record of the total amount of the transaction appears on the customer's bank or access card statement)

Accounting and Finance: 2B   ISBN 9780170182041   Cengage Learning Australia

- can withdraw cash at the point of sale terminal (POS), saving time and trouble of visiting a bank; cash withdrawals in-store are also safer than at ATMs
- cash withdrawal via EFTPOS in-store can be available outside the more restrictive normal banking hours (although ATM withdrawals can be made at any time).

Disadvantages of EFTPOS: trader

Disadvantages of using EFTPOS for the trader include:
- initial establishment cost of setting up the system with the trader's own bank (includes equipment, data telephone lines, compatible sales/EFTPOS software)
- ongoing service charges (which may be based on the number or value of transactions, with a minimum monthly charge); this needs to be evaluated against gains in having no bad debts and the cost of operating own accounts receivable system
- potential for fraudulent use of cards (by customers using stolen cards or cards on which security details have been electronically altered); liability for losses may be shared by both the store and the access card provider
- any system that uses the internet is at risk from interference by hackers its (operation and information)
- loss of function during to power outages or computer system failure; businesses need to have back-up power and manual trading systems so that trading can continue in event of computer or power failure.

Disadvantages of EFTPOS: customer

Disadvantages of using EFTPOS for the customer include:
- potential for misuse of financial or personal details leading to fraudulent use
- potential for overspending beyond financially safe limits leading to financial hardship – even bankruptcy
- need to check bank accounts regularly to ensure no fraudulent transactions.

BILL PAYMENTS – ELECTRONIC PAYMENT SYSTEMS

Agencies such as post offices, pharmacies and banks can accept payment from customers on behalf of another business (a third party). The customer makes the payment at the approved agency, which then transmits the amount paid (less a commission fee) to the business that provided the goods or service. The customer may pay by cash, cheque or credit card.

Benefits of using an electronic payments system for the trader or merchant include increased cashflow as customers have the capacity to make payments offsite and maybe outside the business's normal trading hours.

Benefits for the customer of using electronic payments systems include:
- the possible capacity to make payments outside the business's normal trading hours
- no need to physically attend the business premises or incur costs of writing and posting a cheque
- certainty of payment (compared to posted cheques) as a receipt is issued by the agency at the time of payment.

Disadvantages of using electronic payments systems for the trader or merchant include:
- increased expenses as the agencies charge a commission on funds collected
- necessity of regular reconciliation of electronic receipts through the agency.

SALE OF PRODUCTS USING THE INTERNET

Many businesses have set up websites or online stores so customers can view and purchase goods from their catalogue of products or services for sale. The customer pays for goods online using a credit card, direct transfer of funds from their bank or another payment system (such as PayPal).

If the transaction involves goods, the physical delivery of the goods can then be made by courier or post on the next available working day. The business website can include detailed information of products and services using text, graphics, sound and movies.

EXAMPLE:

www.amazon.com

Example 6.1

Products sold via the internet include books from online bookstores. A large online store is Amazon, which offers a wide range of books (both new and second-hand) as well as a number of other products. This type of business can be located anywhere, as no physical shop is needed for customer access. Retail shops are usually located in retail areas, which charge higher rental costs. Storage can be centralised, with savings in staff and other overhead costs. If the transaction involves purchase of services, access to the service can begin immediately.

https://invest.etrade.com.au

Example 6.2

Services sold via the internet include online share trading. An example of a business operating in this field is E*Trade Australia, a firm set up by the ANZ Bank. Many banks have a similar sort of business. Once the online account is established and the payment authorised, the customer can begin using the service. As the business does not need a physical area to display and sell their services, the operation can be centralised and operated with minimal staff, significantly reducing overheads.

Firms that do not necessarily carry out their transactions on the net may nonetheless use it as a medium for their sales message. A good example of this is the real estate industry. Houses for rent and sale can be viewed online by potential buyers or tenants, who can take a 'virtual' tour of the property to see whether it suits them, read a summary of important information (number of bedrooms and bathrooms, size of block, parking available, etc.), see a floorplan and even view an interactive map of the location.

EXAMPLE:

www.ljhooker.com.au

Example 6.3

LJ Hooker, a nationwide real estate firm, has an extensive website with information on the various services it offers. Through this website property buyers, for example, can select the area and type of property they are after and view and compare the properties that this firm has to offer that meet their requirements. They can also research the availability of finance through the agent. Having perhaps drawn up a shortlist of properties they are interested in, they can contact the agent and arrange to physically visit these before making a decision.

Benefits of electronic payment systems: trader

Benefits of using electronic payment systems for the trader or merchant include:
* lower operating costs as business or the warehouse/dispatch can be located in non retail areas
* no loss of stock from customer or employee theft (as in a retail stores)
* all information and pricing can be easily updated online (cheaper and quicker than altering in-store labeling and advertising or print catalogues and price lists).

Accounting and Finance 2B   ISBN 9780170182041   Cengage Learning Australia

Benefits of electronic payment systems: customer

Benefits of using electronic payment systems for the customer include:
- access to goods and services from anywhere in the world
- access to goods and services at any time, not just during normal trading hours.

Disadvantages of electronic payment systems

Disadvantages of using electronic payment systems for traders or merchants include the possibility that losses caused by fraudulent purchasers may not be fully recoverable from the card provider.

Disadvantages of using electronic payments systems for the customer include the possible loss of security of personal and financial details due to security breaches in the business's computer system.

CREDIT CARDS

Credit cards are issued by banks and other organisations to people and businesses to enable them to pay for goods and services without having to use physical cash (notes and coins). They are cards linked to a bank account with a line of credit; the customer has to pay the amount back to the bank (with interest where applicable). After assessing an applicant's credit worthiness, the card company will issue the card with a maximum credit limit. Sometimes the card company will also set a purchasing limit for individual transactions. If a transaction would lead to the credit limit being exceeded, authorisation to the trader will be refused and the purchaser will not be able to complete the purchase.

Usually on a set day each month the credit card company will issue a statement to the cardholder showing all transactions and the total amount owing. The statement sets a due date for payment, with a minimum amount that must be paid by that date. If the minimum amount is not paid by the due date, authorisation for future transactions can be stopped immediately. For some cards no interest is charged as long as the total amount due is paid on time. Others start to charge interest immediately after each purchase. Interest on credit cards is usually charged at a higher rate compared to other forms of borrowing. Most card companies charge their cardholders an annual fee. Many offer incentives for use, such as giving 'frequent flyer' points for purchases made using the card.

Businesses may either immediately send the data from the credit card sale electronically at the time of sale or at frequent intervals (daily or weekly). The credit card company transfers the sale transaction amount (less commission) in a very short time (usually within a day) into the business's bank account.

Benefits of credit cards

Benefits of using credit cards for the trader or merchant are similar to those of using EFTPOS.

Benefits of using credit cards for the customer are similar to those of using EFTPOS, as well as:
- capacity to borrow small amounts of money to make purchases without having to apply for a loan
- a record of the transactions made appears on the customer's credit card statement.

Disadvantages of credit cards

Disadvantages of using credit cards for the trader are similar to those of using EFTPOS.

Disadvantages of using credit cards for the customer are similar to those of using EFTPOS, plus the money borrowed has a high cost if amounts owing on the card are not paid by the due date (the interest rate on credit cards can be at least twice that applicable for personal loans).

DEBIT CARDS

There is also a type of access card known as a *debit card*. These require the customer to deposit an amount of money into a special debit card account. Each time the debit card is used, the sale value is deducted from the balance until the balance is used up.

The benefit of debit cards to the merchant is similar to credit cards.

The benefit of debit cards to the customer is also similar to credit cards with the additional advantage that they cannot overspend since they must have adequate funds in the account before using it. The losses that might be incurred by someone stealing the card are restricted as future transactions are limited to the unused amount on the card.

Police issue fake credit card warning

Police say false credit cards circulating in Queensland are high-quality copies and retailers will find it difficult to spot them.

They say 26 people, including a number on the Gold Coast, have been arrested for credit card fraud over the past couple of months.

Detective Superintendent Brian Hay says the fraud is part of an international operation and he has urged retailers to report suspicious behaviour.

'If someone comes into you and does a test run with a credit card to buy one, two, three, four gift cards and processes that and the transaction is successful, then they leave the store and come back in and says, 'oh I'd like to buy another four, five thousand dollars worth of those same gift cards', rather than get excited about the sale we'd rather they express concern and start to be more vigilant and take in more account of what's going on,' he said.

Source: ABC News website, www.abc.net.au/news/stories/2009/01/22/2471675.htm, posted 22 January 2009.

Commentary

In the scenario outlined by Superintendent Hay, the original credit card purchase was presumably authorised by the apparent issuer of the card. What else do you think the trader might do if they became suspicious when asked to accept the card for a larger amount?

ONLINE BANKING

Individuals and businesses can arrange with their banks and other financial institutions to conduct banking transactions via the internet. Once the online access is set up, customers can make many types of online adjustments. This may include:

- changing the account details held with their bank, such as address, phone number, etc.
- making one-off payments to creditors online
- transferring money between various bank accounts
- setting up direct debits for regular payments
- checking all transactions and the balances of their accounts.

Accounting and Finance: 2B   ISBN 9780170182041   Cengage Learning Australia

Benefits of online banking: business

Benefits of using online banking for the banking business include:

- reduced costs because less staff are needed to conduct the transactions over the banking counter; online staff can be located anywhere in the country or even overseas, where salaries may be lower
- potential to have fewer branches situated in highly visible locations (with consequentially higher rents) and to locate data processing centres in commercial areas with lower rents
- reduced processing, printing and mailing costs of bank statements because customers can print their own statements from home.

Benefits of online banking: customer

Benefits of using online banking for the customer include:

- convenience of accessing banking information at any time, in any location (including interstate or overseas) and not being restricted to visiting a bank in normal bank operating hours
- reduced costs by not having to buy and post cheques for payments
- immediate provision of documentary proof
- rapid speed of payment – transactions are effected almost instantaneously.

Risks of online banking: bank

Risks of using online banking for the bank include:

- potential for fraudulent access of customer accounts using stolen access data; liability for losses is an expense of the bank unless it can prove the customer was negligent
- potential for interference from hackers – any system that uses the internet is at risk from its operation and information being interfered with by hackers
- loss of function due to power outages or computer system failure – businesses need to have back-up power and systems so trading can continue in the event of computer or power failure.

Disadvantages of online banking: customer

Disadvantages of using online banking for the customer include:

- potential for loss of personal and financial information from others who have obtained information fraudulently – liability for losses may be shared by the bank and the customer depending on negligence
- potential for interference from hackers – any system that uses the internet is at risk from its operation and information being interfered with by hackers
- loss of function due to power outages or computer system failure
- lack of personal interaction – it is often helpful to be able to speak directly to a person if you have a question or a complaint (though it is still usually possible to go in to the local branch and speak to a bank employee).

REALITY CHECK 6.2

Electronic Banking for Small Business – We Have a Problem!

Small business operators using electronic banking services are not adequately protected from fraud and other online hazards.

The Small Business Development Corporation (SBDC) is calling for changes to the Australian Securities and Investment Commission's (ASIC) EFT Code of Conduct to better protect small business operators using electronic banking services.

Acting Managing Director Mr Bruce Macfarlane says many small business operators are not aware of their rights and responsibilities under the Code and are not adequately protected from fraud and other online hazards.

'The ASIC Code of Conduct provides protection for small business operators who use their personal bank accounts for business transactions, but it does not protect those who maintain separate business and personal accounts,' Mr Macfarlane said.

The SBDC, through its Ready Response Network, recently undertook a survey of small business operators to establish the extent of this problem.

From the 100 responses received:

- 95 per cent reported using electronic banking for business purposes and 81 per cent conducted most or all of their business banking electronically.
- 87 per cent maintained separate personal and business bank accounts and 79 per cent reported having personal and business accounts linked or accessible through the same electronic platform.
- 10 per cent of respondents have been victims of credit or debit card fraud, with 16 per cent experiencing problems with mistaken payments.
- Only 34 per cent of respondents were aware that different rules, terms and conditions applied to personal and business accounts.

Mr Macfarlane says that while banks often accepted liability when there was no error by the small business operator, respondents reported delays and costs that impacted on their business.

'In several instances, respondents reported significant losses and disruptions to business operations following successful hacking and phishing attacks,' Mr Macfarlane said.

'An overwhelming ninety-six per cent of those completing our survey did not have, or were not aware of having an insurance policy that protected them from fraud or other losses if their business banking account was compromised,' Mr Macfarlane said.

The SBDC is calling for the ASIC Code of Conduct to be extended to cover all small business transactions.

'Small businesses are substantial users of electronic banking services; they are cautious and aware of potential security risks and in most cases have systems to mitigate those risks,' Mr Macfarlane said.

'As consumers of banking products, small business operators should have the same rights and responsibilities as other consumers under the Code.'

The SBDC is also calling for the Code to be compulsory for all providers of electronic banking services.

'The legal rights of customers should not vary depending on whether a particular financial institution has subscribed to the Code.' Mr Macfarlane said.

Source: Small Business Development Corporation, media release, 26 October 2007, www.sbdc.com.au/publications/mediareleases.asp?newsid=210.

DIRECT DEBITS

Individuals can instruct their banks to make regular payments from their bank account to another business. This is for a standard payment amount that is due to be paid regularly at a set date. The bank deducts the amount from the customer's account and transmits it electronically to the third party. This may be used for expenses such as rent, house or car insurance, superannuation or life assurance, mortgage or loan repayments and subscriptions to a gym or fitness centre.

Accounting and Finance 2B   ISBN 9780170182041   Cengage Learning Australia

Benefits of direct debit

Benefits of using direct debit for the *trader or merchant* include:
- it ensures receipt of regular amounts owing on time, every time, because the transaction is automated
- it is safer as less cash is held on the premises and reduced time is needed to make bank deposits
- documentation of all transactions can be verified through banking records, reducing risks of internal fraud.

Benefits of using direct debits for the *customer* include that payments of regular amounts owing are always made on time, thereby eliminating the risk of non-payment and incurring any late payment charges.

Disadvantages of direct debit: trader

Disadvantage of using direct debits for the trader or merchant include, in addition to the usual risks of any electronic system, that there is no payment if the customer does not have adequate funds in their account. The trader must reconcile bank accounts frequently to monitor the receipt of amounts due. While the customer's bank will advise their client that there are insufficient funds in the account to make the payment, they will not advise the receiving business of the non-payment.

Risks of direct debit: customer

Risks of using direct debits for the customer include:
- inadequate funds in their account mean the bank will not make the payment due on time, which may incur additional or late payment penalties (while the customer may not be aware of low funds in their account and due payments not occurring)
- a stop payment order to the bank must be made to ensure the bank does not continue making payments; this needs to be timed to ensure all payments due are made, but that no additional payments are made, which might be difficult to recover from the trader.

Example 6.4

EXAMPLE:

The Cratchitt family has for some years supported a child in Tanzania through Plan Australia, an international charity. They have arranged with their bank for the support payments to be directly debited each month against their bank account. Plan has written to the Cratchitts advising them that their sponsored child has now reached the age where he no longer qualifies for assistance and asking if they wish to transfer their sponsorship to another child. The Cratchitts decide that they can no longer afford to provide support (Mr Cratchit has just lost his job). Unless they notify their bank that they wish to discontinue the payments, they will continue to have money automatically withdrawn from their account and it might be difficult to recover any overpayment.

SUMMARY

E-commerce and other forms of e-business have revolutionised the way businesses trade and interact with their customers. They can provide tremendous advantages and cost savings to both trader and customer, but they also create some new problems that need to be adequately planned for and dealt with to ensure that the benefits of the systems outweigh their disadvantages.

Test your knowledge

1 Distinguish between 'e-commerce' and 'e-business'.

2 What are the benefits to a business of e-commerce?

3 What are the risks or disadvantages to a business of e-commerce?

4 Explain the benefits of EFTPOS for both the customer and the trader.

5 What measures are taken to secure EFTPOS transactions?

6 In what ways can a firm use its website to promote its business?

7 What is the difference between a credit card and a debit card?

8 What are the benefits for the customer of online banking?

9 What is a direct debit and for what sort of transactions is it suitable?

Test your understanding

Topic guide
- E-commerce: 6.5–6.8
- EFTPOS: 6.1–6.5
- Bill pay: 6.5–6.8
- Credit cards: 6.3, 6.5
- Online: 6.2, 6.4, 6.9

6.1 What is meant by the term EFTPOS? Explain the benefits and risks for a shopkeeper associated with this type of trading.

6.2 How can a customer use online transactions to make payments for goods and services?

6.3 What are the risks to customers of using credit cards? How can a customer reduce these risks?

6.4 What are the benefits and risks for a small business operator in setting up an online sales and payment facility?

6.5 Complete the table below:

Type of e-commerce	How it works	Benefits	Disadvantages or risks
EFTPOS			
Bill payments: electronic payment system			
Credit cards			
Online banking			
Direct debits			

6.6 Nathan Malthouse is an accounting advisor with Colling Wood Public Accountants in Perth. A local small business in Cottesloe, a men's clothing shop called Pontings, has approached Nathan to seek advice on implementing e-commerce in its business. Pontings has been conducting its transactions with its customers on a cash-only basis but would now like to provide for customers who wish to make purchases without using cash.

The owners of Pontings have limited knowledge about the e-commerce options available although they are aware of credit cards and EPTPOS. They are concerned about the risks involved and the potential to lose money through fraud.

Accounting and Finance: 2B   ISBN 9780170182041   Cengage Learning Australia

Required

As Nathan Malthouse, outline to Pontings the best options for it to meet its customers needs and explain why, considering the type of business it runs and how the business can reduce the risk of losing money through fraud.

6.7 Goldielocks is a small business operating in Albany making and selling a range of food, beer and wine products using local produce. Until now it has relied on selling its items to tourists at the farm and through a shop in the town of Albany. However, local opportunities to expand are limited and it now believes that it must attract customers from further afield, particularly in the major capital cities of Australia. Tourists visiting the farm or shop from elsewhere in Western Australia or the eastern states have commented that they would like to be able to buy the products in their home city. The business has a website, but it is used only to advertise its products and location and does not offer products for sale.

The owner of Goldielocks, Theo Bear, has approached the local public accountant, John B Goode to seek advice on how the business can expand and meet the demands of customers in places further afield, such as Perth. It has been suggested by John B Goode that shopping online is the way to go but the owner is unsure how this would operate and is concerned about never actually receiving cash from the customer and the potential for business fraud.

Required

As John B Goode, public accountant and financial advisor, outline and explain the best options for Goldielocks to meet its customers' needs considering the type of business and explain how the business can reduce the risk of losing money through fraud.

6.8 Giants Furniture is a small business in Pemberton making and selling custom-made furniture. Until now it has been selling its products through local shops and using materials from local suppliers using cash or cheques for payment of accounts. Due to its concern about the logging of forests, the business would like to diversify and produce more environmentally friendly furniture. It still plans to operate in Pemberton but needs to find more suitable ways to pay its suppliers, who will now not all be local businesses.

The owners of Giants Furniture, Sarah Karri and Justine Jarrah, have approached Greg Wood, public accountant, to seek his advice on the most appropriate electronic options for their business. Sarah and Justine are concerned about hackers, computer viruses and other security issues in using electronic means to pay suppliers.

Required

As Greg Wood, public accountant and financial advisor, outline and explain to Giants Furniture the best options for it to meet its business needs, considering the type of business they run and explain how the business can reduce the security risks involved.

6.9 Treble Clef Music shop is a family owned business that operates a retail music store selling musical instruments, sheet music and performed music. At present most customers pay in cash at the shop or, in the case of regular approved customers, buy on account and pay within 30 days. They sell recorded music on CD and, for collectors, vinyl.

It wants to set up EFTPOS and credit card facilities and phase out its debtors system. It also wishes to establish an online music business. It has set up its website so that customers can view the catalogue online. The customers can research details of artists, composers and instrument makers on the firm's website. It now wants to be able to allow customers to order online and pay with a credit card.

The retail store displays a limited range of stock, which is resupplied from the bulk store as required by telephoned orders. Delivery of items purchased online will come from its bulk store, which is located in an industrial suburb. Although experts in their own field, the owners of the business have limited computer knowledge.

Required

Outline the benefits and problems that the owners of this business face in trying to operate online.

Investigation

1   Locate the website of one of Australia's major banks and search for information about the products it offers regarding the following types of electronic commerce:
    *   EFTPOS
    *   bill payments
    *   credit cards
    *   online banking
    *   direct debits.
    a   Describe the main features and benefits of the products the bank offers.
    b   What do the banks suggest to businesses to make electronic commerce secure for any business?

2   Locate the websites of four businesses that offer internet shopping and electronic payment for goods and services. Possible choices might include florists, music stores, auto parts sellers, supermarkets, general retail stores, department stores, electronic goods suppliers or bookshops.
    a   Describe how the businesses have made use of electronic payment systems.
    b   What security measures do they have in place to protect the customer and business?
    c   Explain which website you liked best and why, from a customer's perspective.
    d   Explain which website you thought likely to be most effective, from a business's perspective.

3   Write a report on e-commerce crime as reported on the Fido section of the ASIC website. This can be accessed from the ASIC home page or go direct to Fido (www.fido.gov.au/fido/fido.nsf). Your report should describe:
    a   the illegal actions
    b   the risks to business
    c   the risk to customers
    d   any control measures that both customers and business should take to avoid being affected by these illegal activities.

Essay

You are the owner of a small retail business setting up a shop in a large Perth shopping centre. Outline the ways in which your business might make use of e-business systems. Explain the advantages that you might obtain from each of these, outline the costs and risks and indicate how the risks might be minimised.

Ethics case study

Mack the Knife runs a business selling second-hand books and war medals, memorabilia and pictures on the internet. He has an online catalogue with photographs of most of the items in stock. Where any of these items is defaced or damaged, he is often able to conceal this by the angle from which he photographs them or by 'doctoring' the photos using design software, such as Photoshop.

Mack reasons that he is only doing what all shopkeepers do in displaying his stock to maximum advantage and that when the customers receive the goods they are unlikely to remember what they looked like on the website. Mack is very careful to remove pictures from the website as soon as the item pictured has been sold. His judgement in relation to his customers' reaction seems correct, since he receives very few complaints.
a   How would you assess Mack's actions from an ethical standpoint?
b   What adverse effects might they have on his business?
c   What do you think he should do?

Accounting and Finance 2B   ISBN 9780170182041   Cengage Learning Australia

Chapter 7
PROFIT DETERMINATION

What You Will Learn

After studying this chapter you should be able to:
1 Explain the accrual basis assumption as per the Framework
2 Distinguish between cash and accrual methods of accounting
3 Explain the purpose and nature of balance day adjustments for accruals and prepayments, bad and doubtful debts and depreciation
4 Define accrued expenses, prepaid expenses, accrued income, unearned income, doubtful debts and depreciation
5 Prepare General journal and General ledger entries for balance day adjustments, including accruals and prepayments and bad and doubtful debts

Introduction

In this chapter we will learn about the determination of profit using accrual accounting. We will briefly revisit the accounting period assumption and the recognition criteria for income, expenses, assets and liabilities and consider these using the accrual basis of accounting. The accrual basis will be contrasted with the cash accounting method. The correct application of the recognition criteria using accrual accounting leads to the necessity for balance day adjustments. We will examine the purpose and nature of balance day adjustments for accruals and prepayments, bad and doubtful debts and depreciation. Depreciation will, however, be dealt with in more detail in the next chapter. Finally we will revise the closing of the ledger to determine the profit using the profit and loss summary account (dealt with in detail in Chapter 3).

PROFIT

As indicated in an earlier chapter the profit or loss of a business is determined as the difference between the income and expenses of the business. This profit or loss is considered as a measure of the success of the business operations. When income is greater than expenses the business has made a profit but when the expenses are larger than the income then a loss has been incurred. A profit has the effect of increasing owners' equity while a loss decreases owners' equity. The size of the business profit is often the basis for the amount of the drawings taken by the owners of the business. In addition, if a business can make a profit and some of these profits are retained then it is in a better position to repay debt, purchase new non-current assets and expand and grow the business.

Key Concept 7.1

Profit or loss

The profit or loss of a business is the difference between the income and expenses. When the income is greater than the expenses, the business makes a profit, but when the expenses exceed the income, a loss is made.

Formula 7.1

$$\text{Profit/Loss} = \text{Income} - \text{Expenses}$$

To determine profit, we apply the accounting period assumption (that the life of the business is divided into equal arbitrary periods of time; see Chapter 1), which, if not applied, would mean we would need to wait until the liquidation of the business to determine the profit. The time period for determination of profit is usually one year; in Australia this is generally the financial year from 1 July to 30 June. However, for the purpose of monitoring business performance and control it may be necessary to determine the profit on a more frequent basis, such as every month.

Recognition criteria

Before considering the accrual basis of accounting we must revisit the recognition criteria for income and expenses, which are explained in the AASB Framework for the Preparation and Presentation of Financial Statements.

Income and expense recognition criteria

Income is recognised when there is an increase in future economic benefits related to an increase in an asset or a decrease of a liability that can be measured reliably.

Expenses are recognised when there is a decrease in future economic benefits related to a decrease in an asset or an increase of a liability that can be measured reliably.

It should be noted for both income and expenses that their recognition occurs simultaneously with the recognition of assets or liabilities. This is important: later it will be explained that one of the purposes of balance day adjustments is to correctly account for all the assets and liabilities of the business at balance day (such as amounts owing to employees for wages outstanding and receivables due for interest earned).

Both income and expense items are recognised when there is a degree of certainty that the item will occur and when it can be reliably measured. The recognition criteria for income are further elaborated upon in accounting standards; they indicate that income should be recognised in most cases on the accrual basis.

Accounting and Finance: 2B   ISBN 9780170182041   Cengage Learning Australia

ACCRUAL BASIS ASSUMPTION

The Framework states that financial statements should be prepared on the accrual basis. The effects of transactions and other events are recognised when they occur (and not as cash or its equivalent is received or paid) and they are recorded in the accounting records and reported in the financial reports of the periods to which they relate. Due to the issue of timing (which will be explained in more detail shortly) this can result in the need for balance day adjustments. Accounting reports prepared on the accrual basis are considered to be better because they show all the assets, including resources that involve receiving cash in the future (such as interest receivable) and liabilities including obligations that involve paying out cash in the future (such as accrued wages).

The accrual basis of accounting means that credit transactions are recorded. A credit transaction is one where the good or service has been provided but the cash has not been paid. The sale of goods or rendering of a service is earned at the point of sale. In the case of a trading or service business this takes place when the business has transferred ownership of the goods to the purchaser or has performed the service. For a manufacturing business this can occur earlier in the operating cycle and they may use a 'percentage of completion' approach to recognising income.

 Key Concept 7.2

Accrual basis assumption

The accrual basis assumption is that financial transactions and events should be recorded when they occur and in the accounting period to which they relate.

Cash accounting

Cash accounting is the recognition of income in the period when the cash is received and an expense in the period when the cash is paid. Cash-based accounting therefore does not take into account credit transactions and there are no balance day adjustments. As previously mentioned, the Framework indicates that the accrual basis is the method that should be applied by a business in preparing its financial reports. The cash basis is a simple approach and is most useful only for very small businesses that trade on a cash basis.

Key Concept 7.3

Cash-based accounting

Cash-based accounting recognises income when the cash is received and expenses when the cash is paid.

Example 7.1

EXAMPLE:

Consider the following summarised transactions of Mozart Plumbing for the month of May 2010. GST is disregarded in this example.

- Services were rendered to customers on credit for the value of $3500 completed in May, of which only $2000 had been received by the end of May.
- Salaries for work done in May were paid to employees totalling $1100, but $300 is still owing at the end of May. $200 was paid for salaries owing from April 2010.
- Services were rendered to customers for $12000 cash for work completed in May.
- Paid rent of $600 for the months of May, June and July 2010.
- Received $900 from customers for work completed in April 2010.
- Received a deposit of $500 cash from a customer for work to be done in June 2010.
- Paid $300 for electricity used in March and April 2010. Electricity owing for May was $130.
- Paid $4400 for plumbing materials but used $3700 worth of materials in May.
- Paid for other expenses of $1500 as incurred.

Accounting and Finance: 2B   ISBN 9780170182041   Cengage Learning Australia

Calculation of profit or loss using the cash accounting basis

Cash income	
Receipts from:	
Services rendered on credit in May	$2 000
Debtors (for services rendered on credit in April)	$900
Customers (for services to be rendered in June)	$500
Services rendered for cash in May	$12 000
Total cash received	$15 400
Less Cash expenses	
Payments for:	
Salaries for work done in May	$1 100
Salaries for work done in April	$200
Rent for the months of May, June and July	$600
Electricity used in March and April	$300
Plumbing materials	$4 400
Other expenses	$1 500
Total cash paid	$8 100
Cash-based profit	$7 300

Using the cash basis of accounting in this example all the receipts related to income and all the payments related to expenses are used to calculate the profit or loss. Only those items that *do not* involve cash are excluded. Those items that are excluded are the following (they are either credit transactions or amounts still owing) and these are not bought to account in the month of May under cash accounting:

- services rendered to customers in May on credit on which no cash has been received: $3500
- salaries owing for work done at the end of May: $300
- electricity owing for May: $130.

The cash profit of $7300 is the difference between the total cash received of $15400 and total cash paid of $8100.

Calculation of profit or loss using the accrual accounting basis

Income	
Services rendered (on cash) to customers for work completed in May	$12 000
Services rendered (on credit) to customers for work completed in May	$3 500
Total income	$15 500
Less Expenses:	
Electricity owing for May	$130
Plumbing materials used in May	$3 700
Other expenses as incurred	$1 500
Rent for the month of May (i.e. $600 divided by 3 months)	$200
Salaries for work done in May ($1100 plus $300 still owing)	$1 400
Total expenses	$6 930
Accrual-based profit	$8 570

Under the accrual accounting method the income shown must be that which is earned in May and the expenses incurred in May. Therefore cash and credit transactions can be included but those transactions that relate to another month are excluded. These are:

- cash paid for salaries owing from April 2010: $200
- rent paid for June and July 2010 ($600 × 2/3): $400
- cash received for work completed for customers in April 2010: $900
- cash deposit from a customer for work to be done in June 2010: $500
- cash paid for electricity used in March and April 2010: $300
- cash paid for plumbing materials not used in May ($4400 − $3700): $700.

Accounting and Finance: 2B   ISBN 9780170182041   Cengage Learning Australia

Note also that the $2000 cash received by the end of May as part payment for the work completed on credit totalling $3500 has not been included since the full amount of income earned, $3500, has already been included.

The accrual-based profit of $8570 is the difference between the total income of $15500 and total expenses of $6930.

Differences between accrual and cash accounting		
	Income	**Expense**
Cash accounting	Recorded when cash is **received**	Recorded when cash is **paid**
Accrual accounting	Recorded when **earned**, i.e. at the point of sale (when the transaction occurs and in the period it relates to)	Recorded when **incurred**, i.e. as soon as the item is used or consumed (when the transaction occurs and in the period it relates to)

Customer orders goods or service	Goods sold or service performed	Cash is received

Figure 7.1 Income recognition timeline

Using accrual accounting, income is generally recognised when the goods are delivered or a service is performed.

PURPOSE AND NATURE OF BALANCE DAY ADJUSTMENTS

Accrual-based accounting requires that income and expense be recorded in the correct accounting period. This means when income has been earned (the good or service provided) and expense has been incurred (the good or service used or consumed).

The initial recording of a transaction involving income can take place when cash is received or credit is provided. However, this does not necessarily mean that the good or service has been completely provided. In addition, due to the application of the accounting period assumption, the sale of goods or provision of services may take place over a number of accounting periods. This is the issue of timing: transactions do not always start and finish within the one accounting period and the receipt of money or provision of credit does not always mean that all aspects of the transaction have been completed.

Similarly, the initial recording of an expense transaction may take place when the cash is paid or credit received. Once again this does not necessarily mean that the good or service has been completely provided and also because of the accounting period assumption the transaction may take more than one accounting period to complete.

Summary of the purpose of balance day adjustments

- At balance day some transactions are incomplete and therefore they affect the determination of the profit or loss over more than one accounting period.
- This means that the records for income and expense have to be adjusted so that the correct amount is included in the calculation of the profit or loss.
- It also allows for the correct assets and liabilities to be brought to account.
- This process, called balance day adjustments or adjusting entries, takes place on the last day of the financial period.

Key Concept 7.4

Purpose of balance day adjustments

The purpose of balance day adjustments is to ensure that the income and expenses for the accounting period are correctly recognised.

This diagram shows the place of adjusting entries in this process.

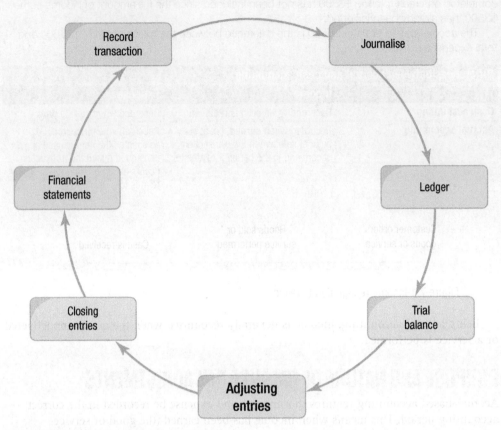

Figure 7.2 Review of the accounting cycle

REALITY CHECK 7.1

Cash versus accrual accounting – the talking point at the recent conference

Mr Barn E Rubble, one of the directors of Bam Bam Pty Ltd, who attended the recent conference on small business, commented that in his opinion cash accounting was the best method as it tied in with the business bank account balance. He went on further to say that cash was the important key to business success.

An accountant, Mr Fred Flint of Stone Accountants, who was attending the conference, overheard this comment and set out a reply to Barn E Rubble. Fred said that 'although cash accounting was a simple method, accrual accounting was in fact a far superior method as it allowed managers, investors and lenders of businesses to see the real picture of business activity and the business's current position'. Fred went on to say that 'accrual accounting showed what had actually happened and bought to account all the business's current assets and liabilities whereas cash accounting did not'.

He explained that it provided a better measure of costs and income and enabled comparisons over time to be meaningful. This, he argued, meant that the users of financial statements had a far better picture of the company's performance as they would be given a more accurate picture of the true profit of the business. Fred pointed out, for example, that cash accounting ignored uncollected income and also those bills yet to be paid. Moreover, cash accounting ignored the expense of the loss of value of non-current assets in the determination of profit.

Accounting and Finance: 2B   ISBN 9780170182041   Cengage Learning Australia

Fred did concede that cash accounting enabled a business to keep a much closer control on its cash position as the focus of cash accounting was very much on cash inflows and cash outflows. Cash accounting, he said, may be useful for those small businesses that were owned and managed by the one person.

Commentary

The arguments for and against cash and accrual accounting are often debated by small business owners. However accrual accounting is usually seen by professional accountants as the more superior method. When a business has no external users and the business is owned by one person then cash accounting is often used, especially if the vast majority of the firm's transactions are actually carried out on a cash basis.

TYPES OF BALANCE DAY ADJUSTMENTS

Balance day adjustments can be categorised as either prepayments or accruals.

Types of balance day adjustments	
Prepayments	**Accruals**
• Prepaid expenses – the cash has been paid but the supply or service not used or consumed	• Accrued expenses – the service or good has been used or consumed but not paid for at balance day
• Unearned income – the cash has been received but the good or service has not been provided	• Accrued income – the good or service has been provided but the cash not received
• Depreciation – the cost has been paid for but the asset has not all been consumed or used	• Bad and doubtful debts – the good or service has been provided but doubt exists as to whether the cash will be received

When accounting for accruals and prepayments it should be noted that when making the required adjusting entry one side of the entry will affect the income or expense and the other side an asset or liability. The cash account is not affected.

Prepaid expenses (including supplies on hand)

In Chapter 2 we introduced the recording of transactions using the manual approach and we indicated that some payments for items such as insurance and supplies can be recorded as an asset at the time of payment. We will now explore this in more detail.

A prepaid expense occurs when a business pays for services or supplies before it uses them. This takes place for such items as insurance, rent, stationery and fuel. For example, it is common business practice to pay for insurance for the forthcoming year and to pay for rent a month or more in advance. A business will also buy stationery and then use it over a period of time. There are two approaches to recording these types of items – the asset method and the expense method. The expense method is to record the item as an expense when paid for and then account for the unused benefit as an asset at balance day. We will, however, use the asset method in this chapter; under this method the good or service will be recorded when paid for as an asset. This is because it represents future economic benefits. In the case of a service prepaid it is called a *prepaid expense* and for supplies purchased ahead of time these are called *stock of supplies*.

Under the asset method, at balance day the business must analyse its prepaid items and consider if any have been used or consumed. If this is the case then the amount used or consumed must be recorded as an expense for the current period and this is the required balance day adjustment. The amount of any prepaid expense still in existence at balance day must be shown in the Statement of financial position as a current asset to be consumed or used in the forthcoming accounting period. The balances in the expense and income accounts created by these adjustments will be closed off to Profit and loss summary in the usual way (see Chapter 3).

Example 7.2

EXAMPLE:

BJ Thomas Art Framing set up business on 1 May and registered for GST. Some of its transactions included paying $990 (GST inclusive) rent on 1 May 2010 for the months of May, June and July. The business also purchased framing supplies of $2200 (GST inclusive) on credit from J Farnham on 1 May 2010.

As a result of the above transactions the business's unadjusted trial balance as at 30 June 2010 showed:

- Prepaid rent: $900 Dr
- Stock of framing supplies: $2000 Dr.

The business had used $1400 worth of framing supplies in the framing of artwork for customers as at 30 June 2010.

Required

a   Prepare the General journal entry to record, using the asset method, the payment on 1 May 2010 and the purchase on credit on 1 May 2010.

b   Prepare the General journal adjusting entry to record the expenses on 30 June 2010.

c   Prepare the entry required on 30 June 2010 to close off the Rent expense and Framing supplies expense accounts to the Profit and loss summary account.

d   Prepare the General ledger Prepaid rent, Stock of framing supplies, Framing supplies expense and Rent expense accounts for the months of May and June 2010.

e   Show how the Prepaid rent and Stock of supplies would be shown in the Statement of financial position as at 30 June 2010.

The amount of prepaid rent ($900 for May, June and July) used as at 30 June 2010 is two months. Therefore, $900 divided by three and multiplied by the two months expired is $600 rent expense.

The entries to record the payment of the prepaid rent and the adjustment required on 30 June 2010 for the rent expense are as follows.

General journal

Date	Account details	Debit $	Credit $
1/5/10	Prepaid rent	900	
	GST outlay	90	
	Cash		990
	Paid rent for May, June and July 2010		
30/6/10	Rent expense	600	
	Prepaid rent		600
	Adjusting entry to record rent expense for the months of May and June 2010		
	Profit and loss summary	600	
	Rent expense		600
	Closing entry		

General ledger

Date	Account details	Debit $	Credit $	Balance $	Dr/Cr
Prepaid rent					
1/5/10	Cash	900		900	Dr
30/6/10	Rent expense		600	300	Dr
Rent expense account					
30/6/10	Prepaid rent	600		600	Dr
	Profit and loss summary		600	0	

Note that the amount remaining in the Prepaid rent account of $300 represents the unused rent for the month of July 2010. The accounting entries and treatment of stock of supplies is the same as prepaid expenses.

Date	Account details	Debit $	Credit $
	General journal		
1/5/10	Stock of framing supplies	2 000	
	GST outlay	200	
	Accounts payable – J Farnham		2 200
	Purchase of framing supplies on credit		
30/6/10	Framing supplies expense	1 400	
	Stock of framing supplies		1 400
	Adjusting entry to record the framing supplies used		
	Profit and loss summary	1 400	
	Framing supplies expense		1 400
	Closing entry		

Date	Account details	Debit	Credit	Balance	Dr/Cr
	General ledger				
	Stock of framing supplies				
1/5/10	Accounts payable – J Farnham	$2 000		$2 000	Dr
30/6/10	Framing supplies expense		$1 400	$600	Dr
	Framing supplies expense				
30/6/10	Stock of framing supplies	$1 400		$1 400	Dr
	Profit and loss summary		$1 400	0	

The $600 remaining in the Stock of framing supplies account represents unused framing supplies to be used in the future.

Points to note about the adjusting entries are:

- The asset accounts of Prepaid rent and Stock of framing supplies are both credited with the used up portion of the item that has now become an expense. The effect of this credit entry is to reduce their value to the correct amount as at 30 June 2010.
- The Rent expense and Framing supplies expense accounts are both debited with the used-up economic benefits and bring to account the accurate amount of these items for the reporting period to 30 June 2010.
- The amounts involved in the adjustment are always exclusive of GST.

The closing entry for both the Rent and Framing supplies expense accounts requires these accounts to be credited so that the amount is transferred out to the Profit and loss summary account and the expense account balance goes to zero.

The $300 Prepaid rent and $600 Stock of framing supplies as at 30 June 2010 are both current assets as these amounts will be used up within the next accounting period. These are reported in the Statement of financial position as at 30 June 2010.

BJ Thomas Art Framing
Statement of financial position as at 30 June 2010

	$
Current assets	
Prepaid rent	300
Stock of framing supplies	600

Prepaid expense

A prepaid expense is a service or supply paid for in advance before it is used or consumed.

Accrued expenses

An accrued expense occurs when a service or good has been used or consumed but not paid for. This can occur for such items as wages and salaries, electricity and interest (expense). In this case the expense item has not been recorded and so the profit would be overstated if no adjustment is made. An adjustment is needed to record the expense in the period in which it occurs. In addition, the amount owing has not been recorded. This liability needs to be shown in the Statement of financial position and, as it will be paid for within the next accounting period, it must be shown as a current liability.

Example 7.3

EXAMPLE:

P Rafter and P Cash own and operate Pat's Sports Store and they are registered for GST. For the year ended 30 June 2010 their Unadjusted trial balance showed the following:

- Wages expense: $19 000 Dr
- Electricity expense: $3 700 Dr.

There were no accrued expenses for wages or electricity as at 30 June 2009.

As at 30 June 2010 the business owed $1200 for wages and this amount was paid on 9 July 2010. There is no GST associated with wages paid. It also owed $300 (GST exclusive) for electricity as at 30 June 2010 and this amount of $300 plus the GST component of $30 was paid on 12 July 2010.

Required

a Prepare the General journal entry to record the adjusting entries required on 30 June 2010.

b Prepare the entry required on 30 June 2010 to close off the Wages expense and Electricity expense accounts to the Profit and loss summary account.

c Prepare the General journal entries required on 9 July and 12 July 2010 to record the payments of wages and electricity respectively.

d Prepare the General ledger Wages payable, Electricity payable, Wages expense and Electricity expense accounts for the year ended 30 June 2010 and show how the payments made on 9 July and 12 July would appear in these accounts.

e Show how the Wages payable and Electricity payable would be shown in the Statement of financial position as at 30 June 2010.

The wages and electricity owing are amounts that at present have not been recorded and therefore no expense or liability has been brought to account. The entries in the records of Pat's Sport Store would therefore be as shown below.

General journal			
Date	Account details	Debit $	Credit $
30/6/10	Wages expense	1 200	
	Wages payable		1 200
	Adjusting entry to record wages owing		
	Electricity expense	300	
	Electricity payable		300
	Adjusting entry to record electricity owing		
	Profit and loss summary	24 200	
	Wages expense		20 200

Accounting and Finance: 2B   ISBN 9780170182041   Cengage Learning Australia

	Electricity expense			300	
	Closing entry				
9/7/10	Wages payable	1 200			
	Cash			1 200	
	Paid wages owing as at 30 June 2010				
12/7/10	Electricity payable	300			
	GST outlay	30			
	Cash			330	
	Paid electricity owing as at 30 June 2010				

General ledger					
Date	Account details	Debit $	Credit $	Balance $	Dr/Cr
Wages expense account					
30/6/10	Balance			19 000	Dr
	Wages payable	1 200		20 200	Dr
	Profit and loss summary		20 200	0	
Electricity expense account					
30/6/10	Balance			3 700	Dr
	Electricity payable	300		4 000	Dr
	Profit and loss summary		4 000	0	
Wages payable account					
30/6/10	Wages expense		1 200	1 200	Cr
9/7/10	Cash	1 200		0	
Electricity payable account					
30/6/10	Electricity expense		300	300	Cr
12/7/10	Cash	300		0	

The points to note about the adjusting entries are:
- The Wages and Electricity expense accounts are both debited as the amounts owing are to be recognised as expenses for the current financial period.
- The Wages payable and Electricity payable accounts are both credited with the amounts owing so as to create a liability as at balance day. Wages payable and Electricity payable can also be called Accrued wages and Accrued electricity respectively.
- With regard to the electricity owing it should be noted that the GST component of $30 is not recorded as GST outlay at balance day. This is because no tax invoice had been issued by the supplier at balance day.
- Remember that wages and salaries are exempt from GST.

With regard to the subsequent period entries and accrued expenses the Wages payable and Electricity payable accounts are both debited when these amounts are actually paid in the new accounting period as well as recording, in the case of Electricity, the GST component. This extinguishes the liabilities as they are now paid. An alternative method of dealing with subsequent payments involves the preparation of reversing entries on the first day of the new accounting period. We will not be using that approach in this textbook.

The closing entry for both the Wages and Electricity expense accounts requires these accounts to be credited so that the amount is transferred out to the Profit and loss summary account and the expense account balance goes to zero.

As at 30 June 2010 the Wages payable of $1200 and Electricity payable of $300 are both current liabilities as it is expected that these amounts would be paid within the next accounting period. These are reported in the Statement of financial position as at 30 June 2010.

Pat's Sport Store
Statement of financial position as at 30 June 2010

Current liabilities	$
Electricity payable	300
Wages payable	1 200

 Key Concept 7.6

Accrued expense

An accrued expense is a service or good that has been used or consumed but not paid for.

Unearned income

Unearned income, sometimes called income in advance, occurs when cash has been received from a customer or client but the good or service has not been provided. The income has not yet been earned in this case. This can occur for such items as rent (revenue), magazine subscriptions and membership fees (revenue). There are two approaches to the recording of these items – the income method and the liability method. Under the income method, when the cash is received it is recorded as income and an adjustment is made on balance day for the unearned income, showing this as a liability.

We will, however, use the liability method. Under this method, when the cash is received from the customer or client it is recorded as a liability. This is because it represents an obligation, for the cash has been received but the good or service not provided. The GST collected is also recorded at this time. On balance day an analysis of the unearned income must be made to determine the proportion that has now been earned. This amount must then be recorded as income for the current period. Any amount still unearned will be shown as a current liability as it is likely that the good or service will be provided within the next accounting period.

Example 7.4

EXAMPLE:

Newcombe Carpenters, which is registered for GST, makes household furniture. The business requires customers to make an advance payment before it will commence any commissioned job.

On 6 May 2010 the business received $4070 (GST inclusive) from Ken Holt, being an advance payment for the making of cabinets. On 12 June the business received $2310 (GST inclusive) from Emma Thompson, being the advance payment for the manufacture of cabinets. During the year the business had recorded $56900 (GST exclusive) in cabinetmaking fees.

It therefore had the following amounts shown in its Unadjusted trial balance as at 30 June 2010:

- Unearned cabinetmaking fees: $5800 (GST exclusive) Cr
- Cabinetmaking fees revenue: $56900 (GST exclusive) Cr.

On balance day 30 June 2010, $3700 (GST exclusive) of the amount of Unearned cabinetmaking fees now represents work completed for customers and is thus revenue earned. The other amount received of $2100 (GST exclusive) is for work still not undertaken at balance day.

Required

a Prepare the General journal entries required, using the liability method, to record the receipts of money on 6 May and 12 June 2010.
b Prepare the General journal entry to record the adjusting entry required on 30 June 2010.
c Prepare the entry required on 30 June 2010 to close off the Cabinetmaking fees revenue account to the Profit and loss summary account.
d Prepare the General ledger Cabinetmaking fees revenue and Unearned cabinetmaking fees accounts for the year ended 30 June 2010.

Accounting and Finance: 2B   ISBN 9780170182041   Cengage Learning Australia

e Show how the Unearned cabinetmaking fees account would be shown in the Statement of financial position as at 30 June 2010.

On balance day it will now be necessary to record the Cabinetmaking fees earned as income and to correct the Unearned cabinetmaking fees to show only the amount of the services still to be completed for customers. The entries required in the records of Newcombe Carpenters would be as follows.

Date	Account details	Debit $	Credit $
	General journal		
6/5/10	Cash	4070	
	GST collected		370
	Unearned cabinetmaking fees		3700
	Receipt of monies for service not performed		
12/5/10	Cash	2310	
	GST collected		210
	Unearned cabinetmaking fees		2100
	Receipt of monies for service not performed		
30/6/10	Unearned cabinetmaking fees	3700	
	Cabinetmaking fees revenue		3700
	Adjusting entry to record cabinetmaking fees now earned		
	Cabinetmaking fees revenue	60600	
	Profit and loss summary		60600
	Closing entry		

Date	Account details	Debit $	Credit $	Balance $	Dr/Cr
	General ledger				
	Unearned cabinetmaking fees account				
6/5/10	Cash		3700	3700	Cr
12/6/10	Cash		2100	5800	Cr
30/6/10	Cabinetmaking fees revenue	3700		2100	Cr
	Cabinetmaking fees revenue account				
30/6/10	Balance			56900	Cr
	Unearned cabinetmaking fees		3700	60600	Cr
	Profit and loss summary	60600		0	

The points to note about the adjusting entry are:
- The Cabinetmaking fees revenue account is credited as the amount is now earned and needs to be recorded as income for the current financial period.
- The Unearned cabinetmaking fees account is debited with the amount of income ($3700) now earned and this amount is transferred to the Cabinetmaking fees revenue account. The Unearned cabinetmaking fees account balance of $2100 as at 30 June 2010 now represents the amount of money received from customers for whom the work has not been performed as at balance day.
- All amounts involved are GST exclusive.

The closing entry for the Cabinetmaking fees revenue account requires it to be debited so that the amount is transferred to the Profit and loss summary account and the income account balance goes to zero.

As at 30 June 2010 the Unearned cabinetmaking fees account balance of $2100 is a current liability as it is expected that this amount represents a service that will be performed within the next accounting period. This is reported in the Statement of financial position as at 30 June 2010 as seen on the following page.

Newcombe Carpenters
Statement of financial position as at 30 June 2010

Current Liabilities	$
Unearned cabinet-making fees	2100

Key Concept 7.7

Unearned income

Unearned income represents cash received for which the good or service has not been provided.

Accrued income

Accrued income or accrued revenue represents a good or service that has been provided at balance day but for which payment has not been received. This can occur for such items as interest (revenue), commission (revenue) and fees (revenue) where no invoice is to be issued as it is not appropriate or the service is ongoing into the next accounting period. An adjustment is needed on balance day to record this income in the period in which it occurs, otherwise the profit for that period will be understated. At the same time an amount owing from the customer, client or supplier needs to be shown in the Statement of financial position as a current asset, as it is expected that the cash will be received within the next accounting period.

Example 7.5

EXAMPLE:

Court and Goolagong are partners in an advertising agency called Kooyong Advertising, which is registered for GST. Clients of the business are usually billed at the completion of the job. However, at the end of the financial year there are a few jobs where this has not occurred. A review of the records reveals that $7800 (GST exclusive) worth of work for clients has been completed but no tax invoice has been issued. In addition, the business has some short-term investments on which interest earned of $800 has not been recorded at balance day. For the year ended 30 June 2010 their Unadjusted trial balance showed the following:

- Advertising revenue: $82 000 Cr
- Interest revenue: $2700 Cr.

There was no accrued revenue for advertising or interest as at 30 June 2009.

The fees owed of $7800 plus the $780 GST collected was received in cash on 10 July 2010 after the issue of a tax invoice. The firm also received in cash the interest revenue of $800, owing on the investment, on 31 July 2010. Remember that there is no GST associated with interest received as financial services are an input-taxed supply.

Required

a Prepare the General journal entry to record the adjusting entries required on 30 June 2010.
b Prepare the General journal entry required on 30 June 2010 to close off the Advertising revenue and Interest revenue accounts to the Profit and loss summary account.
c Prepare the General journal entries required on 10 July and 31 July 2010 to record the receipts from the advertising revenue and interest revenue respectively.
d Prepare the General ledger Accounts receivable, Interest receivable, Advertising revenue and Interest revenue accounts for the year ended 30 June 2010 and show how the receipts made on 10 July and 31 July would appear in these accounts.
e Show how the Accounts receivable and Interest receivable would be shown in the Statement of financial position as at 30 June 2010.

The entries in the records of Kooyong Advertising would therefore be as shown opposite.

Accounting and Finance: 2B   ISBN 9780170182041   Cengage Learning Australia

General journal

Date	Account details	Debit $	Credit $
30/6/10	Accounts receivable	7 800	
	Advertising revenue		7 800
	Adjusting entry to record advertising revenue unrecorded		
	Interest receivable	800	
	Interest revenue		800
	Adjusting entry to record interest revenue unrecorded		
	Advertising revenue	89 800	
	Interest revenue	3 500	
	Profit and loss summary		93 300
	Closing entry		
10/7/10	Cash	8 580	
	GST collected		780
	Accounts receivable		7 800
	Receipt of money owing as at 30 June 2010		
31/7/10	Cash	800	
	Interest receivable		800
	Receipt of money owing as at 30 June 2010		

General ledger

Date	Account details	Debit $	Credit $	Balance $	Dr/Cr
	Advertising revenue account				
30/6/10	Balance			82 000	Cr
	Accounts receivable		7 800	89 800	Cr
	Profit and loss summary	89 800		0	
	Interest revenue account				
30/6/10	Balance			2 700	Cr
	Interest receivable		800	3 500	Cr
	Profit and loss summary	3 500		0	
	Accounts receivable account				
30/6/10	Advertising revenue	7 800		7 800	Dr
10/7/10	Cash		7 800	0	
	Interest receivable account				
30/6/10	Interest revenue	800		800	Dr
31/7/10	Cash		800	0	

The points to note about the adjusting entries are:
- The Advertising and Interest revenue accounts are both credited as the amounts owing are to be recognised as income for the current financial period. These amounts have not previously been recorded as income for the current year.
- The Accounts receivable and Interest receivable accounts are both debited with the amounts owing to create an asset as at balance day. The Accounts receivable in regard to the advertising owing can also be called Accrued advertising revenue and the Interest receivable can also be called Accrued interest revenue.

- With regard to the advertising revenue owing it should be noted that the GST component of $780 is not recorded as GST collected at balance day. This is because no tax invoice had been issued by the business to the client at balance day.

With regard to the subsequent period entries and accrued revenue, the Accounts receivable and Interest receivable accounts are both credited when these amounts are actually received in the new accounting period. In the case of the Accounts receivable it is when this amount is received on 10 July 2010 that the GST component of $780 can be recorded because a tax invoice has now been issued.

The closing entry for both the Advertising and Interest revenue accounts requires these accounts to be debited so that the amount is transferred out to the Profit and loss summary account and the Income account balances brought to zero.

As at 30 June 2010 the Accounts receivable of $7800 and Interest receivable of $800 are both current assets as it is expected that these amounts will be received within the next accounting period. These are reported in the Statement of financial position as at 30 June 2010.

Kooyong Advertising
Statement of financial position as at 30 June 2010

	$
Current assets	
Accounts receivable	7 800
Interest receivable	800

 Key Concept 7.8

Accrued income
Accrued income represents a good or service that has been provided but for which the cash has not been received.

Bad and doubtful debts

Businesses that sell goods and services on credit know that some customers will not be able to repay the amount they owe. When the business is certain that the amount will not be received it is written off as a bad debt. (This was covered in Chapter 2.) A bad debt is an expense as it represents the loss of an economic benefit. This bad debt should ideally be recognised as an expense in the same period as the credit sale. However, this often does not occur as considerable time may elapse from the date of the credit sale to the moment when the firm decides to write off the bad debt. As a result the credit sale can occur in one accounting period and the bad debt in another.

During the course of a year credit sales and fees are recorded as income and as accounts receivable. At balance day amounts owing from accounts receivable will include customers who are likely to become a bad debt in the future. The business may know this is the case from past experience. Therefore the business has earned income but is aware some of this income will not be received in cash. It is appropriate to estimate the amount of income unlikely to be received so that the profit is not overstated. This is done through the allowance for doubtful debts method. This involves the business estimating future bad debts, which are known as *allowance for doubtful debts* and showing this amount in the Statement of financial position. The other side of the entry is to show the income unlikely to be received and this is the *doubtful debts expense*. To show in the Statement of financial position only the gross amount for accounts receivable would not be indicating what the entity considers to be the realisable value of debtors. The business should show the allowance for doubtful debts as a deduction from the gross accounts receivable, which will then show the net accounts receivable, the firm's estimate of realisable value of the debtors.

The first stage in this process is clearly to make an estimate of the doubtful debts.

Accounting and Finance: 2B   ISBN 9780170182041   Cengage Learning Australia

Methods to estimate doubtful debts

Investigate each individual accounts receivable to determine if it is a possible future bad debt. Indicators may be:

- it has been overdue for payment for some time
- a cheque received was dishonoured
- the whereabouts of the debtor is now unknown
- a check of the debtor's credit rating shows that the debtor now has a poor rating.

The ageing of accounts receivable method

Under this method debtors are categorised according to how long the debt has been overdue for payment. Each category is then analysed and percentages applied, based on past experience, to estimate the amount of bad debts. A variation of this method is to apply a percentage, based on past experience, to the total of accounts receivable to determine the amount of likely future bad debts.

Percentage of net credit sales

This method involves applying a percentage, again based on past experience, to estimate the amount of future likely bad debts.

It is important to remember that no matter which method is used the amount of estimated future bad debts – that is, doubtful debts – must exclude any GST collected. This is because in the event of a bad debt the amount of any GST collected can be recovered from the Australian Taxation Office (ATO).

A business that uses the allowance for doubtful debts method will, on balance day, estimate the amount of doubtful debts and raise this amount to be the balance of the Allowance for doubtful debts account. This is done by the following General journal entry:

General journal			
Date	Account details	Debit $	Credit $
	Doubtful debts	XXX	
	Allowance for doubtful debts		XXX
	Adjusting entry		

The Doubtful debts account is an expense account and because it is an estimate of the likely bad debts to result from the current period's credit sale, it takes the place of the Bad debts expense account in the current period.

When a business raises an allowance for doubtful debts the amount of any actual bad debts is off set against this figure. This is done at the end of the accounting period by preparing the following General journal entry:

General journal			
Date	Account details	Debit $	Credit $
	Allowance for doubtful debts	XXX	
	Bad debts		XXX
	Transfer bad debts		

An alternative to this approach is to offset straight away the bad debt when it occurs against the allowance for doubtful debts as seen below:

General journal			
Date	Account details	Debit $	Credit $
	Allowance for doubtful debts	XXX	
	Accounts receivable		XXX
	Write off bad debts		

In this textbook we will use the latter method. The treatment of bad debts under either approach ensures that the bad debt is not closed off to the Profit and loss summary account, thereby treating the item as an expense twice, once in the period (via doubtful debts expense) in which the estimate of future bad debts occurred and again in the period in which it is actually written off.

It must be remembered that the Allowance for doubtful debts account is only an estimate. Therefore the actual bad debts for a period may not equal the allowance that had been established at the end of the previous accounting period. This means that at balance day the adjusting of the allowance for doubtful debts will result in the amount of the Doubtful debts expense being different to the balance of the Allowance for doubtful debts account. This is because it will have to include an additional provision for the previous year (where the actual bad debts exceeded the allowance) or a deduction from this year's expense (where the allowance for last year turned out to be greater than the actual bad debts).

The Allowance for doubtful debts is shown in the Statement of financial position and is offset against the Accounts receivable balance to give the net realisable amount of Accounts receivable.

Example 7.6

EXAMPLE:

Merry Wholesalers Pty Ltd of Perth, which is registered for GST, decided to establish an allowance for doubtful debts as at 30 June 2010. The business had not previously raised an allowance for doubtful debts. The business accountant decided, based on past experience, to set the allowance for doubtful debts at 2% of the Accounts receivable balance.

The business's Unadjusted trial balance as at 30 June 2010 showed the following:
- Accounts receivable: $99 000 (GST inclusive) Dr
- Bad debts expense: $1500 (GST exclusive) Dr*

* Note that as this item is in the Trial balance it means that it has already been recorded and offset against Accounts receivable.

At the end of the next year on 30 June 2011 the only bad debt of $1870 (GST inclusive) for the accounting period occurred. During the year ended 30 June 2011 the only other transactions affecting the Accounts receivable account were credit sales of $120 000 (GST inclusive) and cash received from debtors of $107 130. On 30 June 2011 it was decided to maintain an allowance for doubtful debts at 2% of the balance of Accounts receivable of $110 000.

Required

a   Prepare the General journal entry required on 30 June 2010 to raise the allowance for doubtful debts.

b   Prepare the entry required on 30 June 2010 to close off the Bad debts and Doubtful debts expense accounts to the Profit and loss summary account.

c   Prepare the General journal entry required on 30 June 2011 to write off the bad debt.

d   Prepare the General journal entry required on 30 June 2011 to raise the allowance for doubtful debts.

e   Prepare the General ledger Bad debts expense, Doubtful debts expense, Accounts receivable and Allowance for doubtful debts accounts for the period 30 June 2010 to 30 June 2011.

f   Show how the Accounts receivable and Allowance for doubtful debts would be shown in the Statement of financial position as at 30 June 2010 and 2011.

Step 1

Close off the bad debts to the Profit and loss summary account.

At the beginning of the financial year ended 30 June 2010 the business did *not* use the allowance for doubtful debts method of accounting for bad debts. Therefore, the bad debts written off during the year ended 30 June 2010 of $1500 will be treated as an expense and closed off to the Profit and loss summary account.

Accounting and Finance: 2B   ISBN 9780170182041   Cengage Learning Australia

Step 2

Calculate and record the allowance for doubtful debts as at 30 June 2010 and prepare the closing entry.

At the end of the 30 June 2010 financial year the business had begun to use the allowance for doubtful debts method of accounting for bad debts. The calculation of the allowance for doubtful debts amount as at 30 June 2010 is 2% of $99 000, which is $1980, but from this amount we must exclude GST as this is recoverable from the ATO. This is done by dividing $1980 by 11, which gives $180. The $180 is then subtracted from $1980 to give the allowance for doubtful debts figure of $1800 to be established in the accounting records. Therefore the General journal entries required on 30 June 2010 are as shown below.

General journal			
Date	Account details	Debit $	Credit $
30/6/10	Doubtful debts	1 800	
	Allowance for doubtful debts		1 800
	Adjusting entry to establish the allowance for doubtful debts		
	Profit and loss summary		
	Bad debts		1 500
	Doubtful debts		1 800
	Closing entry		

The Doubtful debts account is an expense and therefore closed off to the Profit and loss summary account. When posted to the General ledger the accounts are as below.

General ledger					
Date	Account details	Debit $	Credit $	Balance $	Dr/Cr
Bad debts account					
30/6/10	Balance			1 500	Dr
	Profit and loss summary		1 500	0	
Doubtful debts account					
30/6/10	Allowance for doubtful debts	1 800		1 800	Dr
	Profit and loss summary		1 800	0	
Allowance for doubtful debts account					
30/6/10	Doubtful debts		1 800	1 800	Cr
Accounts receivable account					
30/6/10	Balance			99 000	Dr

Step 3

Prepare the extract of the Statement of financial position as at 30 June 2010.

The Statement of financial position as at 30 June 2010 would be shown as below.

Merry Wholesalers
Statement of financial position as at 30 June 2010

Current assets	$	$
Accounts receivable	99 000	
Less Allowance for doubtful debts	1 800	97 200

The amount of $97 200 is the net realisable amount to be received from the debtors as at 30 June 2010.

Step 4

Write off the bad debts in the records for the year ended 30 June 2011.

For the year ended 30 June 2011 the business has used the allowance for doubtful debts approach to accounting for bad debts. The GST collected component of $170 ($1870/11) must be excluded from the bad debt written off on 30 June 2011 as this amount is recoverable from the ATO. The bad debts expense is therefore $1700. Therefore, the bad debts for the financial year will be offset against the Allowance for doubtful debts account as seen below. The balance in the Allowance for doubtful debts account is now a $100 credit.

Step 5

Calculate and record the allowance for doubtful debts as at 30 June 2011 and prepare the closing entry.

For the new accounting period, that is the year ended 30 June 2012, we now estimate the new balance for Allowance for doubtful debts account. From 1 July 2011 the balance must be 2% of the Accounts receivable balance of $110000 (GST inclusive). This figure is $2200 but we must now exclude GST of $200 ($2200/11). Therefore, the balance for the Allowance for doubtful debts account is to be $2000 as at 30 June 2011. The adjusting entry to achieve this is the difference between the amount currently in the account, which is $100 credit, as mentioned previously, and what it now should be, which is $2000 credit. Therefore, the adjusting entry in the Allowance for doubtful debts account will be a $1900 credit and the debit entry is $1900 in the Doubtful debts account. These calculations and entries are reflected below in the General journal and General ledger.

General journal			
Date	Account details	Debit $	Credit $
30/6/11	Allowance for doubtful debts	1700	
	GST collected	170	
	Accounts receivable		
	Bad debt written off		1870
30/6/11	Doubtful debts	1900	
	Allowance for doubtful debts		1900
	Entry to adjust the allowance for doubtful debts 2% of debtors		
	Profit and loss summary	1900	
	Doubtful debts		1900
	Closing entry		

General ledger					
Date	Account details	Debit $	Credit $	Balance $	Dr/Cr
Accounts receivable account					
1/7/10	Balance			99000	Dr
30/6/11	Credit sales	120000		219000	Dr
	Cash		107130	111870	Dr
	Allowance for doubtful debts		1700	110170	Dr
	GST collected		170	110000	Dr
Doubtful debts account					
30/6/11	Allowance for doubtful debts	1900		1900	Dr
	Profit and loss summary		1900	0	
Allowance for doubtful debts account					
1/7/10	Balance			1800	Cr
30/6/11	Accounts receivable	1700		100	Cr
	Doubtful debts		1900	2000	Cr

Accounting and Finance: 2B   ISBN 9780170182041   Cengage Learning Australia

It should be noted that because this business is now using the allowance for doubtful debts method of accounting for bad debts there is no closing entry for the year ended 30 June 2011 for bad debts.

Alternative method for writing off bad debts

An alternative method for writing off bad debts is to write bad debts off to a Bad debts account and then, at the end of the financial year, transfer the balance in the Bad debts account to the Allowance for doubtful debts account as seen below.

General journal			
Date	Account details	Debit $	Credit $
30/6/11	Bad debts	1 700	
	GST collected	170	
	Accounts receivable		1 870
	Bad debt written off		
	Allowance for doubtful debts	1 700	
	Bad debts		1 700
	Transfer bad debts on balance day		

As you can see, the end result is the same as the bad debts for the year are finally transferred into the Allowance for doubtful debts account on the debit side.

Step 6

Prepare the extract of the Statement of financial position as at 30 June 2011.

Merry Wholesalers
Statement of financial position as at 30 June 2011

Current assets	$	
Accounts receivable	110 000	
Less Allowance for doubtful debts	2 000	97 200

Note that the amount shown for the Allowance for doubtful debts is the balance figure in the account at this date and *not* the amount of the adjusting entry $1900 for the year ended 30 June 2011.

Depreciation

Accounting Standard AASB 116 Property, Plant and Equipment defines depreciation as the systematic allocation of the depreciable amount of an asset over its useful life. Depreciable non-current assets must be depreciated because they have limited lives. Depreciation is a cost allocation process where the cost of the asset is apportioned over the asset's useful life. A non-current asset is an item that has future service potential or economic benefit to the business. The cost is initially recorded as an asset but these future service potentials or economic benefits are gradually used up over the asset's life. The using up of economic benefits represents an expense called *depreciation.*

The accounting procedure for depreciation on balance day is to debit the Depreciation expense account and credit the Accumulated depreciation account. This entry results in an expense being charged, which has the effect of reducing owner's equity and reflecting the using up of the economic benefits during the past accounting period that were embodied in the asset. The credit entry sets up a contra account, which will reduce the book value of the asset and this will be shown in the Statement of financial position. Note that no entry is made to reduce the original cost of the asset. That is, the asset account is *not* credited. (The nature of and accounting procedures for depreciation will be covered in more depth in Chapter 8.)

Key Concept 7.9

Depreciation

Depreciation is the systematic allocation as an expense of the depreciable amount of an asset over its useful life.

Summary of balance day adjustments	
Balance day adjustment	**Adjusting entry**
Prepaid expenses	Dr Expense Cr Prepaid expense (Asset)
Stock of supplies	Dr Expense Cr Stock of supplies (Asset)
Accrued expenses	Dr Expense Cr Accrued expense/Expense payable
Unearned income	Dr Unearned income (Liability) Cr Income
Accrued income	Dr Accrued income/Income receivable (Asset) Cr Income
Doubtful debts	Dr Doubtful debts Cr Allowance for doubtful debts
Depreciation	Dr Depreciation Cr Accumulated depreciation

EXAMPLE:

Example 7.7

Ponting Electrical Supplies and Electricians had the following Trial balance as at 30 June 2010. The business is registered for GST. The business distinguishes between electrical materials used by its electricians when completing an electrical job and electrical supplies sold over the counter at its retail outlet.

Ponting Electrical Supplies and Electricians
Trial balance as at 30 June 2010

Account	Debit $	Credit $
Cash	18 000	
Accounts receivable	25 000	
Electrical materials (Asset)	8 000	
Services fees revenue		248 000
Salaries and wages	98 000	
Interest revenue		300
Accounts payable		20 000
Prepaid rent	19 000	
General expenses	46 000	
Plant and equipment (at cost)	322 500	
Drawings – Ponting	75 000	
Capital – Ponting		215 000
Retained profits – Ponting		60 000
Short-term investment	5 000	
Unearned service fees revenue		12 500
Allowance for doubtful debts		600
GST payable		4 100
Advertising expenses	8 900	
Interest expenses	3 100	

Accounting and Finance 2B   ISBN 9780170182041   Cengage Learning Australia

Term-loan from bank (due 2019)		40 000
Office administration expenses	59 000	
Other occupancy expenses	15 400	
Vehicle expenses	16 500	
Sales (Electrical supplies)		285 000
Cost of sales (Electrical supplies)	153 700	
Inventory (Electrical supplies)	12 400	
	885 500	885 500

Additional information as at 30 June 2010

- Salaries and wages owing amount to $900.
- Rent expired during the past financial year is $17 200.
- Unearned service fees revenue at balance day is now $9800.
- Interest revenue owing amounts to $150.
- A bad debt of $220 is to be written off.
- The Allowance for doubtful debts account is to be set at 5% of the Accounts receivable balance.
- Electrical materials (Asset) used during the financial year amounted to $7500.

Required

a Prepare the General journal adjusting entries required on 30 June 2010.
b Prepare the General journal closing entries required on 30 June 2010.
c Prepare the General ledger accounts as at 30 June 2010 after entering the balances from the Trial balance and posting the General journal entries above.
d Show how the Current assets and Current liabilities would be shown in the Statement of financial position as at 30 June 2010.

Workings

- Unearned service fees revenue now earned: $12 500 − $9800 = $2700
- Allowance for doubtful debts: Accounts receivable balance $25 000 − 220 = $24 780 × 5% = $1239/11 = $112.64. Therefore, $1239 − $112.64 = $1126 (rounded)
- Doubtful debts: $1126 − 400 = $726

General journal			
Date	**Account details**	**Debit $**	**Credit $**
30/6/10	Salaries and wages expenses	900	
	Salaries and wages payable		900
	Adjusting entry		
	Rent expense	17 200	
	Prepaid rent		17 200
	Adjusting entry		
	Unearned services fees revenue	2700	
	Services fees revenue		2700
	Adjusting entry		
	Interest receivable	150	
	Interest revenue		150
	Adjusting entry		
	Allowance for doubtful debts	200	
	GST collected	20	
	Accounts receivable		220
	Bad debt written off		
	Doubtful debts	726	
	Allowance for doubtful debts		726
	Adjusting entry		

Electrical materials expense			7 500	
	Electrical materials (Asset)			7 500
Adjusting entry				
Sales (Electrical supplies)			285 000	
Services fees revenue			250 700	
Interest revenue			450	
	Profit and loss summary			536 150
Closing entry				
Profit and loss summary			426 926	
	Doubtful debts			726
	Electrical materials expense			7 500
	Rent			17 200
	Salaries and wages			98 900
	Interest expense			3 100
	Vehicles expense			16 500
	Other occupancy expenses			15 400
	Office administration expenses			59 000
	General expenses			46 000
	Advertising expenses			8 900
	Cost of sales (Electrical supplies)			153 700
Closing entry				
Profit and loss summary			109 224	
	Retained profits – Ponting			109 224
Transfer profit				
Retained profits – Ponting			75 000	
	Drawings – Ponting			75 000
Transfer drawings				

General ledger					
Date	Account details	Debit $	Credit $	Balance $	Dr/Cr
Allowance for doubtful debts account					
30/6/10	Balance			600	Cr
	Accounts receivable	200		400	Cr
	Doubtful debts		726	1 126	Cr
Cash account					
30/6/10	Balance			18 000	Dr
Accounts payable account					
30/6/10	Balance			20 000	Cr
Plant and equipment account					
30/6/10	Balance			322 500	Dr
Capital – Ponting account					
30/6/10	Balance			215 000	Cr
Short-term investment account					
30/6/10	Balance			5 000	Dr
GST payable account					
30/6/10	Balance			4 100	Cr
30/10/10	Accounts receivable	20		4 080	Cr
Term-loan from bank (due 2019) account					
30/6/10	Balance			40 000	Cr
Inventory (Electrical supplies) account					
30/6/10	Balance			12 400	Dr

Accounting and Finance: 2B   ISBN 9780170182041   Cengage Learning Australia

Accounts receivable account

30/6/10	Balance			25 000	Dr
	Allowance for doubtful debts		200	24 800	Dr
	GST payable		20	24 780	Dr

Doubtful debts account

30/6/10	Allowance for doubtful debts	726		726	Dr
	Profit and loss summary		726	0	

Electrical materials (Asset) account

30/6/10	Balance			8 000	Dr
	Electrical materials expense		7 500	500	Dr

Electrical materials expense account

30/6/10	Electrical materials (Asset)	7 500		7 500	Dr
	Profit and loss summary		7 500	0	

Unearned service fees revenue account

30/6/10	Balance			12 500	Cr
	Service fees revenue		2 700	9 800	Cr

Service fees revenue account

30/6/10	Balance			248 000	Cr
	Unearned service fees revenue		2 700	250 700	Cr
	Profit and loss summary	250 700		0	

Prepaid rent account

30/6/10	Balance			19 000	Dr
	Rent expense		17 200	1 800	Dr

Rent expense account

30/6/10	Prepaid rent	17 200		17 200	Dr
	Profit and loss summary		17 200	0	

Salaries and wages expense account

30/6/10	Balance			98 000	Dr
	Salaries and wages payable	900		98 900	Dr
	Profit and loss summary		98 900	0	

Salaries and wages payable account

30/6/10	Salaries and wages expense		900	900	Cr

Interest revenue account

30/6/10	Balance			300	Cr
	Interest receivable		150	450	Cr
	Profit and loss summary	450		0	

Interest receivable account

30/6/10	Interest revenue	150		150	Dr

Interest expenses account

30/6/10	Balance			3 100	Dr
	Profit and loss summary		3 100	0	

Sales (Electrical supplies) account

30/6/10	Balance			285 000	Cr
	Profit and loss summary	285 000		0	

Vehicle expenses account					
30/6/10	Balance			16 500	Dr
	Profit and loss summary		16 500	0	
Other occupancy expenses account					
30/6/10	Balance			15 400	Dr
	Profit and loss summary		15 400	0	
Office administration expenses account					
30/6/10	Balance			59 000	Dr
	Profit and loss summary		59 000	0	
General expenses account					
30/6/10	Balance			46 000	Dr
	Profit and loss summary		46 000	0	
Advertising expenses account					
30/6/10	Balance			8 900	Dr
	Profit and loss summary		8 900	0	
Cost of sales (Electrical supplies) account					
30/6/10	Balance			153 700	Dr
	Profit and loss summary		153 700	0	
Drawings – Ponting account					
30/6/10	Balance			75 000	Dr
	Retained profits – Ponting		75 000	0	
Retained profits – Ponting account					
30/6/10	Balance			60 000	Cr
	Profit and loss summary		109 224	169 224	Cr
	Drawings	75 000		94 224	Cr
Profit and loss summary account					
30/6/10	Sales (Electrical supplies)		285 000	285 000	Cr
	Services fees revenue		250 700	535 700	Cr
	Interest revenue		450	536 150	Cr
	Doubtful debts	726		535 424	Cr
	Electrical materials expense	7 500		527 924	Cr
	Rent	17 200		510 724	Cr
	Salaries and wages	98 900		411 824	Cr
	Interest expense	3 100		408 724	Cr
	Vehicles expense	16 500		392 224	Cr
	Other occupancy expenses	15 400		376 824	Cr
	Office administration expenses	59 000		317 824	Cr
	General expenses	46 000		271 824	Cr
	Advertising expenses	8 900		262 924	Cr
	Cost of sales (Electrical supplies)	153 700		109 224	Cr
	Retained profits – Ponting		109 224	0	

Accounting and Finance 2B   ISBN 9780170182041   Cengage Learning Australia

Ponting Electrical Supplies and Electricians
Statement of financial position (Extract) as at 30 June 2010

	$	$
Current assets		
Cash		18 000
Accounts receivable	24 780	
Less Allowance for doubtful debts	1 126	23 654
Electrical materials (Asset)		500
Inventory		12 400
Short-term investments		5 000
Prepaid rent		1 800
Interest receivable		150
Current liabilities		
Accounts payable		20 000
GST payable		4 080
Salaries and wages payable		900
Unearned service fees revenue		9 800

Test your knowledge

1 Explain the recognition criteria for income.

2 Explain the recognition criteria for expenses.

3 What is the accrual basis of accounting?

4 What is the cash accounting basis?

5 What is the purpose of balance day adjustments?

6 Define prepaid expense.

7 Define accrued expense.

8 Define unearned income.

9 Define accrued income.

10 What is the purpose of accounting for doubtful debts?

11 What is the Allowance for doubtful debts?

12 Define depreciation.

13 What is the purpose of closing entries?

Test your understanding

Topic guide

- Cash versus accrual profit: 7.1, 7.2
- Prepaid expenses: 7.3–7.5
- Accrued expenses: 7.6–7.8
- Prepaid expenses and accrued expenses: 7.9, 7.10
- Accrued revenue: 7.11–7.13
- Unearned revenue: 7.14–7.16
- Accrued revenue and unearned revenue: 7.17

- Accrued revenue, unearned revenue, accrued expenses and prepaid expenses: 7.18
- Doubtful debts: 7.19–7.22
- Accrued revenue, unearned revenue, accrued expenses, prepaid expenses and doubtful debts: 7.23, 7.24
- All balance day adjustments: 7.25–7.27

7.1 The following information relates to Indira Gandhi Children's Wear for the year ended 30 June 2010:
- As at 1 July 2009 the Accounts receivable was $13 800 Dr.
- Total sales was $45 000, of which $35 000 was sales on cash and the balance was credit sales.
- $9400 cash was received from accounts receivable.
- Total operating expenses were $21 000, of which depreciation on non-current assets was $1500 and $18 000 was paid in cash.
- Of the $18 000 paid in cash $700 relates to prepaid rent.
- $1200 is owing in salaries as at 30 June 2010.

Required
Calculate the profit or loss for the year ended 30 June 2010 using the cash accounting basis and accrual accounting basis.

7.2 Julia Roberts Financial Planning Consultants had the following transactions for the month of October 2009. The business is not registered for GST.
- Paid $3700 for office supplies on 1 October 2009 but used only $840 worth of supplies in October 2009.
- Fees for services rendered to customers on credit was $5600, for work completed in October, of which only $3800 cash had been received by the end of October 2009.
- Paid insurance of $912 for the months of October, November and December 2009.
- Paid $3400 to employees for wages for work done in October but $840 is still owing at the end of October. Paid $760 for wages owing from September 2009.
- Fees received in cash were $9500 for services rendered to customers for work completed in October 2009.
- Received a deposit of $740 cash from a customer for work to be done in November 2009.
- Received $2400 cash from customers for work completed on credit in September 2009.
- Paid $600 for electricity used in July, August and September 2009. Electricity owing for October was $210.
- Paid for other expenses of $2980 as incurred.

Required
Calculate the profit or loss for October 2009 using the cash accounting basis and accrual accounting basis.

7.3 Raindrops Traders, providers of mobile phones, set up business on 1 February 2010. The business is registered for GST. A transaction on 1 February 2010 included paying $1100 (GST inclusive) insurance for the six months from February to July inclusive. The firm also purchased stationery worth $330 (GST inclusive) on credit from Powderfinger Suppliers on 1 February 2010. The business had used $80 worth of stationery as at 30 June 2010.

Required
a Prepare the General journal entry to record the payment on 1 February 2010 and the purchase on credit on 1 February 2010. Use the asset method to record prepayments.
b Prepare the General journal adjusting entry to record the expenses on 30 June 2010.
c Prepare the entry required on 30 June 2010 to close off the Insurance expense and Stationery expense accounts to the Profit and loss summary account.

Accounting and Finance: 2B   ISBN 9780170182041   Cengage Learning Australia

d   Prepare the General ledger Profit and loss summary, Prepaid insurance, Stock of stationery, Stationery expense and Insurance expense accounts for the period February to June 2010.

e   Show how the Prepaid insurance and Stock of stationery would be shown in the Statement of financial position as at 30 June 2010.

7.4   Lois Lane Mechanical Repairs Trial balance as at 30 June 2009 showed the following balances: Prepaid insurance $1500 and Stock of oil supplies $760. It paid its annual insurance premium of $4730 (GST inclusive) on 1 November 2009. During the year ended 30 June 2010 it also paid the following amounts (GST inclusive) for oil supplies:

1 September 2009	$891
1 December 2010	$935
1 March 2010	$1 012
1 June 2010	$913

On balance day, 30 June 2010, the amount of oil supplies on hand was valued at $150 (GST exclusive). The business uses the asset method of recording all prepaid expenses.

Required

a   Prepare the General ledger accounts for the Profit and loss summary, Prepaid insurance, Insurance expense, Stock of oil supplies and Oil supplies expense for the period 1 July 2009 to 30 June 2010. Use the asset method to record prepayments.

b   Show how the Prepaid insurance and Stock of oil supplies would appear in the Statement of financial position as at 30 June 2010.

7.5   An extract of the Trial balance of Clark Kent Florists showed the following as at 30 June 2009.

Unadjusted trial balance (extract) as at 30 June 2009

Account	Debit $	Credit $
Prepaid rent	1 950	
Stock of wrapping paper	2 900	

During the year ended 30 June 2010 the following cash transactions took place:
- 1 July 2009 paid $3080 (GST inclusive) for wrapping paper supplies.
- 1 October 2009 paid $3245 (GST inclusive) for wrapping paper supplies.
- 31 August 2010 paid $11 000 (GST inclusive) being the annual rent for the business.
- 1 March 2010 paid $3575 (GST inclusive) for wrapping supplies.

As at balance day the records of the business showed that $6600 worth of wrapping supplies had been used during the year ended 30 June 2010.

Required

a   Prepare the General journal entries to record the payments made during the year ended 30 June 2010. Use the asset method to record prepayments.

b   Prepare the General journal entry required on 30 June 2010 to record the balance day adjustments and close off the Rent expense and Wrapping paper expense accounts to the Profit and loss summary account.

c   Prepare the General ledger Profit and loss summary, Prepaid rent, Stock of wrapping supplies, Wrapping paper expense and Rent expense accounts for the year ended 30 June 2010.

d   Show how the Prepaid rent and Stock of wrapping paper supplies would be shown in the Statement of financial position as at 30 June 2010.

7.6 Bravo Traders (makers of surfboards) is owned and operated by John Chance and registered for GST. For the year ended 30 June 2010 the business records showed that Salaries expenses were $84 200 Dr and Gas supplies expenses was $3680 Dr. There were no accrued expenses for salaries or gas as at 30 June 2009.

As at 30 June 2010 the business owed $2800 for salaries and this amount was paid on 6 July 2010. It also owed $620 (GST exclusive) for gas supplies as at 30 June 2010 but no tax invoice had been received at this time. The amount of $620 owing for the gas supplies plus the GST component of $62, as shown on the tax invoice received, was paid on 18 July 2010.

Required

a Prepare the General journal entry to record the adjusting entries required on 30 June 2010.

b Prepare the entry required on 30 June 2010 to close off the Salaries expense and Gas supplies expense accounts to the Profit and loss summary account.

c Prepare the General journal entries required on 6 July and 18 July 2010 to record the payments of salaries and gas supplies respectively.

d Prepare the General ledger Profit and loss summary, Salaries payable, Gas supplies payable, Salaries expense and Gas supplies expense accounts for the year ended 30 June 2010 and show how the payments made on 6 July and 18 July would appear in these accounts.

e Show how the Salaries payable and Gas supplies payable would be shown in the Statement of financial position as at 30 June 2010.

7.7 Virgil Tibbs is the owner of Night Suppliers, makers of bedroom furniture. He asks you to prepare the adjusting entries for the year ended 30 June 2010. As at 30 June 2010 the following amounts were shown in the General ledger:

• Wages expense: $160 000 Dr
• Water usage expense: $1200 Dr.

The staff is paid $6700 per fortnight for working Monday to Friday each week. The 30 June 2010 fell on a Tuesday of the second week of the pay fortnight. The pay fortnight had begun on 22 June 2010 and the staff are next due to be paid on Friday 3 July. Virgil also advised that he owes the Water Corporation $1450 (GST exclusive) for water usage during the past six months for which the invoice had not been received as at 30 June 2010.

On 3 July 2010 the staff are paid the wages owing and on 29 July 2010 the water usage account is paid including the GST component of $145.

Required

a Prepare the General journal to record the adjusting entries required on 30 June 2010.

b Prepare the entry required on 30 June 2010 to close off the Wages expense and Water usage expense accounts to the Profit and loss summary account.

c Prepare the General journal entries required on 3 July and 29 July 2010 to record the payments for the expenses of wages and water usage respectively.

d Prepare the General ledger Profit and loss summary, Wages payable, Water usage payable, Wages expense and Water usage expense accounts for the year ended 30 June 2010 and show how the payments made on 3 July and 29 July would appear in these accounts.

e Show how the Wages payable and Water usage payable would be shown in the Statement of financial position as at 30 June 2010.

7.8 Bogart Jewellery had the following balances in its General ledger at 1 June 2010:

• Telephone expense: $1800 Dr
• Interest expense: $1800 Dr.

As at 1 July 2009 the business had a term loan of $40 000 outstanding at an interest rate of 6% per annum. Interest of $600 per quarter is paid on 1 August, 1 November,

Accounting and Finance 2B   ISBN 9780170182041   Cengage Learning Australia

1 February and 1 May every year. The next interest payment is to be made on 1 August 2010.

The last telephone bill of $660 (GST inclusive) was received on 31 March 2010 and this was for the usage over the four months prior to that date. The business expects its next telephone bill to arrive on 31 July 2010 and that this will be $800 (GST exclusive) and that the telephone usage over the four months will be even. As at 30 June 2010 no tax invoice had been received for the telephone expense. The telephone company's tax invoice was received and paid on 31 July 2010 and it was for $880 (GST inclusive).

Required

a Prepare the General ledger Profit and loss summary, Interest payable, Telephone expense payable, Interest expense and Telephone expense accounts for the month ended 30 June 2010 and show how the payments made on 31 July and 1 August 2010 would appear in these accounts.

b Show how the Interest payable and Telephone expense accounts would be shown in the Statement of financial position as at 30 June 2010.

7.9 The following information relates to Joan Arc Sports Store on 30 June 2010:

Trial balance (extract) as at 30 June 2010

Account	Debit $	Credit $
Cash	25 000	
Prepaid rent	12 360	
Inventory	46 500	
Accounts payable		36 500
Stationery supplies (asset)	2 540	
Wages expense	89 700	
Loan from bank (due 2019)		100 000
Accounts receivable	48 900	

Rent of $13 596 (GST inclusive) was paid on 28 August 2009 for the year 1 September 2009 to 31 August 2010.

Additional information as at 30 June 2010

- Rent expired during the financial year was $10 300.
- Wages owing was $5600.
- Stationery supplies unused were valued at $500.

Additional information for July 2010

- Paid the wages owing of $5600 on 8 July 2010

Required

a Prepare the General journal entry to record the payment made for rent in advance on 28 August 2009.

b Prepare the General journal entries for the balance day adjustments on 30 June 2010.

c Prepare the closing General journal entries for the items above on 30 June 2010.

d Prepare the Profit and loss summary, Prepaid rent, Stationery supplies (asset), Wages expense, Rent expense, Wages payable and Stationery expense accounts as they would be shown in the ledger after the posting of the adjusting and closing entries. Show how the transaction on 8 July 2010 would affect these accounts.

e Show how the current asset and current liability accounts would appear in the Statement of financial position as at 30 June 2010 after the adjustments have been made.

Accounting and Finance 2B   ISBN 9780170182041   Cengage Learning Australia

7.10 The following information relates to Helen Keller Chocolate Store on 30 June 2010:

Trial balance (extract) as at 30 June 2010

Account	Debit $	Credit $
Inventory	74000	
Prepaid insurance	8760	
Bank overdraft		24100
Accounts payable		48900
Advertising supplies (asset)	5600	
Electricity expense	14500	
Equipment		250000
Accounts receivable	68700	

The insurance paid in advance of $9636 (GST inclusive) was made on 26 September 2009.

Additional information as at 30 June 2010
- The Prepaid insurance amount of $8760 (GST exclusive) was the annual insurance for the period 1 October 2009 to 30 September 2010.
- Electricity owing was $5600 (GST exclusive).
- Advertising supplies (asset) used during the financial year were $5200.

Additional information for July 2010
- Paid the electricity owing of $5600 plus the GST outlay of $560 on 19 July 2010

Required
a Prepare the General journal entry to record the payment made of insurance in advance on 26 September 2009.
b Prepare the General journal entries for the balance day adjustments on 30 June 2010.
c Prepare the closing General journal entries for the items above on 30 June 2010.
d Prepare the Profit and loss summary, Prepaid insurance, Advertising supplies (asset), Electricity expense, Insurance expense, Electricity payable and Advertising expense accounts as they would be shown in the ledger after the posting of the adjusting and closing entries. Show how the transaction on 19 July 2010 would affect these accounts.
e Show how the current asset and current liability accounts would appear in the Statement of financial position as at 30 June 2010 after the adjustments have been made.

7.11 Peck Plumbers is registered for GST and it specialises in installing plumbing in new homes. Clients of the business are usually billed at the completion of the job, however at the end of the financial year there are a few jobs where this has not occurred. A review of the records reveals that $9400 (GST exclusive) worth of work for clients has been completed but no tax invoice has been issued.

The business also has a short-term investment which on balance day the interest of $600 for the previous three months has not been received. For the year ended 30 June 2010 their Unadjusted Trial balance showed the following:
- Plumbing service revenue: $140000 Cr
- Interest revenue: $1940 Cr.

There was no accrued revenue for plumbing services or interest as at 30 June 2009.

The amount owing as at 30 June 2010 of $9400 (GST exclusive) plus the GST collected of $940 for plumbing service revenue was received in cash on 21 July 2010 when the tax invoice was issued. In addition the amount owing from interest revenue of $600 was received in cash on 31 July 2010 as well as the interest earned for the month of July of $150.

Accounting and Finance: 2B   ISBN 9780170182041   Cengage Learning Australia

Required

a Prepare the General journal entry to record the adjusting entries required on 30 June 2010.

b Prepare the entry required on 30 June 2010 to close off the Plumbing service revenue and Interest revenue accounts to the Profit and loss summary account.

c Prepare the General journal entries required on 21 July and 31 July 2010 to record the receipts from the Plumbing service revenue and Interest revenue accounts respectively.

d Prepare the General ledger Profit and loss summary, Accounts receivable, Interest receivable, Plumbing service revenue and Interest revenue accounts for the year ended 30 June 2010 and show how the receipts of 21 July and 31 July would appear in these accounts.

e Show how the Accounts receivable and Interest receivable would be shown in the Statement of financial position as at 30 June 2010.

7.12 The business of Jimmy Stewart Lawyers bills clients at the completion of a job. As at 30 June 2009 accrued revenue for services rendered to clients for legal services was $6800 (GST exclusive) and this was received in cash on 16 July 2009 plus the GST collected component of $680.

During the year ended 30 June 2010 the business earned $284 000 (GST exclusive) in legal fees from clients and also $24 500 (GST exclusive) from commission work. On 30 June 2010 work completed for which no tax invoice had been issued was as follows:

- Legal fees revenue: $4800 (GST exclusive)
- Commission revenue: $840 (GST exclusive).

The accrued legal fees revenue of $4800 plus the GST collected component of $480 was received in cash when the tax invoice was issued on 17 July 2010. The accrued commission revenue plus the GST collected was received in cash on 26 July 2010.

Required

a Prepare the General journal entry to record the adjusting entries required on 30 June 2010.

b Prepare the entry required on 30 June 2010 to close off the Legal fees revenue and Commission Revenue accounts to the Profit and loss summary account.

c Prepare the General journal entries required on 17 July and 26 July 2010 to record the receipts from the Legal fees revenue and Commission revenue accounts respectively.

d Prepare the General ledger Profit and loss summary, Accounts receivable, Interest receivable, Legal fees revenue and Commission revenue accounts for the year ended 30 June 2010 and show how the receipts made on 17 July and 26 July 2010 would appear in these accounts.

e Show how the Accounts receivable and Commission receivable would be shown in the Statement of financial position as at 30 June 2010.

7.13 Raquel Welsh Accountants showed the following amounts in its Trial balance as at 30 June 2010.

Trial balance (extract) as at 30 June 2010

Account	Debit $	Credit $
Interest revenue		3480
Accounting service fees		278 000

Additional information

- The last interest payment from the bank was on 30 April 2010 and the next payment is due on 31 July 2010. The business has estimated that at current interest rates $1000 is owing from interest revenue on 30 June 2010.
- Work completed for clients for which no tax invoices have been issued amounts to $6900 (GST exclusive).

The interest received of $1500 on 31 July 2010 included the amount of $1000 owing on 30 June 2010. On 20 July 2010 the business issued tax invoices totalling $9460 (GST inclusive), which included the amounts owing as above on 30 June 2010. The cash was received on 29 July 2010.

Required

a   Prepare the General ledger Profit and loss summary, Accounts receivable, Interest receivable, Accounting fees revenue and Interest revenue accounts on 30 June 2010 and show how the transactions on 20 July, 29 July and 31 July 2010 would be recorded.

b   Show how the Accounts receivable and Interest receivable would be shown in the Statement of financial position as at 30 June 2010.

7.14   A Jolie Adventure Tours, which is registered for GST, receives payment from its customers in advance before a tour begins. The last receipt from a customer, being an advance payment for a tour in July of $3850 (GST inclusive), was received on 27 June 2010. As at 30 June 2010 the business's Unadjusted Trial balance included the following amounts:
   • Adventure tour fees revenue: $154 000 (GST exclusive) Cr
   • Unearned adventure tour fees revenue: $54 200 (GST exclusive) Cr.
      On balance day 30 June 2010, $42 000 of the amount of Unearned adventure tour fees revenue represented tours completed and was thus revenue earned.

Required

a   Prepare the General journal entry to record the receipt of monies on 27 June 2010. Use the liability method to record revenue received in advance.

b   Prepare the General journal entry to record the adjusting entry required on 30 June 2010.

c   Prepare the entry required on 30 June 2010 to close off the Adventure tour fees revenue account to the Profit and loss summary account.

d   Prepare the General ledger Profit and loss summary, Unearned adventure tour fees revenue and Adventure tour fees revenue accounts for the year ended 30 June 2010.

e   Show how the Unearned adventure tour fees revenue account would be shown in the Statement of financial position as at 30 June 2010.

7.15   Audrey Hepburn Fashion House makes high-fashion clothes. It expects payment in advance for large orders. The following financial events took place during the year ended 30 June 2010:
   • 1 July 2009 – amount of Unearned fashion fees was $8900 (GST exclusive).
   • 30 November 2009 – received $33 000 (GST inclusive) cash for advanced order of fashion clothes.
   • 31 December 2009 – sold $30 800 (GST inclusive) worth of fashion clothes on cash.
   • 1 April 2010 – received $49 500 (GST inclusive) cash for advanced order of fashion clothes.
   • 30 May 2010 – sold on credit $37 400 (GST inclusive) worth of fashion clothes.
   • 30 June 2010 – filled $50 000 (GST exclusive) worth of Unearned fashion fees orders during the past financial year.

Required

a   Prepare the General ledger Profit and loss summary, Unearned fashion fees revenue and Fashion fees revenue accounts for the year ended 30 June 2010. Use the liability method to record revenue received in advance.

b   Show how the Unearned fashion fees account would be shown in the Statement of financial position as at 30 June 2010.

7.16   Jenny Lopez Manufacturers makes designer shoes, but it only uses a part of its factory. The unused part of the factory is rented out to P Cruz, who is required to pay in advance each quarter rental of $7480 (GST inclusive) for each three-month period. During the year ended 30 June 2010 rental money was received on 31 July 2009, 31 October 2009, 31 January 2010 and 30 April 2010. As at 1 July 2009 Unearned rent revenue was $2266.

Accounting and Finance: 2B   ISBN 9780170182041   Cengage Learning Australia

Required

a Prepare the General journal entry to record the receipt of cash on 30 April 2010.
Use the liability method to record revenue received in advance.

b Prepare the General journal entry to record the adjusting entry required on 30 June 2010.

c Prepare the entry required on 30 June 2010 to close off the Rent revenue account to the Profit and loss summary account.

d Prepare the General ledger Profit and loss summary Unearned rent revenue and Rent revenue accounts for the year ended 30 June 2010.

e Show how the Unearned rent revenue account would be shown in the Statement of financial position as at 30 June 2010.

7.17 The following information relates to Alan Ladd Travel Agency on 30 June 2010. The business is registered for GST.

Trial balance (extract) as at 30 June 2010

Account	Debit $	Credit $
Cash	56 800	
Unearned fees revenue		14 600
Inventory	34 800	
Accounts payable		28 600
Fees revenue		134 000
Mortgage (due 2019)		85 000
Accounts receivable	41 200	
Interest revenue		1 200

The most recent client to pay for a tour in advance was on 20 June 2010 and the amount paid was $2310 (GST inclusive). This amount is included in the Trial balance figure of $14 600.

Additional information as at 30 June 2010

• Some clients pay in advance for some part of the service. Of the Unearned fees revenue amount of $14 600, $12 000 now represents tasks completed for clients during the past financial year.

• Interest revenue owing was $450.

Additional information for July 2010

• The Interest revenue owing as at 30 June 2010 of $450 was received on 31 July 2010.

Required

a Prepare the General journal entry to record the receipt of $2310 on 20 June 2010.

b Prepare the General journal entries for the balance day adjustments on 30 June 2010.

c Prepare the closing General journal entries for the items above on 30 June 2010.

d Prepare the Profit and loss summary, Unearned fees revenue, Fees revenue, Interest revenue and Interest receivable accounts as they would be shown in the ledger after the posting of the adjusting and closing entries. Show how the transaction on 31 July 2010 would affect these accounts.

e Show how the Current asset and Current liability accounts would appear in the Statement of financial position as at 30 June 2010 after the adjustments have been made.

7.18 The following information relates to Roden Cutler Architects on 30 June 2010. The business is registered for GST.

Trial balance (extract) as at 30 June 2010

Account	Debit $	Credit $
Cash	23 500	
Unearned consulting fees revenue		35 600
Equipment and furniture	146 000	
Accounts payable		37 500
Consulting fees revenue		235 000
Mortgage (due 2017)		105 000
Accounts receivable	56 400	
Commission revenue		13 400
Salaries expense	164 000	
Prepaid rent	56 500	

The most recent client to pay in advance for a consulting service paid $2035 (GST inclusive) on 23 June 2010. This amount is included in the Trial balance amount of $35 600.

Additional information as at 30 June 2010
- Clients usually pay in advance for some part of the consulting service. Of the Unearned consulting fees revenue amount of $35 600, $26 800 now represents tasks completed for clients during the past financial year.
- Commission revenue owing is $3500 (GST exclusive) for which no tax invoice has been issued.
- Salaries owing is $6500.
- The Prepaid rent of $56 500 was for the period 1 August 2009 to 31 July 2010.

Additional information for July 2010
- Received the Commission revenue owing as at 30 June 2010 of $3500 plus the GST collected of $350 on 24 July 2010.
- The Salaries owing of $6500 were paid on 7 July 2010.

Required
a Prepare the General journal entry required on 23 June 2010 to record the receipt of $2035.
b Prepare the General journal entries for the balance day adjustments on 30 June 2010.
c Prepare the closing General journal entries for the items above on 30 June 2010.
d Prepare the Profit and loss summary, Unearned consulting fees revenue, Consulting fees revenue, Commission revenue, Rent expense, Prepaid rent, Salaries expense, Salaries payable and Commission receivable accounts as they would be shown in the ledger after the posting of the adjusting and closing entries. Show how the transactions on 7 July and 24 July 2010 would affect these accounts.
e Show how the current asset and current liability accounts would appear in the Statement of financial position as at 30 June 2010 after the adjustments have been made.

7.19 Kels Pty Ltd of Perth, which is registered for GST, had bad debts totalling $870 (GST exclusive) for the year ended 30 June 2009 and the amounts concerned had been recorded and offset against Accounts receivable. The company did not raise an allowance for doubtful debts but decided to establish such a procedure for the following financial year. It was decided to set the allowance for doubtful debts to be 1.5% of the Accounts receivable balance. The Trial balance as at 30 June 2009 showed:
- Accounts receivable: $74 910 (GST inclusive) Dr.

Accounting and Finance: 2B   ISBN 9780170182041   Cengage Learning Australia

Required

a Prepare the General journal entry required on 30 June 2009 to raise the allowance for doubtful debts.

b Prepare the entry required on 30 June 2009 to close off the Bad debts and Doubtful debts expense accounts to the Profit and loss summary account.

c Prepare the General ledger Profit and loss summary, Bad debts expense, Doubtful debts expense, Accounts receivable and Allowance for doubtful debts accounts as at 30 June 2009.

d Show how the Accounts receivable and Allowance for doubtful debts would be shown in the Statement of financial position as at 30 June 2009.

7.20 Elise Pty Ltd established an Allowance for doubtful debts account on 30 June 2009 of $1500. Its Accounts receivable balance as at 30 June 2009 was $75 000 (GST inclusive). On 30 June 2010 the only bad debt of $1430 (GST inclusive) for the accounting period occurred. During the year ended 30 June 2010 the other transactions affecting the Accounts receivable account were credit sales of $97 900 (GST inclusive) and cash received from debtors of $84 000. On 30 June 2010 it was decided to raise an allowance for doubtful debt to be 2% of the balance of Accounts receivable.

Required

a Prepare the General journal entry required on 30 June 2010 to write-off the bad debt.

b Prepare the General journal entry required on 30 June 2010 to raise the allowance for doubtful debts.

c Prepare the entry required on 30 June 2010 to close off the Doubtful debts expense account to the Profit and loss summary account.

d Prepare the General ledger Profit and loss summary, Doubtful debts expense, Accounts receivable and Allowance for doubtful debts accounts for the year ended 30 June 2010.

e Show how the Accounts receivable and Allowance for doubtful debts would be shown in the Statement of financial position as at 30 June 2010.

7.21 Rhian Pty Ltd had the following balances in its Trial balance as at 1 July 2009:

Trial balance (extract) as at 1 July 2009

Account	Debit $	Credit $
Accounts receivable	67 000	
Allowance for doubtful debts		1 005

The company is registered for GST and during the year ended 30 June 2010 the following took place:
- Total credit sales: $76 120 (GST inclusive)
- Cash received from debtors: $69 800
- Bad debt written off on 1 May 2010: $913 (GST inclusive).

It was decided to raise an allowance for doubtful debts of 1.5% of Accounts receivable as at 30 June 2010.

Required

a Prepare the General journal entry required on 1 May 2010 to write off the bad debt.

b Prepare the General journal entry required on 30 June 2010 to adjust the allowance for doubtful debts.

c Prepare the entry required on 30 June 2010 to close off the Doubtful debts expense account to the Profit and loss summary account.

d Prepare the General ledger Profit and loss summary, Doubtful debts expense, Accounts receivable and Allowance for doubtful debts accounts for the year ended 30 June 2010.

e   Show how the Accounts receivable and Allowance for doubtful debts would be shown
     in the Statement of financial position as at 30 June 2010.

7.22 Monet Pty Ltd is registered for GST and during the year ended 30 June 2010 the following
      events took place:
      • The allowance for doubtful debts balance as at 1 July 2009 was $2400.
      • Bad debt, the only one for the financial year, of $2970 (GST inclusive) was written off
        on 1 April 2010.
      • The accounts receivable balance as at 30 June 2010 was $139 700 (GST inclusive).
      • The Allowance for doubtful debts is to be adjusted to 2% of the Accounts receivable as
        at 30 June 2010.

Required
a   Prepare the General journal entry required on 1 April 2010 to write off the bad debt.
b   Prepare the General journal entry required on 30 June 2010 to adjust the allowance for
     doubtful debts.
c   Prepare the entry required on 30 June 2010 to close off the Doubtful debts expense
     account to the Profit and loss summary account.
d   Prepare the General ledger Profit and loss summary, Doubtful debts expense, Accounts
     receivable and Allowance for doubtful debts accounts for the year ended 30 June 2010.
e   Show how the Accounts receivable and Allowance for doubtful debts would be shown
     in the Statement of financial position as at 30 June 2010.

7.23 The following information relates to Lionel Rose Enterprises on 30 June 2010. The business
      is registered for GST.

Trial balance (extract) as at 30 June 2010

Account	Debit $	Credit $
Accounts receivable	56 900	
Unearned rental fees revenue		18 720
Rental fees revenue		23 500
Allowance for doubtful debts		500
Interest revenue		1 800
Gas expense	8 700	
Prepaid insurance	7 600	
Insurance expense	2 400	

Additional information as at 30 June 2010
• The business rents out some of its vacant warehouse space. The amount of $18 720 (GST
  exclusive) was rent received in advance for the period 1 February 2010 to 31 January 2011.
• Interest revenue owing is $750 (GST exclusive).
• Gas expense owing is $1080 (GST exclusive).
• The Prepaid insurance of $7600 (GST exclusive) was for the period 1 November 2009 to
  31 October 2010.
• The allowance for doubtful debts is to be adjusted to 2% of the balance of Accounts
  receivable as at 30 June 2010.

Additional information for July 2010
• Received on 31 July 2010 Interest revenue of $930 including the amount owing as at 30
  June 2010 of $750.
• Paid the Gas expense tax invoice received on 30 July 2010 of $1650 (GST inclusive),
  including the amount owing on 30 June 2010 of $1080 (GST exclusive) plus the GST
  component of $108.

Accounting and Finance 2B   ISBN 9780170182041   Cengage Learning Australia

Required

a   Prepare the General journal entries for the balance day adjustments on 30 June 2010.

b   Prepare the closing General journal entries for the aforementioned items on 30 June 2010.

c   Prepare the General journal entries required for the transactions in July 2010.

d   Prepare the General ledger accounts, including the Profit and loss summary account, that are required after the posting of the aforementioned adjusting and closing entries.

e   Show how the transactions in July 2010 would appear in the appropriate General ledger accounts.

f   Show how the current asset and current liability accounts would appear in the Statement of financial position as at 30 June 2010 after the adjustments have been made.

7.24   The following information relates to Bowral Enterprises on 30 June 2010. The business is registered for GST.

Trial balance (extract) as at 30 June 2010

Account	Debit $	Credit $
Allowance for doubtful debts	870	
Unearned membership fees revenue		140 000
Membership fees revenue		230 000
Accounts receivable	45 000	
Commission revenue		24 000
Electricity expense	9 100	
Prepaid rent	14 300	
Fuel and oil supplies (asset)	18 700	

Additional information as at 30 June 2010

- A bad debt of $440 (GST inclusive) was written off on 30 June 2010.
- Some customers pay a membership fee for the whole year beginning on 1 January each year. The amount of $140 000 (GST exclusive) is the annual total amount paid by those customers on 1 January 2010.
- Commission revenue owing is $3600 (GST exclusive).
- Electricity expense owing is $980 (GST exclusive).
- The Prepaid rent of $14 300 (GST exclusive) was for the period 1 February 2010 to 31 January 2011
- The allowance for doubtful debts is to be adjusted to 1.5% of the balance of Accounts receivable as at 30 June 2010.
- The fuel and oil still on hand as at 30 June 2010 was worth $2600.

Additional information for July 2010:

- Received $3600 plus $360 GST collected on 15 July 2010 the Commission revenue owing on 30 June 2010.
- Paid the Electricity expense tax invoice received on 31 July 2010 of $1536 (GST inclusive), including the amount owing on 30 June 2010 of $980 (GST exclusive) plus the GST component of $98

Required

a   Prepare the General journal entries for the balance day adjustments on 30 June 2010.

b   Prepare the closing General journal entries for the items above on 30 June 2010.

c   Prepare the General journal entries required for the transactions in July 2010.

d   Prepare the General ledger accounts, including the Profit and loss summary account, that are required after the posting of the adjusting and closing entries above.

e   Show how the transactions in July 2010 would appear in the appropriate General ledger accounts.

f   Show how the current asset and current liability accounts would appear in the Statement of financial position as at 30 June 2010 after the adjustments have been made.

7.25   The following is the Trial balance of Gilchrest Lawyers as at 30 June 2010. The business is registered for GST.

Trial balance as at 30 June 2010

Account	Debit $	Credit $
Cash	45 080	
Accounts receivable	56 000	
Services fees revenue		341 000
Commission revenue		15 600
Accounts payable		15 400
Prepaid general insurance	8 900	
Other general expenses	46 000	
Furniture and equipment (at cost)	365 000	
Drawings – Gilchrest	104 000	
Capital – Gilchrest		200 000
Retained profits – Gilchrest		42 000
Unearned service fees revenue		85 000
Allowance for doubtful debts		980
GST payable		5 200
Selling expenses	34 000	
Interest expenses	4 200	
Term-loan from bank (due 2019)		97 000
Office administration expenses	105 000	
Occupancy expenses	34 000	
	802 180	802 180

Additional information as at 30 June 2010
- Interest expense owing amounts to $820.
- General insurance expired during the past financial year is $7100.
- Unearned service fees revenue at balance day is now $14 200.
- Commission revenue owing amounts to $2560 (GST exclusive).
- The Allowance for doubtful debts account is to be set at 3% of the Accounts receivable balance.

Additional information for July 2010
- Paid the $820 on 31 July 2010 relating to the Interest expense owing on 30 June 2010.
- Received on 7 July 2010 the $2560 (GST exclusive) plus the GST collected component of $256 relating to the Commission revenue owing on 30 June 2010.

Required
a   Prepare the General journal adjusting entries required on 30 June 2010.

b   Prepare the General journal closing entries, including the transfer of profit/loss and transfer of the Drawings account balance, required on 30 June 2010.

c   Prepare the General journal entries required on 7 July and 31 July 2010.

Accounting and Finance: 2B   ISBN 9780170182041   Cengage Learning Australia

d   Prepare the General ledger accounts including the Profit and loss Summary, Drawings and Retained profit accounts after entering the balances from the Trial balance and posting the General journal entries required earlier and show how the entries required on 7 July and 31 July 2010 affect either the Interest payable or Commission receivable accounts.

e   Show how the Current assets and Current liabilities would be shown in the Statement of financial position as at 30 June 2010.

7.26 The following is the Trial balance of the Tom Starcevich Music Store as at 30 June 2010. The business is registered for GST.

Trial balance as at 30 June 2010

Account	Debit $	Credit $
Bank overdraft		24 980
Accounts receivable	13 400	
DJ revenue		14 700
Paper supplies (Asset)	8 970	
Electricity expenses	15 400	
Advertising expenses	67 800	
Interest expenses	6 420	
Mortgage from bank (due 2019)		138 500
General expenses	170 000	
Land (at cost)	340 000	
Premises (at cost)	289 000	
Drawings – Tom Starcevich	94 000	
Capital – Tom Starcevich		596 000
Administration expenses	145 000	
Occupancy expenses	67 850	
Distribution expenses	24 100	
Sales		567 000
Cost of sales	165 000	
Inventory	87 500	
Rent revenue		7 600
Accounts payable		68 700
Prepaid insurance	12 400	
Retained profits – Tom Starcevich		62 000
Unearned rent revenue		12 400
Allowance for doubtful debts		460
GST payable		14 500
	1 506 840	1 506 840

Additional information as at 30 June 2010
- Electricity expense owing amount to $870 (GST exclusive).
- Prepaid insurance now expired is $12 000 (Insurance expense is part of Occupancy expenses).
- The business rents out some spare shop store space and the rent is received in advance each three months. The amount of $12 400 for Unearned rent revenue represents the three-month period from 1 June 2010.
- $6800 (GST exclusive) is owing from DJ work performed in June 2010 but for which no tax invoice has been issued as at 30 June 2010.
- A bad debt of $484 (GST inclusive) is to be written off.
- The Allowance for doubtful debts account is to be set at 6% of the Accounts receivable balance.
- Paper supplies (Asset) used during the financial year amounted to $6780.

Additional information for July 2010
- Paid $1050 Electricity expense on 11 July 2010, including the amount of $870 (GST exclusive) plus the GST outlay of $87 for Electricity payable owing on 30 June 2010
- Received $6800 (GST exclusive) plus the GST collected of $680 on 17 July 2010 relating to the DJ revenue owing on 30 June 2010

Required
a Prepare the General journal adjusting entries required on 30 June 2010.
b Prepare the General journal closing entries, including the transfer of Profit/loss and transfer of the Drawings account balance, required on 30 June 2010.
c Prepare the General journal entries required on 11 July and 17 July 2010.
d Prepare the General ledger accounts including the Profit and loss summary, Drawings and Retained profits account for as at 30 June 2010 after entering the balances from the Trial balance and posting the General journal entries.
e Show how the Current assets and Current liabilities would be shown in the Statement of financial position as at 30 June 2010.

7.27 The following is the Trial balance of the Arthur Hall Bookshop as at 30 June 2010. The business is registered for GST.

Trial balance as at 30 June 2010

Account	Debit $	Credit $
Cash	35 400	
Accounts receivable	18 900	
Stationery supplies (Asset)	2 500	
Book club membership fees revenue		43 000
Shop wages expenses	142 000	
Interest revenue		1 450
Accounts payable		58 400
Prepaid shop rent	48 900	
General expenses	56 000	
Fixtures and fittings (at cost)	654 000	
Drawings – A Hall	89 000	
Capital – A Hall		680 000
Retained profits – A Hall		45 000
Long-term investment	13 540	
Unearned book club membership fees revenue		25 400
Allowance for doubtful debts		780
GST payable		8 970
Marketing expenses	24 700	
Interest expenses	4 520	
Mortgage from bank (due 2019)		136 500
Administration expenses	87 540	
Occupancy expenses	34 500	
Transport expenses	21 300	
Sales		458 700
Cost of sales	156 700	
Inventory	68 700	
	1 458 200	1 458 200

Additional information as at 30 June 2010
- Shop wages owing amount to $900
- The rental agreement requires the business to pay a year in advance at 1 October each year. The amount of $48 900 was the annual rent paid on 1 October 2009. Rent expense is a part of Occupancy expenses.
- The Book club membership fees for members are payable every three months in advance. The amount of Unearned book club membership fees revenue of $25 400 was received on 1 May 2010.
- Interest revenue owing amounts to $654
- A bad debt of $154 (GST inclusive) is to be written off
- The Allowance for doubtful debts account is to be set at 5% of the Accounts receivable balance
- Stationery supplies (Asset) used during the financial year amounted to $1840

Additional information for July 2010
- Paid on 8 July 2010 the Shop wages expense of $1500, which includes the amount of $900 owing on 30 June 2010
- Received on 31 July 2010 $950 Interest revenue, which includes the $654 amount owing on 30 June 2010

Required
a   Prepare the General journal adjusting entries required on 30 June 2010.
b   Prepare the General journal closing entries, including the transfer of Profit/loss and transfer of the Drawings account balance, required on 30 June 2010.
c   Prepare the General journal entries required on 8 July and 31 July 2010.
d   Prepare the General ledger accounts, including the Profit and loss summary account, after entering the balances from the Trial balance and posting the General journal entries required above.
e   Show how the Current assets and Current liabilities would be shown in the Statement of financial position as at 30 June 2010.

Investigation

Select one of the following industries and use the internet to find a company within that industry (perhaps one that you are familiar with):
- media
- retail
- building
- engineering.

Search its website for its annual report and then answer the following questions:

1   When is balance day?

2   What was the profit for the current year?

3   What types of balance day adjustments does the company appear to have made?

4   What is the amount of Accounts receivable?

5   What is the amount of the Allowance for doubtful debts and what is its percentage of Accounts receivable?

6   What was the amount of bad debts for the year?

7   What is the amount of Prepaid expenses and which expenses have been affected?

8   What is the amount of Accrued expenses and which expenses have been affected?

9   What is the policy of the company on the recognition of revenue?

10 Does the company appear to have changed its revenue recognition policy?

Essay

Discuss the importance of the accrual basis of accounting and balance day adjustments to the users of financial statements including in your answer the following:

- an explanation of the recognition criteria for income and expense
- a description of the accrual basis of accounting
- an explanation of the purpose of balance day adjustments
- a description of the various types of adjusting entries
- an explanation of the purpose of accounting for doubtful debts.

Ethics case study

William Tell Manufacturers Pty Ltd makes furniture. One of the owners, Bill Tell, who is the managing director, wants to expand the business. The business has not been as profitable in recent years and this has been reflected in a declining share value.

Bill Tell asks the general manager, Robert Loxley, to determine how the expansion can be funded. One option, which Robert Loxley favours, is for the business to borrow more money and he is considering approaching the North Bank. The business, however, already has an existing loan from the East Bank and the loan agreement with them requires that the business has a debt-to-equity ratio not greater than 70 per cent. At present the business debt-to-equity ratio is 65 per cent. To borrow the required amount of $200 000 would mean that the debt to equity ratio would rise to 75 per cent, which is over the permitted limit.

The general manager instructs the firm's accountant, Arthur King, on 30 June to amend the balance day adjustments for this financial year as follows:

- Alter the allowance for doubtful debts from 5% of Accounts receivable to only 1%.
- Delay any writing off of bad debts until the new financial year.
- Do not record any expenses owing at balance day.
- Show all unearned income as earned at balance day.
- Reduce the amount of depreciation to be charged this year.
- Show all rent and insurance prepaid as expired even though they have both been paid six months in advance as at 30 June.
- Show all research and development costs as an intangible asset and not as an expense for this financial year.

Arthur has estimated that the above manipulations will increase profits and hence the equity in the Statement of financial position of the business, so that the debt-to-equity ratio will decrease to 59 per cent. In this way the business will be able to borrow the extra $200 000 required and keep its debt-to-equity ratio below 70 per cent.

The general manager owns some shares in the company, though he is not a director. He has been considering selling his shares in the business due to the declining profitability.

Arthur is uncomfortable with the instruction from the general manager, which would result in a large increase (on paper) in the profitability of the business compared with previous years.

Required

1   Who are the stakeholders in this case?

2   Describe the ethical problems for Arthur.

3   What are the consequences for Arthur if he does nothing about this issue?

4   What alternatives are available to Arthur?

5   What would you suggest that Arthur do in this case?

Chapter 8

ACCOUNTING FOR NON-CURRENT ASSETS

What You Will Learn

After studying this chapter you should be able to:

1 Define and explain the nature of depreciation expense
2 Explain the purpose and nature of the balance day adjustment for depreciation
3 Explain the nature of a depreciable non-current asset
4 Determine the cost of a depreciable non-current asset
5 Identify the most appropriate method of depreciation to select for a given non-current asset
6 Identify and calculate the over- or under-depreciation on an asset sold
7 Explain the factors that contribute to a non-current asset having a limited life
8 Explain the factors that need to be considered when determining how to depreciate a non-current asset
9 Calculate the amount of depreciation using the straight line or reducing balance method
10 Prepare the General journal and General ledger entries to account for depreciation
11 Prepare the General journal and General ledger entries to account for the disposal of a non-current asset

Introduction

This chapter is concerned with the concept of depreciation and the procedures for the disposal of non-current assets. Some costs incurred by a business are not recorded as expenses because they contain future economic benefits; these costs are called *capital expenditures*. These capital expenditures are recorded as assets and some of these assets, called non-current assets, contain economic benefits that benefit more than one accounting period.

Over a period of time these non-current assets contribute towards the earning of income and the future economic benefits contained in those assets that have limited lives are gradually used up. The consumption of these economic benefits is an expense called *depreciation*. Accounting standard AASB 116 Property, Plant and Equipment defines depreciation as 'the systematic allocation of the depreciable amount of an asset over its useful life'. In this chapter we examine this definition considering the nature of depreciation, its purpose, the characteristics of a depreciable asset and the methods of depreciation. When a non-current asset is disposed of, accounting standards require that the gain or loss be reported in the profit or loss of the business. We shall also examine the accounting procedures involved in this process.

THE NATURE OF A DEPRECIABLE NON-CURRENT ASSET

Key Concept 8.1

Depreciable non-current asset
A depreciable non-current asset is an item of property, plant and equipment that has a limited life.

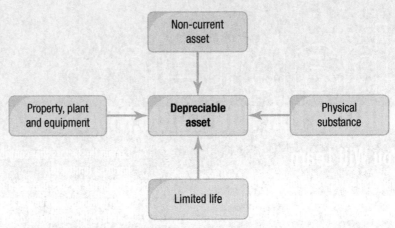

Figure 8.1 Characteristics of depreciable assets

Non-current assets

A depreciable asset is a non-current asset that loses value over time. An asset is defined in the AASB Framework as a resource controlled by the entity as a result of past events and from which future economic benefits are expected to flow to the entity. A current asset (for example, inventory and accounts receivable) is an asset from which future economic benefits will flow to the business within the next accounting period. All other assets are non-current assets and these can be divided into categories, such as investments, intangible assets, natural resources and property, plant and equipment.

Investments, intangible assets and natural resources

An investment is an asset from which the business expects to generate income each period and also on which to make a profit on when sold. An investment is not expected to be used up over a period of time and is therefore not depreciated. Examples of investments are fixed term bank deposits and marketable securities, such as shares and debentures in companies.

Intangible assets are assets that have no physical form but which provide future benefit to the business. Examples of intangible assets are patents, goodwill and trademarks. Intangible assets are amortised (i.e. the depreciable value of an intangible asset is allocated to each year of the asset's life) rather than depreciated because they do not suffer from wear and tear or obsolescence.

Another non-current asset that does not suffer from wear and tear or obsolescence is a natural resource, such as a mine or forest. These resources are also amortised.

Physical substance

A depreciable non-current asset is an asset that has a physical substance. Property, plant and equipment is defined in AASB 116 as tangible items held for use in the production or supply of goods or services, for rental to others or for administrative purposes that are expected to be used during more than one period. Examples are equipment, machinery and vehicles. A tangible item is one that can be seen and touched.

Limited life

Depreciable non-current assets have a limited life. As property, plant and equipment has a physical substance it therefore has a finite life. For example, non-current assets (such as buildings, furniture and fixtures and fittings) have a limited life span, as over a period of time they will deteriorate. The economic benefits embodied in these assets are used up over their useful life. However, land does not have a finite life and is therefore not a depreciable non-current asset.

COST OF A DEPRECIABLE NON-CURRENT ASSET

The issue of what is included in the cost of a depreciable non-current asset is outlined in AASB 116. The standard states that a cost should be recognised as an asset when it is probable that the future economic benefits of the item will flow to the business and the asset can be reliably measured.

The accounting standard also says that property, plant and equipment must be recorded at cost. It further outlines that the cost of an asset is:
- the cash or cash equivalents paid
  or
- the fair value of the other considerations given in exchange for the asset when it was acquired.

The cost of property, plant and equipment, as detailed in accounting standards, includes:
- the purchase price, including import duties and non-refundable purchase taxes, after deducting trade discounts and rebates
- any costs directly attributable to bringing the asset to the location and condition necessary for it to be capable of operating in the manner intended by the management of the business, including site preparation, installation and assembly and testing prior to operation.

Purchase price

The purchase price of an asset is usually the invoice price (less trade discount) excluding GST (as the latter is a refundable tax). The cost of an asset (i.e. the purchase price) is the amount of consideration given to acquire the asset or the cost of constructing the asset. The consideration is most often the cash paid but it can also include non-monetary items, such as the trade-in value given for an old asset disposed. The cost of constructing an asset can include direct labour, direct materials, factory overhead and other construction costs.

Costs attributable to an asset

The costs attributable to an asset are those that are necessary to get the asset ready for use as it is intended to be used. Apart from those mentioned previously, other costs to get the asset ready for use could include professional fees, legal fees, stamp duty, insurance while in transit and freight to get the asset to the business.

 Key Concept 8.2

Cost of a depreciable non-current asset

The cost of a depreciable non-current asset includes its purchase price plus any costs directly attributable to bringing the asset to the location and condition necessary for it to be used as intended.

Difference between an asset and an expense

Costs that increase the future economic benefits of a resource are recorded as an asset. Some costs do not increase the future economic benefits of the asset but only bring the asset back to its full use as intended. These costs are expenses as they bring benefit for the current accounting period and are often recurring or annual costs. They represent a consumption or using up or loss of an economic benefit in the form of an outflow of an asset, depletion of an asset or increase in a liability. Examples of costs associated with non-current assets that are expenses and not assets are:

- repairs and maintenance
- insurance
- vehicle registration
- day-to-day servicing of equipment, machinery and vehicles
- the consumption of consumables, such as fuel and oil.

The difference between an asset and an expense is important, as to incorrectly record a cost will result in an incorrect calculation of profit or loss, as well as the incorrect recording of non-current assets in the Statement of financial position.

Accounting Standard AASB 116 states that costs incurred after the initial acquisition of an asset that result in an increase in the future economic benefits that flow from the asset are to be recorded as an asset. These costs can include:

- major overhauls
- extraordinary repairs
- reconditioning of assets
- additions and extensions.

These expenditures must extend the asset's life or increase its income-earning capacity, service potential or productivity.

Cost, revaluation and impairment loss

In some instances a non-current asset can be shown at a value other than cost. This can occur when there is an impairment loss or revaluation.

An impairment loss results in the write-down of a non-current asset from its carrying amount to its recoverable amount. The latter is what you would get for the asset if you disposed of it – or its considered useful value to the business.

An item of property, plant and equipment can be revalued either upwards or downwards to its fair value. AASB 116 defines fair value as the amount for which an asset could be exchanged between knowledgeable, willing parties in an arm's-length transaction. This is therefore the current market value of an asset.

Accounting and Finance: 2B   ISBN 9780170182041   Cengage Learning Australia

THE NATURE OF DEPRECIATION EXPENSE

Depreciable non-current assets must be depreciated because they have limited lives. The causes of depreciation or the factors that can contribute to non-current assets having a limited life are:

- the usage of the asset
- wear and tear of the asset beyond the ability of repairs and maintenance to rectify. This can occur due to its continued physical use or as a result of it remaining idle
- technical obsolescence due to the advent of new technologies that make the asset inefficient
- commercial obsolescence due to a decline in the demand for the use of the asset in producing goods or services
- legal or other similar limits on the use of an asset.

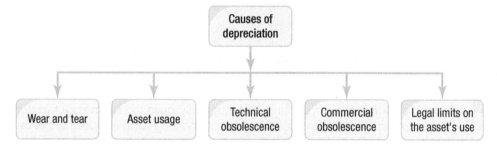

Figure 8.2 Causes of depreciation of non-current assets

Depreciation is a cost-allocation process whereby the cost of the asset is apportioned over the asset's useful life. A non-current asset is an item that has future service potential or economic benefit to the business. The cost is initially recorded as an asset but these future service potentials or economic benefits are gradually used up over the asset's life for the reasons outlined above. The Framework states that an expense is a decrease in economic benefits during the accounting period in the form of outflows or depletions of assets. Thus the using up of economic benefits represents an expense and depreciation is therefore an expense. It must be emphasised, however, that it is not a cash transaction. No resources flow into or out of a business as a result of depreciation.

The application of the accounting period assumption (that the life of a business is divided up into equal arbitrary periods of time to enable the calculation of profit or loss) requires that the depreciation of a non-current asset be recognised in a systematic way in each accounting period.

Misconceptions about depreciation

There are a number of misconceptions surrounding the concept of depreciation. These include:

- that depreciation determines the market value of an asset
- that depreciation sets aside an amount of money equivalent to the replacement cost of the asset.

Accounting and Finance 2B   ISBN 9780170182041   Cengage Learning Australia

Depreciation does not determine the market value of an asset

The term depreciation is often confused with the idea of valuing an asset. Non-accountants refer to the decline in the current value of an asset as depreciation. Depreciation is usually applied under the historical cost accounting system. This system records and values an asset at its original cost when acquired and no account is taken of the change in value of the asset – that is, its market value. Depreciation allocates the original cost of an asset and not a market value. Nor is depreciation the difference between the current or market value of an asset at the start and end of the accounting period. Depreciation is a cost allocation method and not a valuation method.

Depreciation does not set aside money for the replacement of an asset

As indicated earlier, depreciation is a non-cash expense. There is no cash payment made to any external party in relation to depreciation. The only cash payment concerning the asset is made when it is first purchased. Depreciation is therefore not a source of cash. Accumulated depreciation is also not a fund of cash but rather the economic benefits of the asset used up in the past. Depreciation does not provide for an asset's replacement with a new item. Depreciation does, however, have the effect of retaining capital in the business. Depreciation as an expense results in the profit of the business being reduced. This, in turn, means that less is available to the business owners to take as drawings or dividends.

 Key Concept 8.3

Depreciation

AASB 116 defines depreciation as the systematic allocation of the depreciable amount of an asset over its useful life.

REALITY CHECK 8.1

'Depreciation – Not funds for the future!'

A small business proprietor, Mr Wrong, owner of a cottage industry business in the south-west of Western Australia, made the comment at a business breakfast that depreciation was very useful in that it not only gave the business a taxation deduction for an expense but it also set aside cash for the long-term replacement of the asset. Furthermore, he indicated that it allocated funds that would enable the business to meet the cost of buying a new asset as depreciation determined the current market value of an asset.

The local accountant, Ms Wright, who also attended the business breakfast, overheard this comment and replied that this was not correct. She explained that the charge for depreciation is an expense that is therefore offset against income in the process of determining the profit or loss of a business. It is an *allowable deduction* for the purpose of determining the taxable income for a business. This, she said, does mean that profits are retained within the business and that depreciation does reduce the amount available for distribution to the owners. However, this does not necessarily mean that the profits are retained for the purposes of replacing assets. She then went on to explain more about depreciation and made the following comments.

'The charge for depreciation does not set aside anything – it generates nothing. The funds to replace a non-current asset come from the income generated by the business through the cash inflow that results from income-earning activity. Depreciation is only an internal *transfer* and does not involve the business bank account or an external party. There is no money being paid or received by anyone.'

'Depreciation involves the allocation of the asset's original cost over its useful life. This is based on the concept of historical cost accounting and not market or replacement values. At the end of the asset's useful life only the original cost of the asset has been allocated and this would probably be insufficient to purchase a replacement some time in the future.'

Accounting and Finance 2B   ISBN 9780170182041   Cengage Learning Australia

Commentary

This case study highlights the mistaken belief of some people that depreciation accounting is about saving money to replace assets. The purpose of depreciation is not to set aside funds for asset replacement but rather to allocate the original cost of an asset over its useful life.

FACTORS AFFECTING THE DETERMINATION OF DEPRECIATION

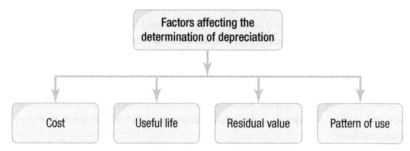

Figure 8.3 Factors affecting the determination of depreciation

Cost

The cost of an asset is the amount of cash or cash equivalents paid or the fair value of the other considerations given to acquire an asset at the time of its acquisition or construction. This represents the purchase price plus those costs to get the asset ready for use by the business. The depreciable amount of an asset is the cost of the asset less its residual value. It is the depreciable amount that is allocated over the asset's useful life.

Useful life

The useful life of an asset is defined in Accounting Standard AASB 116 as the period over which an asset is expected to be available for use by an entity, or the number of production or similar units expected to be obtained from the asset by an entity. The estimated useful life is therefore the expected time that the asset will be used by the entity. In estimating this amount the business should take into consideration the factors that contribute to the depreciation of an asset as previously outlined.

Residual value

The residual value of an asset is defined in AASB 116 as the estimated amount that an entity would currently obtain from disposal of the asset, after deducting the estimated costs of disposal, if the asset were already of the age and in the condition expected at the end of its useful life – in other words, the amount that the business expects to obtain for the asset at the end of its useful life. This amount is sometimes called the *trade-in price* or *salvage value*. As with the estimated useful life, the residual value should be estimated taking into consideration the causes of depreciation.

Pattern of use

The pattern of use is determined by the nature of the depreciable asset. Is it one that will provide the same utility throughout its life or one whose income-earning contribution will decline with age? This concept will be explored later when we consider alternative methods of depreciation.

Accounting and Finance: 2B   ISBN 9780170182041   Cengage Learning Australia

PURPOSE AND NATURE OF THE BALANCE DAY ADJUSTMENT FOR DEPRECIATION

As with other balance day adjustments, depreciation is necessary so that the expenses for the accounting period reflect those that have been incurred during the period and that the correct unallocated value for assets is shown in the balance sheet of the business. The cost of the asset was paid when the asset was acquired and it would be incorrect to record all of this as an expense at that time. An adjusting entry (that is, depreciation) is necessary so that this cost is allocated as an expense over the asset's useful life. In addition, the carrying amount (that is, the cost less the accumulated depreciation) of property, plant and equipment shown in the balance sheet will reflect the economic benefits still contained in the asset at balance date.

To record depreciation requires a balance day adjustment in which the depreciation account is debited as an expense. As depreciation is only an estimate, it would be incorrect to record the credit entry in the non-current asset account. Instead an *accumulated depreciation* account is credited, which reflects the used economic benefits of the non-current asset and will be shown as a deduction from the cost of the asset in the Statement of financial position.

The balance day adjustment for raising depreciation is recorded in the General journal as follows:

General journal				
Date	Details		Debit	Credit
30 June	Depreciation expense		XX	
	Accumulated depreciation			XX
	(Yearly depreciation)			

In the Income statement the depreciation would be classified as an operating expense and placed in the appropriate category of expenses, for example:

Income statement (extract) for the year ended 30 June

	$	$
Operating expenses		
Selling and distribution expenses		
Depreciation on shop fixtures and fittings	XX	
General and administration expenses		
Depreciation on office equipment	XX	

In the Statement of financial position the accumulated depreciation would be deducted from the non-current asset to which it relates and shown as follows:

Statement of financial position (extract) as at 30 June

	$	$
Non-current assets		
Machinery (at cost)	XX	
Less Accumulated depreciation on machinery	XX	XX

METHODS OF DEPRECIATION

There are a number of methods of depreciation that can be selected, such as the straight line, reducing balance, sum-of-the-years digits and units-of-output methods. It should be noted that the method selected by a business for financial reporting purposes may be

Accounting and Finance 2B ISBN 9780170182041 Cengage Learning Australia

different from the method used for income taxation calculation purposes. In this book we will study only the straight line and reducing balance methods.

When selecting which method of depreciation to use, AASB 116 states that the business must consider the pattern in which the economic benefits embodied in the asset are expected to be used up. This will result in the asset's cost being allocated in a manner that reflects the benefits to be obtained from the asset. This, in turn, will be reflected in its pattern of use and pattern of earning revenue.

Key Concept 8.4

Selecting the appropriate method of depreciation
The method of depreciation chosen to use when depreciating an asset should be based on the pattern in which the economic benefits embodied in the asset are expected to be used up.

Straight line depreciation

The straight line depreciation method allocates the depreciable amount of an asset in an even way throughout the asset's useful life. That is, an equal amount of depreciation is allocated in each accounting period. This method is appropriate when the pattern of use of an asset is uniform from one period to the next and where the benefits obtained from the asset are the same each period. The asset will earn an even

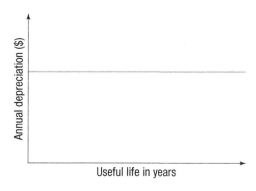

Figure 8.4 The straight line depreciation method

amount of revenue over its useful life. It is particularly appropriate for depreciating furniture, fixtures and fittings and buildings. This method of depreciation is simple and widely used.

To calculate the amount of depreciation each period using the straight line method the following formula is used:

$$\frac{\text{Cost} - \text{Estimated residual value}}{\text{Estimated useful life}}$$

The amount of annual depreciation calculated can be expressed as a percentage. This is determined as follows:

$$\frac{\text{Annual depreciation amount} \times 100}{\text{Cost}}$$

This percentage is then applied to the cost of the asset to determine the annual depreciation each year.

Example 8.1

EXAMPLE:

McManus and Bell are partners in a sporting goods business. They are depreciating the furniture and fixtures at their shop in South Fremantle. The furniture and fixtures were bought on 1 December 2011 at a purchase invoice price of $55000 (GST inclusive) paid for in cash. Delivery and installation costs of $660 (GST inclusive) were also paid in cash on 1 December 2011. The items are to be depreciated on the straight-line method, their residual value is estimated at $2000 (GST exclusive) and the estimated useful life is ten years.

Required

- Calculate the annual depreciation.
- Prepare the General journal entries to purchase the asset on 1 December 2011.
- Prepare the General journal entries for depreciation for the years ended 30 June 2012 and 2013.
- Prepare the General journal entries to close off the depreciation account to the P&L summary account for the years ended 30 June 2012 and 2013.
- Prepare the General ledger accounts for Furniture and fixtures, Depreciation on furniture and fixtures and Accumulated depreciation on furniture and fixtures.
- Show how the asset would appear in the Statement of financial position as at 30 June 2012 and 2013.

The first item to be determined is the value of the non-current asset as follows:

	Total (GST inclusive)	GST outlay	Costs to record – GST exclusive
Invoice price	$55 000	$5 000	$50 000
Delivery and installation	$660	$60	$600
Total	$55 660	$5 060	$50 600

The delivery and installation costs will be recorded as part of the non-current asset's value as these costs are directly attributable to bringing the assets to the location and condition necessary for them to be capable of operating in the manner intended by the management of the business and these would be added to the invoice price. The costs to be recorded in the asset account are GST exclusive, in this case a total of $50 600, and it is this value that will be used to calculate the depreciation. The entry in the General journal is therefore:

General journal			
Date	Account details	Debit $	Credit $
1/12/11	Furniture and fixtures	50 600	
	GST outlay	5 060	
	Cash		55 660
	Purchase of non-current assets		

To depreciate the asset we first calculate the annual depreciation which, using the straight-line formula, is as follows:

$$\frac{\text{Cost less estimated residual value}}{\text{Estimated useful life}}$$

Therefore:

$$\frac{\$50\,600 \text{ less } \$2\,000}{10 \text{ years}}$$

$$\frac{\$48\,600}{10 \text{ years}}$$

$$= \$4860$$

When we depreciate the assets at the first balance day, which in this case is 30 June 2012, we must determine the number of months over which to depreciate the asset. We have calculated the depreciation for 12 months but it may be that in the first year the firm has not owned the asset for 12 months and therefore we should depreciate it for only a proportion of the 12 months. In this case, as the item was purchased on 1 December 2011 and balance day is 30 June 2012, the business has owned the asset for seven months and must depreciate it, therefore, by the proportion of $\frac{7}{12}$, as follows:

$$4860 \times \frac{7}{12} = \$2835 \text{ depreciation for seven months}$$

Therefore, $2835 is used in the entry in the General journal to raise depreciation on 30 June 2012 as follows:

General journal			
Date	**Account details**	**Debit**	**Credit**
30/6/12	Depreciation on furniture and fixtures	$2835	
	Accumulated depreciation on furniture and fixtures		$2835
	Depreciation charges on balance day		

The entry on 30 June 2013 will be exactly the same, except that in that year the firm will have owned the asset for a full year and therefore can depreciate the asset by the annual depreciation of $4860. The entry is:

General journal			
Date	**Account details**	**Debit**	**Credit**
30/6/13	Depreciation on furniture and fixtures	$4860	
	Accumulated depreciation on furniture and fixtures		$4860
	Depreciation charges on balance day		

Depreciation is an expense account and so is closed off on balance day to the Profit and loss summary account. The depreciation account will be credited and the P&L summary account debited as follows for each of the two balance days in this question:

General journal			
Date	**Account details**	**Debit**	**Credit**
30/6/12	P&L summary	$2835	
	Depreciation on furniture and fixtures		$2835
	Closing entry		
30/6/13	P&L summary	$4860	
	Depreciation on furniture and fixtures		$4860
	Closing entry		

When posted to the General ledger the result is as follows:

General ledger					
Date	**Account details**	**Debit**	**Credit**	**Balance**	**Dr/Cr**
Furniture and fixtures					
1/12/11	Cash	$50600		$50600	Dr
Depreciation on furniture and fixtures					
30/6/12	Accumulated depreciation on furniture and fixtures	$2835		$2835	Dr
	P&L summary		$2835	0	
30/6/13	Accumulated depreciation on furniture and fixtures	$4860		$4860	Dr
	P&L summary		$4860	$0	
Accumulated depreciation on furniture and fixtures					
30/6/12	Depreciation on furniture and fixtures		$2835	$2835	Cr
30/6/13	Depreciation on furniture and fixtures		$4860	$7695	Cr

Note how the depreciation entries have no affect on the Furniture and fixtures account. The presentation in the Statement of financial position appears as follows:

McManus and Bell
Statement of financial position (extract) as at 30 June 2012

	$	$
Non-current assets		
Furniture and fixtures (at cost)	$50 600	
Less Accumulated depreciation	$2 835	$47 765

McManus and Bell
Statement of financial position (extract) as at 30 June 2013

	$	$
Non-current assets		
Furniture and fixtures (at cost)	$50 600	
Less Accumulated depreciation	$7 695	$42 905

Please note that the value of the Furniture and fixtures is always shown at its original cost each year (in this case $50 600) and that the Accumulated depreciation increases each year to reflect the economic benefits used up each year.

Key Concept 8.5

Straight line depreciation
The straight line depreciation method allocates the depreciable amount of an asset in an even way throughout the asset's useful life and is calculated as cost minus estimated residual value, which equals the depreciable amount divided by the estimated useful life.

Formula 8.1

Straight-line depreciation

$$\frac{\text{Cost} - \text{Estimated residual value}}{\text{Estimated useful life}}$$

Reducing balance depreciation

The reducing balance depreciation method allocates more of the depreciable amount of an asset in its early years and less as it ages. This method, sometimes called the *diminishing balance method*, is appropriate to those assets where the pattern of use is such that the benefits obtained from the asset will be more in its early years and less in its later years. This will be reflected in the asset's revenue-earning capacity, as more revenue will be earned in the asset's early years and less each year as it ages. As these

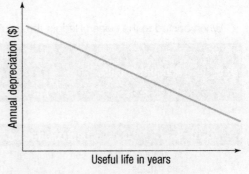

Figure 8.5 The reducing balance method of depreciation

kinds of assets age they usually require more repairs and maintenance and are more likely to break down. This method is particularly appropriate for depreciating machinery and equipment. This depreciation method is sometimes selected for taxation purposes when it is desired to write off more depreciation in the early years of an asset's life, compared with the straight line method, thereby gaining an earlier tax advantage.

Accounting and Finance: 2B   ISBN 9780170182041   Cengage Learning Australia

To calculate reducing balance depreciation the following formula is used to calculate the rate of depreciation:

$$1 - N\sqrt{\dfrac{\text{Residual value}}{\text{Cost of asset}}}$$

N represents the estimated useful life of the asset.

You will not be required to remember or apply this formula in this textbook. You will be given the percentage rate of depreciation in all questions and examples. The formula to calculate the annual depreciation expense by the reducing balance method is as follows:

(Cost of the asset − Accumulated depreciation) × Given % rate of depreciation

It should be noted that using this method the residual value is not subtracted from the cost of the asset.

The percentage rate used for the reducing balance method can also be determined by calculating the annual rate for the straight line method and then multiplying this percentage by 1.5. This will give approximately the same answer as the reducing balance formula above and will write down the asset over approximately the same period of time. This approach is recognised by the Australian Taxation Office in its schedule of tax-permitted depreciation rates.

EXAMPLE:

Example 8.2

Keith and Cliff Richards are partners in Richards Suppliers, a manufacturer of audio CDs in Sydney. They purchased machinery on 1 January 2012 for an invoice price of $111 000 (GST inclusive) cash and also paid $2200 for testing and assembly of the asset, as well as $440 for annual insurance. The assets were estimated to have a residual value of $5000 and estimated useful life of eight years. They decided to depreciate the assets on the reducing balance method at the rate of 15 per cent per year.

Required

- Calculate the annual depreciation for the years ended 30 June 2012, 2013 and 2014.
- Prepare the General journal entries to purchase the asset on 1 January 2012.
- Prepare the General journal entries for depreciation for the years ended 30 June 2012, 2013 and 2014.
- Prepare the General journal entries to close off the depreciation account to the P&L summary account for the years ended 30 June 2012, 2013 and 2014.
- Prepare the General ledger accounts for Machinery, Depreciation on machinery and Accumulated depreciation on machinery from 1 January 2012 to 30 June 2014.
- Show how the asset would appear in the Statement of financial position as at 30 June 2012 and 2013.

The cost of the asset for this business is determined as follows:

	Total (GST inclusive)	GST	Costs to record – GST exclusive
Invoice price	$111 000	$10 091	$100 909
Testing and assembly	$2 200	$200	$2 000
Total	**$113 200**	**$10 291**	**$102 909**

The testing and assembly costs are included in the cost of the machinery as they are essential to the establishment and operation of the asset. However, the insurance cost of $440 is not included as it is an ongoing cost and will need to be renewed annually. The insurance cost is an expense. The entry to purchase the asset is therefore:

General journal			
Date	Account details	Debit	Credit
1/1/12	Machinery	$102909	
	GST outlay	$10291	
	Cash		$113200
	Purchase of non-current assets		

The calculation of the annual depreciation of the machinery is as follows:

Balance day	Cost	Accumulated depreciation	Carrying amount	Rate	Months depreciated	Annual depreciation
30 June 2012	$102909	$0	$102909	15%	6 months	$7718
30 June 2013	$102909	$7718	$95191	15%	12 months	$14279
30 June 2014	$102909	$21997	$80912	15%	12 months	$12137

It is important to remember that when using the reducing balance method of depreciation the residual value is not subtracted from the cost. The accumulated depreciation is subtracted from the cost to give the carrying amount and it is this amount that is multiplied by the depreciation rate of 15%. Note how the amount of depreciation reduces each year as the carrying amount, or reduced balance, also decreases. Also note that the amount to be depreciated of $102909 is net of GST. At the first balance day of 30 June 2012, because the asset has only been owned for six months, the full amount of depreciation of $15436 cannot be raised in the records. The $15436 is found by calculating the cost of the asset of $102909 less accumulated depreciation of zero, which gives the carrying amount of $102909, which is then multiplied by the rate of 15%. As the asset has only been owned for six months we multiply the proportion of 6/12 by $15436 and this gives $7718.

The General journal entries to raise depreciation each year and close it off to the P&L summary account are as follows:

General journal			
Date	Account details	Debit	Credit
30/6/12	Depreciation on machinery	$7718	
	Accumulated depreciation on machinery		$7718
	Depreciation charges on balance day		
30/6/12	Profit and loss summary	$7718	
	Depreciation on machinery		$7718
	Closing entry		
30/6/13	Depreciation on machinery	$14279	
	Accumulated depreciation on machinery		$14279
	Depreciation charges on balance day		
30/6/13	Profit and loss summary	$14279	
	Depreciation on machinery		$14279
	Closing entry		
30/6/14	Depreciation on machinery	$12137	
	Accumulated depreciation on machinery		$12137
	Depreciation charges on balance day		
30/6/14	Profit and loss summary	$12137	
	Depreciation on machinery		$12137
	Closing entry		

Accounting and Finance 2B   ISBN 9780170182041   Cengage Learning Australia

The General ledger appears as follows:

Date	Account details	Debit	Credit	Balance	Dr/Cr
General ledger					
Machinery					
1/1/12	Cash	$102909		$102909	Dr
Depreciation on machinery					
30/6/12	Accumulated depreciation on machinery	$7718		$7718	Dr
	Profit and loss summary		$7718	$0	
30/6/13	Accumulated depreciation on machinery	$14279		$14279	Dr
	Profit and loss summary		$14279	$0	
30/6/14	Accumulated depreciation on machinery	$12137		$12137	Dr
	Profit and loss summary		$12137	$0	
Accumulated depreciation on machinery					
30/6/12	Depreciation on machinery		$7718	$7718	Cr
30/6/13	Depreciation on machinery		$14279	$21997	Cr
30/6/14	Depreciation on machinery		$12137	$34134	Cr

The presentation in the Statement of financial position is as follows:

Richards Suppliers
Statement of financial position (extract) as at 30 June 2012

	$	$
Non-current assets		
Machinery	$102909	
Less Accumulated depreciation as at 30 June 2013	$7718	$95191
Non-current assets		
Machinery	$102909	
Less Accumulated depreciation as at 30 June 2014	$21997	$80912
Non-current assets		
Machinery	$102909	
Less Accumulated depreciation	$34134	$68775

It should be noted that the ledger accounts and journal entries are exactly the same, whatever method of depreciation is used. Only the calculation of the depreciation amount is different.

Key Concept 8.6

Reducing balance depreciation

The reducing balance depreciation method allocates more of the depreciable amount of an asset in its early years and less as it ages. It is calculated as cost minus accumulated depreciation multiplied by the given rate of depreciation.

Formula 8.2

Reducing balance depreciation

(Cost of the asset − Accumulated depreciation) × Rate of depreciation

ACCOUNTING FOR THE DISPOSAL OF AN ASSET

When a depreciable asset is not useful any longer it will be disposed of and, according to AASB 116, it must be *derecognised*. Derecognition can occur when the asset is disposed of or when no future economic benefits are expected from the use or disposal of the asset. The latter situation is often referred to as 'scrapping the asset'. Disposal of a depreciable asset may occur when the asset is sold for cash or credit or traded in.

When the depreciable asset is disposed of, the carrying amount of the asset must be written off, the proceeds (if any) recorded and the gain or loss arising on disposal included in the profit or loss for the period. The gain or loss is the difference between the net disposal proceeds and the carrying amount.

To account for the disposal of a depreciable asset, a number of approaches to the recording in the journal and ledger accounts may be taken. We will use one approach, which is to employ a sale of asset account. The sale of asset account will record the cost of the asset, the accumulated depreciation on the asset sold and the proceeds from the disposal of the asset.

Steps to record the disposal of an asset

- Ensure that the depreciation of the asset disposed of has been calculated right up to the time of its disposal. This may require the calculation and recording of depreciation for a part of the year since the asset was last depreciated (usually the previous 30 June).
- Record the proceeds, if any, from the disposal of the asset in the Sale of asset account.
- Transfer the cost of the asset from the Asset account to the Sale of asset account.
- Transfer the accumulated depreciation of the asset to the Sale of asset account.
- Determine if there is a gain or loss on the disposal of the asset and transfer this amount to the Gain or loss on disposal of asset account.
- At balance day, transfer (by closing entry) the gain or loss on disposal of the asset and the depreciation expense accounts to the Profit and loss summary account.

Example 8.3

EXAMPLE:

The Statement of financial position as at 30 June 2011 for Benaud and Miller showed the following:

Benaud and Miller
Statement of financial position (extract) as at 30 June 2011

	$	$
Non-current assets		
Motor vehicles (at cost)	108 000	
Accumulated depreciation	60 000	48 000

Three motor vehicles were originally purchased on 1 July 2007 at a total cost of $108 000 with a residual value of $6000 each and a useful life to the business of six years. They have been depreciated using the straight-line method. However, after only 4.5 years the fleet of vehicles was sold on 31 December 2011 for $55 000 (GST inclusive) cash.

Required

- Prepare the General journal entry to record the necessary depreciation raised on the fleet of motor vehicles sold on 31 December 2011.
- Prepare the General journal entries required to record the sale of the motor vehicles on 31 December 2011.
- Prepare the General journal entry necessary on 31 December 2011 to transfer the gain or loss on the sale of the motor vehicles.
- Prepare the General journal entries required on 30 June 2012 to close off the Depreciation on motor vehicles and Gain/loss on sale of motor vehicles accounts.

Accounting and Finance 2B   ISBN 9780170182041   Cengage Learning Australia

- Prepare the following General ledger accounts from 1 July 2011 to 30 June 2012:
  - Motor vehicles
  - Depreciation on motor vehicles
  - Accumulated depreciation on motor vehicles
  - Sale of motor vehicles
  - Gain/loss on sale of motor vehicles.

To complete this example we shall follow the steps outlined above.

Step 1

First we need to calculate the depreciation on the fleet of vehicles sold right up until the time of the sale of the vehicles. The vehicles were last depreciated on 30 June 2011 and so we need to depreciate them for a further six months until 31 December 2011 as follows:

Annual depreciation using the straight-line formula:

$$\frac{\text{Cost less estimated residual value}}{\text{Estimated useful life}}$$

Therefore:

$$\frac{\$108\,000 \text{ less } \$18\,000}{6 \text{ years}}$$

$$\frac{\$90\,000}{6 \text{ years}}$$

This equals $15 000 annual depreciation.

Therefore, six months depreciation is $15 000 multiplied by 0.5 (that is, half a year).
This equals $7 500.

You will note that first we determined the annual depreciation and then the proportion of depreciation for six months. This amount of $7 500 can now be added to the Accumulated depreciation on motor vehicles figure of $60 000 shown in the Statement of financial position as at 30 June 2011. This is done by preparing a General journal entry on 31 December 2011, as seen below, and then posting this to the General ledger accounts, also seen further below.

General journal			
Date	Account details	Debit $	Credit $
31/12/11	Depreciation on motor vehicles	7 500	
	Accumulated depreciation on motor vehicles		7 500
	Depreciation raised for six months up to time of sale of motor vehicles		

The total of $67 500 ($60 000 plus $7 500) is now the total accumulated depreciation on the motor vehicles right up to the time of sale on 31 December 2011. This is reflected in the Accumulated depreciation on the motor vehicles account (as seen further below).

To record the sale of a non-current asset we use a Sale of asset account (sometimes called a Disposal of asset account). The Sale of asset account is usually named after the asset being sold, so in this case we shall call the account the Sale of motor vehicles account. The purpose of this account is to determine the gain or loss on the sale of the non-current asset, which is the difference between the proceeds from the sale of the asset and the carrying amount of the asset sold. Therefore, in the Sale of asset account we shall record:
- the proceeds from the sale of the asset
- the original cost of the asset sold
- the accumulated depreciation on the asset sold.

These entries are now seen below.

Step 2

The next step is to record the receipt of cash from the sale of the fleet of motor vehicles. Cash receipts are recorded as a debit in the Cash account. GST must be collected and so this amount of $5000 (that is, $55000/11) is recorded as a credit to reflect that it is a current liability. The amount exclusive of GST, that is, $50000 ($55000 – $5000), is recorded as the proceeds in the Sale of motor vehicle account. This is shown in the General journal entry below:

General journal			
Date	Account details	Debit $	Credit $
31/12/11	Cash	55000	
	GST collected		5000
	Sale of motor vehicles		50000
	Cash received from sale of motor vehicle fleet		

Step 3

Our next entry is to transfer the original cost of the asset now sold into the Sale of motor vehicles account. The cost of the motor vehicles is currently a debit in the Motor vehicles account and therefore this account will be credited by $108000 to transfer this amount out and into the Sale of motor vehicles account.

General journal			
Date	Account details	Debit $	Credit $
31/12/11	Sale of motor vehicles	108000	
	Motor vehicles		108000
	Transfer of original cost of motor vehicle fleet now sold		

Step 4

The next step is to transfer the $67500 accumulated depreciation on the motor vehicle fleet sold, as previously calculated, from the Accumulated depreciation on motor vehicles account into the Sale of motor vehicles account. This amount is currently a credit in the Accumulated depreciation on motor vehicles account and so it will be debited and the credit will be in the Sale of motor vehicles account. The general entry is seen below.

General journal			
Date	Account details	Debit $	Credit $
31/12/11	Accumulated depreciation on motor vehicles	67500	
	Sale of motor vehicles		67500
	Transfer the accumulated depreciation on the motor vehicle fleet now sold		

Step 5

To determine the gain or loss on the sale of the motor vehicles we must find the difference between the carrying amount of the motor vehicles now sold and the proceeds from the sale of the motor vehicles. This is done as shown below:

Original cost of motor vehicles sold	$108000
Less Accumulated depreciation on motor vehicles sold	$67500
Carrying amount of motor vehicles sold	$40500

Accounting and Finance: 2B ISBN 9780170182041 Cengage Learning Australia

This amount of $40500 is subtracted from the Proceeds from sale of motor vehicles (GST exclusive) figure of $50000 to give an amount of $9500 as seen below.

Proceeds (GST exclusive) from sale of motor vehicles	$50000
Less Carrying amount of motor vehicles sold	$40500
Gain on sale of motor vehicles	$9500

If the proceeds amount is greater than the carrying amount then the result is a gain, but if the proceeds are less than the carrying amount then the result is a loss. In this case the $9500 is a gain and this is reflected in the Sale of motor vehicles account seen below. The amount of $9500 is a credit balance in the Sale of motor vehicles account so this account will be debited and the credit will be to the account titled, in this case, Gain on sale of motor vehicles. If it had been a loss, the account would have been called Loss on sale of motor vehicles. The entry for the $9500 is as follows.

General journal			
Date	Account details	Debit $	Credit $
31/12/11	Sale of motor vehicles	9500	
	Gain on sale of motor vehicles		9500
	Transfer the gain on the motor vehicle fleet now sold		

Step 6

The next step involves the entries required on the next balance day, being 30 June 2012. The two entries necessary are to close off the Depreciation on motor vehicles and Gain on sale of motor vehicles accounts to the Profit and loss summary account. These General journal entries are seen below.

General journal			
Date	Account details	Debit $	Credit $
30/6/12	Profit and loss summary	7500	
	Depreciation on motor vehicles		7500
	Closing entry		
30/6/12	Gain on sale of motor vehicles	9500	
	Profit and loss summary		9500
	Transfer gain on sale of motor vehicles during the financial year		

The above General journal entries can now be posted to the required General ledger accounts:

General ledger					
Date	Account details	Debit	Credit	Balance	Dr/Cr
Motor vehicles					
1/7/11	Balance			$108000	Dr
31/12/11	Sale of motor vehicles		$108000	$0	

Depreciation on motor vehicles						
31/12/11	Accumulated depreciation on motor vehicles	$7500			$7500	Dr
30/6/12	Profit and loss summary			$7500	$0	

Accumulated depreciation on motor vehicles						
1/7/11	Balance				$60000	Cr
31/12/11	Depreciation on motor vehicles			$7500	$67500	Cr
	Sale of motor vehicles	$67500			$0	

Sale of motor vehicles						
31/12/11	Motor vehicles	$108000			$108000	Dr
	Accumulated depreciation on motor vehicles			$67500	$40500	Dr
	Cash			$50000	$9500	Cr
	Gain on sale of motor vehicles	$9500			$0	

Gain on Sale of motor vehicles						
31/12/11	Sale of motor vehicles			$9500	$9500	Cr
30/6/12	Profit and loss summary	$9500			$0	

Sale of a non-current asset on credit

When an asset is sold on credit the entries required in the General journal and General ledger are very similar to the sale of an asset for cash. The only difference is in the entry that records the proceeds from the sale of the asset.

Using the above example, if the motor vehicles had been sold on 31 December 2011 to J Heathridge on credit for $55000 (GST inclusive) the entry in the General journal would have been as follows rather than what was shown previously:

General journal			
Date	Account details	Debit $	Credit $
31/12/11	Accounts receivable – J Heathridge	55000	
	GST collected		5000
	Sale of motor vehicles		50000
	Cash received from sale of motor vehicle fleet		

Scrapping of an asset

When an asset is disposed of because it has been fully depreciated and no cash, credit or trade-in is received, it is said to be scrapped. This usually occurs at the end of the asset's life, although it can occur before this time. When an asset is scrapped there will be no General journal entries required to record proceeds from the disposal. In other respects, however, the journal entries required will be the same.

Example 8.4

EXAMPLE:

Status Quo Suppliers have decided to scrap an item of equipment on 30 June 2011 that originally cost $15000. The equipment had been fully depreciated and on 30 June 2011 it had an accumulated depreciation balance of $15000. Its accountant needs to show the General journal entries required to dispose of the equipment and prepare the Equipment, Accumulated depreciation on equipment and Disposal of equipment accounts.

The steps required are very similar to the sale of an asset except there are no proceeds and no gain or loss to record. As this is the case the value of the asset ($15000) and the accumulated depreciation on the asset ($15000) will be the same. Therefore, the asset value and

Accounting and Finance: 2B   ISBN 9780170182041   Cengage Learning Australia

accumulated depreciation amount can be offset against each other. The General journal and General ledger accounts would be as follows:

General journal			
Date	**Account details**	**Debit $**	**Credit $**
30/6/11	Accumulated depreciation on equipment	15 000	
	Equipment		15 000
	Equipment scrapped		

General ledger					
Date	**Account details**	**Debit**	**Credit**	**Balance**	**Dr/Cr**
	Equipment				
30/6/11	Balance			$15 000	Dr
	Accumulated depreciation on equipment		$15 000	$0	
	Accumulated depreciation on equipment				
30/6/11	Balance			$15 000	Cr
	Equipment	$15 000		$0	

If the asset is scrapped before it is fully depreciated and/or there are expenses involved in its disposal, then a loss on disposal will be recorded. Suppose in the above example the equipment was scrapped and it cost $330 (GST inclusive) to dispose of the item and the equipment had only been depreciated to $14 500. If so, the entries to dispose of the equipment would be as follows. We will assume that the accumulated depreciation has been raised in the records right up to the time of disposal.

General journal			
Date	**Account details**	**Debit $**	**Credit $**
30/6/11	Disposal of equipment	15 000	
	Equipment		15 000
	Cost of equipment scrapped		
	Accumulated depreciation on equipment	14 500	
	Disposal of equipment		14 500
	Accumulated depreciation on equipment scrapped		
	Disposal of equipment	300	
	GST outlay	30	
	Cash		330
	Costs to dispose of equipment scrapped		
	Loss on disposal of equipment	800	
	Disposal of equipment		800
	Loss on disposal of equipment		

The Loss on disposal of equipment was determined as follows:

Original cost of equipment sold	$15 000
Less Accumulated depreciation on equipment sold	$14 500
Carrying amount of equipment sold	$500
Add Costs to dispose of equipment	$300
Loss on disposal of equipment	$800

Accounting and Finance: 2B   ISBN 9780170182041   Cengage Learning Australia

The General ledger accounts would be as follows including the closing off of the Loss on disposal of equipment account.

General ledger					
Date	Account details	Debit	Credit	Balance	Dr/Cr
Equipment					
30/6/11	Balance			$15000	Dr
	Sale of equipment		$15000	$0	
Accumulated depreciation on equipment					
30/6/11	Balance			$14500	Cr
	Sale of equipment		$14500	$0	
Sale of equipment					
30/6/11	Equipment	$15000		$15000	Dr
	Accumulated depreciation on equipment		$14500	$500	Dr
	Cash	$300		$800	Dr
	Loss on disposal of equipment		$800	$0	
Loss on disposal of equipment					
30/6/11	Disposal of equipment	$800		$800	Dr
	Profit and loss summary		$800	$0	

Trade-in of a non-current asset

When an asset is traded-in the entries required are very similar to the sale of an asset for cash. A trade-in refers to a situation where a business effectively exchanges its old asset(s) for new asset(s). The business receives an allowance or trade-in for the old assets and this amount is subtracted from the cost of the new assets purchased.

Example 8.5

EXAMPLE:

Morgan and Freeman Traders have traded in a motor vehicle on 30 June 2011 (which originally cost them $40000) for a new motor vehicle costing $55000 (GST inclusive). The old motor vehicle had been depreciated right up to the time of the trade-in and the accumulated depreciation was $30400 as at 30 June 2011. The trade-in allowance received on the old motor vehicle was $7700 (GST inclusive). Its accountant needs to prepare the General journal entries to dispose of the motor vehicle and post to the ledger accounts:

- Motor vehicle
- Accumulated depreciation on motor vehicle
- Disposal of motor vehicle
- Accounts payable.

The General journal entries and General ledger accounts required would be as follows:

General journal			
Date	Account details	Debit $	Credit $
30/6/11	Disposal of motor vehicle	40000	
	Motor vehicle		40000
	Cost of motor vehicle disposed		
	Accumulated depreciation on motor vehicle	30400	
	Disposal of motor vehicle		30400
	Accumulated depreciation on motor vehicle disposed		

Motor vehicle		50 000	
GST outlay		5 000	
Accounts payable			55 000
Cost to purchase new motor vehicle			
Accounts payable		7 700	
GST collected			700
Disposal of motor vehicle			7 000
Trade-in received on disposal of motor vehicle			
Loss on disposal of motor vehicle		2 600	
Disposal of motor vehicle			2 600
Loss on disposal of motor vehicle			

General ledger					
Date	Account details	Debit	Credit	Balance	Dr/Cr
Motor vehicle					
30/6/11	Balance			$40 000	Dr
	Disposal of motor vehicle		$40 000	$0	
	Accounts payable	$50 000		$50 000	Dr
Accumulated depreciation on motor vehicle					
30/6/11	Balance			$30 400	Cr
	Disposal of motor vehicle	$30 400		$0	
Disposal of motor vehicle					
30/6/11	Motor vehicle	$40 000		$40 000	Dr
	Accumulated depreciation on motor vehicle		$30 400	$9 600	Dr
	Accounts payable		$7 000	$2 600	Dr
	Loss on disposal of motor vehicle		$2 600	$0	
Accounts payable					
30/6/11	Motor vehicle		$55 000	$55 000	Cr
	Disposal of motor vehicle	$7 700		$47 300	Cr

You will note that the GST outlay related to the purchase of the new motor vehicle and the GST collected related to the trade-in allowance received on the old motor vehicle are shown separately as per the requirements of the Australian Taxation Office and the preparation of a Business Activity Statement (i.e. they cannot simply be netted off against each other).

The Loss on disposal of motor vehicle was determined as follows:

Original cost of motor vehicle sold	$40 000
Less Accumulated depreciation on motor vehicle sold	$30 400
Carrying amount of motor vehicle sold	$9 600
Trade-in proceeds (GST exclusive) from sale of motor vehicle	$7 000
Less Carrying amount of motor vehicle sold	$9 600
Loss on sale of motor vehicle	$2 600

This is a loss because the carrying amount of $9600 is greater than the trade-in proceeds of $7000.

Accounting and Finance: 2B   ISBN 9780170182041   Cengage Learning Australia

OVER- OR UNDER-DEPRECIATION ON AN ASSET SOLD

The residual value, useful life and method of depreciation chosen for an asset involve estimation and opinion. If the estimates and opinions had been perfectly accurate then, when the asset is disposed of, there would be no gain or loss to record. This of course is highly unlikely and the resultant gain or loss means that the business has over- or under-depreciated the asset.

Over-depreciation

A gain on disposal of an asset means it has been over-depreciated.

Example 8.6

EXAMPLE:

Clint East Wood Suppliers sold an asset on 30 June 2011, which originally cost $50000 and had been depreciated by $45000, for $7700 (GST inclusive) cash. Depreciation had been charged right up to the time of the sale of the asset on 30 June 2011. We need to determine if the asset was under- or over-depreciated.

The table below shows the calculation of the actual result, which is a Gain on sale of asset of $2000, and compares this with the result had the estimations and opinions involved in the calculation of depreciation been perfectly accurate. Remember that the original cost and the proceeds from the sale of the asset are actual amounts and not estimates. If the estimates and opinions involved had been perfectly accurate then no gain or loss would result.

To determine if we have over- or under-depreciated the asset sold let us assume that there is no gain or loss under the perfect scenario and therefore the only amount that can be inaccurate is the accumulated depreciation.

The accumulated depreciation should have been $43000 not $45000 and therefore we have charged too much depreciation – that is, over-depreciated the asset by $2000. This $2000 over-depreciation equates to the Gain on sale of asset of $2000.

	Actual result	Perfect scenario
Original cost of asset sold	$50000	$50000
Less Accumulated depreciation on asset sold	$45000	$43000
Carrying amount of asset sold	$5000	$7000
Proceeds (GST exclusive) from sale of asset	$7000	$7000
Gain on sale of asset	$2000	$0

Under-depreciation

A loss on disposal of an asset means it has been under-depreciated.

Example 8.7

Clint East Wood Suppliers sold another asset on 30 June 2011, which originally cost $70000 and which had been depreciated by $65000, for $4400 (GST inclusive) cash. Depreciation had been charged right up to the time of the sale of the asset on 30 June 2011. We need to determine if the asset was under- or over-depreciated.

	Actual result	Perfect scenario
Original cost of asset sold	$70000	$70000
Less Accumulated depreciation on asset sold	$65000	$66000
Carrying amount of asset sold	$5000	$4000
Proceeds (GST exclusive) from sale of asset	$4000	$4000
Loss on sale of asset	$1000	$0

Accounting and Finance: 2B   ISBN 9780170182041   Cengage Learning Australia

In this example the asset has been depreciated by $65000 but had the calculations been done accurately, the accumulated depreciation should have been $66000. Therefore, the asset has been under-depreciated by $1000, which equates to a Loss on sale of asset of $1000.

Test your knowledge

1   Define 'depreciation'.

2   What is a depreciable non-current asset?

3   Define 'property, plant and equipment'.

4   State the costs that are included in the value of a depreciable non-current asset.

5   What is included in the purchase price of a depreciable asset? Give examples to explain your answer.

6   Explain your understanding of what is included in those 'costs directly attributable to bring the asset to the location and condition necessary for it to be used as intended'. Give examples to explain your answer.

7   List and describe the causes of depreciation. Give examples to explain your answer.

8   Explain why depreciation does not calculate the market or current value of an asset.

9   Does depreciation set aside cash for the replacement of the asset? Explain.

10 State and describe the four factors that must be considered to determine depreciation.

11 What is the purpose of the balance day adjustment for depreciation?

12 What factor determines which depreciation method is selected for a given asset? Give examples to explain your answer.

13 Distinguish between straight line and reducing balance depreciation in terms of manner of calculation and effect.

Test your understanding

Topic guide
- Straight line depreciation: 8.1–8.4
- Reducing balance depreciation: 8.5–8.7
- Both depreciation methods: 8.8–8.11
- Incorporate all balance day adjustments: 8.12
- Disposal of assets (scrap asset): 8.13–8.15
- Disposal of assets (cash or credit sale of asset): 8.16–8.23
- Disposal of assets (trade-in asset): 8.24–8.28

Note: Where necessary, round all calculations to the nearest dollar.

8.1   Sun Dance Kid Pty Ltd purchased computer equipment worth $88000 (GST inclusive) on 1 July 2011 for cash. It was estimated that the residual value of the equipment would be $9000 and its estimated useful life eight years. It decided to depreciate the asset using the straight line method.

Required
a   Prepare the General journal entry to show the purchase of the equipment.
b   Calculate the annual depreciation for the years ended 30 June 2012 and 2013.
c   Prepare the General journal entry to raise depreciation on 30 June 2012 and 2013.

    d Prepare the General journal entry to close the Depreciation on equipment account to the Profit and loss summary account on 30 June 2012 and 2013.

    e Prepare the following General ledger accounts for the period 1 July 2011 to 30 June 2013:
- i   Equipment
- ii Depreciation on equipment
- iii Accumulated depreciation on equipment.

    f   Show how the Equipment and Accumulated depreciation on equipment would appear in the Statement of financial position as at 30 June 2012 and 2013.

8.2   Butch and Cassidy Traders purchased office furniture on 1 July 2011 for the invoice price of $66000 (GST component $6000) on credit from P Newman Pty Ltd. The furniture was to be depreciated using the straight-line method, with a residual value of $3000 and an estimated useful life of nine years.

Required

    a Prepare the General journal entry to show the purchase of the furniture.

    b Calculate the annual depreciation for the years ended 30 June 2012 and 2013.

    c Prepare the General journal entry to raise depreciation on 30 June 2012 and 2013.

    d Prepare the General journal entry to close the Depreciation on furniture account to the Profit and loss summary account on 30 June 2012 and 2013.

    e Prepare the following General ledger accounts for the period 1 July 2011 to 30 June 2013:
- i   Furniture
- ii Depreciation on furniture
- iii Accumulated depreciation on furniture.

    f   Show how the Furniture and Accumulated depreciation on furniture would appear in the Statement of financial position as at 30 June 2012 and 2013.

8.3   Snowy Doc is the owner of The Seven White Corporation, which acquired warehouse plant and equipment on 1 November 2011 at a cost of $110000 (GST component $10000) on credit from Happy Ltd. The initial delivery and handling costs to get the asset to the business cost $770 (GST component $70), paid in cash, and the installation and assembly costs to prepare the plant and equipment ready for use were $1100 (GST component $100), also paid in cash. The residual value was expected to be $12000 and the useful life eight years.

Required

    a Prepare the General journal entry to raise depreciation on the plant and equipment on 30 June 2012 and 2013.

    b Prepare the General journal entry to close the Depreciation on plant and equipment account to the Profit and loss summary account on 30 June 2012 and 2013.

    c Prepare the following General ledger accounts for the period 1 July 2011 to 30 June 2013:
- i   Plant and equipment
- ii Depreciation on plant and equipment
- iii Accumulated depreciation on plant and equipment.

    d Show how the Plant and equipment and Accumulated depreciation on plant and equipment would appear in the Statement of financial position as at 30 June 2012 and 2013.

8.4   Viggo Aragorn, owner of Rings Pty Ltd, purchased a motor vehicle on 1 December 2011 at a cost of $42900 (GST component $3900) paying cash. In addition it was necessary to pay the following costs in cash at the time of the purchase:
- annual insurance of $550 (GST component $50)
- annual vehicle registration of $660 (GST component $60)

Accounting and Finance: 2B   ISBN 9780170182041   Cengage Learning Australia

- air conditioning and window tinting of $3300 (GST component $300)
- legal costs to acquire the motor vehicle of $220 (GST component $20).

It was decided to depreciate the motor vehicle using the straight line method and it was anticipated that the asset's useful life would be six years and its residual value $8000.

Required

a Prepare the General journal entry to raise depreciation on the motor vehicle on 30 June 2012 and 2013.

b Prepare the General journal entry to close the Depreciation on motor vehicle account to the Profit and loss summary account on 30 June 2012 and 2013.

c Prepare the following General ledger accounts for the period 1 July 2011 to 30 June 2013:
 i Motor vehicle
 ii Depreciation on motor vehicle
 iii Accumulated depreciation on motor vehicle.

d Show how the Motor vehicle and Accumulated depreciation on motor vehicle would appear in the Statement of financial position as at 30 June 2012 and 2013.

8.5 Julie Poppins is owner of Sound of Music Productions, which purchased production machinery on 1 July 2011 on credit from Mary Andrews Ltd at a cost of $220000 (GST inclusive). The machinery was expected to have an estimated salvage value of $60000 and useful life of nine years. The machinery was to be depreciated using the reducing balance method at the rate of 15% per annum.

Required

a Prepare the General journal entry to show the purchase of the machinery.

b Calculate the annual depreciation for the years ended 30 June 2012 and 2013.

c Prepare the General journal entry to raise depreciation on the machinery on 30 June 2012 and 2013.

d Prepare the General journal entry to close the Depreciation on machinery account to the Profit and loss summary account.

e Prepare the following general ledger accounts for the period 1 July 2011 to 30 June 2013:
 i Machinery
 ii Depreciation on machinery
 iii Accumulated depreciation on machinery.

f Show how the Machinery and Accumulated depreciation on machinery would appear in the Statement of financial position as at 30 June 2012 and 2013.

8.6 George Martin is the owner of Beetals Pty Ltd. The business purchased an item of processing plant and equipment on 1 July 2011 worth $57200 (GST component $5200), paying cash. The asset was expected to have a useful life of seven years at which time its residual value was anticipated to be $21550. The asset is to be depreciated using the reducing balance method at the rate of 15% per annum.

Required

a Prepare the General journal entry to show the purchase of the plant and equipment.

b Calculate the annual depreciation for the years ended 30 June 2012 and 2013.

c Prepare the General journal entry to raise depreciation on the plant and equipment on 30 June 2012 and 2013.

d Prepare the General journal entry to close the Depreciation on plant and equipment account to the Profit and loss summary account on 30 June 2012 and 2013.

e Prepare the following General ledger accounts for the period 1 July 2011 to 30 June 2013:
 i Plant and equipment
 ii Depreciation on plant and equipment
 iii Accumulated depreciation on plant and equipment.

f   Show how the Plant and equipment and Accumulated depreciation on plant and equipment would appear in the Statement of financial position as at 30 June 2012 and 2013.

8.7   Clapton Hendrix Traders purchased a delivery truck worth $94 600 (GST component $8600) on credit from Cream Pty Ltd on 1 October 2011. On 1 October 2011 the following costs were also incurred and paid for in cash:
- annual vehicle registration $748 (GST component $68)
- annual insurance $561 (GST component $51)
- alterations to enable the truck to be used over long distances $2530 (GST component $230).
    The delivery truck was estimated to have a residual value of $33 300 at the end of its expected useful life of seven years. The delivery truck was to be depreciated using the reducing balance method at the rate of 20% per year.

Required
a   Prepare the General journal entry to show the purchase of the delivery truck.
b   Calculate the annual depreciation for the years ended 30 June 2012 and 2013.
c   Prepare the General journal entry to raise depreciation on the delivery truck on 30 June 2012 and 2013.
d   Prepare the General journal entry to close the Depreciation on delivery truck account to the Profit and loss summary account on 30 June 2012 and 2013.
e   Prepare the following General ledger accounts for the period 1 July 2011 to 30 June 2013:
    i   Delivery truck
    ii   Depreciation on delivery truck
    iii Accumulated depreciation on delivery truck.
f   Show how the Delivery truck and Accumulated depreciation on delivery truck would appear in the Statement of financial position as at 30 June 2012 and 2013.

8.8   An extract of Madonna Suppliers' Statement of financial position as at 1 July 2011 showed the following:

Statement of financial position (Extract) as at 1 July 2011

	$	$
Non-current assets		
Machinery (at cost)	95 000	
Less Accumulated depreciation	34 200	60 800
Fixtures and fittings	40 000	
Less Accumulated depreciation	7 400	32 600

The Machinery is being depreciated using the reducing balance method at the rate of 20% per annum. The Fixtures and fittings are depreciated on the straight-line method, with an estimated useful life of ten years and residual value of $3000.

Required
a   Calculate the annual depreciation for Machinery and Fixtures and fittings for the years ended 30 June 2012 and 2013.
b   Prepare the General journal entry to raise depreciation on the Machinery and Fixtures and fittings on 30 June 2012 and 2013.
c   Prepare the General journal entry to close the Depreciation on machinery and Depreciation of fixtures and fittings accounts to the Profit and loss summary account on 30 June 2012 and 2013.

Accounting and Finance: 2B   ISBN 9780170182041   Cengage Learning Australia

d   Prepare the following General ledger accounts for the period 1 July 2011 to
30 June 2013:
  i   Machinery
  ii   Fixtures and fittings
  iii Depreciation on machinery
  iv   Depreciation on fixtures and fittings
  v   Accumulated depreciation on machinery
  vi   Accumulated depreciation on fixtures and fittings.
e   Show how the Machinery and Fixtures and fittings and associated Accumulated
depreciation would appear in the Statement of financial position as at 30 June 2012
and 2013.

8.9   Elvis Bear, owner of Heartbreak Hotel Pty Ltd, purchased industrial cooking equipment on
1 February 2012 at a cost of $119 900 (GST inclusive) from L Tender Ltd. A loan of $119 900
from the Rock Bank Ltd was arranged to enable the purchase of this equipment. The
equipment was to be depreciated using the diminishing balance method at the rate of 20%
per year and was estimated to have a residual value of $20 000 and a useful life of nine years.

The business also purchased office furniture on 1 May 2012 at a cost of $13 200
(GST inclusive) paying cash. The office furniture was to be depreciated using the
straight-line method with a useful life of ten years and a residual value of $2000.

Required
a   Prepare the General journal entry to show the purchase of the equipment and office
furniture.
b   Calculate the annual depreciation on the equipment and office furniture for the years
ended 30 June 2012 and 2013.
c   Prepare the General journal entry to raise depreciation on the equipment and office
furniture on 30 June 2012 and 2013.
d   Prepare the General journal entry to close the Depreciation on equipment account and
Depreciation on office furniture to the Profit and loss summary account on 30 June 2012
and 2013.
e   Prepare the following General ledger accounts for the financial period 1 July 2011 to
30 June 2013:
  i   Equipment
  ii   Office furniture
  iii Depreciation on equipment
  iv   Depreciation on office furniture
  v   Accumulated depreciation on equipment
  vi   Accumulated depreciation on office furniture.
f   Show how the Equipment and Office furniture and related Accumulated depreciation
would appear in the Statement of financial position as at 30 June 2012 and 2013.

8.10 The following is an extract from the unadjusted Trial balance of Ben Hall and Sons:

Trial balance (extract) as at 30 June 2011

Account	Debit $	Credit $
Workshop machinery	98 000	
Accumulated depreciation on workshop machinery		47 000
Furniture and fittings	46 000	
Accumulated depreciation on furniture and fittings		12 600

Additional information as at 30 June 2011
- The Furniture and fittings are being depreciated on the straight-line method. Their residual value was estimated at $3000 and useful life at ten years.
- The workshop machinery is being depreciated at a rate of 30% on the reducing balance method.

Required

a Prepare the necessary journal entries to account for the depreciation of both assets at 30 June 2011.

b Prepare the closing entry necessary on 30 June 2011.

c Show the following ledger accounts after all transactions:
  i Depreciation on workshop machinery
  ii Accumulated depreciation on workshop machinery
  iii Depreciation on furniture and fittings
  iv Accumulated depreciation on furniture and fittings.

d Show how both assets would appear in the Statement of financial position as at 30 June 2011.

8.11 The following is an extract from the unadjusted Trial balance of Moondyne Joe Traders:

Trial balance (extract) as at 30 June 2011

Account	Debit $	Credit $
Plant and equipment	190000	
Accumulated depreciation on plant and equipment		35000
Office furniture	15000	
Accumulated depreciation on office furniture		6400

Additional information as at 30 June 2011
- The plant and equipment are being depreciated on the reducing balance method. Their residual value was estimated at $3000 and useful life at ten years. The depreciation rate is 20 per cent per year.
- Office furniture is depreciated using the straight line method. It has an estimated useful life of ten years and is expected to have no residual value.

Required

a Prepare the necessary journal entries to account for the depreciation of both assets at 30 June 2011.

b Prepare the closing entry necessary on 30 June 2011.

c Show the following ledger accounts after all transactions:
  i Depreciation on plant and equipment
  ii Accumulated depreciation on plant and equipment
  iii Depreciation on office furniture
  iv Accumulated depreciation on office furniture.

d Show how both assets would appear in the Statement of financial position as at 30 June 2011.

e The owner would like, for tax purposes only, to depreciate the office furniture on the reducing balance method to obtain accelerated tax benefits. What annual percentage rate should he use that would be equivalent to the straight line rate that he is using for his financial accounts?

Accounting and Finance: 2B   ISBN 9780170182041   Cengage Learning Australia

8.12 The following is the unadjusted Trial balance of Tom Roberts Paint Supplies.

Trial balance as at 30 June 2011

Account	Debit $	Credit $
Cash	31 200	
Selling expenses	12 100	
Capital – T Roberts		178 000
Drawings – T Roberts	23 400	
Mortgage from Streeton Ltd		56 800
Interest expense	4 900	
Sales		288 000
Administration office expenses	17 500	
GST collections		25 800
GST outlays	24 800	
Electricity expense	14 600	
Discount allowed	2 500	
Office salaries	69 600	
Motor vehicle	75 000	
Accumulated depreciation on motor vehicle		21 800
Bad debts	800	
Commission revenue		2 560
Accounts receivable	41 300	
Allowance for doubtful debts		760
Loss on sale of motor vehicle	500	
Telephone expenses	1 100	
Accounts payable		21 780
Prepaid rent	12 400	
Cost of sales	123 000	
Plant and machinery	132 000	
Accumulated depreciation on plant and machinery		38 000
Shop wages	48 900	
Interest revenue		2 100
Petty cash	1 100	
Sales returns	4 500	
	635 600	635 600

Additional information as at 30 June 2011
- The Plant and equipment are being depreciated on the reducing balance method. Their residual value was estimated at $9000 and useful life at eight years. The depreciation rate is 18 per cent per year.
- The Motor vehicle is being depreciated on the straight line method and its useful life is ten years and estimated residual value $4000.
- The rent expired during the current year was $11 000.
- Electricity owing at balance day is $700 (exclusive of GST).
- The allowance for doubtful debts was to be 2% of the Accounts receivable balance.
- Accrued commission revenue is $500 (GST exclusive).

Required

a   Prepare the necessary balance day adjustments as at 30 June 2011 in the General journal.

b   Prepare the closing entries necessary on 30 June 2011 in the General journal.

c   Prepare the General journal entries on 30 June 2011 to close the Drawings – Tom Roberts account and to transfer the profit or loss to the Capital – Tom Roberts account.

d   Prepare the Profit and loss summary account for the year ended 30 June 2011.

8.13   The following is an extract of the Statement of financial position of R Laver Supplies as at 1 July 2011.

Statement of financial position (extract) as at 1 July 2010

	$	$
Non-current assets		
Furniture (at cost)	38 000	
Less Accumulated depreciation	36 000	2000

The furniture had been purchased on 1 July 2000. Its estimated residual value was $2000 and useful life ten years. On 30 June 2011 it was decided to scrap the furniture. The furniture would only need to be depreciated by $2000 during the year ended 30 June 2011.

Required

a   Prepare the General journal entry to raise depreciation on the furniture for the year ended 30 June 2011.

b   Prepare the General journal entries to scrap the furniture on 30 June 2011.

c   Prepare the Furniture and Accumulated depreciation on furniture accounts for the year ended 30 June 2010.

8.14   B Cable and P Farmer are partners in Chadwick Traders and on 1 July 2011 it was decided to scrap an item of equipment. The original cost of the equipment was $12000 (exclusive of GST) and as at 1 July 2011 it had been depreciated by $9200. It cost $220 (GST component $20), paid in cash, to dispose of the item of equipment.

Required

a   Prepare the General journal entries to dispose of the equipment on 1 July 2011.

b   Prepare the Disposal of equipment account required on 1 July 2011.

8.15   The following is an extract of the Statement of financial position of Constable Traders as at 1 July 2011.

Statement of financial position (extract) as at 1 July 2011

	$	$
Non-current assets		
Motor vehicle (at cost)	76 000	
Less Accumulated depreciation	56 800	19 200

The motor vehicle was originally purchased on 1 July 2003 and was estimated to have a residual value of $5000 after its useful life of ten years. It is being depreciated on the straight line method. The motor vehicle was destroyed by fire on 30 June 2012. It was not insured. It cost the business $550 (GST component $50) to dispose of the burnt-out vehicle and this was paid on 30 June 2012.

Accounting and Finance: 2B   ISBN 9780170182041   Cengage Learning Australia

Required

a Prepare the General journal entry to depreciate the motor vehicle for the year ended 30 June 2012.

b Prepare the General journal entry to record the cost of disposing of the motor vehicle on 30 June 2012.

c Prepare the General journal entries to dispose of the motor vehicle on 30 June 2012.

d Prepare the Disposal of motor vehicle account for the year ended 30 June 2012.

8.16 On 1 July 2004 Walker and Rioli purchased for their business fixtures and fittings at a cost of $35000 (GST exclusive). These non-current assets were expected to have a useful life of ten years at which time their salvage value would be $3000. The assets were to be depreciated using the straight line method. On 30 June 2011 the fixtures and fittings were sold for $13970 (GST inclusive) cash. They had not been depreciated for the year ended 30 June 2011.

Required

a Prepare the General journal entry to raise depreciation for the year ended 30 June 2011.

b Prepare the General journal entries to account for the sale of the fixtures and fittings on 30 June 2011.

c Prepare the General journal entry on 30 June 2011 to transfer the gain or loss on the sale of the fixtures and fittings to the Profit and loss summary account.

d Prepare the Sale of fixtures and fittings account for the year ended 30 June 2011.

8.17 The General ledger records of S Michael Stores showed the following accounts as at 1 July 2011:

Furniture account					
Date	Account details	Debit	Credit	Balance	Dr/Cr
1/7/11	Balance			$54000	Dr

Accumulated depreciation on furniture account					
Date	Account details	Debit	Credit	Balance	Dr/Cr
1/7/11	Balance			$37456	Cr

The furniture was being depreciated using the straight-line method and the residual value had been estimated as $2500 and useful life at 11 years. On 30 June 2012 the furniture was sold for $12980 (GST component $1180) cash.

Required

a Prepare the General journal entry to raise depreciation for the year ended 30 June 2012.

b Prepare the General journal entries to account for the sale of the furniture on 30 June 2012.

c Prepare the General journal entry on 30 June 2012 to transfer the gain or loss on the sale of the furniture to the Profit and loss summary account.

d Prepare the Sale of furniture account for the year ended 30 June 2012.

8.18 Olivia N John Traders acquired processing machinery on 1 July 2006 worth $120000 (GST exclusive). The machinery was estimated to have a salvage value of $45000 and useful life of seven years. The depreciation rate was set at 15% per year using the reducing balance method. On 30 June 2011 the machinery was sold for cash of $47300 (GST component $4300).

Required

a Prepare the General journal entry to raise depreciation for the year ended 30 June 2011.

b Prepare the General journal entries to account for the sale of the machinery on 30 June 2011.

c Prepare the General journal entry on 30 June 2011 to transfer the gain or loss on the sale of the machinery to the Profit and loss summary account.

d Prepare the Sale of machinery account for the year ended 30 June 2011.

e Was the asset sold under- or over-depreciated and, if so, by how much?

8.19 The General ledger records of M Hines Suppliers showed the following as at 1 July 2011:

Plant account					
Date	Account details	Debit	Credit	Balance	Dr/Cr
1/7/11	Balance			$156000	Dr

Accumulated depreciation on plant account					
Date	Account details	Debit	Credit	Balance	Dr/Cr
1/7/11	Balance			$123284	Cr

The plant was purchased on 1 July 2004 and its estimated residual value was $26000 and useful life nine years. It was being depreciated using the reducing balance method at the rate of 20 per cent per annum. On 30 June 2012 the plant was sold to H Reddy on credit for $24970 (GST inclusive).

Required

a Prepare the General journal entry to raise depreciation for the year ended 30 June 2012.

b Prepare the General journal entries to account for the sale of the plant on 30 June 2012.

c Prepare the General journal entry on 30 June 2012 to transfer the gain or loss on the sale of the plant to the Profit and loss summary account.

d Prepare the Sale of Plant account for the year ended 30 June 2012.

e Was the asset sold under- or over-depreciated and, if so, by how much?

8.20 Icehouse Pty Ltd had the following balances in the General ledger on 1 July 2011:

- Motor vehicle: $73000
- Accumulated depreciation on motor vehicle: $41875.

  The motor vehicle is being depreciated on the straight-line method; its estimated residual value is $6000 and useful life eight years. On 30 April 2012 the motor vehicle was sold for cash of $28105 (GST component $2555).

Required

a Prepare the General journal entry to raise depreciation on 30 April 2012.

b Prepare the General journal entries to account for the sale of the motor vehicle on 30 April 2012.

c Prepare the General journal entry on 30 June 2012 to transfer the gain or loss on the sale of the motor vehicle to the Profit and loss summary account.

d Prepare the Motor vehicle, Accumulated depreciation on motor vehicle and Sale of motor vehicle accounts for the year ended 30 June 2012.

e Was the asset sold under- or over-depreciated and, if so, by how much?

8.21 Border and Hughes, partners in Chappell Traders, show the following non-current asset in their Statement of financial position as at 1 July 2011:

Non-current assets	
Delivery truck (at cost)	$140000
Less accumulated depreciation on delivery truck	$92978

The delivery truck is being depreciated using the reducing balance method at 18 per cent per annum. On 31 March 2012 the business sold the delivery truck to I Redpath on credit for $33990 (GST inclusive).

Required

a   Prepare the General journal entry to raise depreciation on 31 March 2012.

b   Prepare the General journal entries to account for the sale of the delivery truck on 31 March 2012.

c   Prepare the General journal entry on 30 June 2012 to transfer the gain or loss on the sale of the delivery truck to the Profit and loss summary account.

d   Prepare the Delivery truck, Accumulated depreciation on delivery truck and Sale of delivery truck accounts for the year ended 30 June 2012.

e   Was the asset sold under- or over-depreciated and, if so, by how much?

8.22   On 1 August 2007 Bright Meats purchased production machinery paying $154990 (GST component $14090) cash. At the same time the business had to pay testing and assembly costs of $2200 (GST component $200) cash. The asset was to be depreciated using the reducing balance method at the rate of 22 per cent per year.

   However, after only approximately four years the business decided to sell the machinery so that it could upgrade to new technology. The machinery was sold to Hans Ltd on 1 September 2011 for $64900 (GST component $5900).

Required

Prepare the following accounts for the period 1 August 2007 to the 30 June 2012:

a   Machinery

b   Depreciation on machinery

c   Accumulated depreciation on machinery

d   Sale of machinery

e   Gain/loss on sale of machinery.

8.23   On 1 November 2003 Charming Traders acquired office furniture and fittings costing an invoice price of $86999 (GST component $7909) on credit from Prince Pty Ltd. Charming Traders also had to pay freight and delivery costs to get the new furniture to its shop and this cost $627 (GST component $57). This amount was paid in cash. These non-current assets were expected to have a useful life of ten years at which time their residual value would be $4600. Depreciation is being charged each year on the straight line method.

   On 31 May 2011 the business sold the furniture and fittings for $29700 (GST component $2700) cash.

Required

Prepare the following accounts for the period 1 November 2003 to 30 June 2011:

a   Furniture and fittings

b   Depreciation on furniture and fittings

c   Accumulated depreciation on furniture and fittings

d   Sale of furniture and fittings

e   Gain/loss on sale of furniture and fittings.

8.24   Vertigo Cleaning purchased an industrial cleaning machine on 1 July 2004 at a cost of $31900 (GST inclusive) on credit from Rocky Pty Ltd. The machine was to be depreciated using the straight line method and its useful life was estimated to be nine years and residual value $1300.

   After approximately seven years the machine was traded in for a new machine on 30 June 2011. The new cleaning machine cost $36960 (GST inclusive) purchased from Northwest Ltd. The trade-in allowance received for the old machine was $9240 (GST inclusive).

Required

a   Prepare the General journal entry to raise depreciation on 30 June 2011.

b   Prepare the General journal entries to account for the disposal of the cleaning machine on 30 June 2011.

c Prepare the General journal entry on 30 June 2011 to show the purchase of the new cleaning machine and trade-in of the old machine.

d Prepare the General journal entry on 30 June 2011 to transfer the gain or loss on the sale of the cleaning machine to the Profit and loss summary account.

e Prepare the Cleaning machine, Accumulated depreciation on cleaning machine, Northwest Ltd and Sale of cleaning machine accounts for the year ended 30 June 2011.

f Was the asset sold under- or over-depreciated and, if so, by how much?

8.25 The Statement of financial position as at 1 July 2011 for Braveheart Manufacturers showed the following:

Statement of financial position (extract) as at 1 July 2011

	$	$
Non-current assets		
Plant machinery (at cost)	165 000	
Less Accumulated depreciation on plant machinery	117 362	47 638

The plant machinery is being depreciated using the reducing balance method at 22 per cent per year. On 30 June 2012 the plant machinery was traded in on a new item of plant machinery costing $189 200 (GST component $17 200). The trade-in allowance, provided by R Roy Ltd for the old plant machinery, was $55 000 (GST component $5000).

Required

a Prepare the General journal entry to raise depreciation on 30 June 2012.

b Prepare the General journal entries to account for the disposal of the plant machinery on 30 June 2012.

c Prepare the General journal entry on 30 June 2012 to show the purchase of the new plant machinery and trade-in of the old machine.

d Prepare the General journal entry on 30 June 2012 to transfer the gain or loss on the sale of the plant machinery to the Profit and loss summary account.

e Prepare the Plant machinery, Accumulated depreciation on plant machinery, R Roy Ltd and Sale of plant machinery accounts for the year ended 30 June 2012.

8.26 Bravo Producers purchased a delivery truck on 1 October 2004 for an invoice price of $93 500 (GST inclusive) on credit from Grande Pty Ltd. The truck was modified through the setting up of a sleeping cabin for drivers on long-distance hauls at a cost of $6820 (GST inclusive) and this was paid for in cash. The annual registration of $715 (GST inclusive) and annual insurance $748 (GST inclusive) were also paid in cash at that time. The estimated useful life of the delivery truck was nine years and its expected residual value was $7500. The asset was depreciated on the straight line method.

On 30 June 2011 the delivery truck was traded in on a new truck, which cost $104 500 (GST inclusive) from Shane Ltd. The trade-in allowance received for the old truck was $24 970 (GST inclusive).

Required

a Prepare the General journal entry to raise depreciation on 30 June 2005.

b Prepare the General journal entries to account for the disposal of the delivery truck on 30 June 2011.

c Prepare the General journal entry on 30 June 2011 to show the purchase of the new delivery truck and trade-in of the old machine.

d Prepare the General journal entry on 30 June 2011 to transfer the gain or loss on the sale of the delivery truck to the Profit and loss summary account.

e Prepare the Delivery truck, Shane Ltd, Accumulated depreciation on delivery truck and Sale of delivery truck accounts for the year ended 30 June 2011.

8.27 Gale and McPherson are partners in a fashion design and manufacturing business called Crawford's Fashions. They bought factory machinery on credit from Craig Bond Ltd costing $166 980 (GST component $15 180) on 1 October 2004. At the same time they paid cash of $3630 (GST component $330) to have the machinery installed and assembled and also paid cash of $275 (GST component $25) to have the machinery transported to their factory in Cannington. The machinery was to be depreciated using the reducing balance method at the rate of 22 per cent per year.

On 31 August 2010 the business traded in the old machine on a new machine from Halle Ltd costing $209 000 (GST component $19 000). This price included all delivery and installation costs but the company's general insurance premium was increased by $2200 (GST component $200) per annum, paid in cash on 31 August 2010. The trade-in allowance received for the old machine was $31 900 (GST component $2900). The new machinery was also to be depreciated on the reducing balance method at the rate of 22 per cent per year.

Required

a Prepare the Machinery, Halle Ltd, Depreciation on machinery, Accumulated depreciation on machinery, Disposal of machinery and Gain/loss on disposal of machinery accounts for the financial period 1 October 2004 to 30 June 2011.

b Show how the Machinery and Accumulated depreciation would appear in the Statement of financial position as at 30 June 2011.

8.28 Connery Traders purchased a delivery motor vehicle for its business on 1 September 2002 costing $75 900 (GST inclusive) paying cash. The asset was estimated to have a useful life of 11 years and a residual value of $5000. The business depreciates its motor vehicle using the straight line method.

Approximately eight years later, on 31 July 2010, the business traded in the old motor vehicle for a new one costing $93 500 (GST inclusive). The new motor vehicle purchased from Bond Ltd was expected to have a useful life of ten years, at which time its residual value would be $6500. The trade-in allowance received for the old motor vehicle was $23 980 (GST inclusive).

Required

a Prepare the Motor vehicle, Bond Ltd, Depreciation on motor vehicle, Accumulated depreciation on motor vehicle, Disposal of motor vehicle and Gain/loss on disposal of motor vehicle accounts for the period 1 October 2004 to 30 June 2011.

b Show how the Motor vehicle and Accumulated depreciation on motor vehicle would appear in the Statement of financial position as at 30 June 2011.

c Did the business over- or under-depreciate the original delivery motor vehicle? Explain your answer.

Investigation

1 Select one of the following industries and use the internet to find a company within that industry (perhaps one that you are familiar with):
- transport
- retail
- tourism and leisure
- telecommunications.

Search the company's website for its annual report and then answer the following questions:

a What was the total amount of depreciation expense for the current year?

b What is the total value of the non-current assets at the date of the statement of financial position?

c What types of non-current assets does this business have?

d   What were the components of the property, plant and equipment as at the date of the Statement of financial position?

e   What methods of depreciation have been used by this business?

f   At what value(s) are the property, plant and equipment valued (cost, fair value, etc.)?

g   Have any items of property, plant and equipment been disposed of during the past year and, if so, was there a gain or loss on disposal?

h   Were there any new items of property, plant and equipment purchased during the year? If so, what was purchased and for how much?

2   Visit your local small shopping centre and select five businesses of your choice. Observe each business and make a list of the non-current assets that it uses and then ask the proprietor these questions:

a   Does the business have other non-current assets that are not at the retail shop?

b   Does the business own or lease these non-current assets?

c   What depreciation methods are used for each type of asset?

d   How did the business owner or manager determine the residual value and useful life of each asset?

Essay

A non-accounting person was heard saying 'Depreciation is an exact process that shows the decline in the current value of an asset and enables a business to provide for its replacement'.

Comment on this statement in essay format, explaining if you agree or disagree. In your answer outline the following points:

- a definition of depreciation
- the purpose of depreciation and why there is a need for a balance day adjustment
- the nature of a depreciable asset and the factors that contribute to the depreciation of such assets
- whether depreciation determines the market value of an asset
- whether depreciation sets aside cash for the replacement of an asset.

Ethics case study

Bruce Hoyle, Neville Galaxy and Joy Town are directors in a small proprietary company making fashion clothing for the Australian market. Their general manager, Lisa Twain, has directed the accountant, Frank Harper, to adjust the depreciation expense recorded by changing the residual value and useful lives of the company's machinery. Until now, based on past experience, the residual value of the machinery has always been ten per cent of the original cost of the asset and the useful life has always been seven years. This policy has usually resulted in only a small gain or loss on disposal of the asset. Lisa has now directed that the residual value be 15 per cent of the original cost of the asset and that the useful life be extended to ten years.

Frank Harper questions the reason for this and is told that there is a need to show improved profits. Further questioning reveals that this is being done at the request of one of the directors, Bruce Hoyle, who is planning to sell his share in the business in the near future.

Required

a   Who are the stakeholders in this case?

b   Explain what the ethical problem is for Frank.

c   What are the consequences for Frank if he does nothing about this issue?

d   What alternatives are available to Frank?

e   What would you suggest that Frank do in this case?

Accounting and Finance: 2B   ISBN 9780170182041   Cengage Learning Australia

Chapter 9

ADVANCED FINANCIAL REPORTING

What You Will Learn

After studying this chapter you should be able to:

1 Explain the need for the classification of income and expenses and outline the manner in which these elements are classified in financial statements

2 Explain the need for the classification of assets and liabilities and outline the manner in which these elements are classified in financial statements

3 Explain the significance of balance day adjustments on the financial statements of a business

4 Produce a classified income statement for trading/ merchandising and service businesses, based on a post-adjustment Trial balance

5 Produce a classified statement of financial position (balance sheet) for a business, based on a post-adjustment Trial balance

Introduction

In Chapter 3 we covered the production of simple statements indicating the financial performance, in terms of profitability, of a small business over a financial period and its financial position, in terms of assets, liabilities and owner's equity, at the end of that period. As was briefly mentioned in that chapter, it is usual to arrange the information presented in these reports in a certain way in order to make that information more understandable and useful. This process is known as *classification*.

Classification of financial information may be said to serve three purposes:

- the information is made clearer and easier to understand
- analysis and interpretation of the information is facilitated
- accountability is facilitated — those responsible for particular areas or functions within the business are able to evaluate the performance of their area of responsibility, enabling measures to be taken to improve performance in the future.

Key Concept 9.1

Classification

Classification is the process of presenting information in financial statements in a manner that groups or arranges the information in order to facilitate understanding, analysis and accountability within the organisation.

CLASSIFICATION

Even small businesses – which probably don't have separately managed departments and may even be under the control of a single person (typically the owner) – can derive benefit from classification. For example, classifying a business's expenses will help an owner or manager understand the factors that are leading to the firm's success or failure and will hence enable them to make changes that may be necessary to ensure greater success. We will examine the specific benefits of the classification of reports in more detail below in the sections dealing with the two main statements, the Income statement and the Statement of financial position.

The other modification to the simple financial statements covered in Chapter 3 arises from balance day adjustments (BDAs), which were dealt with in Chapters 7 and 8. The purpose of BDAs (including those relating to non-current assets and their disposal) is to allocate revenue and expenses to the accounting periods in which they should be recognised, as opposed to those in which the payments representing that revenue and those expenses may have been made or received. These BDAs will clearly have an impact on:

* the Income statement – by creating, increasing or diminishing items of revenue, or creating, increasing or diminishing items of expense
* the Statement of financial position – by creating, increasing or diminishing assets or liabilities and increasing or diminishing equity through their net effect on the profit for the period.

We will show these effects in more detail in the relevant sections below.

CLASSIFIED INCOME STATEMENTS

The fundamental purpose of an Income statement is to help the user (in the case of a small business, the owner or manager) to make controlling decisions that will improve the profit performance of the firm in the future. This is achieved, in part, by reviewing and analysing the firm's past performance. In particular, the user needs to be able to identify those parts of the firm's business that are capable of improvement and develop strategies for making those improvements. Performance will usually be evaluated by making comparisons – with past performance, with the firm's budget and with other firms in the same industry – either on an individual basis (seldom available) or on the basis of published industry averages or standards. In any case it is helpful to categorise income and expenses.

Classification of income

In the case of income, the classification process is relatively simple, since most firms only have a few separate sources of income. As we have seen already, firms show each income source separately and distinguish between the revenue gained from the firm's trading operations (sales or fees) and other income, such as interest earned, rent revenue and gains on sale of assets.

Merchandising firms show a separate calculation of the gross profit from their trading operations. Sales and purchase returns may be shown as separate items in the Trading statement section of the Income statement so that a judgement can be made as to whether or not they are higher than they should be. If they are, this might indicate inefficiencies in the purchasing or selling systems that should be investigated further.

There are two other ways in which income (specifically 'revenue') may be classified:

- Sales (or fees) may be divided into *cash* or *credit*. This enables the owner/manager to assess the relative significance of the credit sales to the overall income. Expenses specific to credit sales (such as discounts allowed or bad and doubtful debts) can be related to the total value of credit sales to inform judgements on the effectiveness of the firm's management of debtors. Future strategic decisions can be evaluated. For example, if the firm is proposing to try and boost sales by offering additional discounts to credit customers, the relative significance of the credit sales in the greater scheme of things will be an important factor in the decision, as will be the estimated cost by way of the extra discounts allowed. To enable this distinction to be made, there need to be separate ledger accounts for 'Cash sales' and 'Credit sales'.

- Sales (or fees) may be divided into particular *product categories* to judge the relative significance of each category to the firm's total earnings. For example, a hardware store may wish to show separately its sales of timber, paints, tools and garden products; an accounting firm may want to distinguish between fees earned for financial accounting, investment advice and preparation of taxation returns. Especially in the case of merchandising firms, product categories can help identify each category's contribution to gross profit. (An example of this is shown in Example 9.1.)

This sort of classification requires separate accounting for the different categories of revenue and their related costs and its practicality will depend on the complexity of the classification and the nature of the firm's recording systems. A small grocery store maintaining a manual accounting system may find that categorising its sales imposes an impossible clerical burden on the accountant, while a used-car dealer, even if using a manual system, might find it quite easy to record sales under different headings (e.g. passenger vehicles, light commercial, 4WD).

We have mentioned Gain on sale of an asset as an item that would be included in the Other operating income account. If there were to be a loss on disposal, this would be shown as an expense under whichever classification the other expenses related to that asset were recorded.

🔑 Key Concept 9.2

Classification of income and expenses

Income is classified to distinguish revenue from gains and possibly to divide revenue according to manner of payment or type of product or service. Expenses are classified on a functional or departmental basis.

Example 9.1

EXAMPLE:

Millie's Pills is a pharmacy selling prescription and non-prescription medicines, vitamins and other dietary supplements and a wide range of other products, including cosmetics and other hair and beauty products. Customers pay with cash, EFTPOS or credit card. The firm has surplus funds invested in short-term bank deposits. At the end of the first quarter of the year on 30 September 2010, its ledger contains the following balances:

	$
Sales, credit: prescription medicines	89000
Sales, cash: prescription medicines	23000
Sales, credit: non-prescription medicines	98000
Sales, cash: non-prescription medicines	46000
Sales, credit: dietary supplements	51000
Sales, cash: dietary supplements	15000
Sales, credit: hair and beauty products	78000
Sales, cash: hair and beauty products	22000
Sales, credit: miscellaneous	41000
Sales, cash: miscellaneous	16000
Interest revenue	450
Cost of sales, prescription medicines	45000
Cost of sales, non-prescription medicines	56000
Cost of sales, dietary supplements	19200
Cost of sales, beauty products	28800
Cost of sales, miscellaneous	20000

In its simplest form, Millie's Pills' Income statement for the period would appear as follows:

Millie's Pills
Income statement for the quarter ended 30 September 2010

	$	$
Sales		479000
Less Cost of sales		169000
Gross profit		310000
Add Other operating income – Interest		450
Total income		310450

If the firm were to distinguish between cash and credit sales, the statement might look something like this:

Millie's Pills
Income statement for the quarter ended 30 September 2010

	$	$
Sales: Cash		122000
Sales: Credit		357000
Total sales		479000
Less Cost of sales		169000
Gross profit		310000
Add Other operating income – Interest		450
Total income		310450

To show separately the different sources of revenue, the statement could be drawn up as follows:

Millie's Pills
Income statement for the quarter ended 30 September 2010

	$	$
Sales: Prescription medicines	112000	
Non-prescription medicines	144000	

Accounting and Finance: 2B   ISBN 9780170182041   Cengage Learning Australia

Dietary supplements	66000	
Beauty products	100000	
Miscellaneous products	57000	479000
Less Cost of sales		169000
Gross profit		310000
Add Other operating income – Interest		450
Total income		310450

Finally, a comprehensively classified income statement showing the nature of the various product sales and their contribution to the overall gross profit could be as follows:

Millie's Pills
Income statement for the quarter ended 30 September 2010

	Prescription medicines $	Non-prescript medicines $	Dietary supplements $	Beauty products $	Miscellaneous products $	TOTAL $
Sales: Cash	23000	46000	15000	22000	16000	**122000**
Credit	89000	98000	51000	78000	41000	**357000**
Total sales	112000	144000	66000	100000	57000	**479000**
Cost of sales	45000	56000	19200	28800	20000	**169000**
Gross profit	67000	88000	46800	71200	37000	**310000**
Other operating income: Interest						**450**
Total income						**310450**

As this example has shown, the production of this sort of classified statement requires a good deal of detailed recording. However, it will allow the owner or manager to assess the relative importance of the various products and evaluate the effect of measures taken to try to improve performance in the future.

The presentation of the Income statement for a service business is generally a good deal simpler since there is usually not a trading statement ending in a gross profit. Fees may be classified according to source and other revenue and income items will be shown separately.

Example 9.2

EXAMPLE:

Harry Flash Electrics has the following account balances in its ledger at the end of the financial year on 31 December 2009:

Fees: Domestic jobs	$102000
Fees: Commercial jobs	$149000
Fees: Appliance installations	$24000
Discount revenue	$450
Gain on disposal of asset	$1220

The income section of the firm's Income statement would be as follows:

Income statement for Harry Flash Electrics for the year ended 31 December 2009

	$
Fees: Domestic	102000
Commercial	149000
Appliance installations	24000
Total fees	275000

Other income: Discount revenue	450
Gain on disposal	1 220
Total income	276 670

Classification of expense

Important though income classification may be for some businesses, it is fair to say that the classification of expenses has a wider application. For one thing, most businesses will have a much greater number of expenses than sources of revenue, so grouping them in a systematic manner will make a greater contribution to the 'understandability' of the statement. In addition, individual employees or managers usually have more control over the expenses in their area than over any aspect of revenue and it is therefore more critical for them (and for those seeking to evaluate their performance) to be able to isolate the expenses in that area.

The basis of classification will depend on the nature of the business and the way it is organised. As previously noted, a merchandising business will already have classified its expenses into those directly included in the Cost of sales (i.e. the purchase of stock; customs duty, if any; freight inwards, including transit insurance) on one hand and other operating expenses not directly related to the purchase of inventory on the other. These other operating expenses, which will be deducted from the total income to arrive at the profit for the period, are also commonly classified or grouped.

In a large business that has several departments with a manager responsible for each, it is usual to group the expenses on a departmental basis so that each manager is able to see the expenses for which they are personally responsible. If there is a significant transport section with a transport manager, all expenses relating to transport will be grouped; office expenses may be shown together for the benefit of the office manager; selling expenses for the sales manager; finance expenses for the finance manager; and so on.

A small business – particularly a sole trader – is less likely to have a number of managers in charge of its separate functions, but it will still find it convenient to classify the expenses on a functional basis to facilitate comparison with other sets of figures and enable the owner to be aware of the relative significance of the various cost centres of the business.

EXAMPLE:

Example 9.3

Pinafore Consultants has the following accounts in the 'Expenses' section of its ledger:
Bad debts
Depreciation of motor vehicles
Loss or disposal of asset (motor vehicle)
Depreciation of office equipment
Discount allowed
Fuel and oil
Insurance: office equipment
Insurance: motor vehicles
Interest expense
Motor vehicle registration
Motor vehicle repairs and maintenance
Rent
Salaries and wages
Sundry office costs.

The owner, J Porter, wants to separately identify the firm's vehicle expenses and its finance costs. All other expenses are to be classified as 'General administration expenses'. The classification of expenses in the firm's Income statements would therefore be as follows:

Operating expenses	$	$	$
Motor vehicle expenses			
Depreciation of motor vehicle	XXX		

Accounting and Finance: 2B   ISBN 9780170182041   Cengage Learning Australia

	$	$	$
Fuel and oil	XXX		
Insurance for motor vehicle	XXX		
Registration	XXX		
Loss on disposal	XXX		
Repairs and maintenance	XXX	XXX	
Finance expenses			
Bad debts	XXX		
Discount allowed	XXX		
Interest	XXX	XXX	
General administration expenses			
Depreciation of office equipment	XXX		
Insurance of office equipment	XXX		
Rent	XXX		
Salaries and wages	XXX		
Sundry office costs	XXX	XXX	XXX

Note the presentation of the statement in three columns for greater clarity, the first being the amounts of the expenses under each heading, the second (for the subtotals) being the sum of the accounts under each heading and the third being the sum of the subtotals (i.e. the total operating expenses), which will be deducted from the total income to give the profit for the period.

Another example is given below with a different basis of classification. In this case, the business owns its premises and wishes to show costs associated with the building separately. It also wishes to identify selling and distribution costs and finance expenses, the remainder being grouped together as 'General expenses'. The ledger includes the following expense accounts:

Advertising
Bad debts
Building maintenance
Delivery van costs
Depreciation, buildings
Depreciation, delivery vans
Depreciation, office furniture and equipment
Discount allowed
Insurance general
Insurance, buildings
Insurance, delivery vehicles
Interest expense
Loss on disposal
Municipal rates
Office wages and salaries
Sales commissions
Sales salaries
Sundry office expenses.

The 'Loss on disposal' arose from the sale of a delivery van.

The expenses section of the Income statement would look like this:

Operating expenses	$	$	$
Selling and distribution			
Advertising	XXX		
Delivery van costs	XXX		
Depreciation, delivery van	XXX		
Insurance, delivery vehicles	XXX		
Loss on disposal	XXX		
Sales commissions	XXX		
Sales salaries	XXX	XXX	

	Dr	Cr	
Building expenses			
Building maintenance	XXX		
Depreciation of buildings	XXX		
Insurance for buildings	XXX		
Municipal rates	XXX	XXX	
Finance expenses			
Bad debts	XXX		
Discount allowed	XXX		
Interest expense	XXX	XXX	
General expenses			
Depreciation, office furniture and equipment	XXX		
Insurance, general	XXX		
Office wages and salaries	XXX		
Sundry office expenses	XXX	XXX	XXX

We are now in a position to set out a comprehensive example including the classification of both revenue and expenses. If you are asked to prepare a classified statement and not given any guidance as to the classification (particularly the classification of expenses), it will be a matter of examining the list of accounts and using common sense to decide on what would be the most logical groupings. Under those circumstances, there will not necessarily be one 'right' answer – as long as the classification is reasonable, it will be acceptable.

Example 9.4

Ruddigore Enterprises has provided you with the following extract from its Trial balance, after all adjustments have been made, at the end of the financial year on 30 June 2010. You are required to prepare a classified income statement for the firm for the year ended on that date.

	Dr $	Cr $
Accounting fees	3 600	
Advertising	18 900	
Bad debts	1 100	
Cost of sales	298 500	
Discount expense	3 800	
Discount revenue		2 800
Doubtful debts	1 200	
Freight inwards	23 400	
Freight outwards	11 400	
Gain on sale of asset		2 200
Insurance	18 900	
Interest expense	2 400	
Office wages	63 000	
Postage and stationery	900	
Rent expense	48 000	
Rent revenue		6 000
Sales commissions	34 250	
Sales returns	8 700	
Sales salaries	97 000	
Sales: Cash		145 000
Sales: Credit		540 000
Telephone	2 700	

Accounting and Finance: 2B   ISBN 9780170182041   Cengage Learning Australia

In the absence of any instructions on how the expenses are to be classified, we will need to examine the list to see what categories suggest themselves. Some of the expenses (i.e. Cost of sales, Sales returns and Freight inwards) will be included in the Trading statement section. Looking at the other expenses, there are several associated with selling and the distribution of goods to customers, so it would seem sensible to have a category called 'Selling expenses' or 'Selling and distribution'. There are some financial expenses that could be grouped together and it is probably reasonable to group the rest together under the heading of 'General' or 'Administration' expenses. On this basis, the Income statement will appear as follows:

Ruddigore Enterprise
Income statement for the year ended 30 June 2010

	$	$	$
Sales: Cash			145 000
Credit			540 000
			685 000
Less Sales returns			8 700
			676 300
Less Cost of sales			321 900
Gross profit			354 400
Add Other operating income			
Discount revenue		2 800	
Gain on sale of asset		2 200	
Rent revenue		2 500	7 500
Total income			361 900
Less Operating expenses			
Selling and distribution			
Advertising	18 900		
Freight outwards	11 400		
Sales commissions	34 250		
Sales salaries	97 000	161 550	
Finance expenses			
Bad debts	1 100		
Discount expense	3 800		
Doubtful debts	1 200		
Interest	2 400	8 500	
General expenses			
Accounting fees	3 600		
Insurance	18 900		
Office wages	63 000		
Postage and stationery	800		
Rent	48 000		
Telephone	2 700	137 000	307 050
Profit			54 850

Classification of income for a service business will be somewhat simpler than for a merchandising firm (as shown in Example 9.2), but the classification of expenses will be very much the same. The analysis of profit information classified in this manner will be covered in Chapter 11.

CLASSIFIED STATEMENTS OF FINANCIAL POSITION

As we saw in Chapter 3, assets and liabilities are classified on a time basis. Assets likely to be used up or converted into cash in the normal course of business within the next 12 months are classified as 'Current'. Examples of such assets are:

- Cash (in hand or at bank)
- Short-term cash deposits
- Stock of supplies (stationery, cleaning materials, etc.)
- Inventory
- Accounts receivable
- Prepaid expenses
- Accrued revenue

All other assets are non-current. These include:

- Furniture
- Vehicles
- Plant and equipment
- Land
- Buildings
- Investments
- Intangible assets

Intangible assets are assets that do not have a physical existence (i.e. they cannot be touched). These include the value of patents or copyrights, long-term leases that have been paid up-front and goodwill. Goodwill arises when a firm buys another business for a sum greater than the net value of its tangible assets. The extra money is being paid for that business's reputation and customer base, which is shown in the statement of financial position of the purchasing firm as an intangible asset: 'goodwill'.

Similarly, liabilities will be classified according to when it is expected that they must be paid. Current liabilities are debts that must be paid or otherwise discharged in the normal course of business within 12 months of the balance date. These might include:

- Bank overdraft
- Accounts payable
- GST (and other taxes) payable
- Expenses payable
- Revenue received in advance
- Loans repayable within the 12-month period.

Liabilities that must be satisfied outside 12 months from balance date are termed *non-current liabilities*. For most small businesses, long-term loans from banks or other finance institutions would constitute the only type of non-current liability, though any item that represents a quantifiable, present obligation to a third party that will lead to a future outflow of resources from the business should be included as a non-current liability if that outflow is expected to occur later than 12 months from the balance date. As we saw in Chapter 3, if a loan is repayable in instalments over several years, which is usually the case, that part of the loan repayable over the next 12 months will be shown as a current liability while the remainder will be included in non-current liabilities.

The balance day adjustments covered in Chapters 7 and 8 which, as we have seen, have affected the revenue and expenses of the business, have also had an impact on its assets and liabilities by recognising, through accruals and prepayments, amounts owing to and by the business and also reductions in the value of certain assets through depreciation, amortisation and allowance for future bad debts.

The security of any business (i.e. the likelihood of its continued existence) will depend on its capacity to pay its debts when they fall due (i.e. whether it is *solvent*). A business unable to do this is likely to fail financially. By comparing current assets with current liabilities the reader of financial reports will get some idea of the firm's ability to pay

Accounting and Finance 2B   ISBN 9780170182041   Cengage Learning Australia

its debts. Obviously the greater the current assets in relation to the current liabilities, the safer the business is, although an excessive margin of current assets over current liabilities is undesirable from a profit point of view. If the firm has too much money tied up in unproductive assets (such as surplus inventories and accounts receivable), it will not be able to make as much profit as it should. (Further analysis of this aspect of the firm's structure will be carried out in Chapter 11.)

Key Concept 9.3

Classification of Statement of financial position

Assets and liabilities will be classified in the Statement on a time basis as 'current' or 'non-current'.

The following example will illustrate the presentation of the assets and liabilities of a business, together with the owner's equity, in a classified form, which will facilitate judgements about the firm's security.

Example 9.5

EXAMPLE:

Penzance Trading has provided you with this Trial balance taken out after the determination of profit for the year ended 30 June 2010.

Penzance Trading
Trial balance as at 30 June 2010

	Dr $	Cr $
Cash at bank		9500
Accounts payable		43000
Accounts receivable	32000	
Accrued commission revenue	2300	
Wages payable		3000
Accumulated depreciation, plant and equipment		14000
Accumulated depreciation, vehicles		16000
Allowance for doubtful debts		640
Bank loan		120000
Capital – A Pirate		130000
Cash in hand	200	
Drawings	40000	
Goodwill	80000	
GST clearing		3000
Inventory	47000	
Plant and equipment	103000	
Prepaid insurance	6000	
Profit and loss summary (profit for the year)		60160
Stock of stationery	800	
Vehicles	88000	
	399300	399300

The bank loan is repayable in equal instalments over the next five years. During the year the owner contributed an additional $20000 capital.

The items in the Trial balance will now be sorted into current and non-current assets and liabilities and owner's equity before they are entered into the statement. It is customary to list the current assets in order of liquidity (i.e. their ease of conversion into cash) so cash in hand would be the most liquid current asset and prepaid expenses the least. It may also be helpful to list current liabilities in the order in which they may have to be paid.

Note

Note that allowance for doubtful debts and accumulated depreciation, although credit balances, are not shown in the liabilities sections of the statement but as a deduction from the related assets in the assets sections – in effect as 'negative assets'.

As previously noted, it is helpful to include under the equity section a brief statement of the changes in the equity over the year rather than simply showing a single figure for the capital at the balance date.

Bearing all this in mind, the Statement of financial position for this business at the end of the financial year would look like this:

Penzance Trading
Statement of financial position as at 30 June 2010

	$	$
Equity		
Capital at 30/6/2009		110 000
Capital contributed during the year		20 000
		130 000
Add Profit for the year		60 160
Less Drawings		40 000
Capital at 30/6/2010		150 160
Represented by:		
Current assets		
Cash in hand		200
Accounts receivable	32 000	
Less Allowance for doubtful debts	640	31 360
Accrued commission revenue		2 300
Inventory		47 000
Stock of stationery		800
Prepaid insurance		6 000
Total current assets		87 660
Non-current assets		
Plant and equipment, at cost	103 000	
Less Accumulated depreciation	14 000	89 000
Vehicles, at cost	88 000	
Less Accumulated depreciation	16 000	72 000
Goodwill		80 000
Total non-current assets		241 000
Total assets		328 660
Less		
Current liabilities		
Bank overdraft		9 500
Accounts payable		43 000
GST payable		3 000
Wages payable		3 000
Bank loan (1/5 of 120 000)		24 000
Total current liabilities		82 500
Non-current liabilities		
Bank loan (120 000 – 24 000)		96 000
Total non-current liabilities		96 000
Total liabilities		178 500
Net assets		150 160

Accounting and Finance 2B ISBN 9780170182041 Cengage Learning Australia

In conclusion, we will work through a comprehensive example, starting with a post-adjustment Trial balance and using it to produce both the Income statement and the Statement of financial position.

Example 9.6

Iolanthe Fashions
Trial balance as at 30 June 2010 (after balance day adjustments to determine profit for the year ended on that date)

	Dr $	Cr $
Accounts payable		58400
Accounts receivable	29000	
Accumulated depreciation, buildings		100000
Accumulated depreciation, fixtures and fittings)		6000
Advertising	21000	
Allowance for doubtful debts		580
Bank loan (repayable 50% Dec. 2010, 50% Dec. 2011)		160000
Building repairs and maintenance	12800	
Building	400000	
Capital – A Fairy		590000
Cash at bank		18720
Cost of sales	407000	
Depreciation, building	25000	
Depreciation, fixtures and fittings	3000	
Discount allowed	4900	
Discount received		3800
Doubtful debts	900	
Drawings	30000	
Electricity	16000	
Expenses payable		4500
Fixtures and fittings	15000	
Freight inwards	31000	
Freight outwards	24000	
Gain on sale of asset		1500
GST clearing		4600
Goodwill	100000	
Insurance – buildings	11000	
Insurance – general	19000	
Interest expense	40000	
Inventory	38000	
Land	300000	
Office salaries and wages	109000	
Prepaid expenses	4000	
Rates and taxes	3400	
Sales: Cash		632000
Sales: Credit		367000
Sales commissions	43600	
Sales returns	14000	

		$	
Sales salaries		234000	
Stock of stationery		1000	
Sundry office expenses		10500	
		1947100	1947100

The first step is to identify the income and expense accounts and decide on the basis of classification. Expense and revenue accounts are shown in colour in the Trial balance above. From the information given, the only classification of income possible is between cash and credit sales.

As far as expenses are concerned, you have been informed that the firm's owner wishes to group all expenses associated with the building together as 'Occupancy expenses'. Other than that, you may do as you think fit. It would seem reasonable to have headings of 'Selling and distribution', 'Finance' and 'General'. Accordingly, the Income statement will be as follows:

Iolanthe Fashions
Income statement for the year ended 30 June 2010

	$	$	$
Sales: Cash			632000
Credit			367000
			999000
Less Sales returns			14000
			985000
Less **Cost of sales** (includes Freight inwards)			438000
Gross profit			547000
Add **Other operating income**			
Discount revenue		3800	
Gain on sale of asset		1500	5300
Total income			552300
Less **Operating expenses**			
Occupancy expenses			
Building repairs and maintenance	12800		
Depreciation, building	25000		
Insurance, buildings	11000		
Rates and taxes	3400	52200	
Selling and distribution			
Advertising	21000		
Freight outwards	24000		
Sales commissions	43600		
Sales salaries	234000	322600	
Finance expenses			
Discount allowed	4900		
Doubtful debts	900		
Interest	40000	45800	
General expenses			
Depreciation, furniture and fittings	3000		
Electricity	16000		
Insurance, general	19000		
Office salaries and wages	109000		
Sundry office expenses	10500	157500	578100
LOSS FOR THE YEAR			(25800)

Accounting and Finance 2B   ISBN 9780170182041   Cengage Learning Australia

The remaining items in the Trial balance, together with the balance in the Profit and loss summary account of $25800 Dr, can now be used to draw up the Statement of financial position. We have been informed that the owner contributed $50000 of additional capital during the year.

Iolanthe Fashions

Statement of financial position as at 30 June 2010

	$	$
Equity		
Capital at 30/6/2009		540000
Capital contributed during the year		50000
		590000
Less Loss for the year		(25800)
Drawings		(30000)
Capital at 30/6/2010		**534200**
Represented by:		
Current assets		
Accounts receivable	29000	
Less Allowance for doubtful debts	580	28420
Inventory		38000
Stock of stationery		1000
Prepaid expenses		4000
Total current assets		71420
Non-current assets		
Land, at cost		300000
Building, at cost	400000	
Less Accumulated depreciation	100000	300000
Furniture and fittings, at cost	15000	
Less Accumulated depreciation	6000	9000
Goodwill		100000
Total non-current assets		709000
Total assets		780420
Less		
Current liabilities		
Bank overdraft		18720
Accounts payable		58400
GST payable		4600
Expenses payable		4500
Bank loan (1/2 of 160000)		80000
Total current liabilities		166220
Non-current liabilities		
Bank loan (1/2 of 160000)		80000
Total non-current liabilities		80000
Total liabilities		246220
Net assets		**534200**

Accounting and Finance: 2B   ISBN 9780170182041   Cengage Learning Australia

Test your knowledge

1. What is meant by 'classification' of financial statements?

2. What is the general purpose of classifying financial statements?

3. What is the effect of Balance day adjustments on business financial statements?

4. What are the specific benefits of classifying an Income statement?

5. Outline the ways in which income may be classified in an Income statement.

6. Outline the possible bases for the classification of expenses in an Income statement.

7. How are assets and liabilities classified in a Statement of financial position? Give examples to illustrate your explanation.

8. What are the benefits of classifying a Statement of financial position?

9. Would it be true to say that all credit balances in the ledger after the determination of profit will appear in the liabilities or equity sections of the Statement of financial position? Identify and explain any exceptions.

10. What is meant by a 'post-adjustment Trial balance'?

11. What is meant by a 'post-profit-determination Trial balance'?

Test your understanding

Topic guide

- Effect of balance day adjustments: 9.1
- Basis of classification of income: 9.2
- Classified trading account: 9.3–9.5
- Basis of classification of expenses: 9.6, 9.7
- Classification of expenses: 9.8–9.9
- Classified Income statement: 9.10–9.13
- Basis of classification, assets and liabilities: 9.14, 9.15
- Classification of assets and liabilities: 9.16–9.18
- Classified Statement of financial position: 9.19–9.21
- Classified Income statement and Statement of financial position: 9.22–9.23
- Classified Income statement and Statement of financial position with Balance day adjustments: 9.24, 9.25

9.1 Balance day adjustments have an effect on the financial statements of a business produced as at that balance day. For each of the following adjustments, state which accounts are affected and to what category those accounts belong (i.e. asset, liability, income or expense):

a. a computer is depreciated

b. a credit customer who owes $500 is declared bankrupt and the firm is advised it will receive no payment

c. an electricity bill is received for the past two months

d. an annual insurance premium was paid three months ago

e. interest has been earned on a term deposit made with the bank; this will be paid when the deposit matures in two months time

f. one month before balance date, another business, which is renting part of the firm's warehouse space, pays three months rent in advance

g. the firm's actual usage of cleaning materials for the year is reckoned to be $850.

9.2 The ledger of the firm G&S Sports, a shop selling sportswear, shoes and boots and sporting equipment, has the following accounts in the 'Income' section:

a. Sales

b. Interest revenue

Accounting and Finance: 2B   ISBN 9780170182041   Cengage Learning Australia

c   Commission earned

d   Gain on sale of asset

e   Discount received.

For each of these accounts, state where its balance would appear in a classified Income statement. What could the firm do to make its Income statement more useful?

9.3   Kipper Herring has the following balances in its ledger at the end of the financial year on 30 June 2010. Use them to prepare the income section of the Income statement for the firm for that year.

Sales	$573 000
Sales returns	$2 800
Cost of sales	$260 900
Rent revenue	$6 000
Freight inwards	$24 000
Discount revenue	$3 100

9.4   Bob the Brickie has provided you with the following information at the end of the financial year on 30 June 2010:

- Fees earned – credit: $243 000
- Fees earned – cash: $87 000
- Agency commission: $7 800.

Show how the income section of the firm's Income statement for the year ended 30 June 2010 would appear. What benefit might Bob obtain by classifying income in the way that he has?

9.5   The Trial balance for Libby's Liquor Store on 30 June 2010 includes the following balances:

Sales – beer	$295 000
Sales – wine	$263 000
Sales – spirits	$99 000
Cost of sales – beer	$184 000
Cost of sales – wine	$128 000
Cost of sales – spirits	$36 000
Discount revenue	$3 500

Show how the income section of the firm's Income statement for the year ended 30/6/2010 would appear. What benefit might Libby obtain by classifying income in the way that she has?

9.6   Neverland Air Services has the following accounts in the expense section of its ledger. Suggest some appropriate headings under which they could be classified in the firm's Income statement.

- Aircraft maintenance
- Bad debts
- Depreciation of aircraft
- Depreciation of office furniture and equipment
- Fuel and oil
- Insurance – aircraft
- Insurance – general
- Interest expense
- Landing fees
- Office rent
- Office wages
- Pilots' wages
- Postage and telephone
- Sundry office expenses

9.7   The following is an extract from the unclassified Income statement of Peter's Pans:

Operating expenses	$
Accounting fees	3000
Advertising	18000
Depreciation of office equipment	2300
Depreciation of vehicles (sales staff)	9000
Discount allowed	4200
Doubtful debts	1600
Freight outwards	31000
Insurance	25000
Interest paid	12000
Office wages	98000
Postage and stationery	1050
Rent	18000
Sales commission	42000
Sales salaries	206000
Total operating expenses	454950

Required
a   Classify these expenses in an appropriate manner.
b   What do you think the owner of the business might gain from such a classification?

9.8   Using the information contained in the post-adjustment Trial balance of Hook's Hotel, prepare the classified Operating expenses section of the Income statement for the business for the six months ended 31 December 2009.

Trial balance at 31 December 2009 (extract)

	Dr $	Cr $
Advertising	15000	
Cash at bank		10500
Depreciation, bar equipment	7800	
Depreciation, bedroom furniture and fittings	21000	
Depreciation, building	22000	
Depreciation, restaurant furniture and equipment	16700	
Drawings	48000	
Insurance	32000	
Laundry – sheets and towels	3400	
Laundry – tablecloths and napkins	2100	
Office expenses	4500	
Receptionist wages	58000	
Replacement glasses for bar	1200	
Sundry office expenses	12100	
Wages, accommodation	176000	
Wages, bar	162000	
Wages, restaurant	245000	

Hook is keen to evaluate the relative contribution to profit of the three parts of the business – the bar, the restaurant and the overnight accommodation. Are there any items listed above that would *not* be included in the Income statement? Explain your answer.

Accounting and Finance: 2B   ISBN 9780170182041   Cengage Learning Australia

9.9 Lostboys Lighting has provided the following list of balances from its ledger at the end of the financial year on 30 June 2010:

Account	$
Advertising	11 000
Bad debts	600
Bank charges and fees	200
Delivery vehicle expenses	4200
Depreciation, computer	1000
Depreciation, delivery vehicle	6500
Depreciation, office furniture	2700
Discount allowed	1800
Insurance, delivery vehicle	1100
Insurance, general	16 000
Interest expense	2500
Office wages	67 000
Post and telephone	1800
Rent	12 000
Salespersons' wages	176 000
Stationery expense	750

Required

a   Draw up the Operating expenses section (appropriately classified) of the Income statement for Lostboys Lighting for the year ended 30 June 2010.

b   It has been suggested that all the depreciation accounts should be classified together. Comment on this suggestion.

9.10 Nicknax Store has provided the following extract from its Trial balance at the end of the first quarter of the year on 30 September 2010:

	Dr $	Cr $
Advertising	2000	
Cash sales		105 000
Cost of sales	176 000	
Credit sales		206 000
Discount allowed	800	
Discount received		1200
Doubtful debts	200	
Electricity	2800	
Insurance	5000	
Interest paid	1500	
Office wages	16 000	
Postage and stationery	250	
Rent	4500	
Sales commissions	10 000	
Sales staff wages	28 000	

The owner wants to identify selling expenses, finance expenses and general office expenses.

Required

Prepare a classified Income statement for Nicknax Store for the quarter ended 30 September 2010.

Accounting and Finance: 2B   ISBN 9780170182041   Cengage Learning Australia

9.11 Paddiwak Plumbing produces financial statements every six months. At the end of the first six months of the year adjustments were made and a Trial balance was taken out, of which the following is an extract.

Trial balance as at 31 December 2010 (extract)

	Dr $	Cr $
Building repairs	2300	
Commission earned		6800
Depreciation of building	4000	
Depreciation of office equipment	800	
Depreciation of plumbers' tools and equipment	3500	
Depreciation of vehicles	8000	
Fees: Commercial clients		312000
Fees: General public		138000
General office expenses	1100	
Insurance	19000	
Materials used	21500	
Office wages	52000	
Plumbers' wages	235000	
Rates and taxes	1000	
Telephone	4200	
Vehicle expenses	9600	

The vehicles are work vans used by the plumbers.

The owner wants to know the direct costs of providing plumbing services and also costs associated with the building. Other costs can be grouped together under the heading 'General'.

Required

a Prepare an Income statement for Paddiwak Plumbing for the six months ended 31 December 2010.

b Explain the benefit to the owner of separately identifying the direct costs of the service the firm is providing.

9.12 Doggabone Emporium runs a large retail store in a suburban shopping centre. An extract from the post-adjustment Trial balance taken out at the end of the financial year is given below.

Trial balance as at 30 June 2010 (extract)

	Dr $	Cr $
Advertising and promotion	6000	
Bad debts	1300	
Cost of sales	439000	
Credit card commission	15700	
Depreciation of office furniture	1500	
Depreciation of sales fittings	3000	
Discount received		7600
Insurance	31000	
Interest expense	5000	
Office wages	103000	
Postage and stationery	1400	
Rent expense	60000	
Rent revenue		12000
Sales – cash		189000

Accounting and Finance: 2B   ISBN 9780170182041   Cengage Learning Australia

Sales – credit		786 000
Sales commission	47 000	
Sales returns	4 500	
Sales wages	328 000	
Sundry office expenses	4 700	

Required

Prepare an appropriately classified Income statement for Doggabone Emporium for the year ended 30 June 2010.

9.13 Thistleman & Son is a family business providing landscaping design services, mainly for shire and town councils, but also for individuals. At the end of the last financial year the following post-adjustment Trial balance was taken out. Only the income and expenses accounts are shown.

Trial balance as at 30 June 2010 (extract)

	Dr $	Cr $
Accounting fees	2 000	
Consultants' salaries	350 000	
Contractors' wages	110 000	
Depreciation of furniture and equipment	3 200	
Depreciation of vehicles	12 000	
Drafting materials used	4 200	
Electricity	2 900	
Fees: Councils		638 000
Fees: Individuals		163 000
Fuel and oil, vehicles	3 500	
Insurance	28 000	
Interest earned		2 000
Office wages	57 000	
Postage and telephone	1 900	
Repairs and maintenance, vehicles	3 800	
Staff bonus and entertainment	3 000	
Staff training	5 000	
Stationery	750	
Vehicle insurance	3 200	
Vehicle registration	900	

Required

a Prepare an appropriately classified Income statement for Thistleman & Son for the year ended 30 June 2010.

b Explain and justify the basis on which you have classified the expenses.

9.14 Classify the following list of assets and liabilities into 'Current' and 'Non-current'.

Accounts payable

Accounts receivable

Accrued interest revenue

Wages payable

Bank loan (repayable after two years)

Bank term deposit (three months)

Cash at bank (debit balance)

Cash in hand

Fees received in advance

Goodwill

Accounting and Finance: 2B   ISBN 9780170182041   Cengage Learning Australia

GST clearing (credit balance)
Motor vehicle
Office furniture
Prepaid insurance
Stock of cleaning materials

In what order would you list the Current assets and Current liabilities in the Statement of financial position? Explain your answer.

9.15 Draw up a table with the headings given below and list under the appropriate heading the debit and credit balances that follow.

Account	Current asset	Non-current asset	Current liability	Non-current liability

Ledger balances as at 30 June 2010

	Dr $	Cr $
Accounts payable		32000
Accounts receivable	18000	
Accrued interest	1500	
Accumulated depreciation, plant and equipment		56000
Accumulated depreciation, vehicles		32000
Allowance for doubtful debts		360
Bank loan (2013)		60000
Cash at bank		2500
Cash in hand	400	
Expenses payable		1300
GST clearing		2400
Inventory	39000	
Investments (long-term)	30000	
Patents	20000	
Plant and equipment	96000	
Prepaid rent	3000	
Stock of stationery	600	
Vehicles	59000	

If you were told that the bank loan is repayable in equal instalments over the next three years, how would that affect the classification of that item in the Statement of financial position?

9.16 Ilkleymoor Supplies has provided you with the following extract from its Statement of financial position at 31 March 2010.

Statement of financial position (extract) as at 31 March 2010

	$	$
Assets		
Accounts receivable		21000
Accrued revenue		4000
Cash at bank		12500
Cash in hand		200
Furniture and fittings, at cost	16000	
Less Accumulated depreciation	7000	9000
Goodwill		50000
Inventory		24000

Motor vehicles, at cost	46 000	
Less Accumulated depreciation	19 000	27 000
Prepaid expense		2 000
Total assets		149 700
Liabilities		
Accounts payable		18 000
Expenses payable		1 800
Bank loan		50 000
Debt to Toyotas R Us		25 000
GST payable		3 200
Revenue in advance		1 100
Total liabilities		99 100

The bank loan is repayable in equal instalments over the next five years. The debt to Toyotas R Us, for the recent purchase of a vehicle, is due in 30 days.

Required

a Redraw this part of the Statement with assets and liabilities appropriately classified.

b Briefly explain the basis on which you have classified the assets and liabilities.

9.17 Use the extract from the Trial balance given to produce the assets and liabilities sections of the financial statement for this business at 30 June 2010, appropriately classified.

Fran's Fotographs
Trial balance as at 30 June 2010 (extract)

	Dr $	Cr $
Accounts payable		2 700
Accounts receivable	12 400	
Accumulated depreciation, office furniture		1 900
Accumulated depreciation of photographic equipment		9 000
Bank loan		30 000
Cash at bank	6 500	
Cash in hand	500	
Accumulated depreciation of vehicle		13 000
Expenses payable		1 600
GST clearing		3 500
Office furniture	5 400	
Photographic equipment	38 000	
Prepaid insurance	4 000	
Revenue in advance		1 000
Stock of materials	9 800	
Vehicle	29 000	

The bank loan is repayable equally over the next three years.

9.18 Tuck's Traders has provided you with the following extract from its Trial balance at 30 September 2009.

Trial balance as at 30 September 2009 (extract)

	Dr $	Cr $
Accounts payable		32 000
Accounts receivable	37 000	
Accrued commission	3 000	
Accumulated depreciation, buildings		65 000

Accumulated depreciation, office furniture		1 500
Accumulated depreciation, plant and equipment		26 000
Allowance for doubtful debts		400
Buildings	350 000	
Cash at bank		12 000
Cash in hand	250	
Goodwill	100 000	
GST clearing		2 800
Land	200 000	
Office furniture	8 000	
Plant and equipment	56 000	
Prepaid insurance	4 000	
Stock of stationery	1 250	
Term deposit (March 2010)	20 000	
Wages payable		1 800

Required

a   Prepare the classified assets and liabilities sections of the Statement of financial position as at 30 September 2009.

b   Explain the significance of the accounts 'Allowance for doubtful debts' and 'GST clearing'.

9.19   Contrary Garden Centre has provided you with the following Trial balance taken out after the determination of profit for the year ended 30 June 2010.

Trial balance as at 30 June 2010

	Dr $	Cr $
Accounts payable		28 000
Accrued interest expense		3 000
Accumulated depreciation, computer system		1 500
Accumulated depreciation, furniture and fittings		2 000
Accumulated depreciation, plant and equipment		54 000
Bank loan		200 000
Capital – Mary Q		50 000
Cash at bank	13 700	
Cash in hand	300	
Commission accrued	2 000	
Computer system	3 000	
Drawings	40 000	
Fergie's Forklifts		60 000
Furniture and fittings	9 000	
Goodwill	60 000	
GST clearing		4 500
Inventory	87 000	
Plant and equipment	235 000	
Prepaid rent	4 000	
Profit and Loss summary		51 000
	454 000	454 000

The bank loan is repayable in five equal annual instalments. The debt to Fergie's Forklifts relates to a recent purchase of plant and must be paid in 60 days.

Required

Prepare a Statement of financial position for Contrary Garden Centre as at 30 June 2010.

Accounting and Finance: 2B   ISBN 9780170182041   Cengage Learning Australia

9.20 A post-profit-determination Trial balance for Cherries Chockies is given below. The business makes and sells a variety of handmade chocolates and similar confectionery from its premises in the south-west of WA. It also supplies a number of other retailers.

Trial balance as at 30 June 2010

	Dr $	Cr $
Accounts payable		31000
Accounts receivable	16000	
Accumulated depreciation, buildings		80000
Accumulated depreciation, plant and equipment		64000
Allowance for doubtful debts		400
Buildings	350000	
Capital – C Herries		250000
Cash at bank	12500	
Cash in hand	500	
Drawings	55000	
Expenses payable		2600
GST clearing		1000
Inventory of finished product	35000	
Inventory of raw materials	23000	
Land	150000	
Mortgage loan		250000
Patents	30000	
Plant and equipment	145000	
Prepaid expenses	4800	
Profit and loss summary		142800
	821800	821800

The mortgage loan is repayable in equal instalments over the next ten years.

Required

Prepare a Statement of financial position for Cherries Chockies as at 30 June 2010.

9.21 Tom Piper Transport prepares financial reports every six months. The Trial balance at 31 December 2009 is given below.

Trial balance as at 31 December 2009

	Dr $	Cr $
Accounts payable (fuel company)		7600
Accounts receivable	18000	
Accumulated depreciation, buildings		81000
Accumulated depreciation, furniture		1300
Accumulated depreciation, trucks		83000
Accumulated depreciation, workshop equipment		11000
Allowance for doubtful debts		500
Bank loan (repayable 2012)		150000
Buildings	250000	
Capital – T Piper		300000
Cash at bank		24000
Drawings	50000	
Expenses payable		3400
Fees received in advance		5000
Furniture	4200	

	Dr	Cr
Gotcha Finance		100 000
GST clearing		2 900
Land	100 000	
Prepaid insurance	6 000	
Profit and loss summary	22 000	
Stock of fuel	6 500	
Trucks	258 000	
Workshop equipment	55 000	
	769 700	769 700

The amount owing to Gotcha Finance relates to two trucks purchased during the past year. It is to be repaid in monthly instalments of $5000 each.

The owner contributed an additional $50 000 in capital during the past six months.

Required

a   Prepare a classified Statement of financial position for Tom Piper Transport as at 31 December 2009.

b   Explain the meaning of the debit balance in the Profit and loss summary account.

c   Comment on the relationship between the firm's Current assets and Current liabilities. Is this likely to cause the firm any problems?

9.22   Heydiddle Traders has provided you with the following Trial balance taken out after all balance day adjustments for the period had been made.

Trial balance as at 30 June 2010

	Dr $	Cr $
Accounts payable		24 700
Accounts receivable	33 000	
Accumulated depreciation, fixtures and fittings		11 000
Accumulated depreciation, office furniture		4 100
Advertising	8 200	
Allowance for doubtful debts		420
Bank loan (repayable 2014)		60 000
Capital – Anna Fiddle		60 000
Cash at bank	17 600	
Cash in hand	200	
Commission earned		4 000
Cost of sales	328 000	
Depreciation, fixtures and fittings	2 200	
Depreciation, office furniture	980	
Doubtful debts	520	
Drawings	50 000	
Expenses payable		2 200
Fixtures and fittings	28 900	
Freight outwards	11 500	
Insurance	18 000	
Interest expense	6 000	
Inventory	41 820	
Office furniture	9 800	
Office wages	56 000	
Postage and telephone	2 400	
Prepaid expense	6 500	

	Dr	Cr
Rent	24 000	
Sales – cash		236 000
Sales – credit		342 000
Sales salaries	96 000	
Sundry office expenses	2 800	
	744 420	744 420

Required

a Prepare an appropriately classified Income Statement for Heydiddle Traders for the year ended 30 June 2010.

b Prepare a classified Statement of financial position for Heydiddle Traders as at 30 June 2010.

9.23 The Proprietor of Dumpty Accountants has provided you with the following Trial balance, taken out after having made balance day adjustments at the end of the first six months of the year.

Trial balance as at 31 December 2009

	Dr $	Cr $
Accountants' salaries	702 000	
Accounts payable		1 500
Accounts receivable	29 800	
Accumulated depreciation of vehicles		31 000
Accumulated depreciation, furniture and equipment		3 800
Advertising	8 000	
Allowance for doubtful debts		200
Bank loan		40 000
Capital – H Dumpty		60 000
Cash at bank	3 500	
Cash in hand	200	
Depreciation, furniture and equipment	1 600	
Depreciation, vehicles	12 000	
Discount allowed	3 200	
Doubtful debts	500	
Drawings	71 000	
Expenses payable		3 600
Fees – audit		268 000
Fees – financial accounting		424 000
Fees – taxation affairs		389 000
Furniture and equipment	15 600	
Insurance	28 000	
Interest earned		200
Office wages	131 400	
Postage and telephone	6 500	
Prepaid expense	4 700	
Professional development costs	9 600	
Rent	36 000	
Short-term deposit	20 000	
Stationery	2 300	
Stock of stationery	900	
Subscriptions to professional associations	4 000	

Sundry office expenses	7200	
Vehicle expenses	4300	
Vehicles	119000	
	1221300	1221300

The vehicles are used exclusively by the accountants for their consultancy work. The bank loan is repayable 50% in May 2010 and 50% in May 2011.

Required

a   Prepare an appropriately classified Income statement for Dumpty Accountants for the six months ended 31 December 2009.

b   Prepare a classified Statement of financial position for Dumpty Accountants as at 31 December 2009.

c   Why do you think Dumpty has chosen to record separately the three different sources of fees earned by the firm?

9.24   Girlpower Shoes ends its financial year on 30 June. The Trial balance for the firm at the end of the last financial year is shown below.

Trial balance as at 30 June 2010

	Dr $	Cr $
Accounts payable		32540
Accounts receivable	13000	
Accumulated depreciation, computer system		1000
Accumulated depreciation, fixtures and fittings		4630
Advertising	13200	
Allowance for doubtful debts		300
Bad debts	440	
Mortgage loan		150000
Capital – B Doll		50000
Cash at bank		22400
Cash in hand	400	
Computer system	3500	
Cost of sales – men's shoes	219900	
Cost of sales – women's shoes	333600	
Discount expense	3400	
Discount revenue		9800
Drawings	52000	
General expenses (including depreciation)	6000	
Fixtures and fittings	18700	
Gain on sale of asset		2500
Goodwill	100000	
Interest expense	14600	
Inventory	41000	
Office wages	92800	
Postage and stationery	800	
Prepaid insurance	29900	
Rent	36000	
Sales – men's shoes		372000
Sales – women's shoes		536000
Sales returns – men's shoes	2800	

Accounting and Finance: 2B   ISBN 9780170182041   Cengage Learning Australia

Sales returns — women's shoes	3 800	
Sales salaries	195 000	
Telephone	3 200	
	1 187 200	1 187 200

The owner contributed an additional $10000 capital during the year. The mortgage loan is repayable in equal instalments over the next five years. Doll wants to be able to see the relative contributions to gross profit of her two categories of sales.

Additional information

- Insurance prepaid at 30/6/10 was in fact $4900.
- $3200 wages were owing to employees at 30/6/10.
- Allowance for doubtful debts is to be adjusted to 2% of accounts receivable.
- The Computer system is to be depreciated at 30% reducing, the Fixtures and fittings at 10% straight-line method.
- The owner contributed an additional $10000 capital during the year.
- The mortgage loan is repayable in equal instalments over the next five years.
- Doll wants to be able to see the relative contributions to gross profit of her two categories of sales.

Required

a   Adjust the Trial balance to take account of the balance day adjustments.

b   Prepare an appropriately classified Income statement for Girlpower Shoes for the year ended 30 June 2010.

c   Prepare a classified Statement of financial position for Girlpower Shoes as at 30 June 2010.

d   Briefly outline what these statements tell you about Girlpower Shoes' profitability and stability.

9.25   Below is the Trial balance of Chrissy Presence for the year ended 30 June 2010.

	Dr $	Cr $
Accounts payable		42 190
Accounts receivable	51 340	
Allowance for doubtful debts		1 500
Computer systems at cost	48 000	
Accumulated depreciation on computer systems		23 000
Shop equipment at cost	65 000	
Accumulated depreciation on shop equipment		25 000
Building	800 000	
Mortgage loan		200 000
Capital San Claus		719 000
Cash and cash equivalents	22 300	
Sales		975 550
Discount expense	750	
Bad debts	975	
Shop wages	108 500	
Shop expenses	78 000	
Bank charges	2 200	
Office expenses	54 000	

Building maintenance	16 900	
Shop cleaning	21 400	
Advertising	15 000	
Drawings	69 900	
Fax and phone expenses	6 700	
Maintenance computer systems	12 300	
Inventory	107 800	
Sales returns	14 200	
Goodwill	90 000	
Profit on sale of equipment		600
Interest expense	2 675	
Cost of sales	398 900	
	1 986 840	1 986 840

Additional information
- $780 of the Advertising paid is for the following month of July.
- Shop Wages of $1500 remain accrued for the period.
- Depreciate both the Shop equipment and the Computer systems at 15% on cost.
- Adjust the Allowance for doubtful debts to be 3% of receivables.
- 0.5% of the current inventory needs to be written off as expired.
- 75% of the Building maintenance covers the shop operations.

Required
a Adjust the Trial balance to include the balance day requirements.
b Prepare an appropriately classified income statement for Chrissy Presence for the year ended 30 June 2010.
c Prepare a classified Statement of financial position for Chrissy Presence as at 30 June 2010.
d Comment on the profitability and liquidity of the business for the year.

Essay

You are setting up a small retail business. List the accounts that you would expect to have in the business's ledger and show how the information in these accounts might be classified in the firm's financial statements. What would be the benefit of classifying the presentation in this way?

Ethics case study

Yeoman Guard is a small consultancy business advising large companies on security matters. The owner, A Merryman, prepares detailed classified financial statements on a monthly basis for his own information and a similarly detailed set of reports once a year for the benefit of some family members who have invested in the business. Also once a year he prepares a greatly simplified (not classified) Income statement, which supports his personal income tax return for the year.

What do you think Merryman's obligations are with regard to the provision of financial information to:
a his family investors?
b the Australian Taxation Office?

Do you think that what he is currently doing enables him to meet these obligations?

Accounting and Finance: 2B   ISBN 9780170182041   Cengage Learning Australia

Chapter 10

ELECTRONIC PROCESSING OF FINANCIAL TRANSACTIONS

What You Will Learn

After studying this chapter you should be able to:
1. Identify the widespread application of technology in the accounting process
2. Understand the nature of electronic processing of transactions for a service or retail business
3. Understand the nature of electronic processing of balance day adjustments
4. Produce useful financial reports, including balance day adjustments from electronically recorded financial transactions
5. Identify the efficiency of accounting software in the processing and reporting of financial information

Introduction

Imagine a world without computers! Over the past 20 years computers have revolutionised business practices. The speed and accuracy of computers have improved financial recording, financial reporting and accountability. The technology expedites the input process, the classification process and the presentation process.

Information technology providers have developed software to meet the needs of small and large businesses. Two well-known accounting software providers, MYOB and Reckon, have designed educational versions of accounting software. Both of these products are designed to replicate double entry processing based on the accounting entity principle. Accounting software simulates all the processes learnt through manual practice. This chapter will identify the strengths of computer-based accounting. Several examples will be developed to highlight features of MYOB and Reckon (QuickBooks) related to the processing of financial transactions covered in the course.

GETTING STARTED

Both MYOB and QuickBooks are easily learned. After a few introductory sessions, users can improve their skills independently using manuals or online support. Using the program's command centres, familiar accounting functions can be performed in a double entry context. These functions include cash receipts, cash payments, bank reconciliations, sales, purchases, payroll, stock management, taxation (including GST), inventory records, accounts receivable, accounts payable, audit trails, financial reports and analysis.

Chart of accounts

A computer-based accounting program usually operates on a predetermined chart of accounts. The set charts of accounts can be tailored to suit the specific requirements or nature of the business. A chart of accounts is flexible, allowing for the addition of extra accounts and the deletion of unwanted accounts. To aid processing of data, accounts are categorised into assets, liability, income, expense and equity and given identifying numbers.

Abiding by the rules

We know from manual accounting that every transaction will have an impact on at least two accounts in the firm's ledger (i.e. double entry accounting). Often a single transaction may affect multiple accounts. Using an airline as an example, when a flight sale is electronically registered and a credit card is used to pay for the ticket, several things will immediately occur. Processing the flight by use of credit card might incur charges by the credit provider and the transaction will attract goods and services tax. Assuming a domestic flight was offered at $740 (including GST) and incurred a merchant fee of one per cent for use of the credit card, the following account types would be affected:

Bank account	Asset
Flight sales	Income
GST collected	Liability
Bank charges	Expenses

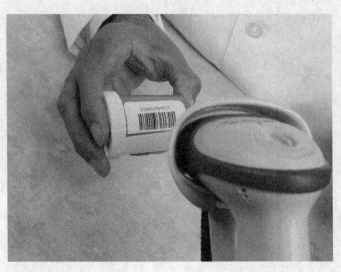

An airline has such transactions occurring 24 hours a day, initiated from countless origins worldwide and all having similar impacts as the above scenario. By use of networked programs these myriad transactions are managed and can be used to produce the reports required by management. Timely data allows management to efficiently use all its resources.

Data management

Peculiar challenges of data management arise when all transactions are electronically dependent. Power failures, viruses, network failures and security breaches can cripple transaction capacity and function. Reliable data management is critical, including comprehensive and immediate accessibility and security and integrity

Accounting and Finance: 2B   ISBN 9780170182041   Cengage Learning Australia

of data using the most efficient and up-to-date hardware and software. A wide range of businesses – from banks, phone companies, mining companies and national retail chains down to small retailers and service firms – are largely dependent on technology to drive all aspects of their operations. Ineffective data processing services can result in severe financial losses and loss of business credibility.

Key Concept 10.1

Data management
Reliable data management and protection is essential to the success of businesses whose systems are dependent on electronic data processing.

The essential accessory for an accountant: a computer

Computer-based accounting provides real bonuses to both students and practitioners of accounting! Multiple and repetitive manual data entry can be time demanding and tedious. Once a person masters an electronic accounting package, given a working understanding of double entry accounting, time can be allocated more productively to analysis and investment decisions.

USING COMPUTERS TO PROCESS BUSINESS TRANSACTIONS

The following sections go through the steps of setting up and creating a new service business and a new retail business using either MYOB or QuickBooks software. It is assumed that the student will have a small amount of prior knowledge of the software. (The steps are not a course manual in the complete operation of the software.)

When entering suppliers and customers of goods and services it is advisable to create a mock ABN for each, particularly in MYOB (made up of eleven digits). Real businesses are required to do this to meet their taxation requirements (i.e. GST).

Although the 2A and 2B Accounting and Finance courses do not require the completion of Business Activity Statements, processing taxation correctly assists in the electronic completion of these statements when required.

The GST for non-current physical assets is identified in these accounting packages as capital acquisition taxation (CAP) and is always applied at the rate of ten per cent.

To avoid complication in data management it is advisable to enter all the following exercises using the default date shown on the computer (i.e. operate with the current date and ignore any year, month or day written into any exercise).

It is straightforward in both programs to establish a business from the receipt of capital. No previous entries are required. MYOB has default Charts of Accounts for a wide range of business types, both service and retail.

Accounting and Finance 2B   ISBN 9780170182041   Cengage Learning Australia

The examples explained below deal with three situations:

- commencing a service business (laundry/cleaner) and a retail shop (health food) with three items of inventory maintained on a perpetual basis
- setting up an existing business with opening balances.

The first two businesses have GST integrated into all transactions where applicable. PAYG taxation is ignored for these exercises and wages are treated as expenses paid. Note that when entering monetary amounts, dollar signs and commas or spaces are not required, as the software defaults to currency formats (e.g. entering 10000 becomes $10000).

Example 10.1

EXAMPLE:

This task sets up a business for Darryl Kleen, who operates a dry cleaning and laundry business (a service business).

The software packages easily process GST, so this will be included where necessary.

The transactions start by setting up a new business with the contribution of capital. Give the business a distinctive name (e.g. your own name instead of Darryl) as a way to identify the printed reports.

There are seven transactions in this exercise. Consider, in each case, how the manner of data entry using the computer programs differs from what you would have done to enter the transaction manually.

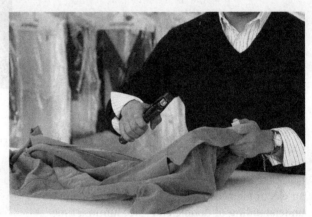

Transaction 1

Paid a capital contribution of $40000 cash (equity).

MYOB	QuickBooks
Create a new company	Create a new company
Add in an ABN 11 345 543 334 (mock)	Skip Interview on first screen
Conversion month is the month of data input	Select – Individual Tax Return
Select a **SERVICE** business	Select Financial Year – July
Use chart of accounts for a dry cleaner	Choose industry as Service Business
Save to your directory	Click Finish and save your data file to your
Command Centre	directory
Accounts	Create two new accounts:
Accounts List	
Use the **Edit** function to give the Equity account personal	• an Equity called Darryl Kleen (or your
name (your name)	name) – Owner's Equity
Close	• a Bank account called Cheque Account
	On Home page select Record Deposit and
From **Command Centre**	deposit $40000 into Darryl Kleen (or your
Select **Banking**	name) – Owner's Equity
Receive Money	
Select Equity Shareholders Capital	
The memorandum (Memo) provides a space for a narration related to this transaction.	
Navigate the screens using **Tab**	
To select accounts, highlight the blue downward arrows around in **Accounts**	
Enter $40000	
check **Amount Received**	
Tab	
Record	

Transaction 2

Pay for dry cleaning equipment $11000 (inclusive of GST) purchases from Acme Suppliers Pty Ltd (remember, taxation is Capital Acquisition: CAP).

MYOB	QuickBooks
Command Centre Banking Spend money Payee set up supplier with card information and ABN number Select account 1-2610 Dry cleaning equipment at cost Enter $11000 Select GST (CAP) choices on screen inclusive use blue downward arrows GST 10% Enter the amount of $11000 to check (use cheque, EFTPOS, credit card) Check amount paid Tab around screen Record Close screen An alternative to this entry could appear as a Purchase using the **Miscellaneous format**. Details of the Supplier can be set up as a **New Creditor** with key data of the Creditor, as well as GST entering paid today. The ledger account reports appear in columnar format and at any time the operator can enter transactions by selecting **Transaction Journal** or by going to **Reports**, selecting **Accounts**, and selecting **General ledger detail**	*(Remember – Capital Acquisition – CAG in QuickBooks and CAP in MYOB)* Create three new Fixed Asset accounts called • Dry cleaning equipment (header account) • At cost (sub account) • Accum Dep (sub account) On Home page select Write Cheque for $11000 (inc. GST) Payee: ACME Supplies (type Supplier) Account: at cost Tax Code: CAG Save and Close

Transaction 3

Pay for Office supplies for $187 (inclusive of GST) purchased from Sands Supplies.

MYOB	QuickBooks
Command Centre Banking Spend money Set up supplier with card information as payee Select account Office Supplies as an expense and amount paid inclusive of GST Check Amount paid Record Close screen Purchases if using a trade creditor Select GST tax code Enter amount Use memo as narration Cost of sales Purchase supplies 5–1000 GST paid will be identified ($17) as a debit entry against future GST liabilities Tab Record Close screen Note: This transaction could be set up as purchase of an asset rather than an expense, later requiring a balance day adjustment.	On Home page select Write Cheque for $187 (inc. GST) Payee: Sands Supplies Account: Office Supplies Tax Code: NCG Save and Close

Transaction 4

Enter sales of Dry Cleaning $150 per day for five days, cash held in the safe and entered daily into undeposited funds account as the manager has insufficient time to bank daily.

MYOB	QuickBooks
Command Centre	Create Cash Sale
Enter Sales	Edit Preferences → Sales & Customers → Company
Use the service format	Preferences → Untick Use Undeposited Funds as a
Select account for Income	default deposit account.
Dry Cleaning Revenue	On Home page select Create Sales Receipts
Create a new customer (Cash)	Optional: Create a Customer called Cash Customer
Enter GST inclusive	Tick: Amounts include Tax
Check amounts of sales and GST	In Item type: Create a Service called Dry Cleaning
Enter amount $150 paid today	Sales
Check Payment Details	Description: Dry Cleaning Sales
Select Group funds in Undeposited funds	Rate: 0.00
Tab screen	Tax Code: GST
The cash will be held in the business until banked	Account: Dry Cleaning Revenue (type Income)
at the end of the week	Bank Received Money from Cash Sales
Sales revenue will be recorded $136.36	On Home page select Record Deposits
Record	Select all money to be deposited and click on OK
Tab screen	Check date
Repeat four times (four separate invoices simulating	Save and Close
five days in total)	
GST collected 2–1310 as a credit entry becomes a	
current liabilities GST	
$13.64	
Paid today and check details to hold in Undeposited	
funds	
Record each separately	
Entering the payment into the Undeposited Funds	
account will necessitate a transfer when banked	
Go to Banking	
Prepare Banking	
Tick check each amount	
This will create a bank deposit	
Record	

These multiple entries simulate the transactions that occur daily in a business when a customer pays for the sale and is offered evidence of the transaction. It is a legal requirement of the business to provide a GST 'docket' (tax invoice). The docket is, in effect, a receipted sales invoice.

Note that all documents are numbered in sequence for audit purposes and have GST and date details automatically recorded.

Obviously, for purposes of internal control, cash takings should be banked regularly (see Chapter 4).

Transaction 5

A dissatisfied cash customer is refunded their payment for a previous service. The amount of the disputed service is $22.00 (GST inclusive). A 'return or allowance' will need authorisation as part of the internal control of the business. The return can be treated as a cash refund or as a credit adjustment to an invoice if it was a credit transaction.

MYOB	QuickBooks
Command Centre	On Home page select Refunds and Adjustments
Sales	Select Customer Cash Customer
Make a Sale (negative)	Select Item Dry Cleaning Sales
Select customer	In Rate type in $22.00
Cash	Click on Save and Close
Use the customer and enter a negative sale for the	Select Give a Refund and click on OK
agreed amount (–$22). This transaction has the effect	Check details and click on OK
of reversing the sales revenue and the GST record.	
Dry Cleaning Revenue	
4–1000 (negative)	
The GST will enter as a negative and reduce the	
liability owing as GST	
Record	
Close	
It will be necessary, once this negative sale is	
recorded, to select:	
Sales	
Sales Register	
Select	
Returns and Credits	
A Credit Note appears in red	
Apply the allowance as a cash refund (bottom left on	
screen) or if the original sale was on credit apply the	
allowance to the accounts receivable.	
Record	
Close	
Applying a cash refund in the sales register will	
diminish the cheque account by $22.00.	

Transaction 6

Enter prepayment of insurance (Good Insurance Company) to cover two months at $55 per month inclusive of GST. This entry forms the basis of a balance day adjustment at the end of this exercise.

MYOB	QuickBooks
Command Centre	On Home page select Write Cheque $110
Banking	Create Payee: Good Insurance Company
Set up supplier of services card information with ABN	Create Account: Prepaid Insurance (type Other
number (Good Insurance Company)	Asset)
Spend money	Tax Code: NCG
Make a payment of $110	Click Save and Close
Prepaid Insurance (Asset)	
Inclusive GST	
Memo: Two months insurance	
Identify the payee Insurance Provider by entering business	
details	
Tab around screen	
Paid today	
Check Amount Paid	

Record
Close
Could be entered as a
Purchase
Miscellaneous
with a creditor identified being paid today
Accounts selected (Prepaid Insurance) $110 amount
GST selected
Access
Reports (top of screen)
Select
Accounts
Select
Accounts Summary and view the **Columnar format of the ledger accounts**

Transaction 7

Balance day adjustment for one month's insurance expense.

MYOB	QuickBooks
Command Centre	Click on Company menu, select Make General
Accounts	journal Entries
Journal Entry	Account: Prepaid Insurance Dr $50
Use the expense account	Account: Create Property Insurance (sub
Property Insurance 6–6020 debit $50	account under Insurance expense) Cr $50
Select Prepaid Insurance credit $50	Save and Close
Add memo	
One month insurance	
Tab	
Record	
Close	

You will have noted that the entry of all of these transactions is considerably less laborious and complicated than it would have been using a manual accounting system. In many cases the computer will make the double entry automatically, guided by the field in which the transaction is being entered. In every case, the transaction will be entered immediately into the ledger account, rather than having to be entered first into the journal from which postings must then be made to the ledger.

Reports

MYOB	QuickBooks
Select Reports	Click on Report Centre
Index to reports	**Trial balance**
Accounts	Select Accountant and Taxes
Find Trial balance	Click on the Trial balance and select date range
Display	Note: A date range allows you to drill down and
Close	view the transactions for that period.
Select Reports again	**Profit & Loss**
Reports	Select Company and Financial
Accounts	Click on Profit and Loss Standard and select
Find Profit Report	date range
Repeat	**Balance Sheet**
Find Balance Sheet	Select Company and Financial
Profit Report	Click on Balance Sheet and select date range
Print reports as required	Note: In Modify choosing a date range
Close	will allow you to drill down and view the
Exit	transactions for that period.
Automatically saves	

Once all the transactions have been entered you are able to access a wide range of reports, which can be produced instantly without any need for balancing and transcription of balances. Go to **Reports** and view or print the financial statements: Trial balance, Profit statement and Balance sheet.

Accounting and Finance 2B   ISBN 9780170182041   Cengage Learning Australia

Review your transactions

- Compare your results with those of your peers and note the differences. If necessary you can identify any differences and attempt to use the system to correct errors.
- View the ledger accounts; you will find they are shown as columnar accounts.
- Contemplate the GST situation and determine whether this business owes GST to, or is owed GST by, the Australian Taxation Office.
- Enter a transaction for Drawings or partners' salaries and process journal entries to distribute the profit based on the Partnership Act or as a result of an agreement made (to the current accounts).

 Key Concept 10.2

Reports

Computer-processed data is constantly updated and instantly available for compilation into timely reports that enhance business owners' or managers' capacity for informed decision-making.

EXAMPLE:

Example 10.2

This is a longer exercise focusing on inventory management. The software system needs to be informed about each individual stock item. In retail stores it is usually the barcode facility that triggers the recording of all stock movements and, in a fundamental way, initiates the accounting process leading ultimately to the production of reports for analysis purposes.

This example is based on a health food store. GST is included in relevant transactions. Additional transactions of allowances, stock write-off and balance day adjustments have been included.

There are 17 transactions in this exercise. As in Example 1, consider how the data entry would have been different using a manual system.

MYOB	QuickBooks
Create a new company	Create a new company
Current month as conversion month	Skip Interview on first screen
Select 12 months accounting period	Select Individual Tax Return
Add ABN number (mock)	Select Financial Year: July
Select Retail	Choose industry as Product Sales/Retail
Select Health Food	Click Finish and save your data file to your directory
Remember to **Save** in your own directory	Create two new accounts: an Equity called Owner's
The system defaults to the current date providing a continuous sequence to record data	Equity and a Bank account called Cheque Account
Select GST, where applicable, for each entry	

Transaction 1

Set up Capital for the owner contributing $50 000. Edit the Capital account with the owner's name (use your own name to identify the printed reports).

MYOB	QuickBooks
Command Centre	On Home page select Record Deposit and deposit
Banking	$50 000 into Owner's Equity
Receive money	
Select Equity	
Owners' Shareholders Equity	
3–1000 account will be credited	
$50 000	

Cheque Account will be automatically adjusted to a
$50000 debit balance
Record
Close screen

Transaction 2

Pay rent on shop $19800 for six months (inclusive of $1800 GST) to supplier Kalgoorlie Rentals.

MYOB	QuickBooks
Command Centre	On Home page select Write Cheque $19800 (inc. GST)
Banking	Create Payee: Kalgoorlie Rentals
Set up supplier by use of Card system or when the	Create Account: Prepaid rent (type Other Asset)
transaction is initiated with ABN	Tax Code: NCG
Make a payment	Click Save and Close
Bank account will be reduced by $19800	
Select GST inclusive	
Add in a new asset account	
Prepaid Rent 1–1405	
Select GST 10%	
Use memo to identify rent paid for six months	
Alternatively a credit supplier could be created as a	
miscellaneous service with paid today.	
Use Tab to navigate screen	
Record	
Close	

Transaction 3

Purchase store equipment ($22000) from Furniture Mart Pty Ltd on credit with $10000 paid as part payment today. The item will be inclusive of GST.

MYOB	QuickBooks
Command Centre	Create three new Fixed Asset accounts called:
Purchases	• Store Equipment (header account)
Miscellaneous	• At cost (sub account)
Create **new** supplier as Furniture Mart Pty Ltd	• Accum. Dep. (sub account)
allocating an ABN number for tax purposes	On Home page select Enter Bills for $22000 (inc. GST)
Inclusive **GST (CAP)**	Payee: Furniture Mart Pty Ltd (type Supplier)
	Account: at cost
Select account	Tax Code: CAG
Store Equipment at cost 1–2610	Save and Close
$22000	
Select GST – CAP will be automatically created $2000	Part Payment on Bill of $10000:
Tab screen	On Home page select Pay Bills
Enter $10000 paid today	Click on Invoice to be paid
Record	Select Payment Method: Cheque
Close	Select Payment Account: Cheque Account
	Choose Payment Date
	Choose Pay Selected Bills
	Click Done

Transaction 4

Enter the stock database.

MYOB	QuickBooks
To operate this store it is necessary to use the	Note: Turn on Inventory Tracking
Inventory Command Centre and establish a	Edit menu → Preferences → Items and Inventory →
database related to the items available for sale.	tick Inventory and purchase orders are active.
Inventory Command Centre to set up these items	
and suppliers (vendors) as the business	
Buys	
Sells	
Stocks	

Accounting and Finance 2B   ISBN 9780170182041   Cengage Learning Australia

Add the below items, remembering to show GST being applicable or not applicable and providing the suppliers' ABN numbers:

Buys	Cost of sales 5–1000
Sells	Income 4–1000
Stock	Merchandise Inventory 1–1300

Complete the card information for buying and selling detail for each item

Both QuickBooks and MYOB track stock through the Perpetual Inventory method. When the item is purchased for cash the Inventory Asset account is debited and the Cheque account is credited. When inventory is sold for cash a revenue account is credited and the Cheque account is debited. The *average cost* of the item is calculated, the Inventory asset account is credited and the Cost of goods sold account is debited with that *average cost* (in other words, both packages use the *Weighted average* method of inventory costing; see Chapter 2)

Suppliers' details

Jenny's Organics, Northcliffe, WA Blueberries	ABN 11 723 417 847 (mock)
Sentinel Pharmaceuticals, Melbourne, Vic Fish Oil	ABN 11 732 714 748 (mock)

Transaction 5

Make purchases from above suppliers on credit of:
* Jenny's Organics: Blueberries, 50 units
* Sentinel Pharmaceuticals: Fish Oil Tablets, 100 units.

MYOB	QuickBooks
Command Centre	Item no: 0001
Purchases	Description: Blueberries 250g
Select Supplier	Cost: $2.50
Create new suppliers as each invoice is processed	Purchase Tax Code: NCF
Select Invoice format for	COGS Account: Cost of Goods Sold
Item select (bottom of screen)	Sales Price: $5.00
Entering	Tax Code: FREE
Item code 001 Blueberries	Income Account: Sales
Cost: $2.50	Asset Account: Inventory Asset
Purchase Tax Code: GST Free	Item No: 0002
Sales Price: $5.00	Description: Fish Oil Tabs (100)
Purchase 50 units	Cost: $8.00 (inc. GST)
Credit transaction	Purchase Tax Code: NCG
Check total $125.00	COGS Account: Cost of Goods Sold
Item code 002 Fish Oil tablets	Sales Price: $12.00 (inc. GST)
Description: Fish Oil Tabs (100)	Tax Code: GST
Cost: $8.00 (inc. GST)	Income Account: Sales
Sales Price: $12.00 (inc. GST)	Asset Account: Inventory Asset
Purchase 100 units	
Credit transaction	On Home page select Enter Bills (credit purchase)
Repeat for each supplier	Payee: Jenny's Organics (type Supplier)
(two separate invoices)	Item: 0001
GST only on Fish Oil tablets	Qty: 50
Check total $800.00	Save and Close (Check total $125.00)

Accounting and Finance 2B   ISBN 9780170182041   Cengage Learning Australia

Leave as credit transaction – not paid	On Home page select Enter Bills (credit purchase)
Tab screen to check all details	Payee: Sentinel Pharmaceuticals (type Supplier)
Note the use of a Purchase Order authority	Item: 0002
Record each transaction for each supplier	Qty: 100
Close screen after all Purchases	Save and Close (Check total $800.00)

Transaction 6

Enter a series of Sales transactions as below.

MYOB	QuickBooks
Command Centre	Create Cash Sale
Sales	Edit Preferences → Sales & Customers → Company
Enter a Sale	Preferences → Untick Use Undeposited Funds as a
Create new customers including a card file for	default deposit account
Cash customers	On Home page select Create Sales Receipts
Use the stock item numbers to build each invoice	Optional: Create a Customer called Cash Customer
Enter each invoice using the details below	Tick: Amounts include Tax
Tab to navigate the screen	Item: 0001 Qty: 10
Remember to enter GST or NT where applicable and	Item: 0002 Qty: 8
Paid today for cash customers	Deposit to: Cheque Account
Record each of the three transactions	Save and Close (Check total $146.00)
Close Sales screen	
Invoice 001	Create Invoice (credit sale)
Command	On Home page select Invoices
Sales	Customer: Job: City Health Club
Make a sale	Item: 0001 Qty: 6
Create a Cash Customer	Item: 0002 Qty: 4
Use the invoice format for items	Save and New (Check total $78.00)
Enter the item number, volume and selling price on	
each line of the invoice	Create Invoice (credit sale)
	Customer: Job: Vibrant Life Services
001 Qty 10 Selling price $5	Item: 0001 Qty: 12
002 Qty 8 Selling price $12.00 inc. GST	Item: 0002 Qty: 18
Complete invoice and then paid today	Save and Close (Check total $276.00)
Check total ($146.00)	
Record Tab	
Command Sales	
Invoice 002	
Command	
Sales	
Make a sale	
Create a new customer	
City Health Club allocate a mock ABN number	
Do not enter paid today credit transaction	
Item 001 Qty 6 prices as above	
Item 002 Qty 4	
Check total $78.00	
Record	
Invoice 003	
Command	
Sales	
Make a sale	
Create a new customer	
Vibrant Life Services (identifying an ABN)	
Credit transactions	
Item 001 Qty 12	
Item 002 Qty 18	
Check total $276.00	
Do not enter paid today	
Record	
Close	

Accounting and Finance 2B   ISBN 9780170182041   Cengage Learning Australia

Transaction 7

Five units of Blueberries item 001 deteriorated and were written off.

MYOB	QuickBooks
Command	Write off 5 units of Blueberries, which were spoilt
Inventory Adjustments	On Home Page select Adjust Quantity on Hand
Enter minus (–5) units of item 001 allocated to 6–4800 Shrinkage/Spoilage	Adjustment Account: Shrinkage/Spoilage (type Expense)
This entry adjusts the inventory on hand and adjusts the value from an asset to an expense	Type Item 0001: New Qty 17 (Check total $–12.50)
Record	Save and Close

Transaction 8

Three containers of Fish Oil Tablets were found to be missing at stocktake – apparently stolen.

MYOB	QuickBooks
Command	Write off 3 items of Fish Oil, which were apparently stolen
Inventory	On Home Page select Adjust Quantity on Hand
Adjustments enter	Adjustment Account: Shrinkage/Spoilage (type Expense)
Enter minus (–3) units of item 002 allocated to 6–4800 Shrinkage/Spoilage	Type Item 0002: New Qty 77 (Check total $–21.82)
This entry adjusts the inventory on hand and adjusts the value from an asset to an expense	Save and Close
Record	

Stock losses internal control

Discuss issues of Internal Control and how to minimise stock losses by deterioration (blueberries) or theft (fish oil tablets). Possibly review Chapter 4 to discover potential solutions to the problems of 'shrinkage'.

Transaction 9

Pay the following accounts.

Supplier	Purpose/Account	Amount
Accounting Western Numbers	Accounting Fees	$330 inc. GST
Health Foods Australia Pty Ltd	Subscription Magazine	$44 inc. GST

MYOB	QuickBooks
Command	On Home page select Write Cheque
Banking	Create Payee: Western Numbers
Make a payment	Amount: $330.00 (inc. GST)
Use memo to record details	Create Account: Accounting
Give each supplier an ABN	Tax Code: NCG
Accounting Fees 6–1050	Click Save and Close
Subscription magazine 6–1400	
Record	On Home page select Write Cheque
Separate payments	Create Payee: Food Australia
Tab around screen	Amount: $44.00 (inc. GST)
or	Create Account: Subscriptions
Command Purchases	Tax Code: NCG
Create suppliers for purchases via Purchases	Click Save & Close
miscellaneous	
Include GST	
Enter details above	
Paid today	
Record	
Close screen	

Accounting and Finance: 2B   ISBN 9780170182041   Cengage Learning Australia

Transaction 10

Make payments of all outstanding amounts to suppliers.

MYOB	QuickBooks
Purchases	On Home page select Pay Bills
Select	Click on Invoices to be paid for each supplier
Pay bills	Select Payment Method: Cheque
Select each Supplier and pay outstanding amounts	Select Payment Account: Cheque Account
Enter the amount paid on each invoice to clear the	Choose Assign Cheque number
account	Choose Payment Date
Record	Choose Pay Selected Bills
Close	Click Done
	Allocate Cheque number and click OK
Note: Invoices can be used to show the creation of	Click Done
discounts and payments due within set periods.	Note: This will create a cheque for each supplier.

Transaction 11

Renew stock supplies and purchase on credit from the Suppliers as below (on credit).

MYOB	QuickBooks
Command	
Purchases	
Make a purchase	
Select Supplier	
Jenny's Organics Northcliffe WA	
Blueberries	
Invoice format	
Item	
Credit transaction	
001 × 60 units	
Original purchase price	
Record	
Command	
Purchases	
Select Supplier	
Sentinel Pharmaceuticals, Melbourne, Vic.	
Fish Oil inc GST	
Invoice format item	
Credit transaction	
002 × 150 units	
Record	
Close	

Transaction 12

Add new stock item: 003 100% Grape Juice 1 litre, cost price $3.10, selling price $4.80, exempt from GST, Supplier Lily Hill Winery WA, Purchase 100 units.

MYOB	QuickBooks
Use the Inventory Command Centre to set up new	Item No: 0003
item and supplier (vendor) as the business	Description: 100% Grape Juice
Buys	Cost: $3.10
Sells	Purchase Tax Code: NCF
Stocks	COGS Account: Cost of Goods Sold
the above item, remembering to show GST being	Sales Price: $4.80
applicable or not applicable and providing the	Tax Code: FRE
suppliers' ABN numbers.	Income Account: Sales
Create new stock line	Asset Account: Inventory Asset
003 Grape Juice	On Home page select Enter Bills (credit purchase)
Buys: Cost of sales 5–1000	Payee: Lily Hill Winery (type Supplier)
Sells: Income 4–1000	
Stock: Merchandise Inventory 1–1300	

Purchases
Select new supplier
Set up information address
Select the Supplier
As above
Purchase 100 units at cost of $3.10 per unit (1 litre)
Add to Inventory account
Trade payable and individual supplier and GST
Record
Close

Item: 0003
Qty: 50
Save and Close (Check total $155.00)

Transaction 13

Enter further sales (two invoices, one for cash and one on credit).

MYOB	QuickBooks
Command	On Home page select Create Sales Receipts
Sales	Optional: Create a Customer called Cash Customer
Find customers and enter invoice	Tick: Amounts include Tax
Note cash and credit sales	Item: 0001 Qty: 12
Cash Sales	Item: 0002 Qty: 8
Paid today	Item: 0003 Qty: 18
Item: 001 Qty: 12	Deposit to: Cheque Account
Item: 002 Qty: 8	Save and Close (Check total $242.40)
Item: 003 Qty: 18	On Home page select Create Invoice (credit sale)
Check total $242.40	Customer: Job: Vibrant Life Services
Paid today	Item: 0001 Qty: 5
Record	Item: 0002 Qty: 18
Sales on credit to	Item: 0003 Qty: 15
Vibrant Life Services Pty Ltd	Save and Close (Check total $313.00)
Item: 001 Qty: 5	
Item: 002 Qty:18	
Item: 003 Qty: 15	
Check total $313.00	
Do not enter paid today	
Record	
Close	

Transaction 14

Record sales return/allowance to Vibrant Life Services for six Fish Oil damaged in transit – credit note was authorised on the previous invoice

MYOB	QuickBooks
Command	6 Fish Oil were damaged on the sale for Vibrant Life
Sales	Services – a return was authorised
Find customer enter	On Home page select Refunds and Adjustments
Negative sale of 6 units of 002 to Vibrant Life Services	Customer: Job: Vibrant Life Services
Check total $72.00	Item: 0002 Qty: 6
Record and then	Save and Close (Check total $72.00)
Select	Select Apply to Tax Invoice
Sales Register	Choose the invoice to apply the credit to
to apply credit note to the invoice	Click Done
See left-hand bottom of screen	
Record	
All stock items are adjusted in the process as are the GST obligations	
View the Sales Transaction Journal to verify entries It is not appropriate to recall invoice and amend as this breaches internal control practice.	

Transaction 15

Make three balance day adjustments.

MYOB	QuickBooks
Command Centre	Bank statement shows a credit transaction of interest earned for the month $38.50
Accounts	Bank statement shows a debit transaction of Bank charges for the month $62.00
Select Journal entry	One month depreciation on Store equipment and Office equipment: $230.00 Store equipment, $70.00 Office equipment
Bank statement shows a credit transaction of interest earned for the month $38.50	Use General journals to enter the following transactions.
Debit	**Interest Received**
Cheque Account	Click on Company menu, select Make General journal Entries
1–1110	Account: Cheque Account Dr $38.50
Credit	Account: Interest Income Cr $38.50 Tax Code: FRE
Interest Income	Save and Close
8–1000	**Bank Charges**
Record	Click on Company menu, select Make General journal entries
Command Centre	Account: Bank Service Charges Dr $62.00 Tax Code: NCF
Accounts	Account: Cheque Account Cr $62.00
Select Journal entry	Save and Close
Bank statement shows a debit transaction of Bank charges for the month $62.00	**1 month depreciation on Store Equipment**
Credit	Click on Company menu, select Make General journal entries
Cheque Account 1–1110	Account: Depreciation Expense Dr $230.00
Debit	Account: accum dep Cr $230.00
Bank Charges	Save and Close
6–1200	
Record	
Command Centre	
Accounts	
Select Journal entry	
One month depreciation on Store equipment: $230.00	
Debit Depreciation 6–1300 $300.00	
Credit Store Equipment	
Accumulated depreciation 1-2620 $230.00	
Record	
Close	

Transaction 16

The owner withdraws $300 cash.

MYOB	QuickBooks
Command Centre	On Home page select Write Cheque
Banking	Create Payee: Owner
Make a payment	Amount: $300.00
Select Owners' Equity Drawings	Create Account: Owners Drawings (type Equity)
3–1200	Click Save and Close
Record	
Close	

Transaction 17

An invoice arrives from Ringers Phone Ltd for the amount of $132 (including GST).

MYOB	QuickBooks
Command	On Home page select Enter Bills (credit purchase)
Purchases	Payee: Ringers Phone Ltd (type Supplier)
Miscellaneous	Account: Telephone
Create a new supplier of a service	Amount: $132.00 (inc. GST)
Add an ABN	Save and Close
Select tax GST inclusive	
Enter details of invoice	

Accounting and Finance: 2B   ISBN 9780170182041   Cengage Learning Australia

Account remains unpaid
Telephone expense
Record
Close

Reports

MYOB	QuickBooks
Reports	Click on Report Centre
Select reports	**Trial balance**
Accounts	Select the Accountant and Taxes
Trial balance	Click on the Trial balance and select date range
Profit Report	Note: A date range allows you to drill down and view
Balance Sheet	the transactions for that period.
Select reports and view/print	**Profit & Loss**
Close	Select the Company and Financial
	Click on Profit and Loss Standard and select date range
	Balance Sheet
	Select the Company and Financial
	Click on Balance Sheet and select date range
	Note: In Modify choosing a date range allows
	you to drill down and view the transactions for
	that period.

Follow-up activities

Having completed the transactions you could compare your reports with those of your peers and determine how a correction would be processed if necessary. You could also:

- make further relevant entries and examine other reports, such as inventory
- create further transactions to extend the exercise
- review results and make decisions about the financial outcomes or future plans of this business
- discuss profitability, liquidity, inventory management and turnover and GST obligations
- discuss the efficiency of electronic processing of data
- trace the double entry processing required for each transaction.

Example 10.3

The purpose of this short task is to set up a business from a given Trial balance (opening accounts). No other transactions have been added, although the exercise could be extended with the addition of some typical transactions.

The task involves creating a business, 'Dollar True', an accounting service with a single owner, Brit Fortune, and to introduce opening balances. The business commences with the following assets and liabilities:

	Debit	Credit
Trade debtors (Fast City Pty Ltd)	$900	
Cheque account	$14 000	
Store equipment at cost	$26 000	
Office equipment at cost	$8 000	
Vehicle at cost	$24 000	
Trade creditor (Providers United Ltd)		$19 000
Mortgage loan		$14 000
Shareholder's equity B Fortune		$39 900

MYOB	QuickBooks
Follow prompts to create a new business	Create a new company called Dollar True
Service	Skip Interview on first screen
Accounting	Select – Individual Tax Return
Conversion month current month	Select Financial Year – July
Create an ABN	Choose industry as Service Business
Save in your directory	Click Finish and save your data file to your directory
Go to Command Centre	Enter the following balances from the Trial balance
Select	below
Setup	Note: If you use the balance field in create new
Balances	Customer or Supplier the transaction is allocated to
Opening balance	Uncategorised Income or Uncategorised Expense
Enter the above amounts	respectively.
Cheque Account	
Trade Debtors	Enter the Customer Balance as follows
Store Equipment at cost	Create a new account called Accounts receivable
Office Equipment at cost	(type Accounts receivable)
Vehicles at cost	Click on Company menu, select Make General journal
Trade Payables	Entries
Bank Loan	Line One
Note the balance remains to be entered to	Account: Accounts receivable Dr $900.00
Shareholders' Equity check	Name: Fast City Pty Ltd
Historical balancing	Line Two
Create new accounts where required	Account: Opening Bal Equity Cr $900.00
Open Reports	Save and Close
Select Trial balance to check entries	
Return to Setup	Enter the Supplier Balance as follows
Balance	Create a new account called Accounts payable (type
Trade Debtors	Accounts payable)
Add a sale	Click on Company menu, select Make General journal
For the Fast City Pty Ltd balance $900	entries
In the control account	Line One
Record	Account: Opening Bal Equity Dr $19000.00
Return to	Line Two
Setup	Account: Accounts payable Cr $19000.00
Balances	Name: Providers United
Trade Creditors	Save and Close
Add a sale	
Providers United Ltd $19000	Enter remaining balances from Trial balance through
To match the control account	General journal
Record	Click on Company menu, select Make General journal
These opening entries are now available to operate	entries
the business	Note: Balance of Equity ($39 900) is allocated to
	Opening Bal Equity account
	Save and Close

SUMMARY

Electronic processing is initiated when a transaction is keyed in to a data entry point. This might be by the use of a barcode reader at a checkout or by keying items at a shop counter. The process is as follows.

- Once the transaction is executed all the relevant 'ledger accounts' are processed.
- The data is then available for reporting purposes. Complicated and repetitive calculations are made in a routine way (e.g. GST or stock movements).
- Multiple business outlets of the same company can be networked. (e.g. a national supermarket) for comprehensive updates across the nation or internationally.
- The following financial and internal control aspects of a business can be facilitated by electronic processing: inventory, sales, purchases, payroll, accounts receivable, accounts payable, cost centres, asset management and taxation (PAYG and GST).
- Judgements can readily be made on profitability, liquidity, stability and performance, including comparisons with budgets.

Maintaining the effectiveness and integrity of the system

- Electronic processing is dependent on competently run systems providing a secure environment for the data to be managed and protected.
- Initial training and ongoing upskilling of network operators and constantly upgrading software and hardware, while essential, both represent financial demands on resources that need to be recouped by more efficient outcomes in data management.
- Virus protection, security of data from hackers, protection of business information from competitors and backup systems are essential aspects of internal control.

Computer-based accounting is efficient and accurate, flexible and dynamic. It accepts, manages, stores, analyses and reports data with a speed and precision that would have been unthinkable just a few years ago. Modern businesses cannot afford to be without it.

Test your knowledge

1 What is a Chart of accounts and why is it important in establishing a computerised accounting system? What features should an EDP Chart of Accounts have?

2 What types of business get the most benefit from employing EDP?

3 What is meant by 'data management'?

4 Outline the benefits to a business of adopting an EDP system.

5 Why is it important to number source documents?

6 List six reports available from either MYOB or Quickbooks and briefly explain the purpose of each.

7 What is the benefit of barcoding inventory items?

8 What inventory costing method is employed by most computerised accounting packages (including MYOB and Quickbooks)?

9 Outline the steps needed to maintain the integrity and efficiency of an EDP system.

Test your understanding

Topic guide
- Simple cash transactions: 10.1
- Service business – simple transactions: 10.2
- Trading business – simple transactions: 10.3
- Trading business, debtors and creditors: 10.4, 10.5
- Trading business, comprehensive, including BDAs, internal control: 10.6, 10.7

10.1 Create an Accounting business for Janine Pound using a computerised accounting package. Ms Pound commences the business with $10000 cash equity. The business aims to generate cash revenue of $800 per day in the first five-day week, inclusive of GST. Expenses paid over this period include rent $990, insurance $110, office expenses $110 and salaries of $2000. All expenses except for salaries are inclusive of GST.

    a   Enter the transactions and print the Balance sheet.

    b   Comment on the account balances following the first week of activity.

10.2 Create a barber shop/beautician business with a computerised accounting package.
Add your name in to the Equity account
Opening entries

Cheque account	$10000
Shop equipment at cost	$12000

Furniture at cost	$5000
Loan	$8000
Equity	$19 000

Transactions in the first week excluding GST:

Payments

Rent	$400
Cleaning	$80
Advertising	$100
Broadband and telephone	$70

Sales (select appropriate accounts for the services provided)

Day 1	$200
Day 2	$300
Day 3	$350
Day 4	$420
Day 5	$380

On Day 5 provide for a donation to 'Shave for a Cure' via a free haircut to the value of $100. Pay GST outstanding to the Australian Taxation Office on Day 5. The owner withdrew $900 on Day 4.

a   Enter all transactions.

b   Print reports for the profit and balance sheet.

10.3   Create a newsagency that sells pencils and pens. Beth Page operates the shop (Good News Pty Ltd). GST is recorded as inclusive in all prices. Enter the following information using a computer accounting package:

- Ms Page has capital of $80 000 invested in the shop ($10 000 cheque account and $70 000 worth of store equipment at cost).
- Set up a stationery supplier, Mark Supplies Pty Ltd.
- All amounts shown are inclusive of GST.
- This business provides pencils at 22 cents each and pens at 44 cents each.
- Good News Pty Ltd buys 800 of each item on credit.

Accounting and Finance 2B   ISBN 9780170182041   Cengage Learning Australia

During the first week:

- Sales of 450 pencils at 99 cents for cash.
- 300 pens were sold to the Sharp River Primary School on credit for $1.32 each.
- In addition, 280 pens were sold for cash $1.21
- Administration expenses paid for the week were $286.
- It was discovered that 20 pens had been stolen from the counter during the week.

Required

a Enter the transactions and view/print the Profit and loss report.

b Discuss the profitability, stock levels and GST commitment of the business.

10.4 Create a new company as a bicycle retailer, Spinning Wheels Pty Ltd, using a computerised accounting package. Bob Bearing is the sole shareholder and business operator, having contributed $30000 cash equity.

Spinning Wheels Pty Ltd will stock the following bicycles:

Model	Cost price	Selling price
Roadtester	$200	$290
Mudraker	$180	$285
Mountain Trailer	$210	$350
Ultimate Racer	$250	$400

The above prices exclude GST. All bicycles are purchased on credit from Cyclist International Pty Ltd, 80 Collins Court Melbourne, ABN 43 418 914 891. The business has numerous cash customers and the following three customers who operate on approved credit:

- Wheels United Pty ltd
- Education Department
- Jim Kidding Pty Ltd.

The only asset of the business is the $30000 contributed by the owner. Enter the following transactions (prices as previously stated; do not forget to add GST in every case).

Day	Transaction
1	Buy on credit from Cyclist International Pty Ltd:
	a 25 Roadtesters
	b 15 Mudrakers
	c 20 Mountain Trailers
	d 15 Ultimate Racers.
2	Sell on credit to the Education Department:
	a 6 Mountain Trailers
	b 6 Mudrakers.
3	Cash sales:
	a 3 Roadtesters
	b 2 Ultimate Racers (prices as above).
4	Credit sales to Jim Kidding Pty Ltd:
	a 8 Roadtesters
	b 4 Mountain Trailers
	c 1 Ultimate Racer
	d A part payment of $1000 is received.
5	A cash customer returns one Roadtester and is refunded the sale price.

6		Cash Sales inc. GST:
		a 4 Roadtesters
		b 3 Ultimate Racers (prices as above)
		c 3 Mudrakers.
7		The business repaired bicycles (open a new account) earning $300 cash (inc GST).
8		Sold a gift voucher to a customer for a friend $200 (customer deposits).
9		Cash purchased a computer for use in the office $3000 (inc GST).
10		Paid rent $990 GST inc.
11		Paid Accounting fees $840 (inc GST).
12		Paid wages $800.
13		Education Department paid their account in full.
14		The gift voucher is presented against the sale of a Mudraker with the remainder owing being paid as cash.
15		The bank advises that $48 has been added to the account as Interest earned.
16		The business donates one Roadtester to the local senior high school as a student prize for academic excellence in accounting.

Required

a   Complete all the entries, access the reports and assess the profitability and liquidity of the business for this first operating period.

b   What is the GST outcome and what processes will occur in regard to GST?

c   What action would be necessary if the shop stocktake does not match the inventory register?

10.5   Create a company, Cornflower Blue Pty Ltd, as a garden nursery retailer with a single shareholder, June Cornflower. June intends to set up an electronic accounting and retail service system so she can barcode all stock items and services. The company commences with the following assets and liabilities:

	Debit	Credit
Accounts receivable	$800	
(Garden City Flowers Pty Ltd)		
Cash at bank	$22 000	
Store equipment	$16 000	
Garden equipment	$40 000	
Vehicle	$22 000	
Valley Supplies Pty Ltd		$18 000
Trade creditor		
Mortgage loan		$30 000
Shareholders' equity		$52 800

Enter the above information into the system. If using MYOB, enter Trade Debtor and Trade Creditor as *previous transactions,* creating the customer and supplier.

Create a stock inventory system selling single units of the following with GST:

001	Flowering plants
002	Ornaments
003	Trees
004	Chemicals
005	Fertilisers

Accounting and Finance: 2B   ISBN 9780170182041   Cengage Learning Australia

Enter the following transactions. All figures shown are GST inclusive. The business will be using the perpetual stock management system.

- Purchased 20 trees from Valley Supplies Pty Ltd at $14.30 each on credit.
- Purchased 50 flowering plants from Jasmine Nursery at $1.43 each on credit.
- Purchased 100 ornaments from Hanoi Pty Ltd at $8.80 each on credit.
- Purchased 50 bags of fertiliser from Bunbury Chemical Pty Ltd at $48.40 per bag for cash.
- Purchased 30 units of chemicals from Western Laboratories at $13.20 per unit on credit.
- Sold for cash 5 trees at $25.30 each and 38 flowering plants $3.30 each.
- Providing landscaping service to local medical centre for $880 (inc GST) cash paid (miscellaneous income).
- Paid water account $660 (including GST).
- Sold for cash 18 bags of fertiliser at $69.30 per bag cash and 15 units of chemicals at $19.80.
- Paid Hanoi Pty Ltd account in full and also received full payment from Garden City Flowers Pty Ltd.
- Banked cash from landscaping contract $990.
- Paid rent $660 (including GST).
- Paid wages $900, PAYG $210 (income tax expense) and $85 superannuation.
- Purchased 80 flowering plants from Jasmine Nursery at $1.50 each on credit.
- Sold for cash 12 trees at $25.45 and 50 flowering plants $3.50.
- Purchased 30 trees from Valley Supplies Pty Ltd at $15.30 each on credit.
- Sold for cash 15 bags of fertiliser at $71.10 per bag cash and ten units of chemicals at $19.90.
- Sold for cash 11 trees at $25.75 each and 35 flowering plants $3.80 each.
- Paid for deposit on family holiday $800.
- Paid fuel expense $220 (including GST) and insurance policy for six months $240 (prepaid for six months, including GST).
- Sold to Garden City Flowers 80 ornaments on credit for $19.50 each.
- Garden City Flowers returned 3 damaged ornaments. Credit given.
- Damaged ornaments credit received from Hanoi Pty Ltd on allowance and a refund was received.

Required

a   Complete all the entries, access the reports and assess the profitability and liquidity of the business for this first operating period.

b   Identify the inventory items that are the best-selling items and suggest strategies that might increase the movement of slower-selling lines.

10.6 Create a computerised ledger for the Lightsout Liquor Store with perpetual inventory and GST and enter into it the following transactions.

Day	Transaction
1	Owner invested $100 000 into Lilydale Perfect Pty Ltd.
	Store equipment for $20 000 paid cash plus GST (CAP).
	The business negotiated a $60 000 lease and paid cash plus GST.
	Create a Petty cash imprest system $200 and a Drawer float of $500.
2	The business paid $1 200 for six months advertising plus GST.
3	The business paid $2 400 for insurance for 12 months plus GST.
4	Purchased on credit from Riverbank Estate (add GST): 20 cartons of chardonnay per carton $150 20 cartons sauvignon blanc $190 20 cartons shiraz $180
5	Purchased for cash (add GST): 20 cartons of chardonnay $120 20 cartons sauvignon blanc $195 20 cartons shiraz $195

Accounting and Finance 2B   ISBN 9780170182041   Cengage Learning Australia

6	Paid wages $500
12	Sold for cash including GST: 15 cartons of shiraz $250 14 cartons sauvignon blanc $296
15	Sold to Perth Central Entertainment on credit: • 15 cartons chardonnay $200 • 14 cartons sauvignon blanc $296
20	One carton of shiraz allowance credit returned to Riverbank Estate $24.50 spent from petty cash on flowers (inc. GST)
22	Damage stock one carton of shiraz written off.
31	Monthly adjustments: • Depreciation on cost at 10% on store equipment • Adjustment insurance and advertising as a cost for one month • Sold an item of store equipment original cost $5000 for $4900 (inc. GST) with accumulated depreciation of $60. Create a Sale of asset account 9-1050 expense

Required

a Print the reports for profit, balance sheet and inventory.

b What would be the consequences for a store like this if the computer system failed all day on a busy trading day? How could the staff continue to trade?

c What could the business do to reduce the likelihood of system failure and to minimise the financial losses if it did occur?

d What legal matters related to taxation could arise in this situation?

10.7 JB Norman opened a computer games store, Electronix, with a deposit of $90000 into the business bank account. A Petty cash account of $200 and $800 Cash float was set up within the business. The following prepayments each for six months were made on the first day:

• Insurance $660 inc. GST

• Advertising $1584 inc. GST

• Shop lease at cost $33000 inc. GST

    The business intends to sell Nintendo, PlayStation and Xbox.

    Store equipment was purchased for $25000 cash plus GST.

Week 1	The business purchased the following stock on credit from Melbourne Games Pty Ltd:
	50 Nintendo DS $105 (inc. GST)
	50 PlayStation 3 $622 (inc. GST)
	50 XBox 360 $388 (inc. GST)
	Cash sale:
	6 Nintendos @ $159 (inc. GST)
	24 PlayStations @ $699
	15 XBox 360 @ $512
Week 2	Cash sale:
	7 Nintendos @$159 (inc. GST)
	12 PlayStations @ $699
	19 XBox 360 $512
	Credit sale (College Secondary):
	5 Nintendos @ $159 (inc. GST)
	5 PlayStations @ $699
	5 XBox 360 @ $512 all sold less 3% discount on selling price
	College Secondary returned a damaged XBox and received a credit on account
	College Secondary paid $2000 on account

Accounting and Finance: 2B   ISBN 9780170182041   Cengage Learning Australia

	The business purchased on credit from Melbourne Pty Ltd:
	30 Nintendos @ $110 (inc. GST)
	50 PlayStations @ $634 (inc. GST)
	20 XBox 360 @ $405 (inc. GST)
Week 3	Cash sale:
	17 Nintendos @ $159 (inc. GST)
	8 PlayStations @ $699
	20 XBox 360@ $512
	Paid in full account of Melbourne Games Pty ltd account less 3% discount for early payment
	Used the Petty cash to buy poster for shop $34.50 (inc. GST)
Week 4	Cash sale:
	10 Nintendos @$159 (inc. GST)
	12 PlayStations @ $699
	8 XBox 360 @ $512
	Installed security camera system in store (asset) $6000 cash (inc. GST)
	Balance day adjustments at end of month: • Allocated depreciation of $400 for the month • Adjusted month's insurance and advertising • Lease cost for the month $420 • Adjusted one XBox not accounted for in a stocktake (written off)

Required

a Complete all the entries.

b Print reports on liquidity, profitability, inventory and a Balance sheet.

c Discuss specific internal control issues that would need watchful attention and identify practices that should be in place for this business to protect liquid assets, inventory and accounts receivable.

10.8 Bill Kingfish owns four suburban fast food (fish and chip) outlets operating under the business name Starfish. He operates the shop his father began 20 years ago. The Starfish shops are well known and have excellent reputations for quality and service. Bill has been puzzled about the comparative profitability of each of the four stores. Profits in the other three shops fluctuate (vary) with staff movements.

a Highlight the obvious problems that could occur when Bill has to employ staff in the three shops he does not directly operate. Bill's accountant suggests that if the shops all operated with a computer software program covering all aspects of the business, he might have better control of his business.

b Develop a flowchart to demonstrate how a computer-based system appropriate for the four shops would operate.

c Highlight the benefits and costs of such a change from the current manual system Bill has in use.

Investigation

Investigate one or more businesses or other organisations (school, charity, sports club, etc.) that uses a computerised accounting system and produce a report for each that explains:

a the sort of accounting package used

b how the data entry is done and by whom

Accounting and Finance: 2B   ISBN 9780170182041   Cengage Learning Australia

c   the reports produced, how they are used and how frequently they are produced

d   measures taken to safeguard data and ensure the continued efficiency of the data processing system

e   the main costs that were involved in setting up the system

f   the main ongoing costs of maintaining the system.

For each entity that you investigate, state what benefits you think it is obtaining from having computerised its accounting and identify any ways in which you think it might be able to improve its systems.

Essay

'If accounting software programs process transactions, accountants need not learn the basics of double entry accounting.'

What are the arguments for and against this statement?

Ethics case study

Vera Smart is a bank loans officer. Vera is a good worker and has lots of friends. She occasionally sees computer records of her friends' credit cards, some of whom have accumulated huge credit card debts. She has password access to customer account balances in the bank. Vera can identify many accounts that are rarely used, some of them with large positive balances. She is often tempted to make temporary internal transfers of balances (for short periods) from the rarely accessed accounts to her friends' accounts to help them meet their obligations. She thinks that by explaining such transfers as 'computer glitches' she would not be held responsible, particularly as many people in the bank have computer access.

Critically evaluate Vera's plan from an ethical point of view. Who might be disadvantaged if she is successful? How might the bank limit or prevent this type of action?

Accounting and Finance 2B   ISBN 9780170182041   Cengage Learning Australia

Chapter 11

FINANCIAL STATEMENT ANALYSIS

What You Will Learn

After studying this chapter you should be able to:

1 Discuss the information needs of various users in relation to the analysis of financial statements
2 Identity possible sources of external and internal information
3 Explain the significance of profitability and risk in the analysis of financial statements
4 Explain the difference between profitability and liquidity

5 Identify the issues to be considered when choosing a benchmark for ratio analysis
6 Identify and apply various ratios that can be used to assess profitability
7 Identify and apply various ratios that can be used to assess liquidity
8 Identify and apply various ratios that can be used to assess leverage
9 Explain the limitations involved in financial statement analysis

Introduction

In previous chapters we considered the way in which accounting information is produced and what the components of financial statements mean. In this chapter we consider the statements themselves and, more specifically, the ways in which they can be analysed.

Accounting is a process of recording and reporting businesses financial transactions. These can then be used by various people to make decisions about the business. This chapter is not intended to be comprehensive in its approach to financial analysis, but it will offer some guidelines on the subject and provide the reader with some basic tools of analysis. We will consider the analysis of the business in three main areas:

- profitability
- liquidity
- leverage.

AREAS OF BUSINESS ANALYSIS

Profitability is the ability of a business to use its resources (assets) to earn profits.

Liquidity is how easy it is for assets to be changed into cash as part of normal business operations. It also refers to the capacity of a business to pay debts when they become due. In order of liquidity, cash in the bank is very liquid. Inventory is not as liquid, as it has to be sold and then the money collected from the purchaser. Non-current assets are not very liquid, as it usually takes much longer to sell and collect the cash proceeds.

Leverage or *gearing* refers to the way a business has financed its assets – whether it has used the owners' own resources (equity) or borrowed funds (liabilities).

Although we will look at ratios in each area, in reality all the ratios are based on the same financial reports (Income statement and Balance sheet). Therefore, the ratios are interdependent, just as the reports are interdependent and a change in one amount (such as sales) affects other amounts (such as profit, equity and maybe debtors).

USERS' INFORMATION NEEDS

It is important to consider the needs of the person for whom the analysis is being undertaken or, in other words, the user group. By using this approach, it is possible to establish the form of analysis that is most appropriate to these needs. Users include the management of the business, owners, potential owners or investors, creditors, bankers, community interest groups, employees and government regulatory agencies.

Management needs performance management information to check how well the business is performing and plan for future business activities.

Owners use ratio analysis to see how well their investment has performed in the past and make decisions about continuing and further investment in the business.

Potential investors need information that they can use to compare this business with other businesses to see where they might invest their money safely and get the best returns.

Creditors who supply goods and services on credit need to evaluate commercial risk – that the business has the liquidity and profitability to repay outstanding amounts and pay them on time.

Bankers and other finance providers who may lend the business money need to ensure that the loans are secure and that the business has the profitability and liquidity to pay the interest and repay the principle of the loan when they are due.

Community interest groups may want to assess a business to ensure that it has the financial stability to fulfil community expectations, such as environment concerns.

Employees want to work for businesses that have long-term viability to advance their careers and make sure that current and future pay entitlements will be paid.

There are many *government regulatory authorities* that are concerned with a business's current and future financial performance. These include taxation as well as environmental, employee relations, superannuation and safety organisations.

Analysing ratios

When analysing ratios results we need to compare the results with some other benchmark. This may be:

- the same business in a previous time period
- the budget for the same time period
- another business – usually in similar industry
- an average of similar types of businesses, known as *industry average*.

Accounting and Finance: 2B   ISBN 9780170182041   Cengage Learning Australia

Evaluating results

When *evaluating* the results it is important to look at the *rate of change* of the components of the formula and what makes up these components. This will help to explain why a ratio has increased or decreased. Mathematically, all formula consists of:

$$\frac{\text{Numerator}}{\text{Denominator}}$$

For example, an *increase* in the result may be caused by one of the following:

- the numerator increasing at a greater rate than the denominator

Numerator	5	6	20% increase
Denominator	10	10	equal
Result	50%	60%	

- the denominator decreasing at a greater rate than the numerator

Numerator	5	5	Equal
Denominator	10	9	10% decrease
Result	50%	55.5%	

- the numerator increasing at a greater rate than the denominator

Numerator	5	6	20% increase
Denominator	10	11	10% decrease
Result	50%	54.6%	

A decrease in the result may be caused by the opposite of any of the above.

We must also look at the financial statements and see which items that make up the numerator and denominator have changed and evaluate which of these may have caused the ratio to increase or decrease.

If the question asks for an explanation as to why the ratio has changed, students should look at the rate of change in the denominator and numerator. For example:

Gross profit	50000	60000	20%
Net sales	150000	175000	17%
Gross profit ratio	33%	34.3%	

The gross profit ratio has increased, which is *good*, because the gross profit has increased at a greater rate than the rate of increase in net sales.

This would be caused by the change (increase) in the cost of sales being relatively less than the change (increase) in net sales. This may be because the average sale price per unit has increased, the business has been able to obtain a better average purchase price per unit or been able to manage its inventory better.

Although, in this course, students will calculate and interpret the ratios one by one, in reality they are all inter-related as they come from the same set of financial reports. Therefore, a change in one can affect a change in other ratios as well. For example, changes in the *Expense ratio* cause a change in the *Profit ratio*.

As we go through each ratio we will explain if a higher result is better or worse for that business.

PROBLEMS OF WORKING FROM LIMITED DATA

Ratios are only as good as the underlying figures used in their calculation. If the accounting reports have not been prepared properly or there have been differences in accounting methods then the ratios will also be inaccurate. People who use the ratio results in their decision-making may not make the best decision.

Problems in assessing performance and financial position when working from limited data can be influenced by the following factors:

1 Ratios may need to be calculated for a number of years before a trend becomes apparent.

2 It is not always possible to compare ratios between companies as different accounting policies may have been chosen that will affect ratio calculations.

Different accounting policies could be:
- cash or accrual accounting
- balance day adjustments
- different methods of accounting for inventory (perpetual or periodic)
- different methods of inventory valuation (Weighted average or First in first out)
- different depreciation methods (straight line or reducing balance) or rates of depreciation.

3 If only some of the information is on the reports it makes it difficult to calculate some ratios. (For example, public companies are not required to show the Cost of sales in their annual accounting reports, therefore the inventory turnover ratio cannot be calculated.)

4 Ratios need to be compared to a standard to be interpreted. This may be ratios from the current period compared to:
- ratios from another time period (past year) of the same business
- budgeted figures for that business over the same time period
- industry averages for similar types of business
- another business in a similar industry.

5 Ratios do not identify the causes of problems. They are based on financial reports that have already happened. What happened in the past is not always an indicator of what will happen in the future. The gross profit ratio may have fallen from 40 per cent to 30 per cent because of a fall in total sales. However, is the fall in total sales due to poor marketing, competition from other businesses or some other factor?

The current ratio is calculated by using the ending balance sheet data. However, the current ratio obtained from this data may not be typical of the current ratio of the business for much of the year as the current ratio can be improved by paying off the creditors a few days before the end of the financial period.

Example 11.1

EXAMPLE:

To help us learn about ratios we will examine the following business.

Bentley Bookshop
Income statement for the years ended 30 June

	Year 1 $		Year 2 $	
Sales (net)		400 000		500 000
Less Cost of sales				
Opening inventory	50 000		80 000	
Purchases (and purchase costs)	380 000		418 000	
	430 000		498 000	
Closing inventory	80 000		40 000	
Total cost of sales		350 000		458 000
Gross profit		**50 000**		**42 000**
Add other income				
Interest received		1 000		2 000
Proceeds from sale of fixtures		–		1 200

Accounting and Finance 2B   ISBN 9780170182041   Cengage Learning Australia

Total income		51000	45200
Less expenses			
Stationery supplies used	10000		11000
Other expenses	29000		31000
		39000	42000
Profit		$12000	$3200

Bentley Bookshop
Balance sheets as at 30 June

	Year 1 $		Year 2 $	
Current assets				
Cash at bank	4400		–	
Accounts receivables	42000		60000	
Inventory	80000		40000	
Prepayments	2000		5000	
Total current assets		128400		105000
Non-current assets				
Property, plant and equipment	184000		205800	
Investments	6000		16000	
Total non-current assets		190000		221800
Total assets		318400		326800
Less Current liabilities				
Bank overdraft	–		4000	
Accounts payable	26000		40000	
Total current liabilities		26000		44000
Non-current liabilities				
Mortgage	100000		100000	
Total non-current liabilities		100000		100000
Total liabilities		126000		144000
Net assets		192400		182800
Equity				
Capital		192400		182800
Total equity		192400		182800

Other information
Total assets for the previous year was $309200.

PROFITABILITY

Key Concept 11.1

Profitability and profit ratio

Profitability is the ability of a business to use its resources (assets) to earn profits. (It is different from operating profit.) As it is expressed as a percentage, it is easier to compare one result with another.

The profit (margin) ratio measures the amount of operating profit as a percentage of net sales.

Formula 11.1

$$\text{Profit (Margin) ratio} = \frac{\text{Profit}}{\text{Net sales}}$$

The answer is shown as a percentage.

Net sales are gross sales (which include both cash and credit sales) less sales returns. The profit (margin) ratio is considered to be more informative than the amount of operating profit as it is a measure by which we can compare two different accounting periods or businesses. This shows the capacity of a business to control all costs (cost of sales and expenses) compared to its net sales.

Formula	Year 1	Year 2
$\dfrac{\text{Profit (after income tax)} \times 100}{\text{Net revenues}}$	$\dfrac{12\,000 \times 100}{400\,000} = 3.0\%$	$\dfrac{3200 \times 100}{500\,000} = 0.64\%$

Evaluating the results

The profit margin ratio for Bentley Bookshop has decreased, which means the business is earning less profit per sales dollar even though sales are increasing. This is not good.

For this business, profit has decreased while sales have increased by 25 per cent from $400000 to $500000. Both of these elements have caused the ratio to decrease.

Possible reasons for changes in the profit ratio	
Increases	**Decreases**
• Greater rate of increase in profit than the rate of increase in sales	• Greater rate of increase in sales than the rate of increase in profit
• Higher sales prices, expenses constant	• Higher expenses, no increase in sales price
• Increase in volume of sales, no change in purchase prices per unit or other expenses	• Decrease in volume of sales, no change in purchase prices per unit or other expenses
• Decreases in expenses due to better management	• Increases in expenses due to poor management
• Increase in gross profit, expenses constant	• Decrease in gross profit, expenses constant

Formula 11.2

$$\text{Gross profit ratio} = \frac{\text{Gross profit}}{\text{Net sales}}$$

The answer is shown as a percentage.

The *gross profit ratio* measures the amount of profit as a percentage of net sales. This ratio is considered to be more informative than just the amount of gross profit as it is a measure by which we can compare two different accounting periods or businesses. This shows the capacity of a business to control the total cost of sales compared to its net sales. The total cost of sales includes not only purchases but both opening and closing inventory. Other costs relating to cost of purchasing goods for sale, such as customs duty and freight inwards, should be included as part of the cost of sales.

Bentley Bookshop
Income statement (extract) for the years ended 30 June

	Year 1		Year 2	
Sales	404000		503500	
Less Sales returns	4000	400000	3500	500000
Less Costs of sales				
Opening inventory	50000		80000	
Plus purchases	372000		409000	
Customs duty	5000		5500	

Accounting and Finance 2B   ISBN 9780170182041   Cengage Learning Australia

Freight inwards	3 000		3 500	
Subtotal	430 000		498 000	
Less Closing inventory	80 000		40 000	
Total cost of sales		350 000		458 000
Gross profit		50 000		42 000

Formula	Year 1	Year 2
$\dfrac{\text{Gross profit} \times 100}{\text{Net revenues}}$	$\dfrac{50\,000 \times 100}{400\,000} = 12.5\%$	$\dfrac{42\,000 \times 100}{500\,000} = 8.4\%$

The gross profit ratio is decreasing, which means the business is earning less gross profit per sales dollar, even though sales are increasing. This is not good and may be caused by a number of factors. In the example above, gross profit has decreased, while net sales have increased. Both of these changes would cause the ratio to decline.

Possible reasons for changes in the gross profit ratio

Increases	Decreases
• Greater rate of increase in gross profit than the rate of increase in sales	• Greater rate of increase in sales than the rate of increase in gross profit
• Higher sales prices, cost of sales constant	• Higher cost of sales, no increase in sales price
• Increase in volume of sales, no change in purchase prices per unit	• Decrease in volume of sales, no change in purchase prices per unit
• Higher closing stock, causes lower cost of sales, higher gross profit	• Lower closing stock, causes higher cost of sales, lower gross profit
• Decrease in purchase costs, sales constant	• Increase in purchase costs, sales constant
• Selling a higher proportion of higher-margin stock items	• Selling a higher proportion of lower-margin stock items

Formula 11.3

$$\text{Expense ratio} = \frac{\text{Total expenses}}{\text{Net sales}}$$

The answer is shown as a percentage.

The *expense ratio* measures the amount of expense as a percentage of net sales. This ratio is considered to be more informative than the amount of total operating expenses as it is a measure by which we can compare two different accounting periods or businesses. This shows the capacity of a business to control all expenses compared to its net sales.

Formula	Year 1	Year 2
$\dfrac{\text{Total expenses} \times 100}{\text{Net sales}}$	$\dfrac{39\,000 \times 100}{400\,000} = 9.75\%$	$\dfrac{42\,000 \times 100}{500\,000} = 8.4\%$

The expense ratio is decreasing, which means the business is incurring fewer expenses per sales dollar, even though sales are increasing. This is good.

Possible reasons for changes in the expense ratio

Increases	Decreases
• Greater rate of increase in expenses than the rate of increase in sales	• Greater rate of increase in expenses than the rate of increase in sales
• Higher sales prices, expenses constant	• Higher expenses, no increase in sales price
• Increase in volume of sales, no change in expenses per unit	• Decrease in volume of sales, no change in expenses per unit
• Lower closing stock, causes higher cost of sales, lower gross profit and profit	• Higher closing stock, causes lower cost of sales, higher gross profit and profit

Accounting and Finance: 2B   ISBN 9780170182041   Cengage Learning Australia

Formula 11.4

$$\text{Rate of return on assets ratio} = \frac{\text{Profit}}{\text{Average total assets}}$$

The answer is shown as a percentage:

Average total assets = (this year's total assets + last year's total assets) divided by 2

The *rate of return on assets* measures the profit of the business as a percentage of average total assets. It shows how effective the use of these assets has been in earning profit. Average assets can be calculated as the assets owned at the beginning of the year plus assets at the end of the year divided by two. If the *rate of return on assets* is greater than the *rate of interest on a loan*, then it may be worthwhile to borrow funds to expand business operations.

Formula	Year 1	Year 2
$\dfrac{\text{Operating profit}}{\text{Average total assets}}$	$\dfrac{12\,000 \times 100}{(309\,200 + 318\,400)/2} = 3.82\%$	$\dfrac{3\,200 \times 100}{(318\,400 + 326\,800)/2} = 1.0\%$

For Bentley Bookshop the rate of return on assets has decreased, which is not good. It means the operating profit has decreased while the average total assets have increased. This business could not justify borrowing money to fund further assets until it has improved its profits.

Possible reasons for changes in the rate of return on assets ratio	
Increases	**Decreases**
• Greater rate of increase in profit than the rate of increase in average total assets	• Greater rate of increase in average total assets than the rate of increase in profit
• Higher sales, expenses constant, assets used constant	• Higher amount of assets, profit steady or declining
• Increase in profit as explained above	• Decrease in profit as explained above

LIQUIDITY RATIOS

Liquidity ratios assist in assessing the business's ability to meet its financial commitments in both the short and long term.

Working capital ratio

Formula 11.5

$$\text{Working capital ratio} = \frac{\text{Current assets}}{\text{Current liabilities}}$$

The answer is shown as a percentage or as a ratio.

The working capital ratio measures the capacity of a business to pay its short-term debts over the next 12 months using its current assets. The current ratio can be improved by paying off creditors just before the balance date. The ideal ratio is greater than 1:1 but preferably less than approximately 2:1. The items that make up current assets do not earn any income (0%), so if the ratio is more than 2:1, although the business would be very liquid, it indicates a 'lost opportunity' to invest more of the surplus in income earning investments.

Formula	Year 1	Year 2
$\dfrac{\text{Current assets}}{\text{Current liabilities}}$	$\dfrac{128\,400}{26\,000} = 493\%$	$\dfrac{105\,000}{44\,000} = 238\%$

This means that for every dollar of liabilities the business has $2.38 (4.93) in assets to pay the amount. The liquidity has decreased as the rate of increase in current liabilities is

Accounting and Finance 2B   ISBN 9780170182041   Cengage Learning Australia

greater than the rate of increase in current assets. Although the ratio has decreased, there are still adequate liquid assets to meet known liabilities due in the next 12 months. Both years represent a 'lost opportunity' to invest surplus current assets in income-earning non-current assets. The business should try to reduce accounts receivable and inventory to improve this ratio.

Possible reasons for changes in the working capital ratio	
Increases	**Decreases**
• Greater rate of increase in current assets than the rate of increase in current liabilities • Higher cash at bank, inventory accounts receivable and current liabilities constant • Just before balance date using cash at bank to pay off creditors or GST summary	• Greater rate of increase in current liabilities than the rate of increase in current assets • Current assets constant but creditors, accrued expenses, GST collections and short-term loans increasing • Leaving excess amounts owing to creditors

Quick asset ratio

Formula 11.6

$$\text{Quick asset ratio} = \frac{\text{Current assets less inventory and prepayments}}{\text{Current liabilities less bank overdraft}}$$

The answer is shown as a percentage or as a ratio.

The quick asset ratio is also known as the *liquid* or *acid test ratio*. This is a modified form of the current ratio. It measures the capacity of the business to pay its liabilities in the short term, usually in the next month or two, using quickly available assets. From the current assets inventory and prepayments are excluded. As stock is sold, it will be replaced by new stock and it is therefore difficult in the short term to reduce the overall amount. Prepayments are excluded because although a current asset, the money has already been paid out and is therefore not available to help pay liabilities. The bank overdraft is excluded from the total current liabilities because, under a normal agreement with the bank, as long as the business keeps under the maximum overdraft limit, it does not have to be repaid in the next one to three months.

Year 1	Year 2
$\dfrac{128\,400 - 80\,000 - 2000}{26\,000} = 178\%$	$\dfrac{105\,000 - 40\,000 - 5000}{44\,000 - 4000} = 150\%$

This means that the business does have sufficient 'quick' assets to pay its immediate liabilities. The ratio has decreased from the first year to the second, indicating that the business's liquidity is decreasing, which, although adequate, is a trend that is not good.

Possible reasons for changes in the quick asset ratio	
Increases	**Decreases**
• Greater rate of increase in quick assets than the rate of increase in short-term liabilities • Higher cash at bank and inventory accounts receivable and current liabilities constant • Just before balance date using cash at bank to pay off creditors or GST summary	• Greater rate of increase in short-term liabilities than the rate of increase in quick assets • Current assets constant but creditors, accrued expenses, GST collections and short-term loans increasing • Leaving excess amounts owing to creditors

Key Concept 11.2

Liquidity essential to a business

The single biggest requirement of an operating business is to maintain adequate liquidity to meet its financial obligations as they fall due.

Accounting and Finance: 2B   ISBN 9780170182041   Cengage Learning Australia

LEVERAGE RATIO

Key Concept 11.3

Debt as a form of funding

For businesses to operate and grow they need funding, not all of which is possible from equity capital. Borrowing money for business purposes is financially responsible. However, borrowing too much increases the financial risk and quickly leads to loss of liquidity and profitability.

Debt to equity ratio

Formula 11.7

$$\text{Debt to equity} = \frac{\text{Total liabilities}}{\text{Total equity}}$$

The answer is shown as a percentage.

The *debt to equity ratio* measures how the business has funded its assets by comparing the total liabilities to the amount of contributed equity. This ratio measures gearing – the greater the company relies on borrowed funds, the less financially safe it is. If the profit decreases or the costs of borrowing increase this will put added pressure on the business's financial stability. If a company's liabilities exceed equity it starts to become highly geared. Some companies have liabilities as high as 95 per cent of assets with only five per cent of equity, but these are highly risky financially. (See the section dealing with sources of finance in Chapter 1.)

Formula	Year 1	Year 2
Total liabilities / Equity (end)	$\frac{126\,000 \times 100}{192\,400} = 65.5\%$	$\frac{144\,000 \times 100}{182\,800} = 78.8\%$

Bentley Bookshop's debt to equity ratio has increased, which is not good, although it is still not highly geared. However, the increase in gearing is not a good trend. In modern business practice if a business could only rely on owner's capital and retained earnings to expand, its growth would be limited. Borrowing money helps a business grow. However, borrowing too much increases the business's financial risk. When a business's debt to equity ratio exceeds 100 per cent it begins to be heading into a financially riskier situation. See also the rate of return on assets to evaluate if a loan is viable.

Possible reasons for changes in the debt to equity ratio	
Increases	Decreases
• Greater rate of increase in total liabilities than the rate of increase in total equity	• Greater rate of increase in total equity than the rate of increase in total liabilities
• Higher drawings relative to profit, reducing equity	• Higher profits and relatively lower drawings

SUMMARY

Ratio	Simple interpretation	If ratio is increasing:	If ratio is decreasing:	Caused by changes in:
Profit	The bigger the more profitable	Profit is increasing at a **higher** rate than the rate of increase in net sales	Profit is increasing at a **lower** rate than the rate of increase in net sales	Sale price Sale volume Purchase price Inventory Expenses
Gross profit	The bigger the more profitable	Gross profit is increasing at a **higher** rate than the rate of increase in net sales	Gross profit is increasing at a **lower** rate than the rate of increase in net sales	Sale price Sale volume Purchase price Inventory

Accounting and Finance 2B   ISBN 9780170182041   Cengage Learning Australia

Expense	The smaller the better	Expenses are increasing at a **higher** rate than the rate of increase in net sales	Expenses are increasing at a **lower** rate than the rate of increase in net sales	Sales Expenses
Working capital	The bigger the more financially safer	Current assets are increasing at a **higher** rate than the rate of increase in Current liabilities	Current assets are increasing at a **lower** rate than the rate of increase in Current liabilities	Cash Debtors Creditors Inventory Balance day adjustments
Quick asset	The bigger the more financially safer	Current assets are increasing at a **higher** rate than the rate of increase in Current liabilities	Current assets are increasing at a **lower** rate than the rate of increase in Current liabilities	Cash Debtors Creditors Inventory Accruals
Debt to equity	The smaller the more financially stable	Liabilities are increasing at a **higher** rate than the rate of increase in Equity	Liabilities are increasing at a **lower** rate than the rate of increase in Equity	Creditors Loans Bank overdraft Capital Drawings Profit

Test your knowledge

1 Explain some of the limitations of using ratio analysis to evaluate financial statements.

2 Evaluating financial statements usually requires a comparison of two or more sets of statements. What are the different types of financial statement that can be used for comparison?

3 What is meant by the terms liquidity, profitability and leverage?

4 Which ratios would you use to evaluate a firm's profitability?

5 What ratios would you use to evaluate a business's liquidity?

6 What is the purpose of using ratio analysis?

7 What ratio would you prepare to assess a business's financial stability?

8 If interest rates were to increase, which ratios would this effect?

9 Explain the difference between profit and profitability.

10 Explain the difference between liquidity and profitability.

Test your understanding

Topic guide
- Profit margin: 11.1–11.5
- Gross profit: 11.1–11.5
- Expense: 11.1–11.5
- Return on assets: 11.6–11.8
- Current ratio: 11.9–11.11
- Quick ratio: 11.12
- Debt/equity: 11.13–11.16
- All ratios: 11.17–11.20

Accounting and Finance 2B   ISBN 9780170182041   Cengage Learning Australia

11.1 Adventure Catering provided the following income statements:

Adventure Catering Income statements for the years ended

	30/6/09 $	30/6/10 $
Sales	220 000	240 000
Less Cost of sales	124 000	127 000
Gross profit	96 000	113 000
Less Expenses	55 000	67 000
Operating profit	41 000	46 000

Required
a   Calculate the profit (margin) ratios for each of the years.
b   Explain whether or not the business has improved its operations from 2009 to 2010.
c   Suggest reasons why the ratios have changed.

11.2 Beijing Bicycles provided the following income statements:

Beijing Bicycles Income statements for the years ended

	30/6/09 $	30/6/10 $
Sales	356 000	428 000
Less Cost of sales	187 000	196 000
Gross profit		
Less Expenses	85 000	46 000
Operating profit		

Required
a   Calculate the gross profit and operating profit for each year.
b   Calculate the profit margin ratios for each of the years.
c   Explain whether or not the business has improved its operations from 2009 to 2010.
d   Suggest reasons why the ratios have changed.

11.3 Albany Art Supplies provided the following income statements:

Albany Art Supplies Income statement for the years ended

	30/6/09 $	30/6/10 $
Sales	130 000	140 000
Less Cost of sales	87 000	109 000
Gross profit	43 000	31 000
Less Expenses	21 000	24 000
Operating profit	22 000	7 000

Required
a   Calculate the gross profit ratios for each of the years.
b   Explain whether or not the business has improved its operations from 2009 to 2010.
c   Suggest reasons why the ratios have changed.

11.4 Brookton Brakes provided the following income statements:

Brookton Brakes Income statement for the years ended

	Budget $	Actual $
Sales	67 000	74 000
Less Cost of sales	46 000	49 000

Accounting and Finance: 2B   ISBN 9780170182041   Cengage Learning Australia

Gross profit		
Less Expenses	14000	15000
Operating profit		

Required

a Calculate the gross profit and operating profit for each year.

b Calculate the expense ratios for the budget and actual results.

c Explain whether the business has improved its actual operations compared to its budgeted projections.

d Suggest reasons why the ratios have changed.

11.5 A client has asked you to help them make a decision about which of these two businesses has the better profitability.

Income statements for the year ended 30 June 2012

	Carnamah Cycles $	Coorow Cycles $
Sales	67000	77000
Less Cost of sales		
Gross profit	21000	30000
Less Expenses		
Operating profit	5000	13000

Required

a Calculate the cost of sales and the expense for each year

b Calculate the gross profit ratios for both businesses.

c Calculate the profit (margin) ratios for both businesses.

d Calculate the expense ratios for each of the years.

e Explain whether the business has improved its actual operations compared to its budgeted projections.

f Suggest reasons why the ratios have changed.

11.6 Calculate return on assets ratios from the following data:

	2013 $	2014 $	2015 $
Operating profit	4000	5000	7000
Total assets	46000	47000	48000

Required

a Calculate the return on assets ratios for the years ended 2014 and 2015.

b Explain whether the business improved its profitability from 2014 to 2015.

c Suggest reasons why the ratios have changed.

d If the bank is prepared to give a loan at 11 per cent per annum is it a good idea for the firm to borrow in order to purchase more assets?

11.7 Calculate return on assets ratios from the following data:

	2016 $	2017 $	2018 $
Operating profit	6000	7000	8000
Total assets	66000	57000	68000

Accounting and Finance 2B ISBN 9780170182041 Cengage Learning Australia

Required
a   Calculate the return on assets ratios for the years ended 2017 and 2018.
b   Explain whether the business has improved its profitability from 2017 to 2018.
c   Suggest reasons why the ratios have changed.
d   Is the trend of profitability for this business increasing or decreasing?

11.8   Analyse the following return on assets ratio data:

	2013 $	2014 $	2015 $
Sales	20000	22000	
Less Expenses	16000		18000
Operating profit		5000	7000
Total equity	26000	28000	27000
Total liabilities	20000	19000	
Total assets	46000		48000

Required
a   Complete the table above by calculating the missing figures.
b   Calculate the return on assets ratios for the years ended 2014 and 2015.
c   Explain whether the business has improved its profitability from 2014 to 2015.
d   Suggest reasons why the ratios have changed.
e   If the bank is prepared to give a loan at 11 per cent per annum is it a good idea for the firm to borrow in order to purchase more assets?

11.9   The owners of the Bunjil Bakery have provided the following information:

	Budget $	Actual $
Current assets		
Cash at bank	2000	
Accounts receivable	14000	12000
Less Provision for doubtful debts	(100)	(200)
Inventory	6000	7000
Current liabilities		
Bank overdraft	–	1900
Accounts payable	19000	17000

Required
The owners have asked for you to calculate the current ratio for both the budget and actual results and to comment on whether the firm's actual liquidity has improved compared to what was planned. Why has the actual liquidity changed?

11.10   The owners of Morawa Motors have provided the following information:

	30/6/09 $	30/6/10 $
Current assets	120000	130000
Current liabilities	97000	109000

The average current ratio for this type of business is 150 per cent.

Required
a   Calculate the current ratio for each year.
b   Comment on whether or not the business's liquidity has improved and how the business compares to the industry average.

Accounting and Finance 2B   ISBN 9780170182041   Cengage Learning Australia

11.11 The following information belongs to a local business

Badgingarra Builders
Balance sheets as at 30 June 2010

	Budget $		Actual $	
Current assets				
Cash at bank			11000	
Accounts receivables	13000		25000	
Inventory	16000		17000	
Prepayments	2500		2700	
Total current assets		31500		55700
Current liabilities				
Bank overdraft	1300			
Accounts payable	26000		32000	
Accrued expenses	2900		4800	
Total current liabilities		30200		36800

Required
a   Calculate the quick asset ratio comparing the budget to the actual result.
b   Comment on whether or not the business's liquidity has improved.

11.12 The following information belongs to a local business

Caron Cartage Contractors
Balance sheets as at 30 June

	2009 $		2010 $	
Current assets				
Cash at bank			12000	
Accounts receivable	12000		30000	
Inventory	15000		13000	
GST outlays	2000		2000	
Total current assets		29000		57000
Non-current assets				
Property, plant and equipment	84000		102000	
Investments	4000		6000	
Total non-current assets		88000		108000
Total assets		117000		165000
Less current liabilities				
Bank overdraft	1200			
Accounts payable	25000		33000	
GST collections	2000		6000	
Total current liabilities		28200		39000
Non-current liabilities				
Loan	70000		80000	
Total non-current liabilities		70000		80000
Total liabilities		98200		119000
Net assets		18800		46000

Accounting and Finance 2B   ISBN 9780170182041   Cengage Learning Australia

Required

a   Calculate the current ratio for both years.

b   Calculate the quick asset for both years.

c   Explain whether the change in the ratios indicates that the business's liquidity has improved.

d   What would be the change in the ratios for 2010 if the business paid off the net amount owing for GST?

e   What would be the change in the ratios for 2010 if the business paid off $10000 owing to accounts payable?

11.13 The owners of Northampton Nurseries provided the following information.

	30/6/09 $	30/6/10 $
Total assets	130000	140000
Total liabilities	63000	89000
Total equity	67000	51000

The average debt to equity ratio for this type of business is 150 per cent.

Required

a   Calculate the debt to equity ratio for each year.

b   Comment on whether or not the business's gearing has improved and how the business compares to the industry average.

11.14 The owners of Perenjori Party Planners provided the following information.

	30/6/09 $	30/6/10 $
Total liabilities	89000	94000
Total equity	77000	65000

The average debt to equity ratio for this type of business is 130 per cent.

Required

a   Calculate the debt to equity ratio for each year.

b   Comment on whether or not the business's gearing has improved and how the business compares to the industry average.

11.15 The owners of Broome Bus Lines provided the following information.

	30/6/19 $	30/6/20 $
Total assets	630000	740000
Total liabilities	265000	
Total equity		152000

The average debt to equity ratio for this type of business is 125 per cent.

Required

a   Complete the table showing total equity and total liabilities.

b   Calculate the debt to equity ratio for each year.

c   Comment on whether or not the business's gearing has improved and how the business compares to the industry average.

11.16 If net sales changed and all other amounts stayed constant, what would be the effect on the following ratios (an increase or decrease)?

Ratio	Increase in sales	Decrease in sales
Profit		
Gross profit ratio		
Expense		

Accounting and Finance 2B   ISBN 9780170182041   Cengage Learning Australia

Return on assets			
Current ratio			
Quick assets ratio			
Debt to equity			

11.17 The following financial statements for the business of Cookies and Cakes are shown below:

Cookies and Cakes
Income statement for the year ended 30 June 2014

	$	$	$
Sales income			90000
Proceeds of sale of assets			18000
Cost of sales:			
Opening inventory	48000		
Purchases	56000		
	104000		
Closing inventory	56000	48000	
Depreciation		9000	
Interest paid		1200	
Other expenses		43800	(102000)
Profit			$6000

Comparative balance sheets as at June

	2014	2013
Accounts receivable	17000	$14000
Accumulated depreciation – buildings	(5000)	(3000)
Accumulated depreciation – sales equipment	(15000)	(9000)
Buildings	60000	60000
Cash at bank	$9000	–
Equipment	36000	30000
Inventory	56000	48000
Land	20000	40000
	$178000	$180000

	2014	2013
Accounts payable	26000	24000
Bank overdraft	–	10000
Capital	152000	146000
	$178000	$180000

Required

A Cheff, the owner of Cookies and Cakes, had been concerned about the size of the bank overdraft at the beginning of the year. Having examined the financial statements of the business, he asked you to comment on the firm's rate of return on assets and to evaluate any alterations in the working capital and liquidity of the business. Calculate the following ratios and comment briefly on the items mentioned by J Cheff:

a working capital/current ratio
b quick asset ratio
c debt to equity ratio
d rate of return on assets.

Accounting and Finance: 2B   ISBN 9780170182041   Cengage Learning Australia

11.18 The summarised Income statement of Valentines Vineyards for the years ended 30 June 2009 and 30 June 2010 are shown below.

	2010	2009
Sales (net)	170000	150000
Less Cost of sales	75000	68000
Gross profit	95000	82000
Less Operating expenses	32000	25000
Profit	63000	57000

Extracts from the Balance sheets are shown below.

	2010	2009
Current assets	25000	20000
Current liabilities	18000	18000
Non-current assets	105000	102000
Non-current liabilities	62000	55000

Prepayments	5000	4000
Bank overdraft	1500	–
Inventory	7000	6000

Required

Calculate the following ratios for the year ended 30 June 2010 by completing the table below:

Ratio	Ratio formulae	Industry average	2010
Gross profit ratio	$\dfrac{\text{Gross profit}}{\text{Net sales}}$	54.66%	
Profit ratio	$\dfrac{\text{Profit}}{\text{Net sales}}$	38%	
Expense ratio	$\dfrac{\text{Total expenses}}{\text{Net sales}}$	16.66%	
Rate of return on assets ratio	$\dfrac{\text{Profit}}{\text{Average total assets}}$	34%	
Working capital ratio	$\dfrac{\text{Current assets}}{\text{Current liabilities}}$	156%	
Quick asset ratio	$\dfrac{\text{CA – inventory and prepayments}}{\text{CL – bank overdraft}}$	120%	
Debt to equity ratio	$\dfrac{\text{Total liabilities}}{\text{Total equity}}$	15%	

Analyse the changes in the profitability, liquidity and leverage of Valentines Vineyards for the 12 months ended 30 June 2010, using the information provided in the question and the ratios as calculated above.

11.19 Palomino's Riding Academy was started by Chris Palomino on 1 July 2010 with capital of $60000. The business has been going well and he now wants to expand by borrowing an additional $90000 at ten per cent per annum to buy some stables.

Accounting and Finance 2B   ISBN 9780170182041   Cengage Learning Australia

The following has been extracted from his business reports for each of the years ended 30 June:

	2012	2011
Current liabilities	50000	50000
Non-current loan	100000	-
Owner's equity	60000	60000
Total liabilities and equity	$210000	$110000
Profit before interest	50000	22000
Less Mortgage interest	12000	-
Profit to owner	38000	22000
Sales	230000	110000

Required

a Based on the information available, calculate Chris's profitability and leverage/gearing for both of the years 2011 and 2012.

b Explain the results of these ratio calculations to Chris and advise him of the risks involved in his plan to borrow a further $90000.

11.20 Sunrise Ballooning needs your help in evaluating its business. It has had difficulty in effectively managing its working capital. It also has experienced declining sales. Below is information extracted from Balance sheets and Income statements for the past three years.

Income statement

	2014	2013	2012
Sales (all credit)	895000	1050000	1200000
Cost of sales	535000	630000	720000
Gross profit			
Less Expenses	224000	217000	325000
Operating profit			

Balance sheet

	2014	2013	2012
Current assets			
Accounts receivable	181000	182000	206000
Inventory	95000	77000	70000
Prepaid expenses	2500	1500	2800
Current liabilities			
Bank overdraft	98000	62000	35000
Accounts payable	235000	195000	176000
Accrued expenses	35000	28000	30000
Total assets	1200000	1340000	1287000
Total liabilities	567000	489000	497000
Net assets			

Accounting and Finance 2B   ISBN 9780170182041   Cengage Learning Australia

Calculate the following ratios using the information on the previous page.

Ratio	Formula	2014	2013	2012
Gross profit ratio	$\dfrac{\text{Gross profit}}{\text{Net sales}}$			
Expense ratio	$\dfrac{\text{Expenses}}{\text{Net sales}}$			
Profit ratio	$\dfrac{\text{Profit}}{\text{Net sales}}$			
Working capital ratio	$\dfrac{\text{Current assets}}{\text{Current liabilities}}$			
Quick asset ratio	$\dfrac{\text{CA} - \text{inventory and prepayments}}{\text{CL} - \text{bank overdraft}}$			

Required

a   Complete the above statement by calculating the missing figures.
b   Calculate the above ratio for each year (correct to two decimal places).
c   Explain the general purpose of each ratio. (What does each ratio measure?)
d   Evaluate the information provided by all the ratios calculated over the past three years by explaining what the ratios reveal about Sunrise Ballooning's profitability and liquidity situation.

Essay

Courtney Jones has just inherited a large sum of money and wants your advice on some investment options. He has heard about using ratios to help analyse a business's financial statements, but does not understand what this means.

   Explain the purpose of ratio analysis, including:
- the difference between liquidity and profitability
- what ratios he could use to measure profitability, liquidity and leverage
- any limitations he should be aware of in using ratio analysis.

Ethics case study

Vern Dodgy is a businessman who runs a second hand goods business. Much of his trading is in cash. He keeps his financial records in a shoe box and gets his friend to prepare financial reports to show his business is profitable and financially stable. At the end of each financial year he writes out cheques to pay GST and other creditors so it appears he has fewer current liabilities. He does his own stocktakes. He prepares one set of financial statements for the tax department, in which he adjusts the closing inventory and only does balance day adjustments if they help lower his taxable profit. He does another set of financial statements to show his bank. In these he adjusts his closing inventory and only uses those balance day adjustments that will show the best profit. He also includes as business expenses as many household costs as he can. He regards his drawings as wages from the business. Vern argues that paying less tax is allowed and because these adjustments are usually non-cash and they help his overall business they should be acceptable.

   Discuss Vern's business practices. How could ratio analysis help end users evaluate businesses like Vern's? What limitations are there on evaluating businesses using ratios?

Chapter 12

PROFESSIONAL ACCOUNTABILITY

What You Will Learn

After studying this chapter you should be able to:

1   Identify professional codes of conduct for accounting practitioners and financial service providers

2   Explain the role and function of the professional accounting and finance associations

3   Explain the nature and purpose of codes of conducts

Introduction

This chapter examines the role and function that accounting and financial service provider professional associations play in enhancing the professions they represent, assisting the individuals they cater for and how they interact in society. We will explore these associations and see how they play a vital role in society and, in particular, the business community. Of specific interest will be the nature and purpose of codes of conduct that apply to their members. We will examine the general focus of these codes of conduct and how they protect the rights of consumers and outline the responsibilities of accounting and financial service provider members.

THE FINANCE INDUSTRY

An examination of the finance industry will show that there is a wide range of financial services and products available from a variety of differing institutions, such as banks, credit societies, insurance companies, superannuation companies, brokers and financial planning and accounting firms. Financial decisions, like all other decisions, are rarely made in isolation. Decision-makers seek information to support their actions. Just as a sportsperson may be trained and advised by a coach, so may a potential investor seek out an expert for guidance in financial matters.

An examination of the finance industry will also highlight the requirement for financial advisors to be licensed under Australian law. The required licence has the intent of producing more confidence in the operation of the financial sector. Financial service providers can also gain credibility by membership of professional associations.

Financial markets are an integral feature of all economies and perform the vital function of facilitating the distribution of capital by bringing together borrowers and lenders. Financial markets are used by participants to either raise funds (e.g. by issuing securities or borrowing) or to invest savings (by buying securities and other financial assets).

The major markets in the Australian financial system include the capital markets (shares and bonds), the money market and the derivatives market. There are also other markets in the financial systems that facilitate the trading of specific financial products, such as the national electricity market.

There are various careers for those who operate in the financial market sectors, ranging from accountants, stockbrokers and bank managers to insurance advisors and general financial advisors.

Financial services providers and investment choices

With a sophisticated, varied and dynamic financial industry, Australian individuals and businesses have considerable choice in making investment decisions. Individuals and businesses need to exercise care in seeking financial services – from bank credit cards to retirement packages. They should compare products available, seek broad advice, ensure service providers are trained, competent and experienced and ensure that service providers belong to professional associations and follow and apply an identified code of ethics.

Occasionally financial choices turn sour. Many factors can be involved, including economic turbulence, greed, corruption, excessive risk and failures in ethical and professional practice. Investors and borrowers are in a more vulnerable position as they generally enter financial transactions or contracts with limited knowledge of products, services and information. Therefore they require protection. All financial service providers must have a licence to operate and there are laws that govern many aspects of the finance industry.

Accounting and Finance: 2B   ISBN 9780170182041   Cengage Learning Australia

LEGAL FRAMEWORK FOR FINANCIAL ADVISORS IN AUSTRALIA

The *Australian Financial Services Reform Act 2001* clarifies the licensing rules and disclosure requirements for financial advisors, particularly in relation to banking, superannuation, securities, insurance and funds management. The legislation provides some protection for users of information. Since 2001 every person or organisation who engages in the activities shown in Figure 12.1 requires an Australian Financial Services licence.

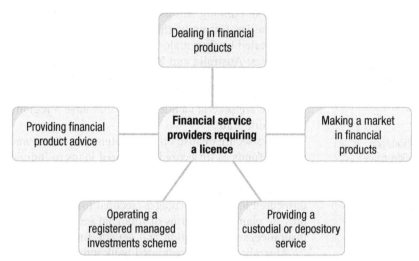

Figure 12.1 Licensed financial service providers

This licence requires that accountants and financial advisors work within a framework of integrity, objectivity, honesty, truthfulness, independence, fairness and reliability. The main objectives of the Act (Chapter 760A) are listed in Figure 12.2.

In Australia, the financial services sector is regulated by the Australian Securities and Investments Commission (ASIC). The Act states, for example, that stockbrokers need to gain specific accreditation, including a university degree in finance or commerce, in order to trade on behalf of clients. Stockbrokers also require extensive experience in the financial services sector.

Many other parts of the finance industry are regulated in some way. The banks are regulated by the Australian Prudential Regulatory Authority (APRA). APRA is responsible for regulating much of the financial industry, including insurance and superannuation companies. There is also the Reserve Bank, which is an Australian government body exercising the authority of a central bank with the major role of ensuring the stability of the Australian financial system.

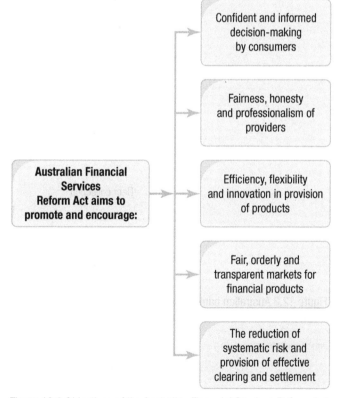

Figure 12.2 Objectives of the Australian Financial Services Reform Act

Accounting and Finance 2B   ISBN 9780170182041   Cengage Learning Australia

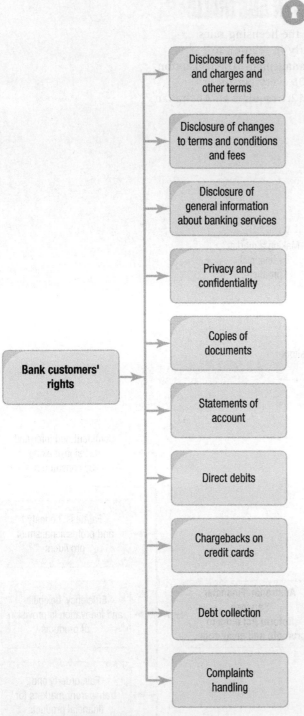

Bank customers' rights

- Disclosure of fees and charges and other terms
- Disclosure of changes to terms and conditions and fees
- Disclosure of general information about banking services
- Privacy and confidentiality
- Copies of documents
- Statements of account
- Direct debits
- Chargebacks on credit cards
- Debt collection
- Complaints handling

Figure 12.3 Australian bank customers' rights

Key Concept 12.1

Regulation of the financial services sector

The financial services sector is regulated by the Australian Securities and Investments Commission (ASIC) and the Australian Prudential Regulatory Authority (APRA).

Bankers

A career in banking will provide a wide variety of job opportunities. Currently, the Australian banking sector is dominated by four major banks operating as public companies: Australia and New Zealand Banking Group, Commonwealth Bank of Australia, National Australia Bank and Westpac Banking Corporation.

There are several smaller banks that have a regional base in one state.

Banks secure deposits paying interest to clients and provide funds as unsecured or secured loans to individuals (personal and mortgage housing loans) and businesses.

Bank finance may be in the form of overdrafts, unsecured loans or mortgages (secured loans). Banks provide many other forms of financial services, including insurance, superannuation and general financial advice.

Australia has a de-regulated bank industry and there are a number of foreign subsidiary banks. However, only a few have a retail banking presence and foreign banks have a more significant presence in the Australian merchant banking sector.

Banking industry association

The Australian Financial Markets Association (AFMA) is the peak industry association for Australia's wholesale banking and financial markets. These markets play a pivotal role in the Australian economy by making it possible for Australian financial institutions and companies to conduct business with each other and with their counterparts overseas.

AFMA represents over 130 industry participants in the wholesale banking and financial markets, including Australian and foreign banks, securities companies, state government treasury corporations, fund managers, traders in electricity and other specialised markets and industry service providers.

All banks in Australia endorse the Australian Banking Association Code of Banking Practice giving customers rights that the bank must observe.

Bank customers have a number of rights under the Australian Banking Code (see Figure 12.3). Further details can be found in the Australian Bankers website.

Banking products and services that are covered by the Code are those provided to individuals and small business customers. Examples are shown in Figure 12.4.

Insurance

Insurance companies are common in the Australian financial industry. The services and products available are usually well defined and the relationship between the service provider and the clients reasonably transparent. Insurance companies provide their customers with cover against the financial consequences of specified events in return for a payment, usually called a *premium*.

Given the wide range of risks covered by insurance policies and the huge amount of premiums paid, the insurance sector is a very significant part of the finance industry. Insurance provides cover over assets and revenue, protection against liability and personnel protection. Examples of insurance include business loss of income, burglary, fire, life insurance, transit insurance, vehicle cover, product liability and workers compensation.

Insurance companies are regulated by APRA.

Superannuation

Australia has a compulsory employer-contributed superannuation scheme. All employers are required to contribute an additional nine per cent of each employee's gross wage or salary into a superannuation fund. In addition, many people, or their employers on their behalf, make voluntary contributions into superannuation to provide for their old age. The superannuation industry in Australia manages billions of dollars in managed accounts. The sector provides a wide range of finance careers.

This industry is also regulated by APRA.

Deposit and transaction accounts

Safe custody facilities

Personal and home loans

Services covered by the Australian banking code

Small business loans

Credit cards and debit cards

Investment loans

Lease financing

Figure 12.4 Services covered by the Australian Banking Code

Financial planners

In recent years financial planners have provided services ranging from salary sacrificing, investment in property development and self-managed superannuation funds to complex share investment schemes and retirement plans.

Financial planners are regulated by the ASIC, which requires all financial planners to have an Australian Financial Services Licence (AFSL).

Brokers

Brokers manage investments for clients. Such clients can be individuals or companies and other large organisations. Brokers offer three different types of service:

- discretionary – managing clients' investments and making decisions on their behalf
- advisory – advising clients about various investment options
- 'execution only' – buying and selling only on the client's instructions without giving advice.

Brokers may specialise in one type of service or offer all three. Across all types of service, brokers would be:

- managing and reviewing clients' investment portfolios
- researching financial markets (working closely with investment analysts who report on how companies and markets are performing)
- answering clients' questions
- keeping clients informed about their investments
- instructing stock market traders to achieve the best market prices
- providing market services to new clients.

In larger companies, brokers specialise in investing in certain markets, such as technology or finance, or in specific regions. Brokers who work for private individual clients may be known as investment managers or wealth managers.

The regulator in action!

ASIC bans broker in rumour crackdown

The corporate regulator has taken its first scalp in its crackdown against spreading false market rumours but has also admitted it does not have all the powers needed to combat the behaviour. The Australian Securities and Investment Commission has banned Richard Macphillamy, of Bondi in Sydney, from providing financial services advice for 18 months after finding he wrote and widely distributed an email falsely claiming that Macquarie Group was struggling to meet withdrawal requests from its cash management trust …

Source: *Australian Financial Review*, 24 March 2009.

LEGAL FRAMEWORK FOR ACCOUNTANTS IN AUSTRALIA

Accountants are required by provisions of taxation law to be licensed with the Tax Agents Registration Board (a government body) if they are to act as tax agents. This enables them to deal with the taxation affairs of individuals or companies, including preparing and submitting annual taxation returns on their behalf. As indicated previously, if an accountant is to act as a financial planner they must have an Australian Financial Services Licence to provide professional advice. Those who wish to be an external company auditor must register with ASIC to undertake auditing of companies. The latter is governed by the *Corporations Act 2001*.

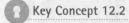 Key Concept 12.2

Regulation of accountants

Accountants are subject to legislative control in their roles as:

- tax agents
- financial advisors
- external auditors.

ACCOUNTANTS AS PROVIDERS OF FINANCIAL SERVICES

Accountants are well known and recognised in the role of providers and communicators of financial information and as financial advisers. Accountants have specialised skills and they are trained to act in informed and professional ways within an ethical framework. Accountants belong to professional associations that provide educational training and services, social activity and legal guidance and their associations have the power to ban members from the profession should they breach ethical standards. The largest providers of accounting services in Australia include Deloittes Touche Tomatsu, Ernst Young, KPMG and Pricewaterhouse Coopers. RSM Bird Cameron is a well-known Western Australian accounting business.

Figure 12.5 Accountants' areas of expertise

Accountants provide expertise in area such as:

- audits – independently examining a business's financial records, processes and reports in order to form an opinion on whether due accounting processes have been followed and whether the information is a true and fair view of the business's financial performance and position
- external reporting – reporting on the financial information of a business to users who may use such information in applying their scarce resources
- insolvency – assisting businesses experiencing trading difficulties, such as liquidity or profitability problems
- taxation – assisting businesses to comply with taxation legislation (accountants specialise in these areas of taxation demands and reporting requirements)
- financial planning – accountants may provide services such as budgeting, investment, mergers, takeovers, deceased estates, leasing and technology systems
- management accounting – promoting business profitability through systems quality and cost accounting of products and or services (these can be specialised areas for accountants)
- information technology – providing advice on appropriate software and hardware in business and protecting the integrity of information
- government – processing and reporting on government businesses and statutory authorities and departments at national, state and local level.

Accounting professional associations

Those working as accountants or as financial service providers in many of the financial sectors are able to join a professional association that will assist them in their careers – both professionally and socially. In most careers there is a need to regularly improve skills and update professional knowledge. Professional associations provide a broad range of career support and social networking opportunities.

There are three professional accounting organisations in Australia and these are:

1 CPA (Certified Practising Accountant) Australia
2 Institute of Chartered Accountants Australia (ICAA)
3 National Institute of Accountants (NIA).

Key Concept 12.3

Professional accounting associations in Australia

Certified Practising Accountant (CPA) Australia

Institute of Chartered Accountants Australia (ICAA)

National Institute of Accountants (NIA)

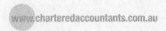

www.charteredaccountants.com.au

www.cpaaustralia.com.au

www.nia.org.au

The benefits of membership of these associations include:

- professional recognition
- international standing
- further training and promotion
- participation in professional activities
- professional and business networking
- meritorious awards
- research grants
- social networking and recreation
- commitment to a code of ethics.

To gain CPA or ICAA membership an aspirant must be a university graduate with a finance or commerce degree as well as mentored experience. In addition, new members must undertake post-graduate training and gain three years professional work experience working under the guidance of a professional member. NIA members can gain their qualifications through Technical and Further Education (TAFE) training and relevant industry experience.

CPA Australia's Member Benefits

Member benefits

CPA Australia creates high-calibre, work-ready individuals of today and the strategic business leaders of tomorrow.

Completing CPA Program ensures you are equipped with an understanding of the dynamic issues facing organisations in a global marketplace. You'll learn how to think strategically, how to position yourself as a leader and gain a global perspective. As a CPA, you will be in demand.

CPA Australia membership also gives you exclusive access to a range of benefits and services, including continuing professional development and special offers.

Keep abreast of the latest industry information and build on your skills and knowledge through CPA Australia's many networking opportunities available through committee and member groups and CPA Program.

The CPA designation is also recognised by a number of overseas membership bodies under agreements with CPA Australia, making an international career easier to pursue.

Special offers are available to members, including:

- AMP banking deals
- American Express card specials
- detailed IBISWorld reports
- savings on *BRW*, *Asset*, *AFR Smart Investor* and *CFO* magazines
- discounted Australian Unity health cover
- ING insurance benefits
- AIG travel insurance discounts
- Europcar car hire discounts.

The information as seen above is provided by CPA Australia Ltd.

FINANCIAL SERVICES PROVIDER PROFESSIONAL ASSOCIATIONS

Those working within the finance industry as service providers are able to join an appropriate professional association. The following is an outline of some of these associations.

Brokers

The Securities and Derivatives Industry Association (SDIA) is the peak industry body representing institutional and retail stockbroking firms. The SDIA promotes among its members high standards, skills and knowledge of securities and derivatives. SDIA aims to effectively represent the securities and derivatives industry in the following way:

- discuss policy and issues with government and regulatory agencies
- consider customer–supplier relationship issues with exchanges, clearing houses and other suppliers
- provide professional recognition for industry practitioners
- promote the securities and derivatives profession
- provide professional education and training
- facilitate the discussion and resolution of industry-wide issues
- ensure members are better informed on issues likely to affect their business
- collect and publish statistics on the industry.

Bankers

The Australian Institute of Banking and Finance (AIBF) is the major banking and finance professional association for Australia and New Zealand. It is dedicated to enhancing the professionalism of its members (and therefore of the financial services industry in general) by increasing knowledge and skills through education and professional development.

Insurers

The National Insurance Brokers Association is a key education and training body for this sector. The aim of the association is to support and encourage members to adopt high standards of professional competence and conduct. There is also the Australian and New Zealand Institute of Insurance and Finance (ANZIIF), which also provides professional development for its members, encourages professional conduct and provides opportunities for business networking.

Superannuation

The superannuation industry's main professional body is the Association of Superannuation Funds of Australia (ASFA). ASFA works to:

- represent the superannuation industry, trustees and, through them, the members of funds
- undertake research and develop policy to improve the administration of superannuation and retirement income for members
- create public awareness of superannuation issues

- provide professional development, education and training for those working in the superannuation industry
- promote best practice in the operation of superannuation funds
- coordinate a range of events, seminars and forums to enable information sharing, debate and networking on superannuation and related issues
- provide a range of information and resources to ensure members are kept up to date on matters affecting the superannuation industry.

Financial planners

Financial planners can be members of the Financial Planners Association (FPA) though they must hold an Australian Financial Services licence. The FPA is the main association for financial planners in Australia. The FPA works toward goals of professional membership, professional conduct and professional accountability. These goals embrace continuing education and encouraging members to operate within a code of ethics.

Benefits of joining the Financial Planners Association (FPA)

Membership of the FPA tells colleagues, clients and Australians:

- that you adhere to high professional standards and a code of ethics and rules
- that you are committed to continuing professional development
- that you put the interests of your clients ahead of all other considerations.

Other benefits include:

- the value placed on FPA membership by the majority of consumers inspiring trust and confidence in you as a professional
- gaining professional certification including FPA practitioner status and CFP certification
- influencing regulatory and professional issues via debate policy formulation and lobbying
- access to a broad range of education and learning opportunities for you as a professional or for your practice
- referrals to your practice via Find a Planner and access to quality discounted consumer brochures
- a dynamic network for the exchange of experience and information via the events and community initiatives of our 31 Chapters.

Source: adapted from 'Why join the FPA?', Financial Planning Association of Australia, November 2007, www.fpa.asn.au/files/PubWhyJoinTheFPA07.pdf.

www.fpa.asn.au

Consequences of misconduct

Where the control exerted by the regulatory authorities is inadequate, or where finance industry managers have disregarded their own codes of conduct, the consequences for investors can be severe.

REALITY CHECK 12.2

Let the buyer beware!

Various news reports and federal court actions revealed during 2008 that a prominent Queensland financial advisory business, Storm Financial Services Pty Ltd, was under surveillance by the Australian Securities and Investments Commission. By March 2009 the business investors voted to have the business liquidated under the company legislation. The major focus in the situation appeared to be on highly geared investors – many on relatively low incomes and elderly – who had arrangements made for them to acquire loans on their properties (houses) and then the funds were applied to buy shares.

The company, formed in 1994, rewarded many investors throughout the boom years. However, when the global economic downturn hit in the final quarter of 2008, a significant loss of equity in property and shares occurred. By September 2009 a Senate hearing of the federal parliament reported that a possible sum of over $3 billion in losses had occurred. An interesting set of allegations implicated three Australian banks in possible careless lending practices. Properties were overvalued to generate loans that were so highly geared that any hint of recession would compromise the borrowers' capacity to repay the loans.

Ponzi schemes

Madoff and Ponzi have almost become household terms. The term 'Ponzi' emerged when an enterprising American called Charles Ponzi initiated a finance scheme during the 1920s offering high returns on a range of investment schemes. Very much pyramid in form, the early returns are actually paid from the capital sums invested as positive publicity attracts increasing numbers of 'gullible' investors.

Many business and legal reports from the USA in the latter part of 2008 exposed Bernard Madoff, a prominent New York financier, as the mastermind of a vast Ponzi-like scheme that had collapsed with the potential of $US65 billion in investor losses. Upon his admission of guilt for fraudulent financial actions Mr Madoff was gaoled for 150 years!

A later report on this investigation in May 2009 revealed that at least $3 billion of investors' losses is estimated, with ASIC pursuing criminal charges for major breaches of the Corporations legislation and ASIC legislation.

 See the Financial Planners Code of Ethics and assess how many of these principles were ignored by Storm Financial Services.

Commentary

The Storm Financial Services and Madoff cases could be further investigated for their background and consequences and from the perspective of investors' responsibilities, professional skills of the providers and their responsibilities, an ethical framework, the extent of legislative regulation, the general economic environment, the ultimate impact such failures have on individuals and systems and whether improvements have been implemented to protect against future similar outcomes.

Often significant collapses of complex business arrangements take many years to resolve with very little benefit to the investors. The above cases and other similar cases obviously occurred within an accounting, banking and legal environment. Other people than the principal (owner) would have been complicit in the actions causing serious distress and loss. Clearly, personal ethical behavioural and professional codes of practice were breached by a number of professional people associated with the businesses (lawyers, bankers, advisors and accountants).

Professional images

A telephone poll by Roy Morgan Research conducted in June 2009 included the following data on the image of various professions:

Occupation	Ratings for ethics and honesty
Nurses	89%
Pharmacists	84%
Doctors	82%
School teachers	76%

Engineers	69%
Dentists	69%
Police	65%
Accountants	51%
Financial planners	25%
Stockbrokers	15%
Insurance brokers	11%
Advertising people	6%
Car salespeople	3%

Source: Roy Morgan Research, ' Roy Morgan Image of Professions survey',
24 June 2009, www.roymorgan.com/news/poll/2009/4387/.

Commentary

It is interesting to note that those professions related to the finance industry are well down the list. Visit the Roy Morgan website and see how the ratings have changed over the years the poll has been running. (Note, 2009 was the first year financial planners were included in the poll.)

- Why do you think that those professions associated with the finance industry rate so low with regards to ethics and honesty?
- What factors might have affected people's opinions of these professions? What role do the media play in this?
- Does the existence of legislation play a part in this result?
- Are the financial services professions so complex and by nature related to activities that seem to involve more potential for criminal activity that they are bound to be perceived in an unfavourable manner?

WORKING WITHIN A CODE OF BEHAVIOUR

Sporting associations have guidelines of expected behaviour for both players and spectators. Tribunals exist to rule on unacceptable behaviour and infringements can be imposed on players. For example, in the Australian Football League players can be banned from playing or fined. Most professional bodies develop codes of behaviour to build confidence by the public in the services offered by the professional group. Ethics is the cornerstone of what accountants do. Clients seek impartial information and depend on accountants to perform their jobs with the highest degree of accuracy and ethical standards. The stability of a free-market system depends to a great extent on competent and ethical financial information providers.

Professional codes of conduct for accountants

The Accounting Professional and Ethical Standards Board (APESB) was established as an independent body in February 2006, as an initiative of CPA Australia and the Institute of Chartered Accountants in Australia (the Institute). CPA Australia, the Institute and the National Institute of Accountants (NIA) are all members of the APESB, with the objectives of producing a code of model ethical behaviour for accountants and to maintain timely debate on topical ethical issues.

The fundamental principles and features identified in the Code are:
- integrity – being straightforward and honest in all professional and business relationships
- objectivity – not allowing professional judgement to be compromised by bias, conflict of interest or the undue influence of others

- professional competence and due care – maintaining professional knowledge and skill at the level required to ensure competent professional service and acting diligently in accordance with applicable standards when providing services
- confidentiality – respecting the confidentiality of information acquired as a result of business relationships and not disclosing any such information to third parties without proper authority
- professional behaviour – complying with relevant laws and regulations and avoiding any action that discredits the profession.

The Code then acknowledges that a broad range of circumstances may potentially threaten compliance with the fundamental principles, such as:

- self-interest threats, which may occur as a result of the financial or other interests of the individual or their family
- self-review threats, which may occur when a previous judgement needs to be re-evaluated by the accountant responsible for that judgement
- advocacy threats, which may occur when an accountant promotes a position or opinion to the point that subsequent objectivity may be compromised
- familiarity threats, which may occur when, because of a close relationship, an accountant becomes too sympathetic to the interests of others
- intimidation threats, which may occur when an accountant may be deterred from acting objectively by threats, actual or perceived.

The following news article shows how some accounting service providers may disregard the law and their professional code of conduct and what the consequences of this sort of action may be.

Accountants face court over laundering charge

by Harriet Alexander

Three partners of a suburban accounting firm and 11 of their clients faced court yesterday accused of participating in the alleged tax evasion scheme which is targeting hundreds of wealthy Australians, including the actor Paul Hogan ...

The firm allegedly put the money through a false invoice scheme, which involved transferring money to overseas financial institutions disguised as business expenses and then returning the same money to Australia in the form of interest-free loans.

The case forms part of Operation Wickenby, an investigation by the Australian Federal Police and Australian Taxation Office into an alleged $100 million tax evasion scheme involving money laundering promoted by Agius, the director of accounting firm PKF Vanuatu ...

Source: *Sydney Morning Herald*, 11 March 2009, www.smh.com.au.

Commentary

The accounting partnership mentioned above will not enhance the image of accountants! The Australian Taxation Office acted on behalf of the public to maintain the integrity of taxation laws in Australia. Both the accountants and the clients apparently acted in a conspiracy to defraud the community and obtain unfair financial advantages.

Identify the breaches of professional practice in this instance.

Professional codes of conduct for financial services providers

The Financial Planning Association of Australia has set professional standards in its Code of Ethics. The Code of Ethics is part of the professional obligations that all members of the Financial Planning Association (FPA) need to adhere to. The full code can be downloaded from the FPA website.

www.fpa.asn.au

Principle 1: Client First

Place the client's interests first.

Placing the client's interests first is a hallmark of professionalism, requiring the financial planner to act honestly and not place personal and/or employer gain or advantage before the client's interests.

Principle 2: Integrity

Provide professional services with integrity.

Integrity requires honesty and candour in all professional matters. Financial planners are placed in positions of trust by clients, and the ultimate source of that trust is the financial planner's personal integrity. Allowance can be made for legitimate differences of opinion, but integrity cannot co-exist with deceit or subordination of one's principles. Integrity requires the financial planner to observe both the letter and the spirit of the Code of Ethics.

Principle 3: Objectivity

Provide professional services objectively.

Objectivity requires intellectual honesty and impartiality. Regardless of the services delivered or the capacity in which a financial planner functions, objectivity requires financial planners to ensure the integrity of their work, manage conflicts and exercise sound professional judgment.

Principle 4: Fairness

Be fair and reasonable in all professional relationships.
Disclose and manage conflicts of interest.

Fairness requires providing clients what they are due, owed or should expect from a professional relationship, and includes honesty and disclosure of material conflicts of interest. It involves managing one's own feelings, prejudices and desires to achieve a proper balance of interests. Fairness is treating others in the same manner that you would want to be treated.

Principle 5: Professionalism

Act in a manner that demonstrates exemplary professional conduct.

Professionalism requires behaving with dignity and showing respect and courtesy to clients, fellow professionals, and others in business-related activities, and complying with appropriate rules, regulations and professional requirements. Professionalism requires the financial planner, individually and in cooperation with peers, to enhance and maintain the profession's public image and its ability to serve the public interest.

Principle 6: Competence

Maintain the abilities, skills and knowledge necessary to provide professional services competently.

Competence requires attaining and maintaining an adequate level of knowledge, skills and abilities in the provision of professional services. Competence also includes the wisdom to recognise one's own limitations and when consultation with other professionals is appropriate or referral to other professionals necessary. Competence requires the financial planner to make a continuing commitment to learning and professional improvement.

Accounting and Finance 2B   ISBN 9780170182041   Cengage Learning Australia

Principle 7: Confidentiality
Protect the confidentiality of all client information.

Confidentiality requires client information to be protected and maintained in such a manner that allows access only to those who are authorised. A relationship of trust and confidence with the client can only be built on the understanding that the client's information will not be disclosed inappropriately.

Principle 8: Diligence
Provide professional services diligently.

Diligence requires fulfilling professional commitments in a timely and thorough manner, and taking due care in planning, supervising and delivering professional services.

Source: Financial Planning Association of Australia, Code of Ethics from the Financial Planning Association's Code of Professional Practice, www.fpa.asn.au.

Test your knowledge

1   List some of the laws and regulations that are in place to control the banking industry.

2   What laws and regulations apply to control the activities of accountants as tax agents and company auditors?

3   What laws and regulations apply to control the activities of financial planners?

4   What is the purpose of accounting and financial service provider professional associations?

5   What is a code of ethics?

6   What is the purpose of a code of ethics?

7   Explain the following in regards to a code of ethics and ethical behaviour:
    a   integrity
    b   confidentiality
    c   competence
    d   objectivity.

Test your understanding

12.1   If you were new to the accounting profession, what services from an accounting professional association would be useful to support you in your career? Create a list of these and investigate how one of the three accounting associations would be able to support your interests.

12.2   An experienced and respected accountant is asked by a wealthy client to make misleading remarks in a press release about the current financial results of the client's business to divert attention from the recent poor performance of the client's business. The accountant refuses. The client then talks to a senior partner of the accounting practice that employs the accountant and requests her to get the accountant to cooperate and make the press release.

    Comment on what should happen and ways in which you, as the partner, should respond. Should you:
• sack the accountant for not supporting a client
• refuse to act for the client any longer
• promote the accountant

Accounting and Finance: 2B   ISBN 9780170182041   Cengage Learning Australia

- give responsibility for this client to another employee within the firm who may be more willing to do what the client wants
- or give another possibility?

12.3 In the following report from a local newspaper fraudulent behaviour has resulted in criminal charges being laid.

What do you think is the ethically correct course of action by management?

Centrelink crackdown on skimpy cash fraud

Centrelink investigators have saved taxpayers more than an estimated quarter of a million dollars as part of a continuing investigation into Western Australia's skimpy barmaids and strippers.

Since March last year, Operation Mariana, together with two other operations, has resulted in estimated savings of $280000 to date, with thirteen workers having their Centrelink payments cancelled or suspended.

Centrelink is also likely to refer the cases of six workers to the Commonwealth Director of Public Prosecutions for prosecution consideration.

Centrelink WA Business Integrity Manager Suzan Anthony said the investigation focuses on skimpy barmaids and strippers in metropolitan Perth and Kalgoorlie.

'The operation is still in progress and we're anticipating further savings and debts from a number of cases,' Ms Anthony said. 'Some of these customers are very clever and will go to extraordinary lengths to hide the fact they're earning an income at the same time as they are on a payment from Centrelink.'

Source: Centrelink Western Australia, Media Release, 11 January 2007, http://www. centrelink.gov.au/internet/internet.nsf/news_room/07wa_cash_fraud.htm.

Required

a Identify the stakeholders in this breach.
b What responsibility do the employers have and is there a case for the prosecution being extended to the employers?
c Do a business's accountants have some responsibility to uphold legislation related to employment and benefits and have they breached their professional codes in other ways?

12.4 You are a recently retired person who has decided to manage your own superannuation funds. You have a good general understanding of finance markets, but you are not an expert. Your situation is complicated somewhat by the fact that your spouse, who is younger than you, is still working and you have a disabled child still living with you, for whom you are able to get certain government allowances.

Identify three financial professionals whose services you might employ and explain what each of them might be expected to do for you. In each case, outline the controls that the professional is subject to that will ensure that they do the job you want of them.

Investigation

1 Visit the website of a financial professional association and discover the answers to following:
   a How do you become a member?
   b What qualifications are required?
   c How do you maintain membership?
   d What training and professional development is offered?
   e How does a client lodge a complaint?
   f What does its code of conduct or code of ethics require?
   g What is the process for dealing with members who are alleged to have breached professional requirements and what are the consequences for the members if they are found to be guilty of such breaches?

Accounting and Finance: 2B   ISBN 9780170182041   Cengage Learning Australia

2   Identify a recent case of default by financial service providers in Australia (search your library or the internet) and research it. Then produce a report in written or electronic form.
   - Describe the circumstances of the case.
   - Identify the nature of failures and the reasons for them.
   - Examine the role of the regulators (both government and professional associations). Did they do what was expected of them? Could they have done better?
   - Explain the consequences for the clients, the service providers and any other stakeholders.

Essay

'Professional associations play a vital role in our society to ensure confidence in the capital markets through regulation and professional training.'

Discuss this statement as it applies to the finance industry, including in your answer the following:
- the role of professional associations, giving some examples to illustrate your answer
- the importance of professional codes of conduct
- the consequences of an absence of active professional associations
- the relationship between the professional associations and other market regulators.

Ethics case study

Consider this dilemma of the chief accountant of a Welshpool engineering firm. The firm is seeking bank finance to update its manufacturing machinery in order to remain competitive in the market. While business is difficult, the company's board of directors are assured by the Chief Executive Officer that bank finance is assured, given that profits are expected to improve by three per cent on the previous year's results. A new sales contract is being finalised for the next period. The accountant is aware that current sales have been sluggish and performance is below the three per cent increase expected. However, if he included the new contract in the current result he could report the desired growth outcome.

The accountant's own remuneration and bonuses, together with those of the CEO depend on improving results. The machinery update is vital for the firm's success in the marketplace and failure to finance this could possibly threaten the firm's existence. There is considerable unemployment in senior accounting, management and engineering positions at the moment!

Discuss your responses to the following questions.
- Should the accountant tell the truth to the bank, irrespective of the consequences?
- Does it really matter if the accountant 'massages' the figures, including sales that will occur in the future?
- Is the self-interest of the accountant a justifiable concern?
- How should the accountant tackle the matter of loyalty to the CEO? Isn't the CEO ultimately responsible for the decision?
- Does the accountant have a responsibility to protect the jobs of employees?
- Who are the stakeholders in this and what are their interests?
- What should the accountant do?

Accounting and Finance: 2B   ISBN 9780170182041   Cengage Learning Australia

Glossary

ABN
Australian Business Number

Account
a record of all transactions affecting a particular item

Accounting controls
measures and systems set up to protect a business's assets and ensure that its records and reports are accurate

Accounting cycle
the process of recording, storing, analysing and acting on financial transactions

Accounting entity
the business entity is viewed as being separate from the owner(s) and the business's records, which are kept separate from the owner(s) records

Accounting equation
the equation expressing the relationship between an entity's assets, liabilities and owner's equity: A = L + OE

Accounting period
useful and comparative time intervals for reporting purposes

Accrual accounting
income and expense are recognised when they take place – income when it is earned (i.e. the point of sale or provision of service) and expense when it is incurred (i.e. used or consumed) – not necessarily when the payments are made or received

Accrual basis assumptions
the assumption that financial transactions and events should be recorded when they occur and in the accounting period to which they relate

Accrued expense
a service or good that has been used or consumed but not paid for

Accrued income
a good or service that has been earned (i.e. provided) but for which the cash has not been received

Adjustment note
a formal document providing evidence of a sale or purchase return or allowance

Administrative controls
the procedures and systems that a business puts in place to ensure its efficient and effective operation and compliance with its set policies

Allowance for doubtful debts
an estimate of future bad debts (i.e. amounts owing by credit customers that are not expected to be paid)

APESB
the Accounting Professional and Ethical Standards Board – a joint independent body sponsored by the three Australian professional accounting associations with a purpose to have a continuing dialogue about ethical and professional standards and to develop and apply a code of practice

Asset
a resource controlled by an entity as a result of a past transaction

ATM
automatic teller machine

B2B
business to business – electronic transactions from one business to another business (e.g. a wholesaler to a retailer). The two companies' computer systems need to be able to interact to allow the transaction to proceed, with all the benefits and risks that are associated with the internet

B2C
business to customer – electronic transactions between a business and its customers

Balance day adjustments
adjusting general journal entries made on balance day to ensure that income and expense accounts are accurate for the accounting period and to bring to account assets and liabilities not previously recorded

Bank reconciliation
the process of comparing the business's cash records with the bank's record of the business's cash account (i.e. the bank statement) and then determining the reason(s) for any difference

BAS
Business Activity Statement – a report sent to the Australian Taxation Office on a regular basis (usually quarterly) with details of GST, PAYG and FBT collections/payments during the period

Broker
a career in finance linking buyers to sellers, most commonly identified as facilitating the sale and purchase of shares and other financial instruments, such as futures and bonds

Cash based accounting
recognises income when the cash is received and expenses when the cash is paid

Chart of accounts
a systematically arranged list of the accounts in a firm's ledger

Cheque
an instruction to a bank to make a payment to a particular person or organisation

Classification
the systematic grouping or arrangement of information in financial statements to facilitate understanding and analysis

Code of ethics
a charter of behaviour determined to be professionally appropriate based on virtues and wide community expectations

Collusion
when two or more people conspire to commit fraud

CPA Australia
the Australian Certified Practising Accountants' professional association – a non-profit incorporated body

Credit card
a card issued by a bank or other financial institution giving the cardholder the ability to borrow from the institution to a set limit for purchases or cash advances

Credit policy
the conditions under which a business will provide credit to its customers

Credit rating
a symbol or alphabetical or numerical rating of a business's or individual's credit history usually provided by an external third party called a credit rating agency

Current asset
an asset that will be used up or turned into cash in the normal course of business within 12 months of the balance date

Current liability
a debt that must be paid within 12 months of the balance date

Cybercrime
any fraudulent action conducted through an online data system which may result in losses by the victim and financial gain by the criminal

Debit card
a card issued by a bank or other financial institution giving the cardholder the ability to access their own funds for purchases

Depreciable non-current asset
an item of property, plant or equipment that has a limited life

Depreciation
the systematic allocation of the depreciable amount of an asset over its useful life

Double entry
the concept that every transaction will have an opposite and equal effect on two or more accounts

Doubtful debts
an estimate of the amount of income unlikely to be received in the current accounting period (provided to ensure that profit is not overstated)

EDP
electronic data processing

EFT
electronic funds transfer

EFTPOS
electronic funds transfer at point of sale

Environmental awareness
acting in a manner that shows consideration and responsibility for the natural and built world in which the business operates, including consideration for the needs of future generations

Equity
the residual interest in the assets after the external liabilities have been subtracted

Ethics
a set of moral principles; a code of conduct

Accounting and Finance: 2A–2B   ISBN 9780170182041   Cengage Learning Australia

Expenses
a decrease in economic benefits of a business during the accounting period in the form of outflows of assets or increases in liabilities that have the effect of reducing the owner's equity (other than the owner withdrawing equity)

Fair value
the amount for which an asset could be exchanged between knowledgeable, willing parties in an arm's length transaction

FBT
fringe benefits tax – a tax applied to the value of non-cash benefits provided by employers to their employees such as private use of a company car, subsidised home loans, discounts on product purchases

Financial planner
a career that provides advice on a wide range of financial decisions from accounting to retirement plans

First in, first out (FIFO)
a method of determining the cost of inventory sold under the perpetual inventory system

Footing the accounts
the process of calculating the balances in a set of T-form accounts and entering these balances into the accounts to enable a trial balance to be taken

General ledger
those accounts in the ledger system that are collated into reports

Going concern
the assumption that a business will continue for the foreseeable future with the value of the assets being based on that assumption

GST
goods and services tax – a sales tax of 10% applied to most goods and services produced in Australia with some specific exceptions, such as basic foodstuffs

Goodwill
an intangible asset representing reputation, customer base and other benefits that may accrue to a firm when purchasing another business

Hacking
unauthorised access to a business's computer system with the intention of stealing or corrupting data

Historical cost
valuation of assets at the amount paid for them at the date of the acquisition

ICAA
the Institute of Chartered Accountants of Australia professional association – a non-profit incorporated body

Income
an increase in economic benefits during the accounting period as a result of inflows or increases of assets or decreases of liabilities that increase the worth of the owner's equity other than those inflows related to contribution by the owner(s)

Income statement
a statement showing details of a firm's income and expenses and the resultant profit or loss for a specified time period

Intangible asset
an asset that does not have a tangible, physical existence (e.g. patents, copyrights, goodwill)

Internal audit
the function of conducting an ongoing investigation, monitoring and review of the internal control systems in place within a business

Internal control
the procedures, policies, processes and systems in place within a business which ensure that the business operations are effective and efficient, the financial records and reports are reliable and the business objectives are achieved

Inventory (stock)
goods held for use, processing or resale

Invoice
a document providing evidence of the credit purchase or sale of a good or service

Journal
a chronological record of financial transactions

Ledger
the book or set of files containing all the accounts

Liability
a present obligation to meet a commitment arising from a past transaction that will deplete resources

Liquidity
the extent to which assets can be turned into cash to meet a firm's payment obligations

Manufacturer
a business fabricating goods from raw materials

Market value
the value of an asset as agreed upon by a seller and buyer

Merchandising firm
a business that earns the bulk of its revenue by reselling inventory at a profit

Monetary assumption
measurement of the elements of financial statements and their reporting shall be in terms of money values (i.e. the currency of the country in which the report is presented)

Mutual agency
the concept that each partner can make binding decisions on behalf of the partnership in the normal course of business activities

MYOB
'mind your own business' – an accounting software package used by many small businesses

Network
a linkage of hardware and software to manage data

NIA
National Institute of Accountants professional association – a non-profit incorporated body

Non-current asset
any asset that is not a current asset

Non-current asset register
a systematic record of all the details pertaining to a number of non-current assets from their acquisition through to their disposal

Non-current liability
a debt that must be paid later than 12 months from balance date

Online banking
a system allowing customers to conduct bank account transactions and obtain information via the internet

Overdraft
an arrangement with a bank to borrow by withdrawing funds from the business bank account over and above the money held in it, up to a specified limit

Partnership
an unincorporated business structure with two to 20 owners trading with a view to profit

Passwords
provide access to protected systems, such as an accounting system

PAYG
Pay As You Go – a system enabling employers to collect income tax from the wages of their employees and remit these monies to the government

Periodic (physical) inventory system
a method of calculating cost of sales based on physical stocktakes at the start and end of a period

Perpetual inventory system
a method of calculating cost of sales based on perpetual updating of the inventory and cost of sales accounts

Petty cash imprest system
a system whereby cash required to pay for small costs is accounted for through a reimbursement of cash to bring the petty cash fund back to the original amount advanced

Phishing
fraudulent actions that purport to originate from genuine businesses with the purpose of convincing customers to provide personal or access information that may be used to steal goods or cash electronically

PIN
personal identification number – used to validate debit or credit card transactions and allow customers to access ATMs and EFTPOS

Prepaid expense
a service or supply paid for before it is used or consumed

Profit-determining account
working ledger account used to determine profit or loss for a particular period (usually called 'Profit and loss summary')

Proprietary company
an organisation formed as a separate legal entity with up to 50 shareholders and no capacity to raise capital from the public

Public company
an organisation formed as a separate legal entity with unlimited shareholders having the capacity to raise funds from the public

Purchase price
usually the invoice price (less trade discount), excluding GST

Purchase return or allowance
the return of, or allowance made on, goods purchased on credit

QuickBooks
an accounting software package produced by Reckon

Receipt
a document providing evidence of a cash payment

Reckon
the brand name of an accounting software business

Reducing balance depreciation
the depreciation method that allocates more of the depreciable amount of an asset in its early years and less as it ages

Redundancy
the loss of a job due to technological or economic changes that make the job unnecessary

Residual value
the estimated amount that an entity would currently obtain from disposal of an asset after deducting the estimated costs of disposal and if the asset was already of an age and in the condition expected at the end of its useful life

Resource conservation
acting in a manner that makes effective use of natural resources and minimises waste

Retailer
a business providing general or specific ranges of merchandise, usually acquired from wholesalers or manufacturers

Sales return or allowance
the return of, or allowance made on, goods sold on credit

Service business
a business that earns revenue by providing a service to customers

Service firm
a business that earns the bulk of its revenue by providing a service for sale to the public

Shareholder
a person or an entity owning legal divisions or proportions of the equity of a company described as shares

Sole trader
an unincorporated form of business structure owned by one person

Source document
the initial record or evidence of a financial transaction

Statement of financial position
a formal statement showing details of a firm's assets, liabilities and equity at a particular point in time

Statutory superannuation
a system requiring employers to contribute a set amount (currently 9%) of every employee's gross wages into a superannuation fund that employees access in retirement

Stocktaking
a periodic physical count of all inventories and comparison with the inventory records and general ledger inventory account balance

Straight line depreciation
the depreciation method that allocates the depreciable amount of an asset evenly throughout the asset's useful life

Subsidiary ledger
a set of records separate from the general ledger that contains all details pertaining to a specific group of accounts, this detail being summarised in the general ledger in a control account

Tangible asset
an asset that has a physical substance

TFN
tax file number – a unique number allocated by the Australian Taxation Office to each Australian taxpayer

Trial balance
listing and totalling of all debit and credit balances in a ledger to identify recording errors and facilitate reporting

Unearned income
cash received for which the good or service has not been provided

Useful life
the period over which an asset is expected to be available for use by an entity, or the number of production or similar units expected to be obtained from the asset by an entity

Virus
deliberate corruption of computer software usually as a result of internet use

Weighted average
a method of determining the cost of inventory sold under the perpetual inventory system

Wholesaler
a business that purchases goods in bulk and sells them to retail businesses, which sell them to individual customers

Accounting and Finance. 2A-2B   ISBN 9780170182041   Cengage Learning Australia

Index

Accounting and Finance: 2A-2B   ISBN 9780170182041   Cengage Learning Australia

Accounting and Finance: 2A–2B   ISBN 9780170182041   Cengage Learning Australia

Accounting and Finance: 2A–2B   ISBN 9780170182041   Cengage Learning Australia

Accounting and Finance: 2A-2B   ISBN 9780170182041   Cengage Learning Australia

Accounting and Finance: 2A-2B   ISBN 9780170182041   Cengage Learning Australia

Accounting and Finance: 2A-2B   ISBN 9780170182041   Cengage Learning Australia

Accounting and Finance: 2A-2B   ISBN 9780170182041   Cengage Learning Australia

Accounting and Finance: 2A–2B   ISBN 9780170182041   Cengage Learning Australia

Accounting and Finance: 2A-2B   ISBN 9780170182041   Cengage Learning Australia